PHONOLOGY
THEORY AND ANALYSIS

PHONOLOGY
THEORY AND ANALYSIS

LARRY M. HYMAN
University of Southern California

HOLT, RINEHART AND WINSTON
New York Chicago San Francisco Atlanta Dallas
Montreal Toronto London Sydney

To My Parents and Grandparents

Library of Congress Cataloging in Publication Data

Hyman, Larry M
    Phonology: theory and analysis.

    Bibliography: p.
    Includes index.
    1. Grammar, Comparative and general—Phonology.
I. Title.
P217.H9   415   74–32172

ISBN 0–03–012141–8

5 6 7 8 9   059   5 4 3 2 1

FOREWORD

"This book deals with *phonology,* the study of the sound systems of language." So begins this book which, true to its subtitle, is concerned with both phonological theory and descriptive analysis, recognizing and demonstrating that every phonological analysis is dependent on theory.

The author's main concern is to reveal "how speech sounds *structure* and *function*" in the languages of the world. All phonological theories have this as their goal; alternative theories are critically examined in reference to this goal. The basic tenets of the theory of generative phonology as proposed by Chomsky and Halle are set against the background of earlier phonologists like Trubetzkoy, Martinet, Jakobson, Sapir, Pike, and Firth. The book thus illuminates the continuity and the breaks between past and present in phonological theory, providing the reader with the theoretical and practical background necessary to understand and analyze phonological phenomena.

The book's primary aim is to serve as a textbook for students of linguistics, but it is more than a textbook. The author objectively assesses and summarizes what has been learned through the ages about the sound systems of human language and also reveals some of the gaps in our knowledge. This is not a book written by someone who has learned his phonology from books; it is written by a working phonologist who has himself struggled with and contributed to phonological theory and analysis. The modifications in current phonological theory which he proposes reflect the author's intimate knowledge of the many languages he has studied. For this reason, the book, while introductory in style and exposition and completely understandable by the novice, will also be of interest to the advanced student and working phonologist.

Little previous knowledge of phonology is assumed; anyone with a rudimentary knowledge of phonetics will have no difficulty. The tables in the appendixes define all the symbols used; both IPA charts of phonetic symbols and distinctive feature matrices are provided.

The book is comprehensive and detailed. Traditional and current concepts and technical terms, such as distinctiveness, redundancy, complementary distribution, neutralization, assimilation, dissimilation, phonetic similarity, free variation, alternation, archiphoneme, segmental and sequential constraints, conjunctive and disjunctive ordering, alpha variables, are carefully explained and exemplified by language data drawn from more than seventy languages from Akan to Zulu.

Phonology is organized into six chapters. Chapter 1 discusses the basic distinction between phonetics and phonology, the notion of levels of representation, and the kinds of evidence which support theoretical hypotheses and analyses. Chapter 2 deals with the basic building blocks of phonology—distinctive features—and provides an historical view of the development of distinctive feature theory. Binary and multivalued features are discussed, as are the articulatory and acoustic correlates of universal phonetic features. Chapter 3 covers alternative approaches to phonological analyses and the nature of the "phoneme." The abstractness of phonological representation is considered. In Chapter 4 the formal representation of phonological analysis is presented. The notion of simplicity is discussed in relation to the formal devices and ordering relations between phonological rules that have been proposed in the literature. In this chapter, some recent proposals for modifications of generative theory—such as those dealing with global rules and derivational constraints—are considered. Chapter 5 deals with the concept of phonological naturalness—of classes of sounds, phonological systems, and rules. The development of the theory of "markedness" is discussed in terms of both synchronic and diachronic "natural" systems and rules.

The first five chapters thus present a comprehensive view of segmental phonology. Chapter 6, a special feature of the book, discusses suprasegmental phenomena. Stress and tone, the kinds of units to which they should be assigned, and the rules that affect them are considered. The syllable, the morpheme, and the word as phonological units are examined, and the concept of the transformational cycle is evaluated.

No description of the contents of this book, however, can suggest the exciting discoveries about the nature of sound systems that await the reader.

VICTORIA A. FROMKIN
University of California, Los Angeles

PREFACE

When faced with the task of teaching an introductory course in phonology, a linguist must decide which of two strategies to follow. First, one may choose to devote the course to one particular theory of phonology, the theory that one personally esteems to be the most adequate—or possibly the "right" approach to the field. Or, the linguist may choose to reflect a wider range of views on the nature of sound systems, a subject that has inspired a number of different theoretical schools of thought.

In writing *Phonology,* my aim has been to present what I feel to be the major advances in the study of phonology over the past several decades. Though I cannot claim to have given each theorist the number of pages deserved, I have attempted to provide a historical perspective on the evolution of phonological study. By incorporating many of the contributions of earlier scholars, as well as discussions of some currently debated issues, I hope I have produced an introduction to the field that is broad enough to satisfy phonologists of different theoretical persuasions.

Because of the rapidly changing scope of phonology and because of the diversity of opinions held about its nature, it is impossible to satisfy all teachers of phonology with one book. In addition, some phonologists may not agree with the relative weight I have given various topics. Most professors would probably agree that it is good to expose students to different points of view. While some may prefer to make "comparative phonological theory" a topic for graduate seminars, devoting more elementary courses to one view of phonology, I have chosen to give the beginning student a more general picture. This should, I hope, enable students to approach the phonological literature (much of which is cited in the text) and make critical judgments on their own. The risk, of course, is that students may be discouraged by the fact that, as in other areas of linguistics, most of the answers are yet to be found.

The last fifty years have taught us a lot about the way sound systems work—and it is expected that the next fifty years will be at least as exciting. I hope that this introductory overview of phonology will contribute to the development of the science.

• • •

Research on the nature of stress and tone (Chapter 6) was supported in part by the Miller Institute for Basic Research in Science, University of California, Berkeley.

I would like to thank John Ohala, Edward Finegan, William Leben, and Stephen Krashen for reading and commenting on parts of an earlier draft of this manuscript. In addition, I would like to express my deepest appreciation to Victoria Fromkin and Meredith Hoffman, whose many detailed criticisms have led to improvements both in style and in content. Finally, I would like to thank members of my phonology classes at the University of Southern California and the University of California, Santa Cruz, whose stimulating response encouraged me to undertake this project.

L.M.H.

CONTENTS

3

PHONOLOGICAL ANALYSIS   59

6

SUPRASEGMENTAL PHONOLOGY   186

PHONOLOGY
THEORY AND ANALYSIS

1

WHAT IS PHONOLOGY?

1.1 Introduction

This book deals with *phonology*, the study of the sound systems of language. In the following chapters, a close look will be taken at the ways in which various languages organize or structure different sounds. Since speech sounds are used to convey meaning, sound systems cannot be fully understood unless they are studied in a wider linguistic context. A language learner, for instance, must master the production and perception of the sounds of a given language. He must also, however, learn *when* to use these sounds. Thus, speakers of English must learn not only the sounds [k] and [s], which are transcribed between phonetic brackets (see below), but also that the [k] of *opaque* changes to [s] when the suffix *-ity* is added to form the word *opacity*. This change of [k] to [s] is as much a part of the sound system of English as is the fact that English contains the sounds [k], [g], [s], and [z].

The goal of phonology is, then, to study the properties of the sound systems which speakers must learn or internalize in order to use their language for the purpose of communication. Thus, when approaching the sound system of a language, it is necessary to study not only the *physical* properties of the attested sounds (that is, how they are made and what their acoustic correlates are), but also the *grammatical* properties of these sounds.

1

1.2 Phonetics and Phonology

Since speech sounds are the product of human anatomy and phys-
iology, it is not suprising to find similarities across languages. In some cases
phonologists are tempted to claim certain *universals* (or at least certain
tendencies) in the sound systems of the world. Thus, all languages appear to
have the vowel [a] in their inventory of sounds. Other vowel sounds, such
as [i] and [u], are extremely common in languages, but are not universal,
while still other vowel sounds, such as [ü], as in French *rue* [rü] 'street,' are
much more restricted in their distribution in the world's languages. In order
to explain why certain sounds occur more frequently than others, one turns
to the field of *phonetics*, the study of speech sounds. Within this field one
might first look to *articulatory phonetics*, the study of how speech sounds are
articulated or produced. It may be that certain sounds require less muscular
effort in their production than other sounds, and since the latter sounds
require greater effort, they are not as frequently found in languages. Nor,
as we shall see (**1.5.2**), are they learned as early in language acquisition as are
sounds requiring less effort. On the other hand, one might look to *acoustic
phonetics*, the study of the physical properties of the sounds that are produced.
In this case, it may be that a certain sound is not as frequently found as
another because it is less acoustically *distinct* from other sounds.

Phonology has been defined as the study of sound systems, that is, the
study of how speech sounds *structure* and *function* in languages. As we shall
see, some speech sounds can be used in a language to distinguish words of
different meanings, whereas other sounds cannot. Thus, Trubetzkoy, one of
the founders of the Prague School of Linguistics, wrote (1939:10): "It is the
task of phonology to study which differences in sound are related to
differences in meaning in a given language, in which way the discriminative
elements . . . are related to each other, and the rules according to which they
may be combined into words and sentences." A phonetic study tells how the
sounds of a language are made and what their acoustic properties are. A
phonological study tells how these sounds are used to convey meaning.

While it may be the case that phonetic explanations readily account for
the relative frequency of sounds, there are many issues in the study of speech
sounds which cannot be resolved by reference to phonetics alone. Because
speech sounds function to convey meaning, speakers sometimes have internal
or mental representations of sounds which are not identical with their
physical properties. That is, there is a *psychological* as well as a physical
(phonetic) side to speech sounds.

In a *phonetic* study of a language, an inventory of sounds is provided.
Part of a phonetic study of English will include a statement that the sound
[θ] occurs but that the sound [x] does not occur. Part of a phonetic study

of German, on the other hand, will include a statement that the sound [x] occurs but that the sound [θ] does not occur. Phoneticians point out that although speech is characterized by a (semi)continuous flow of sounds, speakers segment this continuous speech signal into discrete units. If one were to look at an acoustic record of the pronunciation of the English word *ran* (such as on a spectrogram), one would not observe a pause between the [r] and the [æ], or between the [æ] and the [n]. Nor would one find an abrupt change in the acoustic properties from one sound to the other. Instead, sounds blend into one another, creating transitions from one sound to another. In the above example, the lowering of the velum, which is necessary for the pronunciation of the nasal consonant [n], begins *before* the tip of the tongue reaches the alveolar position required for the articulation of this consonant. As a result, some of the acoustic properties of nasalization which belong to [n] will be realized on the preceding vowel. Because of such resulting transitions, it is impossible to delimit in all cases exactly where one sound begins and another ends. And yet, all speakers of English would agree that the word *ran* consists of three *discrete* sounds.

Since it is not always possible to ascribe a physical reality to the discrete sound units which are transcribed between phonetic brackets, such transcriptions as [ræn], where partial nasalization is not indicated on the vowel, necessarily represent an abstraction from the actual physical record. We shall refer to these discrete units as phonetic *segments* or *phones*. A phonetic study of a language, then, provides an inventory and description of the occurring phonetic segments. However, since speech signals are semicontinuous in nature, and since no two utterances are ever exactly the same, it should be clear that not all of the physical properties of a given form or utterance will ever be included in a phonetic transcription.

A phonological study also refers to the inventory of segments in a language. But stating which phonetic segments occur in a language and which do not is only a superficial part of phonology. As pointed out by Sapir (1925:16–18), two languages can have the same inventory of phonetic segments but have very different phonologies.

As an illustration of this point, consider the status of *ts* in English and German. Compare the German word *Salz* [zalt^s] 'salt' with the English plural form *salts* [sɔlts]. Although one might argue that these two words end with equivalent sound sequences, a closer examination of the two languages reveals that these sequences are analyzed quite differently by speakers of the two languages. The final *ts* of *salts* is considered to be *two* consonants by speakers of English, for two reasons. First, they know that the singular form is *salt* and that the plural form is obtained by adding the additional segment *s*. Second, *ts* is not found at the beginning of English words, unlike the single affricate segment *č* as in *chalk*, which phoneticians break up into a [t] closure and a [š] release. If *ts* were one consonant, it would be expected to occur in all of the general positions where single consonants are found in English. On the other hand, analyzing *ts* as two consonants allows the possibility of identifying *ts* with other consonant sequences such as *ps* and *ks*, which also are not found at the beginning of English words (see Sapir, 1925:20). In other words, there is a *structural* principle in English ruling out sequences of certain consonants followed by [s] in word-initial position. The analysis of *ts* as *t* + *s* therefore fits the pattern or structure of the language.

In German, on the other hand, *ts* (which is frequently written *z* in the orthography) is found in initial position as well as in final position, for example, *Zahl* [t^{s}a:l] 'number.' Because of its relatively free distribution, speakers of German analyze the [t] closure followed by an [s] release as the one segment *t^s*. While *ps* and *ks* are not found at the beginning of German words, *t^s* is found in this position. This difference in the structuring of *ps* and *ks*, on the one hand, and *t^s* on the other, makes German *t^s* different from English *ts*. Since the two are identical phonetically, a purely phonetic study would miss this distinction. It is in a *phonological* study that the difference between *ts* and *t^s* is captured. Thus, it is claimed that English has two *phonological* segments /t/ and /s/ in sequence, while German has, in addition to /t/ and /s/, a phonological segment /t^s/. Such phonological segments or *phonemes* are written between phonemic slashes.

A phonological study thus deals with the *structure* of the phonetic segments in a language. It also deals with the *function* of these segments. In one sense this means determining whether a given sound is used in words of everyday speech or only in a particular style of speech (poetic, archaic, etc.). For example, languages often use exceptional sounds or sound sequences in *ideophones*, a class of forms which express noises, feelings, intensity, etc. The bilabial trill represented orthographically as *brrr* in English and used to convey the idea of one's being cold falls outside the sound system of English. Unlike the sound *b* or the sound *r*, which are phonetic and phonological segments of English, *brrr* does not combine with other sounds to build words. While there is a word *bat* and a word *rat*, there is no English word [ʙæt], where [ʙ] represents this bilabial trill. A bilabial trill does occur in some languages, for example, in the Babanki word [ʙɨ] 'dog,' though it is relatively rare. A second sound occurring only in a single English ideophone is the coarticulated labiovelar stop [k͡p] as found in [k͡pək͡pək͡pə] (the ideophone used to call chickens). The status of [k͡p] in English is quite different from that of the [k͡p] which frequently occurs in West African languages, for example, Igbo [àk͡pà] 'bag.' A purely phonetic study of English *describes* this sound and notes its infrequency in the language. A phonological study points out the limited *function* of [k͡p] in English, that is, the fact that it is permissible only in one ideophone. It therefore differs from [p] and [k] not only quantitatively (that is, in frequency), but also qualitatively. While

English speakers have no difficulty pronouncing the consonants in Igbo [òpì] 'horn' and [áká] 'hand,' they experience great difficulty in reproducing the [k͡p] of [àk͡pà] 'bag.' This is true even for speakers who use the sound to call chickens. This reveals the different *psychological* status of [k͡p] as opposed to [p] and [k]. Like the *brrr* sound, [k͡p] is not part of the sound structure of English. It cannot be used to build words.

1.3 Redundancy and Distinctiveness

The preceding section establishes that there is a difference between phonetics and phonology. While the former is concerned with the physical properties of speech sounds, the latter is concerned with the structure and function of these sounds in conveying meaning. It was said that two languages can have the same phonetic segments, and yet these segments may have different phonological properties in the two languages.

This statement can be better understood by comparing a fragment of the phonologies of English and Thai. English has two kinds of voiceless stops phonetically: aspirated [pʰ, tʰ, kʰ] and unaspirated [p, t, k]. Aspirated stops are found at the beginnings of words. As a result, the word which is written *pin* is pronounced [pʰɪn]. On the other hand, unaspirated stops are found after word-initial *s*. Thus, the word *spin* is pronounced [spɪn], not *[spʰɪn]. That the stop consonant in *spin* is phonetically different from the stop consonant in *pin* can be demonstrated by holding a lit match in front of the mouth: pronouncing the word *spin* makes the flame flutter less than pronouncing the word *pin*.

There are also two series of voiceless stops in Thai: an aspirated series and an unaspirated series. The Thai words [pʰàa] 'to split' and [pàa] 'forest' (Ladefoged, 1971:12) illustrate the same difference between [pʰ] and [p] as in the English words *pin* and *spin*. However, if the comparison were to stop at the observation that English and Thai share a common inventory of aspirated and unaspirated stops, an important phonological distinction would be missed.

In English, the two different *p*s are found in different environments. The fact that one *p* is aspirated and the other is not is predictable from the place it falls within the word. Thus, given the environments,

$$\#\# \underline{\hspace{2em}} \text{ɪn} \qquad\qquad \#\# \text{ s} \underline{\hspace{2em}} \text{ɪn}$$

where ## marks the beginning of a word, it would sound un-English to put [p] instead of [pʰ] in the first blank and [pʰ] instead of [p] in the second blank. The same distribution is observed in the words *tick* and *stick*, pronounced with [tʰ] and [t], and the words *kin* and *skin*, pronounced with [kʰ] and [k]. Since the presence or absence of aspiration can be predicted from the environment of the voiceless stop in a word, aspiration is said to be *redundant* in English.

The difference between English and Thai is that aspiration is not redundant in Thai. Since [pʰ] and [p] both occur in exactly the same environment in 'to split' and 'forest' (namely, at the beginning of a word and before [àa]), it is not possible to predict whether a given *p* will be aspirated or unaspirated in this language. When two words such as [pʰàa] and [pàa] differ only by one sound, they are said to constitute a *minimal pair*. The difference between the two sounds is sufficient to signal a difference in meaning. Examples of minimal pairs in English are *pin* and *bin*, *cat* and *cad*. In Thai, if we pronounce [pʰ] instead of [p] we risk pronouncing a word of a different meaning (for example, 'to split' instead of 'forest'). In English, on the other hand, if we pronounce [pʰ] instead of [p], as in the non-native sounding [spʰɪn], we probably will not be misunderstood, since aspiration is a redundant property predictable from the presence or absence of a preceding [s]. If we pronounce [b] instead of [pʰ], however, a word of a different meaning will result (for example, *bin* instead of *pin*). This means that the difference between [b] and [pʰ] is not redundant in English.

We now begin to appreciate Trubetzkoy's definition of phonology (**1.2**). Since both *p's* are capable of occurring in the same place in a word in Thai, and since the substitution of one for the other results in a word of a different meaning, aspiration is said to be *distinctive* in Thai. Similarly, the difference between [b] and [pʰ] is distinctive in English, though the difference between [p] and [pʰ] is redundant. Trubetzkoy rightly pointed out that the concerns of phonology go beyond those of phonetics. In phonology we are concerned with the distinctive vs. redundant function of speech sounds (or, more correctly, features, as we shall see below). If the goal of phonetics is to understand the physical properties of speech sounds, then the goal of phonology is to understand the ways these sounds function in language.

Phoneticians have long talked about sounds grouping into intersecting classes. Some classes are more general or inclusive (for example, the class of voiced sounds), while some classes are more specific or exclusive (for example, the class of voiceless aspirated stops). While these classes are assumed to be universally available to all languages, they are used differently by different languages (compare the use of aspiration in English and Thai). However, phonologists argue that there are only a certain number of "natural" ways a language can deal with these classes. It should be clear that one way languages differ is in their general inventory of sounds. A language can lack a sound (for example, French does not have [h]) or even a whole series (class) of sounds (for example, English does not have breathy voiced consonants). However a difference in inventory between two languages has not only *phonetic* consequences, but also *phonological* consequences.

As an illustration, consider the case of English and Berber. In the labial series, English has four oral consonants, while Berber, like many languages in North Africa and the Middle East, has only two:

	ENGLISH	BERBER
voiceless stop	p	
voiced stop	b	b
voiceless fricative	f	f
voiced fricative	v	

Berber does not have a [p] or a [v], whereas English does. In English, in order to distinguish [f] from all other consonants, it is necessary to say that it is (1) voiceless, (2) labial, and (3) a fricative. We must specify it as voiceless, because there is a [v] in English which differs from [f] only in that it is voiced. We must specify it as labial, because there is an [s] in English which differs from [f] primarily in that it is alveolar. Finally, we must specify it as a fricative, because there is a [p] in English which differs from [f] primarily in that it is a stop. Thus, three features are required to distinguish [f] from other sounds in English.

In Berber, on the other hand, only two features are needed. In order to specify [f] in Berber, we can say either that it is (1) voiceless and (2) labial or that it is (1) a fricative and (2) labial. In the first case we need not add that it is a fricative, because we know that if a Berber consonant is voiceless and labial, it can only be [f]. It cannot be [p], since this sound does not exist in the language. Similarly, in the second case we need not add that it is voiceless, because we know that if a Berber consonant is a fricative and labial, it can only be [f]. It cannot be [v], since this sound does not exist in the language.

Thus, in English each of these phonetic features is *distinctive* for all these sounds, whereas in Berber there is some *redundancy*. In labial consonants in Berber, voiceless + fricative go together: one can be predicted from the other. In English, each phonetic property has distinctive value. Thus, if one feature is changed, say, voiceless to voiced, a distinctive sound of the language is obtained (for example, [v]). Notice also in Berber that while voiceless + fricative go together in the labial series, voiced + stop also go together. Thus, we find only [b] and not [p]. In summary, the two Berber labials [f] and [b] differ from each other in *two* features, whereas in English, [p] and [b], [p] and [f], [f] and [v], and [b] and [v] each differ from each other in only *one* feature. As a result, there is less redundant information in English than in Berber, for the labial series of sounds.

A child in acquiring his language must learn to recognize which sounds of his language are distinctive and which sounds are redundant. Distinctive sound units, that is, those which are capable of distinguishing words of different meanings, are termed *phonemes*, whereas redundant sounds, that is, those which are predictable from a given environment, are termed *contextual variants* or *allophones* (see **3.1**). As the child learns the phonemes and con-textual variants of his language, he establishes that certain phonetic features are distinctive, whereas others are redundant. Some of these redundancies are language-specific, such as the Berber case just examined. Other redundancies are *universal* (for example, no language has a sound which is both an affricate and nasal). In addition, there are some redundancies which are not universal but which are frequently attested in languages. Thus, most languages only have *voiced* sonorants (that is, nasals, liquids, glides, and vowels) and no *voiceless* ones. Burmese, however, has a complete contrast between voiced and voiceless nasal consonants, as seen in the following examples (Ladefoged, 1971:11):

| [mà] | 'healthy' | [nà] | 'pain' | [ŋâ] | 'fish' |
| [m̥à] | 'order' | [n̥à] | 'nostril' | [ŋ̥â] | 'rent' |

From these words it can be seen that voicing is *distinctive* in nasal consonants in Burmese. Such a situation is relatively rare, and voiceless nasal consonants are among those sounds which are viewed as complex by phonologists. Finally, there are many sounds which are frequently missing from the phonetic inventories of languages, for example, the interdental fricatives [θ] and [ð], the front rounded vowels [ü, ø, œ], the labiovelar stops [k͡p, g͡b, ŋ͡m], and the South African click sounds. As was seen in Berber, gaps in the phonetic inventory of a language partly determine which features are used distinctively and which features are used redundantly.

1.4 Levels of Sound Representation

The preceding sections have illustrated that there are two separate (though interdependent) fields, phonetics and phonology, and that for any given language it is possible to provide either a phonetic description or a phonological description. The units of phonetic description are sound segments (or *phones*), while the units of phonological description are *phonemes*. In order to characterize the relationship between the phonemes of a language and its inventory of phonetic segments, two levels of sound representation are distinguished, a *phonological level* and a *phonetic level*. Phonological representations consist of sequences of phonemes, transcribed between diagonal bars (/ ... /)[1]; phonetic representations consist of sequences of phones, transcribed between square brackets ([...]). Thus the phonological

---

[1] As we shall see in **3.3.2**, grammatical information such as the presence of morphological boundaries plays an important role in phonology and must therefore often be included in phonological representations.

representation of the English word *pin* will be /pɪn/, while its phonetic representation will be [pʰɪn].

Since the phonological level represents the distinctive sound units of a language and not redundant phonetic information (such as the aspiration of the initial [pʰ] of English /pɪn/), it is appropriate to think of it as approximating the *mental* representations speakers have of the sounds of words in their language. As an example, consider the *ch* sounds in German. As seen from the words *lachen* [laxən] 'to laugh' and *riechen* [riːçən] 'to smell,' orthographic *ch* is pronounced both as a velar fricative [x] and as a palatal fricative [ç]. Whether *ch* will be pronounced [x] or [ç] can, however, be predicted from what precedes it: *ch* will be pronounced [x] if it is preceded by a back vowel; it will be pronounced [ç] if it is preceded by a front vowel, a consonant, or zero:

[x]		[ç]	
Buch	'book'	*mich*	'me'
hoch	'high'	*Pech*	'pitch'
noch	'still'	*horch*	'hark!'
Bach	'stream'	*China*	'China'

Because the phonetic difference between [x] and [ç] can be predicted by context, the two sounds are derived from the same unit on the phonological level, that is, from the same phoneme. The phonological identity of the two phonetic realizations [x] and [ç] is of course reflected in German orthography. More important, however, is the claim inherent in deriving these two sounds from the same phoneme; namely, it is claimed that speakers of German mentally "store" [x] and [ç] as one unit in their brain. Since there can never be a contrast between two such sounds found in mutually exclusive environments, the difference between [x] and [ç] can never serve to make a meaning difference between two words. In this sense [x] and [ç] are comparable to the earlier example of [p] and [pʰ] in English. Thus both *lachen* and *riechen* will be represented phonologically with the phoneme /x/, although the /x/ of *riechen* is pronounced [ç].[2]

1.4.1 Phonological and Phonetic Constraints

From the preceding example it should be clear that the phonetic and phonological levels sometimes differ in their inventories. Thus, both [x] and [ç] are part of the phonetic inventory of German, though only /x/ is posited in the phonological inventory. As demonstrated in **1.4**, the exact inventory partly establishes the redundancies in the use of phonetic features in a

---

[2] The choice of representing this single phoneme as /x/ rather than as /ç/ may seem arbitrary at this point, as may some of the solutions which will be discussed below. See Chapter 3 for a survey of the general considerations involved in establishing phonological representations.

language. In the German case, since /ç/ is not an independent phoneme, it is possible to formulate the following redundancy on the *phonological* level: *if a fricative is articulated further back than the alveopalatal region* (that is, where [š] is produced), *then it will be velar*. That is, there is no phonological unit which combines the features fricative and palatal, or fricative and uvular, as would be the case if either /ç/ or /X/ were among the list of German phonemes. Such a restriction on the feature composition of a unit is termed a *segmental constraint*. Since the constraint under discussion here characterizes the phonological level, we can refer to it as a *phonological* segmental constraint.

There are also segmental constraints characterizing the phonetic level of representation. In this case we speak of *phonetic* segmental constraints. If the inventories of both the phonological and the phonetic levels are identical, then the same segmental constraints are said to characterize both levels. However, the two inventories typically differ, as in the German case. Since [ç] does exist on the phonetic level, we cannot state the same restriction as a phonetic segmental constraint. However, the voiced velar fricative [ɣ] is missing from both levels in Standard German. Thus the following segmental constraint characterizes both the phonological and the phonetic levels: *if a fricative is velar, it is voiceless*. This generalization does not, of course, apply to those dialects of German which do have [ɣ].[3]

In addition to segmental constraints, there are also *sequential constraints*, and these too can pertain to either the phonological level or the phonetic level, or both. We thus speak of *phonological* sequential constraints and *phonetic* sequential constraints. That is, on both levels there are restrictions on how segments can be combined sequentially. This may mean that words or syllables can begin with only certain segments or that certain segments cannot occur before or after other segments. Let us first cite a case from English, where the same sequential constraint is found phonologically and phonetically, schematized as follows:

$$
\begin{array}{cccc}
\text{If:} & \#\# & \text{C} & \text{C} & \text{C} \\
 & & \Downarrow & \Downarrow & \Downarrow \\
\text{Then:} & \text{s} & \left\{\begin{matrix} p \\ t \\ k \end{matrix}\right\} & \left\{\begin{matrix} l \\ r \\ y \\ w \end{matrix}\right\}
\end{array}
$$

If a word (##) begins with three consonants in English, then the first consonant must be *s*, the second consonant must be *p*, *t*, or *k*, and the third

---

[3] A situation whereby a language would have a phonetic sequential constraint which is not also a phonological sequential constraint would mean that a certain phoneme, say /p/, is never realized as [p] phonetically. This possibility relates to the question of abstractness in phonology, which is discussed in **3.3.5.**

consonant must be *l*, *r*, *y*, or *w*. Any other word-initial combination of three consonants is unacceptable (for example, *fpl–*, *sfl–*, *spv–*). Notice, however, that this sequential constraint, as written, is not entirely satisfactory. The if-then condition allows word-initial *spl–*, *spr–*, *stl–*, *str–*, *skl–*, and *skr–* clusters. Words such as *spleen*, *spring*, *stroke*, and *scream* show that initial *spl–*, *spr–*, *str–*, and *skr–* are well attested in English. On the other hand, words with initial *skl–*, such as *sclerosis*, are extremely rare and are limited to a handful of learned borrowings. Also, no word in English begins with *stl–*, since *l* cannot follow *t* or *d* (thus we have the words *play* and *clay*, with *pl–* and *kl–*, but no corresponding word **tlay*). Finally, there are severe restrictions on the occurrence of *CCy–* and *CCw–*. When *y* is the third of three word-initial consonants, the following vowel must be *u*, for example, *spew* [spyu], *skew* [skyu].[4] When *w* is the third consonant, the second consonant must be *k*, for example, *square* [skwer]. Thus the precise statement of a sequential constraint can often be quite complex in nature.

While this sequential constraint on word-initial three-consonant clusters pertains to both the phonological and the phonetic levels, the sequential constraints of the two levels sometimes differ in a language. This can mean either (1) that there is a sequential constraint which characterizes the phonological level but not the phonetic level; or (2) that there is a sequential constraint which characterizes the phonetic level but not the phonological level. As an example of the first situation, French disallows many consonant clusters on the phonological level which are nonetheless permitted on the phonetic level. For instance, phonologically there are no word-initial /fn/ or /št/ sequences in the language. However, phrases such as *la fenêtre* 'the window' and *le jeton* 'the token' are pronounced [la fnɛ:tr] and [lə štɔ̃], respectively. On the phonological level, on the other hand, these consonants do not occur in sequence, but rather are separated by a schwa, as seen in the pronunciation of such words in isolation, that is, [fənɛ:tr] and [žətɔ̃]. As will be discussed in **1.4.2**, this phonological /ə/ is sometimes deleted when the phonological representation is converted into the corresponding phonetic one.

As an example of the second situation (that is, where a phonological sequence is not permitted on the phonetic level), consider the case of word-initial *sC–* clusters in Spanish. Phonetically speaking, word-initial sequences

---

[4] There have been a number of proposals for the transcription of English vowels. In capturing the phonetic differences between [uw] as in *fool* and [ʊ] as in *full*, we note that (1) [uw] is longer than [ʊ]; (2) [uw] is dipthongized, while [ʊ] is not; and (3) [uw] is tense, while [ʊ] is lax. In the remainder of this study we shall transcribe this difference as one between tense and lax. That is, the so-called diphthongized vowels will be transcribed as [i, e, u, o] rather than as [iy, ey, uw, ow], while the corresponding nondiphthongized vowels will be transcribed as [ɪ, ɛ, ʊ, ɔ].

of [s] followed by another consonant must be preceded by [ɛ], for example, [ɛspaɲa] 'Spain,' [ɛstufo] 'stove,' [ɛskwela] 'school.' However, this [ɛ] is predictable from the fact that it is required any time a word would otherwise begin with an [sC] sequence. It therefore need not be represented in the phonological representations /spaɲa/, /stufo/, and /skwelo/ (just as aspiration and the difference between [x] and [ç] were not represented phonologically in English and German, respectively). Thus, the sequential constraint against word-initial *sC–* applies only to the phonetic level and not to the phonological level.

1.4.2 Phonological Rules

The reason that phonological constraints sometimes differ from phonetic constraints in a language is that there are *phonological rules* (P-rules) which convert phonological representations into phonetic ones. For example, /la fənɛ:tr/ 'the window' is converted to [la fnɛ:tr] in French by a phonological rule which can be schematized as follows[5]:

$$\text{ə} \rightarrow \emptyset \;/\; \text{V C} \underline{\quad}$$

This rule states that schwa may be deleted (that is, becomes zero or Ø) when the preceding consonant is in turn preceded by a vowel.[6] Thus there are phonological rules, such as this rule of schwa deletion, which relate the phonological and phonetic levels. These rules, which reveal linguistically significant generalizations in phonology, are either *optional* or *obligatory*. The above French rule is optional, since it is possible for the same speaker to pronounce either [la fnɛ:tr] (in fast or allegro speech) or [la fənɛ:tr] (in slow, articulated speech). The Spanish rule which inserts [ɛ] before word-initial /sC/ sequences, and which can be schematized as follows:

$$\emptyset \rightarrow \text{ɛ} \;/\; \#\# \underline{\quad} \text{s C}$$

is, however, obligatory, since [ɛspaɲa] 'Spain' cannot be pronounced *[spaɲa].

Phonological rules can also be divided into those which produce *alternations* and those which do not, a distinction which will be of significance in

---

[5] The segment to the left of the arrow is to be read as the input to be changed by the rule; the segment to the right of the arrow represents the change, while the information to the right of the "environment slash" / indicates the grammatical or phonetic context in which the rule takes place. Thus, in this French rule, /VCə/ is converted to [VC]. For a discussion of notational conventions and the role of formalisms in phonology, see **4.3.1.**

[6] This statement covers only the major cases of schwa deletion in French, a phenomenon which is particularly complex (see Dell, 1973:221–260). Thus, it does not cover examples such as *je t'aime* 'I love you,' which is pronounced [žə tɛ:m] in slow speech, but [štɛ:m] in rapid speech.

the discussion of abstractness in **3.3.5**. A particularly clear example of a rule which produces alternations is seen in the following forms:

we miss you   → [wi mɪš(y)u]
we please you → [wi pliž(y)u]
we bet you   → [wi bɛč(y)u]
we fed you   → [wi fɛǰ(y)u]

The phonetic forms on the right represent possible pronunciations of these forms in American English. In careful speech, speakers may pronounce [wi mɪs yu], etc., but the more rapid the pace, the more likely that forms such as the above will be heard.[7] The following optional rule is therefore needed:

$$
\begin{bmatrix} s \\ z \\ t \\ d \end{bmatrix} \rightarrow \begin{bmatrix} š \\ ž \\ č \\ ǰ \end{bmatrix} / \underline{\quad} y
$$

This rule states that /s/ becomes [š], /z/ becomes [ž], /t/ becomes [č], and /d/ becomes [ǰ] before /y/ (which in turn may be deleted, as indicated by the parentheses in the phonetic transcriptions).

Because of this rule, a word such as *miss* will have two pronunciations. It will be pronounced [mɪs] in a context such as *we miss it* [wi mɪs ɪt], but [mɪš] in a context such as *we miss you*. These alternants of the same word or *morpheme*[8] 'miss' are termed *allomorphs*. Whenever such alternants are conditioned by a phonological rule, the phonetic shape of the allomorphs is *predictable*. Thus, American English speakers say [wi mɪš(y)u], but never *[wi mɪš ɪt]. While many allomorphs are predictable in this way, others are not. A morpheme may have different pronunciations not because of different phonological environments but because of different grammatical environments. Thus, the past tense of the verb *to go* is *went*, and the plural of the noun *mouse* is *mice*. In both of these cases it is not possible to derive one form from the other by means of a general phonological rule. Such cases of irregular allomorphs (known as *suppletion*) therefore differ in a crucial way from the more regular allomorphs derived by phonological rules. While [mɪš] can be derived from /mɪs/ by a general rule of English phonology, [wɛnt] cannot be derived from /go/.

---

[7] The change of /s/ to [š] is also affected by stress. Thus, the /s/ of the phrase *I miss yóghurt* and the word *mis-úse* does not become [š] as readily as in *I miss you*, since the syllable following /s/ is stressed in the first two instances.

[8] A morpheme can be defined for our purposes as a minimal unit of sound carrying meaning. It can consist of a single segment (e.g., the /z/ of *dogs* [dɔgz], which denotes plurality), or of several segments (e.g., /dɔg/).

Because native speakers hear and produce [s] and [š] in the same morpheme (depending on the phonological context), the English language is said to have an *alternation* between [s] and [š]. Whenever there is an alternation, the need for a phonological level distinct from a phonetic one is evident. In this case, speakers are aware of the underlying (phonological) /s/ and are capable of saying [wi mɪs yu] in slow or careful speech. Thus phonological /s/ is sometimes pronounced [s], sometimes [š].

However, there is not always an alternation for each phonological rule. Returning to the [p] vs. [pʰ] distinction discussed earlier, there must be a rule such as the following in English:

$$\begin{bmatrix} p \\ t \\ k \end{bmatrix} \rightarrow \begin{bmatrix} p^h \\ t^h \\ k^h \end{bmatrix} / \#\# -$$

Phonological /p, t, k/ is converted by this rule to phonetic [pʰ, tʰ, kʰ] at the beginning of a word. There are, however, no resulting allomorphs and no alternations of the kind we have just seen. English does include a few remnants of alternations, such as in the words *take* [tʰek] and *mistake* [mɪstek] (where the latter form is derived historically from *mis + take*). In these forms it might be argued that there is an alternation between [tʰ] and [t]. However, in order to maintain this position, it is necessary to demonstrate that native speakers view *take* and the final part of *mistake* as the same morpheme.

In summary, some phonological rules are obligatory, while others are optional; and some phonological rules produce alternations, while others do not. While we shall look in depth at numerous phonological processes in languages in subsequent chapters, the different kinds of operations that phonological rules can perform are summarized below:

1. Phonological rules can change segments (or, as will be seen in Chapter 2, change the phonetic features of segments). In the American English example, /s, z, t, d/ are changed to [š, ž, č, ǰ] before /y/. In terms of phonetic features, alveolar consonants become alveopalatal before the palatal glide /y/.

2. Phonological rules can delete segments. The schwa of French /fənɛːtr/ 'window' is deleted in the phrase [la fnɛːtr] 'the window,' as illustrated earlier.

3. Phonological rules can insert segments. We have seen that Spanish inserts [ɛ] before word-initial /sC/ sequences, for example, /spaɲa/ 'Spain' is pronounced [ɛspaɲa].

4. Phonological rules can coalesce segments. In many languages /ai/ and /au/ are realized respectively as [e] (or [ɛ]) and [o] (or [ɔ]). In such cases the phonetic output is in a sense a "blend" of the two segments in the phonological input: the lowness of /a/ combined with the close tongue position of /i/ and /u/ results in the mid vowels [e] and [o].

5. Finally, there are occasional cases where phonological rules can permute

or interchange segments. This operation, known as *metathesis,* as when *ask* is pronounced [æks], converts phonological /AB/ to phonetic [BA].

1.5 Some Universals of Phonological Systems

Recent phonological studies have revealed a number of common properties shared by the sound systems of the world's languages. One of the major goals of phonologists is to discover *phonological universals.* One such universal, the presence of the vowel /a/ in all languages, has already been mentioned. Other universals (or, in some cases, "universal tendencies") have been hypothesized on the basis of cross-linguistic comparisons of phonological inventories, language acquisition, and language change.

1.5.1 Phonological Inventories

As stated above, certain sounds are found in more languages than others. Cross-linguistic comparisons have been made on the basis of both phonetic and phonological inventories, although we shall look only at the latter. Thus the phonological segment /s/, for instance, is more frequent in the world's languages than is /θ/. In addition, it has been observed that the presence of certain segments in a language often implies the presence of other segments. If a language has /θ/, it can be assumed that it also has /s/. The reverse is not true, since there are languages which have /s/ but do not have /θ/. Such *implicational universals* have been discussed by Jakobson (1941) and Greenberg (1966a). In an implicational universal, X implies Y but Y does not imply X. Thus, to take another example, the consonant /t/ implies the consonant /d/, but /d/ does not imply /t/. That is, it has been suggested that any language which has /d/ also has /t/. There are, however, many languages which have /t/ but do not have /d/ (for example, Finnish, Korean, Southern Paiute).

Ferguson (1966) and Greenberg (1966a) have devoted considerable attention to the status of nasalized vowels in languages. Some languages have a distinctive contrast between oral and nasalized vowels. Thus, the French words *sept* [sɛt] 'seven' and *sainte* [sɛ̃t] 'saint(f.)' differ primarily in that the latter has a nasalized vowel while the former has an oral vowel. Given that both oral and nasalized vowels are found in languages, it is logically possible to imagine four different vowel systems:[9]

    (a) languages with V and Ṽ
    (b) languages with V only
    (c) languages with Ṽ only
    (d) languages with neither

[9] The symbol V stands here for any oral vowel, and the symbol Ṽ for any nasalized vowel.

Of the four possible vowel systems, only the first two are in fact found. French is an example of (a), since it has both oral and nasalized vowels. Italian is an example of (b), since it has only oral phonological vowels.[10] No language has only nasalized vowels (c), and no language has no vowels at all (d). We can conclude that the presence of nasalized vowels *implies* the presence of oral vowels in a language, but not the reverse. Thus X implies Y but Y does not imply X.

Another instance of an implicational universal concerns voiceless and voiced stops. Again, there are four logically possible systems:

   (a) languages with /p, t, k, b, d, g/
   (b) languages with /p, t, k/
   (c) languages with /b, d, g/
   (d) languages with neither series

As in the previous example, only the first two possible stop systems are found. There are languages with voiceless and voiced stops (a), such as English and French; there are also languages with only voiceless stops (b), such as Southern Paiute (Sapir, 1933). No language has only voiced stops (c), and no language has no stops at all (d). Thus, the series /b, d, g/ implies the series /p, t, k/, but the series /p, t, k/ does not imply the series /b, d, g/.[11]

1.5.2 Language Acquisition

We also owe to Jakobson (1941) the observation that, in all languages, sound segments tend to be learned in a relatively fixed order by children. While more recent studies have not always confirmed the details of Jakobson's relative chronology of sound acquisition, certain general tendencies cannot be missed. It can be observed, for instance, that children learning English acquire [f] before they acquire [θ]. A child is quite likely to produce a word such as *thumb* with an initial [f]. As a result, the word *three* may become homophonous with the word *free*. Other general tendencies include the learning of voiceless stops before voiced stops, as well as the learning of front consonants such as [p] and [t] before back consonants such as [k].

[10] Since all languages show a tendency for a vowel to receive at least a slight degree of nasalization in the context of a nasal consonant, the minute nasalization of the two instances of [a] in the word *andante* cannot be said to be a *phonological* property of Italian (see **5.2.5**).

[11] This implicational universal can be extended to include all *obstruents* (i.e., stops, affricates, and fricatives). Notice, however, that some languages may lack one particular member of a series. Thus, Arabic, Berber, Hausa, and several other languages lack /p/ and /v/, although they have /f/ and /b/. In these languages, /t, k, f, s . : . / are said to imply /b, d, g, z . . . /. It still remains true that no language will have a series of voiced obstruents unless it also has a series of voiceless obstruents.

This last tendency is revealed by the predominance of front consonants in the following common forms for 'mother' and 'father' in child language (Jakobson, 1960):

	LABIAL	DENTAL/ALVEOLAR	
nasal	mama	nana	'mother'
oral	papa/baba	tata/dada	'father'

The presence of labial or dental/alveolar consonants in the forms for 'mother' and 'father' is widely attested in the acquisition of unrelated languages. In addition, cross-linguistic investigations of child language indicate a nasal consonant in 'mother' but an oral consonant in 'father.' While the above forms are frequently heard, it is rarely the case that a child refers to his mother as [ŋaŋa] and to his father as [kaka]. The statistical bias in favor of front consonants in the terms 'mother' and 'father' is presumably due to the fact that labial and dental/alveolar consonants are learned before velar consonants. Thus, numerous studies in child language have reported children replacing velars by dental/alveolar consonants. Stampe (1969:446), for instance, reports a child saying [ta] instead of *car* [kar], and [tæt] instead of *cat* [kæt].

Jakobson further made the discovery that there is a correlation between the order in which sounds are acquired by children and the implicational universals noted on the basis of phonological inventories. While a language will not have /b, d, g/ unless it has /p, t, k/, a child will presumably not learn [b, d, g] until he has learned [p, t, k]. This correlation is not accidental, but rather results from the relative complexity of some sounds (for example, [b, d, g]) as compared to others (for example, [p, t, k]).

1.5.3 Language Change

The notion of relative complexity of certain speech sounds over others also plays a role in determining the direction of sound change. While it is a well-known fact that sounds change through time, some sound changes are more frequently attested than others, while still other potential sound changes are not attested at all. For example, the sound change turning [b, d, g] into [p, t, k] has been observed in several language families of the world (for example, in the history of Chinese). This change constitutes part of the consonant shift known as Grimm's Law, which separates the Germanic branch from the rest of the Indo-European languages. On the other hand, a sound change turning all instances of [p, t, k] into [b, d, g] has never been reported. If such a sound change were to take place, the resulting system would include a series of voiced stops but no series of voiceless stops. In other words, the Jakobsonian implicational universal whereby /b, d, g/ implies /p, t, k/ would be violated. As pointed out by Greenberg (1966a:510), any sound change which produces an impossible sound system (such as the one which would result from a change voicing all voiceless stops) is an impossible sound change.

In the study of sound change it becomes apparent, then, that some changes are unidirectional. While X frequently becomes Y, Y rarely (if ever) becomes X. In addition, while a sound X may be frequently observed to change into another sound Y, it may not change into a third sound Z. For example, an aspirated stop easily becomes an affricate (compare English *to* [tʰu], German *zu* [tˢu]). It does not normally become a nasal consonant. Thus, we would not expect the English word *to* to change its pronunciation to [nu], although it could conceivably go the route of German affrication.

Each time a sound change is observed, the relationship between the original sound and the new sound can be examined. If all occurrences of X change to Y, we look for some articulatory or acoustic property shared by X and Y. If only some instances of X change to Y (for example, those which are followed by the sound Z), we again assume a phonetic property shared by X and Y, and then seek to understand the way that Z motivates the sound change in question. In general, sound changes of the first type, which are said to be *context-free*, tend to produce segments which are articulatorily or perceptually less complex, while sound changes of the second type, which are said to be *context-sensitive*, tend to produce more complex segments. Voiced stops can become voiceless in a context-free fashion (thereby producing less complex segments), but voiceless stops cannot become voiced as a context-free sound change. On the other hand, voiceless consonants can become voiced in restricted contexts (producing more complex segments). In particular, [p, t, k] may become [b, d, g] between vowels (for example, the consonant in English *auto* is frequently voiced) as well as after a nasal consonant (for example, Kpelle *ḿ* 'my' + *pólù* 'back' is pronounced [ḿbólù] (Welmers, 1962:73)).

The study of sound change is thus intimately tied to the study of implicational universals and language acquisition. As a final example, the tendency of sounds to be dropped (lost) at the end of words more readily than at the beginning can be cited. The spelling of the French word *rat* 'rat' indicates that there once was a final [t]. The original pronunciation [rat] has become [ra], and not [at]. Similarly, the Proto-Bamileke form [kám] 'crab' has become [ká] in Dschang-Bamileke, and not [ám]. In both cases a final consonant has been lost historically, revealing that consonants are more stable in word-initial position than they are in word-final position. What this means is that a syllable consisting of three segments, consonant-vowel-consonant (CVC), is more likely to become CV than VC. This fact correlates with a universal established by Jakobson and others to the effect that all languages have CV syllables (see **6.1.1.1**). Not all languages have VC syllables. A historical change of all CVC syllables to VC would therefore create an impossible phonological system. Finally, it has been noted in studies in language acquisition that CV is the earliest syllable structure to be acquired by children. All three of these observations (the favoring of CV syllables in phonological systems, in language acquisition, and in language change) are related and are receiving attention from linguists working in each of these areas.

1.6 The Psychological Reality of Phonological Descriptions

In **1.4** we distinguished a phonological level, a phonetic level, and phonological rules converting phonological representations into phonetic ones. The phonological level captures the distinctive sound contrasts of a language, while the phonological rules specify how the underlying phonological units (or *phonemes*) are to be pronounced in the various environments in which they are found. The resulting phonetic level provides a transcription of the sound segments used in actual utterances.

Learning a language, especially one's native language, requires that a person learn the distinctive contrasts on the phonological level, the phonological rules, and the resulting phonetic properties specified by these rules. It is therefore quite appropriate to ask for evidence that the phonological properties described by linguists are in fact learned by speakers—that is, that they are *psychologically real*. While many kinds of evidence have been seen in the literature, only four will be mentioned here.

1.6.1 Linguistic Intuitions

The first kind of evidence comes from the probing of linguistic intuitions. This has been done informally by asking a native speaker (perhaps the linguist himself) for his intuition on some aspect of the phonology of his language. It has also been done employing more sophisticated experimental techniques. As a case in point, let us return to the issue of sequential constraints in phonology. The question is, how do we know that native speakers "know" (in some tacit, not necessarily verbalizable form) the sequential constraints of their language?

According to Chomsky (1964:64) and Chomsky and Halle (1968:380ff), knowledge of these sequential constraints is responsible for the fact that speakers of a language have a sense of what "sounds" like a native word and what does not. Thus, the word *brick* is an English word familiar to all speakers of the language. The word *blick* is equally acceptable (we shall say "well-formed") in its phonological structure, but happens not to be a word of

English (that is, it is nonoccurring). On the other hand, *bnick* is not acceptable in its phonological structure (we shall say "ill-formed"), since /n/ cannot follow /b/ at the beginning of an English word.[12] As the second element in a word, /n/ can only be preceded by /s/ or a vowel.

The *brick*:*blick* opposition shows that two forms which both satisfy the sequential constraints of the language (are well-formed) can differ in that one word occurs in the dictionary or *lexicon* (*brick*), while the other does not (*blick*). Words which are well-formed but are not found in the lexicon are termed *accidental gaps*. On the other hand, the *blick*:*bnick* opposition shows that two words not occurring in the lexicon can differ in that one is well-formed (*blick*) and the other ill-formed (*bnick*). Words which are ill-formed and do not occur in the lexicon are termed *systematic gaps*.

As a final possibility, exceptional words such as *sclerosis* and *sphere* (*skl–* and *sf–* sequences are normally not found word-initially in English) are ill-formed but occur in the lexicon. We therefore have the following four possibilities:

	OCCURRING	NONOCCURRING
well-formed	*brick*	*blick*
ill-formed	*sphere*	*bnick*

It is just an accident that English does not have a word *blick*, but it is not an accident that English does not have a word *bnick*; there is a systematic reason, namely a sequential constraint forbidding *bn–* sequences at the beginning of a word (but see footnote 12). *Bnick* violates the system in a way that *blick* does not. Thus, it would not be surprising if a new product on the market were called *Blick Soap*. It would be quite surprising to find anyone inventing *Bnick Soap*.

While most work on phonological constraints is done on the basis of intuitive judgments about permissible sequences, there is also *experimental* evidence that speakers are aware of sequential constraints in their language. A particularly revealing experimental study is reported by Greenberg and Jenkins (1964). They demonstrate that speakers of English judge nonsense words such as *swit* [swɪt] and *gluck* [glək] to be much more English-like than the nonsense words [čwʊp] and [ðyəŋ], which violate the sequential constraints of the language. What is of interest is that they show that there is a continuum from completely well-formed nonsense words to nonsense words which are aberrant in that they violate not only the sequential constraints

---

[12] Actually, the sequence *bn–* cannot occur at the beginning of a *syllable* in English (see **6.1.2.1**).

but also the segmental constraints, since they contain non-English sounds, for example, [zbüɣ].

1.6.2 Foreign Accents

It is well known that speakers substitute sounds of their own language for the sounds of foreign languages they attempt to speak. The result is that they typically have "foreign accents." Often these accents are directly attributable to the phonological properties of the native language. Thus, speakers of Spanish tend to insert [ɛ] before English words beginning with /s/ followed by another consonant (for example, *I espeak espanish*). This insertion is due to the (improper) operation in English of the spanish ɛ-insertion rule discussed and exemplified in **1.4.2**. Similarly, American English speakers have been known to pronounce the French word *monsieur* [məsyø] as [məšə] and the Spanish word *gracias* [grasyas] as [grašəs]. This substitution can be accounted for on the basis of the phonological rule in American English which derives [š] from /s/ followed by /y/ (see **1.4.2**). The foreign sound substitutions made by Spanish speakers when they speak English and by American English speakers when they speak French or Spanish reveal that the phonological rules in question have an objective reality. That is, phonological analysis, far from being a purely formal study of patterns, makes predictions about how speakers of one language will reproduce sounds of another language.

1.6.3 Speech Errors

While speech errors have long fascinated linguists and nonlinguists alike, it is only recently that attention has been focused on the possibility of using the data of speech errors as an indication of the psychological reality of phonological descriptions. A commonly studied type of speech error—a *spoonerism*—occurs when the initial consonants of two words are interchanged, as when someone says *tips of the slung* instead of *slips of the tongue*. The theoretical interest of such speech errors is discussed in the works of Fromkin (1971, 1973a, b). Spoonerisms can involve interchanging the place of initial consonants, as in the above example; in other examples, a consonant is interchanged with zero, that is, it is transposed, as when someone says *pick slimp* [pɪk slɪmp] instead of *pink slip* [pɪŋk slɪp]. The nasal consonant of the word *pink* has been transferred to the resulting nonsense word *slimp*. But notice that somehow in the transformation from the intended utterance to the speech error, [ŋ] has become [m]. If the velar nasal had been transferred as such, the resulting error would have been *[slɪŋp]. However, this sequence is ill-formed in English, since there is a sequential constraint stating that within a word a nasal consonant is made at the same place of articulation as a following consonant.[13] Thus we have the words *ramp, rant,* and *rank* with [mp, nt, ŋk], but not the words **ranp, *rangt,* and **ramk*. The modification of [ŋ] to [m] which accompanies the speech error thus provides evidence for the reality of this sequential constraint. As pointed out by Fromkin, forms resulting from speech errors generally do not violate the phonological properties of the language.

Speech error phenomena motivate the necessity of a fundamental distinction in the study of language. Speakers of English "know" that the word *pink* should be pronounced [pɪŋk] rather than [pɪk]. The error involved in pronouncing [pɪk] is therefore one of *language use* rather than one in the *knowledge* that the speaker has of the way this word should be pronounced. In other words, the speaker who uttered *pick slimp* did not think that the correct pronunciation of *pink* was [pɪk]. Thus a distinction is necessary between *linguistic competence*, which represents the underlying "system" of a language and aims at revealing the speakers' implicit knowledge, and *linguistic performance*, which represents the way speakers *use* that system (competence) in producing and perceiving utterances. In our phonological descriptions we shall be concerned with competence, that is, the knowledge speakers have of the sound system of their language. On the other hand, the data of performance, such as in speech errors, may very well provide supporting evidence for the reality of phonological analyses.

1.6.4 Language Acquisition

The study of language acquisition is of importance to phonologists, since it is possible to observe the stages children go through as they attempt to discover the phonology of their language. In particular, the errors they make are sometimes quite revealing. For instance, children speaking English have frequently been observed to substitute the sound [w] for [r]. Thus they say *wabbit* instead of *rabbit* and *wight* instead of *right*. However, when adults repeat *wabbit* and *wight* back to the children who normally produce these forms, it is often discovered that the children, capable of *perceiving* the difference between [w] and [r], are annoyed at the adults' use of child language. This ability of the child to perceive a sound distinction which he does not produce is justification for distinguishing a phonological level as opposed to a phonetic level. The phonological level, representing the child's mental representation of words, has the forms *wabbit* and *wight* beginning with /r/.

---

[13] There are some important exceptions to this constraint, as when the negative marker *un-* is prefixed to a labial-initial stem, e.g., *un-predictable* (not **um-predictable*), or when the past tense marker *-ed* is suffixed after a labial nasal, e.g., *strummed* [strəmd], not **[strənd]* or **[strəmb]*. Note, however, that for those speakers who pronounce *pink* as [pɪ̃k], i.e., with a nasalized vowel and no nasal consonant, the speech error change of *pink slip* [pɪ̃k slɪp] to *pick slimp* [pɪk slɪ̃p] may involve only a switch of nasality on the vowels of the two words.

The phonetic level has these forms beginning with [w]. Thus, at this stage in the child's linguistic development, there is a phonological rule merging /r/ with /w/. He keeps track of which words with [w] have a phonological /r/ and which have a phonological /w/, since he will later give up this temporary rule and put in phonetic [r] in the appropriate places.

This example shows that, in language acquisition at least, it is possible to have different phonological representations for the same sound. Thus [w] is sometimes represented as /r/ and sometimes as /w/. A similar example is found in the phonological system of a child isolated for twelve of her fourteen years (Curtiss et al., 1974). In the speech of "Genie," word-initial /sC/ sequences are pronounced either without the initial /s/ or with an inserted [ə] between the consonants, for example, *spoon* [pŭn] or [səpŭn]. In this case such words have been internalized (stored phonologically) with the underlying clusters, but the phonological system is characterized by a phonetic sequential constraint disallowing these clusters on the surface. At this stage in Genie's development, there are two conflicting phonological rules (one of *s*-deletion and one of ə-insertion) which guarantee that [sC] sequences will not appear at the beginning of a word.

1.7 Summary

In this chapter we have distinguished between phonetics and phonology and, in the description of sound systems, between a phonetic and a phonological level. In the following chapters a close look will be taken at these and other aspects of the study of phonology. In Chapter 2 we shall begin by focusing attention on the development of *distinctive feature theory*, which provides the framework most commonly used in the description of phonological and phonetic segments. In Chapter 3 different approaches to phonological analysis will be treated, with particular emphasis on the nature of underlying (phonological) representations. In Chapters 4 and 5 the notions of *simplicity* and *naturalness* will be discussed within the framework of *generative phonology*. Finally, in Chapter 6, stress, tone, and other *suprasegmental* properties of phonology will conclude our study.

2

DISTINCTIVE FEATURE THEORY

2.1 The Need for Distinctive Features

Although the phonological rules in Chapter 1 are all written in terms of segments, such notation is actually only an abbreviation. Rules typically apply to classes of phonetically related segments, and not to arbitrary classes of unrelated segments. Thus, the change of /s, z, t, d/ to [š, ž, č, ǰ] illustrated from American English in the preceding chapter involves something more general than four segments changing into four other segments. In particular, the four phonological segments /s, z, t, d/ have in common that they are alveolar consonants.[1] The four phonetic segments [š, ž, č, ǰ] have in common that they are alveopalatal consonants. Thus, in order to reveal that these two classes of segments are not composed of random members, the American English rule by which the former consonants are converted into the latter consonants before /y/ should, as a first approximation, be written as follows:

Alveolar → Alveopalatal / ___ y
   C   C

[1] Actually, since they are not nasals or liquids, the consonants /s, z, t, d/ have in common that they are alveolar *obstruents* (see **2.4.1**).

If the phonological segments becoming [š, ž, č, ǰ] had been /s, k, b, r/, no general phonetic feature such as alveolar could have been stated; similarly, if /s, z, t, d/ had become [š, g, p, l], no general phonetic feature such as alveopalatal could have been stated. In fact, this is exactly what is expected. Since the two classes /s, k, b, r/ and [š, g, p, l] are composed of arbitrary segments, we should not expect to find languages utilizing these classes. However, the arbitrariness of /s, k, b, r/, as opposed to /s, z, t, d/, is revealed only when an attempt is made to *extract* the phonetic property shared by all of the segments. When a phonetic property can be extracted, a generalization is revealed. When no phonetic property can be extracted, these segments should not be expected to occur as a class in languages.

It is a significant fact about phonological systems that segments typically group themselves into phonetically definable classes. As just seen, they do so in the inputs as well as the outputs of phonological rules (see **1.4.2**). However, while the reformulation of the above rule of American English is superior to the original formulation in Chapter 1 involving individual segments, we still fail to see in this new statement of the rule why the class of alveolar consonants should become alveopalatal before the segment /y/. As stated, it would perhaps make as good sense for this change to be accomplished before the segment /p/ or /r/, etc. In order to reveal the phonetic motivation or "naturalness" of such a change before /y/, the rule must be reformulated again with /y/ restated also in terms of phonetic features:

Alveolar → Alveopalatal / __ Palatal
   C   C   G

Now we see that alveolar consonants become alveopalatal before a palatal glide, which /y/ is. In other words, the phonetic motivation for this rule— rather than an equivalent change taking place before /p/ or /r/—is now made explicit: alveolars become *palatalized* to alveopalatals before a palatal. Thus a full understanding of this process of palatalization is possible only when phonetic features are substituted for segments.

Just as the symbols *C, V, N, L,* and *G* are abbreviations for consonants, vowels, nasals, liquids, and glides, symbols such as *p, t, k, a, i, u* are used as convenient shortcuts for the feature compositions which combine to produce these segments. The symbol *p,* for instance, stands for a consonant which is voiceless, labial, and a stop; the symbol *a* stands for a vowel which is low, central, and unrounded. While such segments will be used in the formulation of phonological rules below, it is important to recognize that the phonetic features are ultimately the factors responsible for the way phonological systems function.

2.2 Trubetzkoy's Theory of Distinctive Oppositions

The study of the phonetic properties of segments is the subject of the various branches of phonetics. As such, this study of how speech sounds are made dates back over two millennia. As phonologists, our interest in phonetic features centers around the question of how the articulatory and acoustic properties of sounds are put to work in various languages—in particular, how they function to convey meaning. We shall begin with the work of Trubetzkoy, one of the founders of the Prague School of Linguistics, which developed in the decade preceding World War II.

Trubetzkoy (1939) attempted a comprehensive taxonomy of the phonetic properties of the distinctive contrasts employed by languages. He was interested not only in how /p/ differs from /b/, but also in what the nature of the contrast was within a given phonological system. Thus, in his *Principles of Phonology*, he classified distinctive oppositions[2] on the basis of (1) their relationship to the entire system of oppositions, (2) the relationship between opposition members, and (3) the extent of their distinctive force.

2.2.1 Bilateral, Multilateral, Proportional, and Isolated Oppositions

The first dichotomy Trubetzkoy draws is between *bilateral* and *multilateral* oppositions. In bilateral oppositions, the sum of the phonetic (henceforth *distinctive*; see below) features common to both members of the opposition is common to these two members only (1939:68). Thus, in English, /p/ and /b/ stand in a distinctive opposition and have in common that they are "oral labial stops." The opposition is bilateral since there are no other consonants in English which come under the heading "oral labial stops." /m/ is not in the same class because it is nasal, and /f/, /v/, and /w/ because they are not stops. In Thai, on the other hand, one finds not only /p/ and /b/ but also /pʰ/. We can still say that /p/ and /b/ stand in a bilateral opposition, but it is necessary to further specify the properties that they have in common as "oral unaspirated labial stops." However, /pʰ/ and /b/ do not stand in a bilateral opposition. They have in common that they are "oral labial stops," but /p/ is also an oral labial stop. Since there is a third segment which shares the properties common to /pʰ/ and /b/, these latter segments are said to be in a *multilateral* opposition.

Another example comes from English /f/ and /b/. The two consonants

---

[2] By opposition is meant a sound difference which results in a meaning difference, as discussed in Chapter 1. Thus there is an opposition between /p/ and /b/ in English, which are said to be *phonemes*, because of such word pairs as *pan* and *ban*.

have in common that they are "labial obstruents" (see footnote 1). This is an example of a multilateral opposition, since /p/ and /v/ are also labial obstruents in English. In Berber, however, which has no */p/ or */v/, /f/ and /b/ stand in a bilateral opposition, since there are no other labial obstruents in the language. Thus, the same phonetic segments distinguished by the same phonetic features can stand in a multilateral opposition in one language and in a bilateral opposition in another language.

Another distinction is made concerning oppositions which, in relation to the whole system, are either *proportional* or *isolated.* Trubetzkoy states (p. 70) that "an opposition is proportional if the relation between its members is identical with the relation between the members of another opposition or several other oppositions of the same system." Otherwise the opposition is said to be an isolated one. In English, the opposition between /p/ and /b/ is proportional, because the relation between its members is identical with the relation between /t/ and /d/ and between /k/ and /g/. On the other hand, the opposition between /l/ and /r/ is isolated, since no other segments in English stand in the same relation as these two opposition members. Whether an opposition is proportional or isolated depends on the language. For example, the relation existing between /t/ and /x/ (that is, alveolar stop : velar fricative, agreeing in voice quality) is isolated in Standard German, since there is no /ɣ/ to correspond with the voiced alveolar stop /d/. In a language with /t/, /d/, /x/, and /ɣ/, the relation between /t/ and /x/ would be a proportional one, since /t/ is to /x/ as /d/ is to /ɣ/. Trubetzkoy concludes (p. 71) that "these different types of oppositions determine the inner order or structure of the phonemic inventory as a system of distinctive oppositions." Thus "proportions" can be stated, such as $p:b = t:d = k:g$, which are said to have "phonological reality" (p. 72).

2.2.2 Privative, Gradual, and Equipollent Oppositions

In classifying oppositions on the basis of the relation between the members of the oppositions, Trubetzkoy recognizes oppositions which are *privative*, *gradual*, and *equipollent* (p. 75). In privative oppositions, one member of the opposition carries a phonetic "mark" which the other member lacks. In other words, it is a question of the presence vs. the absence of a feature. In the opposition /b/ : /p/ in English, /b/ is characterized by the presence of voicing, while /p/ lacks voicing. In the opposition /m/ : /b/, /m/ is characterized by nasality, while /b/ lacks it. In Thai, /pʰ/ has aspiration, while /p/ lacks it, and so on. The opposition member which is characterized by the presence of a mark is said to be "marked," while the member which is characterized by the absence of this mark is said to be "unmarked" (see **5.1.2.1**).

Oppositions in which the members are characterized by different degrees or gradations of the same property are said to be gradual. Thus, in a language such as Yoruba, which has the following seven-vowel system,

i   u
e   o
ε   ɔ
     a

the opposition between /u/ and /o/ is a gradual one, since the vowel /ɔ/ is a third degree of the same property (vowel height). /u/ cannot be said to carry a mark, because there are three values of back rounded vowels—high, mid, and low. In Turkish, on the other hand, where the following vowel system is found.

i   ü   ɨ   u
e   ö   a   o

it is possible to regard the opposition between /u/ and /o/ as a privative one. This possibility results from the fact that there are only two vowel heights that are phonologically relevant in Turkish. The vowel /u/ can therefore be said to have (high) vowel height, whereas the vowel /o/ lacks (high) vowel height. In the binary feature system to be proposed in **2.4** below, the vowels in the first row are viewed as [+high], and the vowels in the second row are [−high].

The third possible relation between members of an opposition results when the members are considered "logically equivalent" (p. 75). In other words, it is not possible to view one as having a mark which the other lacks. Nor is it possible to view the two members as differing by the degree of some phonetic property. Such an example is the opposition in English between /p/ and /t/ or between /t/ and /k/. It is not possible, as in the case of vowel heights, to speak of a continuum from labial to velar, whereby /p/ and /t/ would differ, say, by degree of backness. Unlike vowels, where only the degree of vowel height is involved, different places of articulation in consonants are obtained by discrete changes in the two articulators. Thus, the labial consonant /p/ involves the upper and lower lips, while the consonant /t/ involves the tip of the tongue and the upper teeth. This third category of oppositions is termed equipollent.

In determining the nature of an opposition, it is always important to consider the inventory of distinctive sounds (phonemes) in the language under investigation. We have seen that the same opposition can be privative in one language but gradual in another. For this reason Trubetzkoy distinguishes between "logically" privative, gradual, or equipollent and "actually" privative, gradual, or equipollent. The /u/ : /o/ opposition discussed above is logically gradual (since we know that there are languages with /ɔ/), but may be considered actually privative in a language such as Turkish. This opposition is, of course, actually gradual in Yoruba, which has /ɔ/. Thus, in Trubetzkoy's view, there are phonetic universals (universal relations between sounds), but languages may alter the logical (that is, phonetic) relation between two opposition members in phonological systems.

2.2.3 Constant and Neutralizable Oppositions

Trubetzkoy's (1939) final classification is made according to the extent of the distinctiveness of an opposition (p. 77). He draws a distinction between *constant* and *neutralizable* oppositions. A classic example of a neutralizable opposition comes from Standard German. While there is an opposition between the voiceless consonants /p, t, k, f, s/ and the voiced consonants /b, d, g, v, z/ in some positions of the word in German (for example, *Tier* [tiːr] 'animal' vs. *dir* [diːr] 'to you'), only the voiceless series is found at the end of a word. Although *Rat* 'advice' and *Rad* 'wheel' are written differently, both are pronounced [raːt]. The plural forms *Räte* [rɛːtə] 'advices' and *Rader* [rɛːdər] 'wheels' show a contrast between /t/ and /d/, since these consonants are, with the plural suffixes *–e* and *–er*, no longer at the end of the word. The opposition between /t/ and /d/ is therefore realized phonetically only in certain positions. Where only [t] is found phonetically, the opposition is said to be *neutralized*. On the other hand, when the two members of an opposition can occur in all positions, there is no neutralization. Rather, the opposition is said to be *constant*. In Nupe, for instance, the general phonological structure is CVCV. That is, each syllable consists of a consonant followed by a vowel, with few exceptions. The opposition /t/ : /d/, as exemplified by the verbs /tá/ 'to tell' and /dá/ 'to be soft,' is a constant one, since both opposition members are found in all possible consonant positions (see **5.1.2.1**).

2.3 Jakobson's Theory of Distinctive Features

The importance of Trubetzkoy's work is that he attempted to give a *phonological* analysis of phonetic contrasts. In his framework, it is possible not only to describe the opposition between /p/ and /b/, as in English /pɪn/ and /bɪn/, as one of voicing, but also to characterize it as bilateral, proportional, privative, and neutralizable.[3] With these notions, Trubetzkoy was able to reveal how the same phonetic contrast may structure differently in different languages. Depending on the system, a given opposition may be

---

[3] The opposition between /p/ and /b/ is neutralizable in English because only [p] is found after word-initial /s/, e.g., *spin*, but not **sbin*.

privative in one language but gradual in another (for example, /u/ : /o/ in Yoruba and Turkish).

While Trubetzkoy's concern was to capture the phonological properties of such frequent phonetic contrasts as voicing in consonants and height in vowels, the concerns of Jakobson, another founding member of the Prague School, were somewhat different. Jakobson wanted to develop a theory of phonology which would predict only those oppositions which could be found in languages. In particular, he hypothesized that the presence of certain phonetic oppositions precludes the presence of other oppositions. For example, in works such as Jakobson, Fant and Halle (1952) and Jakobson and Halle (1956) it is maintained that languages do not have contrasts between labialized, velarized, and pharyngealized consonants, that is, /C^w/, /C^{uu}/, and /Ç/, respectively. Jakobson claimed that a given language will contrast only *one* of these three consonant types with a plain /C/. Thus, while there can be an opposition between /C/ and /C^w/, /C/ and /C^{uu}/, and /C/ and /Ç/, one cannot find an opposition between /C^w/ and /C^{uu}/, /C^{uu}/ and /Ç/, or /C^w/ and /Ç/. This mutual exclusiveness of these three kinds of consonants led Jakobson, Fant and Halle to propose that they are merely surface phonetic realizations of the same underlying feature of *flatness* (see below). They hypothesized that there are a limited number of such features, say 12 to 15, which together account for all of the oppositions found in the world's languages.

Since many more than 12 to 15 *phonetic* features are necessary to differentiate the various sounds occurring in languages, it becomes apparent that some of these phonetic features will be "conflated" into the more limited set of *phonological* or *distinctive* features. This represents, then, a major departure from earlier phonetic studies of speech sounds. In the work of other phoneticians and phonologists, there is an assumption that the same features are to be used to characterize phonological contrasts in a language and to describe the phonetic content of various speech sounds. Jakobson's position is that there are certain phonetic distinctions, such as labialization, velarization, and pharyngealization, which are not available per se as phonological features but rather are representative of the more basic phonological feature of flatness. Thus, for the first time, the possibility is entertained that the set of phonological features may not be the same as the set of phonetic features.

2.3.1 Articulatory vs. Acoustic Features

Since the earliest phonetic studies, segments have been classified according to their *articulatory* properties. In consonants, for example, one asks where a sound is made (place of articulation), how it is made (manner of articulation), and what the state of the glottis is (voiced, unvoiced, etc.). (Other factors include what airstream mechanism is involved and whether the velum is raised or lowered.) In vowels, one asks which part of the tongue is raised (front, back, central), how much it is raised (high, mid, low), and whether the lips are rounded. While this is the most common and oldest way of classifying sounds, it is now possible with technological advances to group sounds according to their *acoustic* properties. That is, phonetic features such as the one distinguishing [p] from [b] can be stated either in terms of what is involved in the production of such sounds in the vocal tract or in terms of the characteristics of the acoustic signal which results from the different articulatory gestures. In other words, segments can be similar (or dissimilar) either in the way they are made or in the way they sound, two aspects which of course are related.

While the overwhelming emphasis has been on the articulatory side of phonetics, there are distinct cases where phonological properties cannot be accounted for without considering the acoustic properties of the sounds in question. A simple case is seen in the following data from Fe?fe?-Bamileke:

[vɑp]   'to whip'
[fat]   'to eat'
[čɑk]   'to seek'

In this language, the oral stops [p], [t], and [k] can occur at the end of a word preceded by a low unrounded vowel. In such words the difference between [a] (a front vowel similar to the vowel of French *patte* 'paw') and [ɑ] (a back vowel similar to the *a* sound of *father* in certain dialects of English) is totally redundant: before [p] and [k] we find [ɑ], and before [t] we find [a]. The question is, why?

While a front vowel might be expected to be backed before a back (velar) consonant, the change of /a/ to [ɑ] before [p] is not so easily explained. It would appear that [p] and [k], which function together in this backing process, have some phonetic feature in common—and yet articulatorily they are made at opposite extremes in the oral cavity.

The reason is that [p] and [k] share an acoustic property which [t] does not share with either one. Both [p] and [k], since they are made at the peripheries of the oral cavity (one at the lips and one at the back of the mouth), produce a concentration of energy in the lower frequencies of the sound spectrum (see Fant, 1960 for further discussion). Since alveolar/dental and palatal sounds cut the oral cavity in two, they do not create a large oral cavity, but rather two smaller cavities. Consequently, they have in common a concentration of energy in the upper frequencies of the sound spectrum. This acoustic distinction is directly incorporated into the feature system proposed by Jakobson et al. Labial and velar consonants are said to share the property of *graveness* (low tonality), and alveolars and palatals share the property of *acuteness* (high tonality).

Turning to the vowels [a] and [ɑ], back vowels, like labial and velar consonants, are made at the periphery of the oral cavity, since the tongue is raised in the back of the mouth; front vowels, like dental/alveolar and palatal consonants, are made in a non-peripheral (or medial) part of the oral cavity, since the tongue is raised in the center of the mouth. Consequently, both consonants and vowels differ in this acoustic property of graveness/acuteness, as follows:

GRAVE	ACUTE
labial C's	dental/alveolar C's
velar C's	palatal C's
back V's	front V's

Now that this acoustic property of consonants and vowels has been identified, the Feʔfeʔ forms given above can be accounted for in a straightforward way. Instead of writing a phonological rule in terms of segments, as follows:

$$\text{/a/} \rightarrow \text{[ɑ]} \: / \: \underline{} \begin{Bmatrix} p \\ k \end{Bmatrix} \#\,\#$$

which states that /a/ becomes [ɑ] before word-final [p] and [k], the rule should be written in terms of phonetic features:

$$\begin{array}{lll} \text{Acute} & \rightarrow \text{Grave} \: / \: \underline{} \: \text{Grave} \: \#\# \\ \text{Low V} & \text{Low V} \qquad\quad \text{C} \end{array}$$

An acute low vowel becomes a grave low vowel before a grave consonant. This formulation reveals that the process in question is phonetically motivated: low vowels are changed to agree in graveness with word-final consonants. In this sense, this rule can be compared with the rule of palatalization presented at the beginning of this chapter. Both rules involve cases of *assimilation* by which segments acquire the features of surrounding segments. This assimilation can be either articulatory or acoustic in nature, depending on the feature which is being assimilated. Thus there is a need for both articulatory and acoustic features in phonology (see Hyman, 1973a).

2.3.2 Binary vs. Nonbinary Features

While one innovation of Jakobson and his co-workers was to incorporate acoustic phonetics into phonology, another innovation was to convert all phonological features into binary ones. That is, a feature can have only two values, one of which is designated as [+F] and the other as [−F]. In many cases only a binary approach is phonologically significant, as in those oppositions which Trubetzkoy termed privative. Thus, phonemes are either [+nasal] or [−nasal], though phonetically some sounds may be more heavily nasalized than others. The sound [b] is often said to be more fully voiced in French than in English. For phonological purposes, however, both are [+voice]. Presumably there will be phonetic statements which specify the *degree* of voicing or the *degree* of nasality, etc. But apparently languages will rarely, if ever, use two degrees of voicing or nasality for contrastive purposes.

In other cases, however, the binary nature of a feature may not be as clear. While Trubetzkoy's equipollent oppositions, such as Labial vs. Dental, can easily be reinterpreted as [±labial] and [±dental] (though this is not what Jakobson proposed), Trubetzkoy's gradual oppositions seem to defy binary reinterpretation. Thus, the vowels /i, e, ɛ, æ/ differ in degree of vowel height and would appear to require a scale, say from [1 vowel height] for /æ/ to [4 vowel height] for /i/. However, as will be shown in the discussion of vowel features, Jakobson reinterpreted these four vowel heights in terms of two binary features, Diffuse and Compact. In claiming that all features are binary, including features which are logically gradual from a phonetic point of view, Jakobson made an important break with all previous linguistic analyses of sounds—a break which is still being debated today, as we shall see.

2.3.3 The Distinctive Features of Jakobson and Halle

Since the proposed binary features were designed only to capture the phonological oppositions found in languages, but not necessarily to capture the different phonetic realizations of these oppositions, they are referred to as a set of *distinctive features*. Since these features are not meant to be phonetic features, but rather phonological features, they do not account for every phonetic detail of the phonological segments.

2.3.3.1 The Major Class Features   Perhaps the features which best reveal the motivation of Jakobson's approach are those he set up to classify the major classes of sounds. While traditional phonetics distinguishes consonants, vowels, glides (semivowels/semiconsonants), and liquids, Jakobson et al. proposed two binary features, Consonantal and Vocalic. Like all of Jakobson's features, Consonantal and Vocalic can be defined in terms of either their acoustic or their articulatory correlates. Thus, Jakobson and Halle (1956:29) define these features as follows:[4]

> *Consonantal/non-consonantal:* acoustic—low (vs. high) total energy; articu-latory—presence vs. absence of an obstruction in the vocal tract.

[4] The definitions of these features are given for reference only; for a deeper understanding of the motivation behind these features, as well as their phonetic justification, see Jakobson, Fant and Halle (1952) and Jakobson and Halle (1956).

Vocalic/non-vocalic: acoustic—presence vs. absence of a sharply defined formant structure; articulatory—primary or only excitation at the glottis together with a free passage through the vocal tract.

These two binary features define four major classes of segments, as seen below:

TRUE CONSONANT   VOWEL   LIQUID   GLIDE

$$\begin{bmatrix} +\text{cons} \\ -\text{voc} \end{bmatrix} \qquad \begin{bmatrix} -\text{cons} \\ +\text{voc} \end{bmatrix} \qquad \begin{bmatrix} +\text{cons} \\ +\text{voc} \end{bmatrix} \qquad \begin{bmatrix} -\text{cons} \\ -\text{voc} \end{bmatrix}$$

e.g.   /p/   /a/   /l/   /y/

The class of true consonants (including stops, fricatives, affricates, and nasals) is specified as [+cons, −voc], since they are characterized by an obstruction in the vocal tract and therefore do not permit a free passage of air; the class of vowels, on the other hand, is specified as just the opposite, that is, [−cons, +voc], since there is no obstruction and consequently a free passage of air through the vocal tract. The classes of liquids (for example, /l/ and /r/ sounds) and glides (/w/ and /y/ sounds) are intermediate between these two classes, as can be seen from their feature specifications.

These specifications reveal that true consonants have nothing in common with vowels. On the other hand, vowels and liquids share the feature specification [+voc], and vowels and glides share the feature specification [−cons]. Since true consonants and vowels share neither feature specification in common, it is seen that these two classes have nothing in common except that they are comprised of segments. In other words, these binary features provide a way of revealing "natural classes" of segments:

C + L : [+cons]
C + G : [−voc]
V + L : [+voc]
V + G : [−cons]

The notion of natural class is an important one in phonology, and one which will be dealt with in greater detail in **5.1.1**. For the purposes of the present discussion, it suffices to say that feature specifications are designed to make specific claims about the similarities of classes of segments. These claims are substantiated both by phonetic studies into the articulatory and acoustic properties of sounds and by phonological studies of specific languages.

Thus, if the claim that C + L, C + G, V + L, and V + G share properties in common is correct, languages should be expected to reflect this claim. For example, phonological rules should occur where true consonants and liquids function together in the input—or in the output (see Chapter 5).

As we shall see in **2.4**, the claims made by these particular Jakobsonian features are only partially valid.

2.3.3.2 The Distinctive Features of Vowels   As stated in the previous section, vowels are specified as [−cons, +voc]. In addition, the three parameters of tongue height, tongue position, and lip rounding are accounted for by means of the features Diffuse, Compact, Grave, and Flat, as seen in Table 2.1 (see Halle, 1962:389).

Table 2.1

	i	e	æ	u	o	ɔ	a
consonantal	−	−	−	−	−	−	−
vocalic	+	+	+	+	+	+	+
diffuse	+	−	−	+	−	−	−
compact	−	−	+	−	−	+	+
grave	−	−	−	+	+	+	+
flat	−	−	−	+	+	+	−
voice	+	+	+	+	+	+	+
continuant	+	+	+	+	+	+	+
strident	−	−	−	−	−	−	−
nasal	−	−	−	−	−	−	−

The features Diffuse, Compact, Grave, and Flat are defined by Jakobson and Halle (1956:29) as follows:[5]

> *Compact/diffuse:* acoustic—higher (vs. lower) concentration of energy in a relatively narrow, central region of the spectrum, accompanied by an increase (vs. decrease) of the total amount of energy; articulatory—forward-flanged vs. backward-flanged (the difference lies in the relation between the volume of the resonance chamber in front of the narrowest stricture and behind this stricture).
>
> *Grave/acute:*[6] acoustic—concentration of energy in the lower (vs. upper) frequencies of the spectrum; articulatory—peripheral vs. medial. . . .
>
> *Flat/plain:*[7] acoustic—flat phonemes in contradistinction to the corresponding plain ones are characterized by a downward shift or weakening of some of their upper frequency components; articulatory—the former (narrowed slit) phonemes in contradistinction to the latter (wider slit) phonemes are produced with a decreased back or front orifice of the mouth resonator, and a concomitant velarization expanding the mouth resonator.

[5] The features Voice, Continuant, Strident, and Nasal are dealt with below.
[6] The term Acute refers to segments which are [−grave].
[7] The term Plain refers to segments which are [−flat].

From Table 2.1, the following correlations can be noted between these features and the vowels they specify:

[+ diffuse]   :   high vowels
[− diffuse]   :   mid and low vowels
[+ compact] :   low vowels
[− compact] :   high and mid vowels
[+ grave]   :   back vowels
[− grave]   :   front vowels
[+ flat]   :   rounded vowels
[− flat]   :   unrounded vowels

Two important aspects of this system are that no provision is made for more than two degrees of frontness/backness and that no provision is made for more than three vowel heights. The claims inherent in these proposals are that no language will ever contrast more than two degrees of frontness/backness or more than three degrees of vowel height. Since these features are designed only to capture phonological contrasts in languages, it does not matter that [i] and [a] are really central vowels phonetically or that [ɛ] is a fourth vowel height intermediate between [e] and [æ]. /i/ and /a/ are specified as [+ back]; /ɛ/ is specified as a mid vowel, that is, as [− diffuse, − compact], and differentiated from /e/ by an additional feature, Tense, as defined below (Jakobson and Halle, 1956:30):

> *Tense/lax:*[8] acoustic—higher (vs. lower) total amount of energy in conjunction with a greater (vs. smaller) spread of energy in the spectrum and in time; articulatory—greater (vs. smaller) deformation of the vocal tract away from its rest position.

The vowel /e/ is [+ tense], while the vowel /ɛ/ is [− tense]. Similarly, the vowels /i/ and /u/ are [+ tense], while the corresponding lax vowels /ɪ/ and /ʊ/ are [− tense]. Turning to degrees of frontness/backness, if a language has the two phonemes /u/ (a back rounded vowel) and /i/ (a central unrounded vowel), these can be differentiated on the basis of the specification for the feature Flat: /u/ is [+ grave, + flat], and /i/ is [+ grave, − flat]. On the other hand, if the same language were to contrast /ɯ/ (a back unrounded vowel) and /i/ (a central unrounded vowel), a problem would arise, since both of these vowels would have to be specified as back unrounded, that is, as [+ grave, − flat]. While no language has been shown to have such a contrast, the difference between /ɯ/ and /i/ could conceivably be characterized by specifying the former as [+ tense] and the latter as [− tense]. In such a way, Jakobson's claim that languages do not contrast three degrees of frontness/backness can be maintained (but see **2.5.3**).

---

[8] The term Lax refers to segments which are [− tense].

The four remaining features of the vowel chart, namely Voice, Continuant, Strident, and Nasal, are defined as follows (Jakobson and Halle, 1956:30, 31):

> *Voiced/voiceless:* acoustic—presence vs. absence of periodic low frequency excitation; articulatory—periodic vibrations of the vocal cords vs. lack of such vibrations.
> *Discontinuous/continuant:*[9] acoustic—silence (at least in frequency range above vocal cord vibration) followed and/or preceded by spread of energy over a wide frequency region . . . vs. absence of abrupt transition between sound and such a silence; articulatory—rapid turning on and off of source either through a rapid closure and/or opening of the vocal tract that distinguishes plosives from constrictives [that is, stops and affricates from fricatives].
> *Strident/mellow:*[10] acoustic—higher intensity noise vs. lower intensity noise; articulatory—rough-edged vs. smooth-edged. . . .
> *Nasal/oral (nasalized/non-nasalized):* acoustic—spreading the available energy over wider (vs. narrower) frequency regions by a reduction in the intensity of certain (primarily the first) formants and introduction of additional (nasal) formant; articulatory—mouth resonator supplemented by the nose cavity vs. the exclusion of the nasal resonator.

All of the vowels discussed so far are specified [+voice, +continuant, −strident, −nasal]. While languages have been known to have voiceless as well as nasalized vowels, vowels are universally specified [+continuant] and [−strident]. That is, all vowels are characterized by a continuous air flow, while no vowels are characterized by the kind of high-intensity noise described by the specification [+strident]. Thus, the contrasts between [+continuant] and [−continuant] and [+strident] and [−strident] are limited to consonants.

2.3.3.3 The Distinctive Features of Consonants By consonant is meant, in the Jakobsonian framework, any segment which is *not* specified [−cons, +voc]. That is, any segment which is either [+cons] or [−voc] qualifies as a consonant. One of the great advantages of Jakobson's feature system is that it makes it possible to characterize both consonants and vowels in terms of the same features. Whereas phoneticians speak of vowels as being either front, central, or back but of consonants as being labial, dental, etc., these different placements of the two articulators required to make vowels and consonants are related in Jakobson's system by means of the features Diffuse and Grave. Table 2.2 (see Halle, 1964:396) shows how the same distinctive features already illustrated for vowels capture the

---

[9] Discontinuous segments are [−continuant]; continuant segments are [+continuant]; see below.
[10] The term Mellow refers to segments which are [−strident].

Table 2.2 Distinctive Feature Representation of English Consonants

	p	b	f	v	m	t	d	θ	ð	s	z	n	č	ǰ	š	ž	k	g	l	r	w	y	h
cons	+	+	+	+	+	+	+	+	+	+	+	+	+	+	+	+	+	+	+	+	−	−	−
voc	−	−	−	−	−	−	−	−	−	−	−	−	−	−	−	−	−	−	+	+	−	−	−
diff	+	+	+	+	+	+	+	+	+	+	+	+	−	−	−	−	−	−	+	+	−	−	−
grave	+	+	+	+	+	−	−	−	−	−	−	−	−	−	−	−	+	+	−	−	+	−	+
flat	−	−	−	−	−	−	−	−	−	−	−	−	−	−	−	−	−	−	−	−	+	−	−
voice	−	+	−	+	+	−	+	−	+	−	+	+	−	+	−	+	−	+	+	+	+	+	−
cont	−	−	+	+	−	−	−	+	+	+	+	−	−	−	+	+	−	−	+	+	+	+	+
strid	−	−	+	+	−	−	−	−	−	+	+	−	+	+	+	+	−	−	−	−	−	−	−
nasal	−	−	−	−	+	−	−	−	−	−	−	+	−	−	−	−	−	−	−	−	−	−	−
comp	−	−	−	−	−	−	−	−	−	−	−	−	−	−	−	−	−	−	−	−	−	−	−

contrasts of English consonants.[11] As stated earlier, the features Consonantal and Vocalic distinguish between *true consonants*, which are [+cons, −voc]; *liquids*, which are [+cons, +voc]; and *glides*, which are [−cons, −voc]. In addition, the following correlations between the remaining features and the consonants they specify can be extracted from this chart:

[+diffuse]	:	labial and dental/alveolar consonants
[−diffuse]	:	palatal and velar/back consonants
[+grave]	:	labial and velar/back consonants
[−grave]	:	dental/alveolar and palatal consonants
[+voice]	:	voiced consonants
[−voice]	:	voiceless consonants
[+continuant]	:	fricatives, liquids, glides
[−continuant]	:	stops and affricates
[+strident]	:	noisy fricatives (labiodental, alveolar, alveopalatal), affricates
[−strident]	:	less noisy fricatives (interdental, as well as palatal and velar; see below), stops, liquids, glides
[+nasal]	:	nasal consonants
[−nasal]	:	oral consonants

In addition, aspirated consonants, as well as the glide /h/, are specified as [+tense].[12]

2.3.3.3.1 Primary Articulations This feature analysis is possible only as a result of Jakobson's focus on underlying sound contrasts rather than on surface phonetic contrasts. As an example, consider the consonant chart included in Appendix 1. In this arrangement of consonants, it is necessary to distinguish at least *ten* places of articulation: bilabial, labiodental, interdental, dental/alveolar, alveopalatal, palatal, velar, uvular, pharyngeal, and glottal. It is quite clear, however, that no language will ever *contrast* ten places of articulation. Rather, if one takes a close look at this consonant chart, a number of gaps are observed. Some of these gaps represent impossible feature combinations; for example, voiced glottal stops do not exist. Other gaps represent infrequent feature combinations such as palatal and velar affricates ([c^{ç}, ɟ̌^{j}] and [k^{x}, g^{ɣ}]), which are much less frequent than labiodental, alveolar, and alveopalatal affricates ([p^{f}, b^{v}], [t^{s}, d^{z}], and [č, ǰ] = [t^{š}, d^{ž}]).

Notice that only the fricatives [θ] and [ð] are represented in the interdental position (the affricates [t^{θ}] and [d^{ð}] are also possible, as we shall see below). Thus, only in fricatives is there a potential contrast between interdental and dental/alveolar consonants, that is, /θ/ and /ð/ vs. /s/ and /z/.

[11] Just as the features Continuant and Strident are not used for vowels, the feature Compact is not used for consonants.

[12] Other secondary articulations involve the features Sharp and Checked; see **2.3.3.3.2.**

If one could show that there is an additional feature distinguishing these two pairs of consonants, then it would no longer be necessary to recognize an interdental position as a phonologically relevant distinction. Jakobson et al. (1952, 1956) claim that such a feature does exist, namely Strident, and that /θ/ and /ð/ differ from /s/ and /z/ in that the former are [−strident], whereas the latter are [+strident]. Thus this contrast, which is usually viewed as a difference in place of articulation, can be reinterpreted as a difference in noise components. In fact, this same contrast between [+strident] and [−strident] can be used to differentiate the labial fricatives [φ, β], which are [−strident], and the labiodental fricatives [f, v], which are [+strident]. Finally, the alveopalatals [š, ž] differ from the palatal fricatives [ç, j] in that they are [+strident], whereas the latter are [−strident].

In order to eliminate the labiodental and alveopalatal positions, however, it is necessary to account for the difference between [p, b] and [pᶠ, bᵛ] on the one hand and [c, ɟ] and [č, ǰ] on the other, that is, the difference between stops and affricates. Since the affricates [pᶠ, bᵛ, tˢ, dᶻ, č, ǰ] are characterized by considerable noise (stridency), Jakobson et al. attribute the difference between stops and affricates to this feature: affricates are [+strident], whereas stops are [−strident]. We therefore have the following feature specifications:

	φ	f	θ	s	š	ç	p	pᶠ	t	tˢ	č	c
strid	−	+	−	+	+	−	−	+	−	+	+	−
cont	+	+	+	+	+	+	−	−	−	−	−	−

Thus, the features Strident and Continuant define the oppositions stop/fricative, stop/affricate, and affricate/fricative. By use of the feature Strident, six places of articulation (bilabial, labiodental, interdental, dental/alveolar, alveopalatal, palatal) are reduced to three. We can refer to these three places of articulation as labial, dental, and palatal, bearing in mind that each of these stands for two more precise phonetic places of articulation.

Jakobson, Fant and Halle (1952:24) further propose that the uvular fricative [X] differs from the velar fricative [x] in that it is [+strident], whereas the latter is [−strident]. While this works for the fricative oppositions in these two positions, it is not possible to view the difference between the velar stop [k] and the uvular stop [q] as one of stridency. Harms (1968: 32) uses the feature Flat (see below) to distinguish /k/ and /q/ in Quechua: /k/ is [−flat] and /q/ is [+flat]. This is only possible, however, if there is no opposition between /kʷ/ and /q/, since /kʷ/, being a rounded consonant, is [+flat]. While the Jakobsonian features are not fully adequate to this purpose, it will be shown in **2.4.2.1** that velars and uvulars can be classified under one heading which will be called velar. Thus there are four general positions, each of which subdivides into two more specific phonetic places of articulation distinguished by other features:

LABIAL   DENTAL

Bilabial   Labiodental   Interdental   Dental/Alveolar

PALATAL   VELAR

Alveopalatal   Palatal   Velar   Uvular

These four places of articulation are distinguished by means of the two distinctive features Grave and Diffuse:

	LABIAL	DENTAL	PALATAL	VELAR
Grave	+	−	−	+
Diffuse	+	+	−	−

2.3.3.3.2 Secondary Articulations   Distinctions in consonants with secondary articulations (labialization, palatalization, etc.) are captured by means of the features Flat (defined earlier), Sharp, and Checked, the latter two being defined as follows (Jakobson and Halle, 1956:31):

Sharp/plain: acoustic—sharp phonemes in contradistinction to the corresponding plain ones are characterized by an upward shift of some of their upper frequency components; articulatory—the sharp (widened slit) vs. plain (narrower slit) phonemes exhibit a dilated pharyngeal pass, that is, a widened back orifice of the mouth resonator; a concomitant palatalization restricts and compartments the mouth cavity.

Checked/unchecked: acoustic—higher rate of discharge of energy within a reduced interval of time vs. lower rate of discharge within a longer interval; articulatory—glottalized vs. non-glottalized.

These features define the following sets of consonants with secondary articulations (only the *plus* specifications are of interest here):

	[+flat]	:	labialized, velarized, pharyngealized, and retroflex consonants
	[+sharp]	:	palatalized consonants
	[+checked]	:	glottalized consonants
cf.	[+tense]	:	aspirated and geminate/long consonants

By treating labialized, velarized, pharyngealized, and retroflex consonants all as phonetic manifestations of the feature specification [+flat], the claim is made that no language will ever contrast, say, /tʷ/ and /ṭ/, or /ṭ/ and /tᵚ/. This feature system therefore makes a claim—or prediction—about languages which is not made in feature systems not relating these secondary articulations as realizations of the same underlying property. In this sense, Flat is what has come to be known as a "cover feature," since it can stand for any one of four possible phonological contrasts, depending on the language (see **2.4.2.3**).

2.3.3.4 Summary Jakobson, Fant and Halle's system proposes to account for all of the possible phonological contrasts of languages by means of the following thirteen features (excluding features of tone and stress):

Vocalic	Voice	Checked
Consonantal	Nasal	Grave
Compact	Continuant	Flat
Diffuse	Strident	Sharp
Tense		

These features represent innovations in three areas: (1) the features capture phonological contrasts rather than describe phonetic segments, (2) the features are all binary in nature, and (3) the features are defined primarily in acoustic terms.

2.4 The Distinctive Features of Chomsky and Halle

The distinctive features presented in Chapter VII of *The Sound Pattern of English* (*SPE*), although based to a great extent on the work of Jakobson, Fant and Halle (1952) and Jakobson and Halle (1956), reveal a number of modifications. These modifications are to be found both in the specific set of distinctive features used to capture contrasts and in the conceptualization of these features.

While Jakobson's emphasis was on capturing all the possible phonological contrasts of languages by means of his features, Chomsky and Halle (1968) explicitly distinguish two functions of their features. On the one hand, the distinctive features are designed, like Jakobson's features, to capture the phonological contrasts of languages. On the other hand, they are designed to describe the *phonetic* content of segments derived by phonological rules, as well as underlying segments. This difference, with Chomsky and Halle looking as well at the noncontrastive feature composition of derived segments, will become clear as the modifications they proposed in the set of distinctive features are pointed out.

2.4.1 The Major Class Features

As pointed out in **2.3.3.1**, the Jakobsonian features Consonantal and Vocalic define four major classes of segments: True Consonants, Vowels, Liquids, and Glides. In addition, these features reveal certain similarities between the major classes: true consonants and liquids are [+cons], true consonants and glides are [−voc], vowels and liquids are [+voc], and vowels and glides are [−cons]. These feature specifications therefore predict that segments will group together in just this way, for example, that true consonants and liquids will be subject to certain phonological rules that vowels and glides are not subject to.

There are, however, serious problems with these features, as pointed out by Chomsky and Halle (1968). While the binary features Consonantal and Vocalic provide a means of capturing relations between segment classes in groups of two, there is no straightforward way to group three classes together as opposed to the fourth. In fact, the most natural grouping of these four major classes may be between true consonants, liquids, and glides on the one hand and vowels on the other. That is, phonological properties must often be stated in terms of vowels and nonvowels, as when one gives the general word structure of a language as CVCV (consonant-vowel-consonant-vowel). In such formulae the C stands for either a true consonant, a liquid, or a glide. These consonants have in common that they are usually not syllabic.[13] Vowels, on the other hand, are always syllabic. If one attempts to state a CVCV constraint on word structure in a language, it is necessary to use a disjunction of the following sort (where the braces indicate that *either* one of the specified features *or* the other is to apply):

$$\#\# \quad \left\{ \begin{matrix} [+\text{cons}] \\ [-\text{voc}] \end{matrix} \right\} \quad \begin{bmatrix} -\text{cons} \\ +\text{voc} \end{bmatrix} \quad \left\{ \begin{matrix} [+\text{cons}] \\ [-\text{voc}] \end{matrix} \right\} \quad \begin{bmatrix} -\text{cons} \\ +\text{voc} \end{bmatrix} \quad \dots \#\#$$

Since the class of nonvowels is defined as those segments which are either [+cons] or [−voc], it is necessary to use a disjunction to express the above CVCV word structure constraint. However, in so doing, the generalization which is missed is that every other segment is *syllabic*. Each CV sequence defines a syllable in this language. It therefore cannot be the case that both C and V are syllabic. Rather, if a new feature Syllabic is substituted for the old feature Vocalic, this word structure constraint can be stated much more satisfactorily as follows:

$$\#\# \quad [-\text{syll}] \quad [+\text{syll}] \quad [-\text{syll}] \quad [+\text{syll}] \quad \dots \#\#$$

After providing evidence that languages commonly group segments into vowels and nonvowels, Chomsky and Halle (1968:354) propose, following Milner and Bailey, that the feature Syllabic replace the feature Vocalic. [+syllabic] segments are those constituting a syllabic peak, that is, vowels, syllabic liquids, and syllabic nasals (see Table 2.3); all remaining segments are said to be [−syllabic].

---

[13] A segment will be viewed as syllabic if it constitutes the *nucleus* or *peak* of a syllable (see **6.1.1.1**). Liquids can, of course, be syllabic, as can nasal consonants, as we shall see. Glides, on the other hand, when they "turn" syllabic, become vowels.

While this new feature allows the grouping of true consonants, (non-syllabic) liquids, and glides, as opposed to vowels, there is no feature which allows the grouping of vowels, liquids, and glides, as opposed to true consonants. If such a grouping were to be attempted using the features Consonantal and Vocalic, another disjunction would be required, namely:

$$\left\{ \begin{matrix} [-\text{cons}] \\ [+\text{voc}] \end{matrix} \right\}$$

Vowels, liquids, and glides have in common that their normal state of the glottis is [+voice]. Voiceless vowels, liquids, and glides are attested in languages but are relatively rare. On the other hand, nasal consonants, which, like oral consonants, are specified [+cons, −voc], also have [+voice] as their normal state of the glottis. Voiceless nasals do exist, but again they are relatively rare. Thus it appears that there is a need for a feature which will group vowels, liquids, glides, and nasals together. In order to group these segments together, Chomsky and Halle (1968:302) propose the feature Sonorant: vowels, liquids, glides, and nasals are [+sonorant], defined by a relatively free air passage either through the mouth or through the nose; non–nasal true consonants, which are called *obstruents* (that is, stops, affricates, and fricatives), are [−sonorant]. As we shall observe in later chapters, such a distinction is often utilized by languages in phonological rules. Thus the feature Vocalic is abandoned, and the two new features Syllabic and Sonorant, along with the Jakobsonian features Consonantal and Nasal, define the following major classes of segments:

Table 2.3

	C	V	L	G	N	L̩	N̩
cons	+	−	+	−	+	+	+
syll	−	+	−	−	−	+	+
son	−	+	+	+	+	+	+
nas	−	−	−	−	+	−	+

In Table 2.3, C stands for the class of obstruents, and L̩ and N̩ for syllabic liquids and nasals, respectively. Two things should be noted about this table. First, it can now be seen that glides and vowels differ in precisely the same way as nonsyllabic and syllabic liquids and nasals, that is, G:V = L:L̩ = N:N̩. Second, according to these feature specifications, liquids and nasals differ only in nasality: liquids are [−nasal], while nasals are [+nasal]. This can potentially create a problem, since the above four features do not differentiate nasalized liquids (for example, [l̃], [r̃]) from true nasals (for example, [n]). Here we have the possibility of using the feature Continuant, carried over from Jakobson, whereby liquids are [+cont] and nasals [−cont]. It should, however, be noted that although Chomsky and Halle (1968:303) characterize voiceless vowels (and presumably voiceless liquids, glides, and nasals) as [+sonorant], they are probably best seen as [−sonorant], that is, as obstruents in the case of L̥, G̥, and N̥. This includes /h/, which Chomsky and Halle consider to be a voiceless glide and [+sonorant].

2.4.2 Primary Placement Features for Vowels and Consonants

Chomsky and Halle (1968) retain the features Consonantal (p. 302), Tense (p. 324), Voice (p. 326), Continuant (p. 317), Nasal (p. 316), and Strident (p. 329) from the earlier feature system. In all other cases new features are substituted. The approximate correlations between the two systems, which we shall now discuss in turn, are given below:

CHOMSKY AND HALLE	JAKOBSON ET AL.	
	vowels	*consonants*
[+high]	[+diff]	[−diff]
[+low]	[+comp]	[+flat]
[+back]	[+grave]	$\begin{bmatrix} +\text{grave} \\ -\text{diff} \end{bmatrix}$
[+anterior]	——	[+diff]
[+coronal]	——	[−grave]
[+round]	[+flat]	[+flat]

2.4.2.1 The Features High, Back, and Low The features High, Back, and Low characterize the body of the tongue. They are defined by Chomsky and Halle (1968) as follows:

> High sounds are produced by raising the body of the tongue above the level it occupies in the neutral position; nonhigh sounds are produced without such a raising of the tongue body. (p. 304)
>
> Back sounds are produced by retracting the body of the tongue from the neutral position; nonback sounds are produced without such a retraction from the neutral position. (p. 395)
>
> Low sounds are produced by lowering the body of the tongue below the level that it occupies in the neutral position; nonlow sounds are produced without such a lowering of the body of the tongue. (p. 305)

The neutral position of the body of the tongue is "assumed to be raised and fronted, approximating the configuration found on the vowel [e] [read [ɛ]] in English *bed*" (p. 304). These features are used for both vowels and consonants.

Since in the case of the features High and Low, no segment can be [+high, +low] (for this would imply a sound which is simultaneously both raised and lowered from the neutral position), these features define three possibilities: [+high, −low], [−high, −low] and [−high, +low]. Since [+high] automatically implies [−low] and [+low] implies [−high], we can refer to these three classes as [+high], [−high, −low], and [+low]. Segments which are [+high] include all high vowels; the glides /y/ and /w/; and palatal, palatalized, velar, and velarized consonants. Thus, the segments [i, u, y, w, č, tʸ, k, tʷ] are all [+high]. Segments which are [−high, −low] include mid vowels and uvulars, for example, [e, o, q, R]. Finally, segments which are [+low] include low vowels, pharyngeals and pharyngealized consonants, and glottal (laryngeal) consonants, for example, [æ, a, ḥ, ṭ, h, ʔ]. Thus, the features Diffuse and Compact (the latter of which applied only to vowels in Jakobson's system) are replaced by the features High and Low.

One interesting observation in this change is that precisely the opposite claim is made concerning the relatedness of consonants and vowels. In Jakobson's feature system, labial and dental consonants, along with high vowels, are [+diff], while palatal and velar consonants, along with nonhigh vowels, are [−diff]. In Chomsky and Halle's feature system, palatal and velar consonants, along with high vowels, are [+high], while labial and dental consonants, along with nonhigh vowels, are [−high]:

JAKOBSON ET AL.		CHOMSKY AND HALLE	
[+diffuse]	[−diffuse]	[+high]	[−high]
labials	palatals	palatals	labials
dentals	velars	velars	dentals
high V's	nonhigh V's	high V's	nonhigh V's

Thus there is a fundamental difference in the claim made about the shared properties of consonants and vowels. The only way to resolve this difference is by consulting the world's languages to see how consonants and vowels pattern.

McCawley (1967) cites Maxakali, in which vowels are inserted before syllable-final stops, as follows: [ə] before [p], [a] before [t], [i] before [č], and [ɨ] before [k]. There appears to be in this example a case of tongue body height assimilation[14]. The segments [p, t, o, a] are all [−high], while the segments [č, k, i, ɨ] are all [+high]. The feature High aptly captures this height agreement, while the feature Diffuse makes the opposite—and wrong—prediction that high vowels will go with [p] and [t] and nonhigh vowels with [č] and [k]. With the feature High, it is possible to state that the inserted

[14] Although this conclusion is well-founded, McCawley's report of the Maxakali data is considerably simplified; see Gudschinsky, Popovich and Popovich (1970:82–84).

vowel will be [+high] before a syllable-final [+high] consonant and [−high] before a syllable-final [−high] consonant.

Further evidence is provided by Maran (1971:32ff). In the history of Burmese, the proto syllable-final sequence *ak became [ek] (and later [et]). This change from *a to [e] in the environment of a following velar consonant is argued by Maran to be an agreement in tongue body height. The feature Diffuse would predict that the proto sequences *ap and *at should become, respectively, [ep] and [et], rather than *ak becoming [ek]. However, the vowel *a stays [a] before labials and dentals (although *ap does change to [at]).

The feature Back characterizes velar(ized), uvular, and pharyngeal(ized) consonants as well as back vowels. Segments which are [+back] are characterized by the retraction of the body of the tongue. Front vowels, as well as any consonants produced in front of the velar region (unless they are velarized or pharyngealized), are automatically [−back]. Glottal and glottalized consonants, including [h], are considered to be [−back], since they do not involve the retraction of the tongue body (except, of course, consonants such as the ejective [k'], which is [+back] because it is a *velar* which is glottalized). The following distinctive feature matrices indicate how these features apply to vowels and consonants (where the feature Round distinguishes rounded vowels from unrounded vowels):

	i	e	æ	u	o	ɔ	a
high	+	−	−	+	−	−	−
low	−	−	+	−	−	+	+
back	−	−	−	+	+	+	+
round	−	−	−	+	+	+	−

	p	t	č	k	q	ḥ	ʔ	tʸ	tɯ	ṭ	t'
high	−	−	+	+	−	−	−	+	+	−	−
low	−	−	−	−	−	+	+	−	−	+	+
back	−	−	−	+	+	+	−	−	+	+	−

2.4.2.2 The Features Anterior and Coronal   This second matrix fails to show the difference between [p] and [t], [č] and [tʸ], [k] and [tɯ], [ḥ] and [ṭ], and [ʔ] and [t']. In the case of [p] and [t], the features High, Low, and Back fail to show the difference between labials and dentals. In all of the other cases, the features fail to show the difference between primary place of articulation (palatal, velar, pharyngeal, glottal) and secondary place of articulation (palatalized, velarized, pharyngealized, glottalized).[15] Thus

---

[15] If uvularized consonants exist, there is a potential problem distinguishing the uvular stop [q] from a uvularized [t].

other features are needed to distinguish between primary and secondary articulations.

For this purpose, Chomsky and Halle (1968) introduce the features Anterior and Coronal. These are defined as follows:

> Anterior sounds are produced with an obstruction that is located in front of the palato-alveolar [that is, alveopalatal] region of the mouth; non-anterior sounds are produced without such an obstruction. The palato-alveolar region is that where the ordinary English [š] is produced. (p. 304)
>
> Coronal sounds are produced with the blade of the tongue raised from its neutral position; noncoronal sounds are produced with the blade of the tongue in the neutral position. (p. 304)

Thus labial and dental consonants are [+ant], while all other consonants are [−ant]. Dentals, alveolars, and alveopalatals are [+cor], while all other consonants are [−cor] (including "true palatals," for example, [ç], [y]). While the feature Anterior does not apply to vowels, retroflex vowels (for example, [ɚ] in American English) are [+cor]. These feature specifications are summarized below:

	p	t	č	c	k	q
ant	+	+	−	−	−	−
cor	−	+	+	−	−	−

It should be clear that these features are designed in part to replace the Jakobsonian features Grave and Diffuse. We have already seen the weaknesses of the feature Diffuse. On the other hand, the importance of the feature Grave has already been demonstrated (see Hyman, 1973a). By and large, what Chomsky and Halle attempted to do was to replace Jakobson's acoustically oriented features with articulatorily oriented features. Thus, the feature Grave is discarded with almost no discussion (p. 306). Consonants which are now [+ant] are those which in the earlier system were [+diff]. The feature Coronal, while closely paralleling the old feature Grave (but with opposite value), has no exact equivalent in Chomsky and Halle's framework. [+cor] consonants include dentals, alveolars, retroflex consonants, and alveopalatals. While all of these are [−grave], the [−grave] true palatals (for example, [c, j, y]) are [−cor], according to Chomsky and Halle.[16] With this exception only, a [+grave] segment will be [−cor] and a [−grave] segment will be [+cor] in the Chomsky and Halle system.

2.4.2.3 Secondary Articulations   In addition to changing the features from being essentially acoustically motivated to being articulatory in nature, a more basic modification was introduced. While Jakobson's aim had been

---

[16] J. Hoard and C. Sloat have suggested, in personal communications, that true palatals should also be viewed as [+cor], though we shall not further investigate this possibility here.

to provide only those distinctive features that were necessary to characterize phonemic contrasts in the world's languages, Chomsky and Halle enriched the set of features so as to permit finer phonetic statements. In other words, in addition to capturing underlying contrasts, the features assumed a second function, which was to specify the phonetic content of segments derived by phonological rules (see McCawley, 1967:522–523). Starting with Halle (1959), phonological rules which convert underlying (systematic) phonemic representations to surface (systematic) phonetic representations are stated in terms of binary features. Thus, it now becomes necessary to refer to binary feature specifications which are not distinctive in a given language.

The standard example centers around the Jakobsonian feature Flat. Recall that [+flat] segments include labialized, velarized, and pharyngealized consonants as well as rounded vowels. Jakobson postulated that no language would ever have a contrast between labialized, velarized, and pharyngealized consonants, and therefore, with this "complementary distribution" in the world's languages, the three consonant types were said to be surface manifestations of a broader phonological category of flat consonants. In each language a statement would be required about whether [+flat] referred to [Cʷ], [Cᵚ], or [C̣].

McCawley (1967:524–525) showed, however, that such an approach leads to complications in formulating phonological rules. He cites the case of Arabic, which has pharyngealized consonants which are [+flat] and the three-vowel system /i, a, u/, of which the last is [+flat]. Already we see that [+flat] refers to two different phonetic properties. In addition, vowels which are adjacent to pharyngealized consonants are also pharyngealized, as in the following rule.

$$\text{V} \rightarrow \text{Ṿ} \ / \ \begin{Bmatrix} — \ \text{C̣} \\ \text{C̣} \ — \end{Bmatrix} \quad \begin{matrix} \text{(a)} \\ \text{(b)} \end{matrix}$$

In other words, a vowel becomes pharyngealized before (a) or after (b), a pharyngealized consonant. When one rewrites this rule in terms of features, the following results:

$$[+\text{syll}] \rightarrow [+\text{flat}] \ / \ \begin{Bmatrix} — \begin{bmatrix} +\text{flat} \\ -\text{syll} \end{bmatrix} \\ \begin{bmatrix} +\text{flat} \\ -\text{syll} \end{bmatrix} — \end{Bmatrix}$$

What this now means is that [+flat], in addition to standing for pharyngealization in [−syll] segments in Arabic (that is, consonants), also stands for (1) rounding in [u], (2) pharyngealization in [ị] and [ạ], and (3) rounding *and* pharyngealization in [ụ]. Since the phonology of Arabic will have to provide such "mapping" statements of the [+flat] specification onto these segments, these statements will be quite complex. McCawley (1967) therefore suggests that more specific features relating to lip-rounding and pharyn-gealization be used.[17]

Chomsky and Halle (1968) introduce the feature Round to cover rounded vowels and labialized consonants:

> Rounded sounds are produced with a narrowing of the lip orifice; nonrounded sounds are produced without such a narrowing. (p. 309)

Pharyngealized consonants are taken to be [+back, +low], revealing the retracting and lowering of the body of the tongue in making pharyngealized sounds. This leaves the problem of marking pharyngealization in vowels. If we were to consider the Arabic pharyngealized vowels [i̯] and [u̯] as [+back, +low], it would not be possible to distinguish [i̯] from [a] nor [u̯] from a hypothetical [ɔ]. In addition, one could not distinguish [a] from [a̯], since [a] is already [+back, +low]. It seems to be necessary, then, to introduce another binary feature relating to the position of the tongue root.

Chomsky and Halle (1968) propose a feature Covered (pp. 314–315), identical to Stewart's (1967, 1971) feature Advanced Tongue Root (ATR). Numerous West African languages (for example, Akan, Igbo) show a vowel harmony (see **6.3.1**) which divides vowels into two series, one of which is specified [+advanced tongue root] and one of which is specified [−advanced tongue root]. The latter corresponds, it seems, to pharyngealized vowels. In Igbo, the [+ATR] vowels include /i, e, u, o/, while the [−ATR] vowels include /i̯, a, u̯, ọ/. Since pharyngealized consonants are [−ATR], the rule of pharyngealization of vowels in Arabic can be rewritten as follows:

$$[+\text{syll}] \rightarrow [-\text{ATR}] \Big/ \left\{ \begin{array}{l} \begin{bmatrix} -\text{ATR} \\ -\text{syll} \end{bmatrix} \\ \begin{bmatrix} -\text{ATR} \\ -\text{syll} \end{bmatrix} \underline{} \end{array} \right\}$$

In this proposal, the assimilation of the pharyngealization of the consonant onto a neighboring vowel is revealed in a straightforward way.

One further modification Chomsky and Halle (1968) make is to discard the

---

[17] The status of the feature Flat is not clear as of the writing of this book. If it is a pho-netically valid feature, then languages should be expected to have flatness assimilation rules such as the following:

ɯ → u / Ç __ Ç

That is, a back unrounded vowel is rounded between pharyngealized consonants. In features this would be written:

$$\begin{bmatrix} +\text{syll} \\ -\text{flat} \end{bmatrix} \rightarrow [+\text{flat}] \Big/ \begin{array}{ccc} [+\text{flat}] & \underline{} & [+\text{flat}] \\ \text{C} & & \text{C} \end{array}$$

Some evidence for Flat is presented in Hyman (1972b: 120ff).

feature Sharp, which was used for palatalized (but not palatal) consonants. The feature Sharp was one of the few which did not have an application to both consonants and vowels (compare Compact, which was used only for vowels). The problem inherent in the feature Sharp is revealed when a rule such as

$$
\begin{bmatrix} p \\ t \\ k \end{bmatrix} \rightarrow \begin{bmatrix} p^y \\ t^y \\ k^y \end{bmatrix} / \underline{} i
$$

is formalized in terms of features:

$$
[-\text{syll}] \rightarrow [+\text{sharp}] / \underline{} \begin{bmatrix} +\text{syll} \\ +\text{high} \\ -\text{back} \end{bmatrix}
$$

While this is clearly a case of consonants assimilating to the high front (palatal) position of the vowel [i], the feature specification [+sharp] disguises the similarity between palatalized and high front vowels.[18] In order to remedy this situation, Chomsky and Halle (1968) recognize palatals and palatalized consonants as [+high, −back]. Now the above rule can be rewritten as follows:

$$
[-\text{syll}] \rightarrow \begin{bmatrix} +\text{high} \\ -\text{back} \end{bmatrix} / \underline{} \begin{bmatrix} +\text{syll} \\ +\text{high} \\ -\text{back} \end{bmatrix}
$$

Notice that the labial and dental consonants [p] and [t], which are [−high, −back], must change one feature and become [+high]. The velar consonant [k], which is already [+high], must change one feature specification and become [−back]. A uvular consonant such as [q], which is [−high, +back], would presumably have to change two features to become [+high, −back] if palatalized.

2.4.2.4 Additional Features   Chomsky and Halle (1968) introduce a number of other features, many of which are meant to be only tentative. For example, features are mentioned which are needed to distinguish the clicks of the Khoisan languages of South Africa and of Xhosa and Zulu. Also, features are needed for implosives, nasal release, prenasalization, etc. Even the most cursory glance at the phonetic material presented by Ladefoged (1971) will convince any phonologist that much more work is required on phonological and phonetic features.

---

[18] It also fails to reveal the relationship between palatals, which are [−sharp], and palatalized consonants, which are [+sharp]. Of course, palatalized palatals would be [+sharp].

One last important feature which we shall now look at is Delayed Release,[19] which Chomsky and Halle (1968) define as follows:

> There are basically two ways in which a closure in the vocal tract may be released, either instantaneously as in the plosives [that is, stops] or with a delay as in the affricates. During the delayed release, turbulence is generated in the vocal tract so that the release phase of affricates is acoustically quite similar to the cognate fricative. The instantaneous release is normally accompanied by much less or no turbulence. (p. 318)

Jakobson had originally planned on the feature Strident to distinguish affricates from stops, for example, $[p^f]$ from $[p]$. However, for this to be possible, it would mean that no language would ever contrast affricates such as $[p^\varphi]$ and $[p^f]$ or $[t^\theta]$ and $[t^s]$. Since the fricatives $[f]$ and $[s]$ are $[+\text{strident}]$ (see **2.3.3.3.1**), it follows that affricates released with a similar sound component should be $[+\text{strident}]$ as well. Similarly, since $[\varphi]$ and $[\theta]$ are $[-\text{strident}]$, the corresponding affricates $[p^\varphi]$ and $[t^\theta]$ should be $[-\text{strident}]$. However, recall that Jakobson differentiated stops such as $[t]$ and affricates such as $[t^\theta]$ on the basis of this feature Strident, with the former being minus and the latter plus.

While the inconsistent treatment of $[\theta]$ as $[-\text{strident}]$ but $[t^\theta]$ as $[+\text{strident}]$ presented a problem in itself, the final blow to this approach to affricates came when McCawley (1967:523), basing himself on Li (1946:398), pointed out that Chipewyan contrasts /t/, $/t^\theta/$, and $/t^s/$ as well as the fricatives /θ/ and /s/. While $/t^s/$ can differ from /t/ in stridency, there is no way to distinguish $/t^s/$ and $/t^\theta/$ in such a case. Therefore, the feature Delayed Release is necessary to distinguish in general between affricates and stops, with Strident accounting for the difference between $/t^\theta/$ and $/t^s/$:

	t	t^θ	t^s	θ	s
cont	−	−	−	+	+
strid	−	−	+	−	+
del rel	−	+	+	+	+

The feature Delayed Release contrasts only in sounds produced with a complete closure in the vocal tract, that is, stops vs. affricates.

2.5 Further Remarks and Revisions

While *The Sound Pattern of English* represents one of the most comprehensive treatments of phonological distinctive features accomplished

---

[19] Other linguists have used the opposite feature, Abrupt Release, though we shall follow Chomsky and Halle in this regard.

to date, various phonologists and phoneticians have suggested further modifications since the appearance of this book in 1968. Halle himself has changed his position on some of the issues concerning glottal mechanisms (see **6.2.2.5**). The purpose of this section is to point out a few of the remaining problems inherent in the *SPE* feature system.

2.5.1 The Feature Labial

Although Chomsky and Halle (1968) solve the problem of relating palatals and palatalized consonants to high front vowels, their feature system fails to relate labial and labialized (rounded) segments. It fails first to relate labial consonants such as [p, b, m], which are [+ant, −cor] and [−round], to labialized consonants such as [tʷ] and [kʷ], which are [+round]. It fails also to show the relationship between labials and rounded vowels, since the former are [−round] and the latter [+round].

That there is a need for a feature Labial covering all of the above segments is seen from the following facts from Igbo reduplication (Hyman, 1973a).[20] In Igbo, verb stems, which are of the form CV, reduplicate (that is, become double) with a high vowel in the reduplicated (prefixed) syllable. Thus, the verb /lé/ 'look' reduplicates as [òlílé] 'looking' and the verb /lá/ 'return' reduplicates as [ọ̀lị́lá] 'returning.' From these examples it is seen that the expected reduplicated vowel is [i] when the stem vowel is [e] and [ị] when it is [a] (see the discussion of advanced tongue root in **2.4.2.3**). However, when these stem vowels occur with a labial stem consonant, the reduplicated vowel is, in many dialects, [u] or [ụ], for example:

VERB STEM		DIALECT A	DIALECT B
/bè/	'cut'	[òbìbè]	[òbùbè]
/bà/	'enter'	[ọ̀bịbà]	[ọ̀bụ̀bà]

Dialect A has the older forms, while dialect B has changed [i] and [ị] to [u] and [ụ] under the influence of the labial consonant. Assuming that the rule of dialect B is to be written so as to change unrounded high vowels to rounded high vowels between labial consonants when followed in turn by a nonhigh vowel, we obtain the following using Chomsky and Halle's (1968) features:

$$
\begin{bmatrix} +\text{syll} \\ +\text{high} \end{bmatrix} \rightarrow [+\text{round}] \, / \begin{bmatrix} -\text{syll} \\ +\text{ant} \\ -\text{cor} \end{bmatrix} - \begin{bmatrix} -\text{syll} \\ +\text{ant} \\ -\text{cor} \end{bmatrix} \begin{bmatrix} +\text{syll} \\ -\text{high} \end{bmatrix}
$$

Although the change of [i] to [u] between labial consonants is an assimilation to the labial position, the features Round, Anterior, and Coronal do not

---

[20] Other discussions of the need for a feature Labial include Wang (1968), Zimmer (1969), Anderson (1971), Vennemann and Ladefoged (1971), and Campbell (1974).

permit us to expose this assimilation. If, on the other hand, we were to use the feature Labial, the rule could be rewritten in a more explanatory way:

$$\begin{bmatrix} +\text{syll} \\ +\text{high} \end{bmatrix} \rightarrow [+\text{labial}] \; / \begin{bmatrix} -\text{syll} \\ +\text{labial} \end{bmatrix} \underline{\quad} \begin{bmatrix} -\text{syll} \\ +\text{labial} \end{bmatrix} \begin{bmatrix} +\text{syll} \\ -\text{high} \end{bmatrix}$$

The feature specification [+labial] functions here as a "cover feature" for labial and labialized consonants as well as rounded vowels (see Vennemann and Ladefoged, 1971:18). In fact, the Igbo consonants which condition this assimilation include /p, b, m, f, w, kʷ, gʷ, ŋʷ, k͡p, g͡b/, that is, bilabials, labiodentals, labialized velars, and labiovelars—briefly, any consonant having to do with the lips.

2.5.2 The Treatment of Labiovelars

The labiovelar consonants /k͡p, g͡b, ŋ͡m/ present a problem for Chomsky and Halle's (1968) feature system. It is argued (p. 311) that since Nupe has a surface contrast between [k͡p] and [k͡pʷ], these labiovelars should be considered as velarized labials rather than as labialized velars. That is, their feature specifications are as in (a), not as in (b):

(a) $\begin{bmatrix} +\text{ant} \\ -\text{cor} \\ +\text{back} \\ +\text{high} \end{bmatrix}$ (b) $\begin{bmatrix} -\text{ant} \\ -\text{cor} \\ +\text{back} \\ +\text{high} \\ +\text{round} \end{bmatrix}$

If [k͡p] were treated as in (b), that is, as a velar consonant with extreme rounding, then there would be no way to distinguish [k͡p] and [k͡pʷ]. In addition, there would be no way to distinguish [k͡p] and [kʷ], both of which exist in Igbo. The problem inherent in this approach is that there is no way to view /k͡p/ as equally labial and velar. One of the two features must be chosen as primary, the other as secondary.

Chomsky and Halle (1968) argue that since [k͡pʷ] exists, [k͡p] could not already be considered [+round], that is, a labialized velar. A problem arises, however, when a palatized labiovelar is taken into consideration. Examples of a plain vs. labialized vs. palatalized labiovelar are given below, from Nupe:

[k͡pā]   'to feed'
[k͡pʷà]   'to be plentiful, cheap'
[ēg͡bʸɔ̌]   'bow string'

Chomsky and Halle state (1968:307) that an "inadequacy of the former framework [that is, Jakobson's] is that it provided no explanation for the fact that palatalization, velarization, and pharyngealization are mutually exclusive." Palatalization, which is represented by the features [+high, −back], and velarization, which is represented by the features [+high,

+back], are automatically mutually exclusive in the *SPE* framework, since a segment cannot be simultaneously [−back] and [+back].

However, if [k͡p] and [g͡b] are velarized labials, as Chomsky and Halle (1968) claim, then [k͡pʸ] and [g͡bʸ] should be phonetic impossibilities. If, on the other hand, we consider [k͡pʸ] and [g͡bʸ] to be [−back], as palatalization in their framework would require, then [k͡pʸ] and [pʸ] merge together, as seen in the following distinctive feature matrices:

[p]	[pʷ]	[pʸ]	[k͡p]
$\begin{bmatrix} +\text{ant} \\ -\text{cor} \\ -\text{back} \\ -\text{high} \\ -\text{round} \end{bmatrix}$	$\begin{bmatrix} +\text{ant} \\ -\text{cor} \\ -\text{back} \\ -\text{high} \\ +\text{round} \end{bmatrix}$	$\begin{bmatrix} +\text{ant} \\ -\text{cor} \\ -\text{back} \\ +\text{high} \\ -\text{round} \end{bmatrix}$	$\begin{bmatrix} +\text{ant} \\ -\text{cor} \\ +\text{back} \\ +\text{high} \\ -\text{round} \end{bmatrix}$

[k͡pʷ]	[k͡pʸ]	[kʷ]	[kʸ]
$\begin{bmatrix} +\text{ant} \\ -\text{cor} \\ +\text{back} \\ +\text{high} \\ +\text{round} \end{bmatrix}$	$\begin{bmatrix} +\text{ant} \\ -\text{cor} \\ -\text{back} \\ +\text{high} \\ -\text{round} \end{bmatrix}$	$\begin{bmatrix} -\text{ant} \\ -\text{cor} \\ +\text{back} \\ +\text{high} \\ +\text{round} \end{bmatrix}$	$\begin{bmatrix} -\text{ant} \\ -\text{cor} \\ -\text{back} \\ +\text{high} \\ -\text{round} \end{bmatrix}$

If, however, [k͡pʸ] is considered to be [+back], then it would not be possible to distinguish it from plain [k͡p]. The conclusion which must be drawn is that features are needed to distinguish primary and secondary places of articulation, as well as double places of articulation for coarticulated consonants such as the labiovelars under consideration. It may be necessary, in fact, to return to such traditional features as Labial, Palatal, Velar, etc. (see Wang, 1968; Vennemann and Ladefoged, 1971).

2.5.3 Binarity

Finally, it would not be possible to critically evaluate Jakobson's and Chomsky and Halle's systems without stating a few reservations one might have concerning binary features. The notion that all phonological features are binary has been questioned by a number of phonologists in various ways.[21] One area which is frequently cited is vowel height.

According to Jakobson, three vowel heights only are utilized phonemically by any language. These are distinguished in his system as [+diff, −comp] (high vowels), [−diff, −comp] (mid vowels), and [−diff, +comp] (low vowels). Since no vowel can be [+diff, +comp], only three vowel heights are possible.

[21] See, for instance, Martinet (1965), Wilson (1966), Contreras (1969), and, for an early defense of binarity, Halle (1957).

In Chomsky and Halle's framework, three vowel heights are recognized, which carry the feature specifications [+high, −low] (high vowels), [−high, −low] (mid vowels), and [−high, +low] (low vowels). Again, there is no fourth vowel height, because no vowel can be [+high, +low].

This raises the problem of what to do about languages with four phonetic vowel heights, for example, Danish (Martinet, 1937) or Swedish (Fant, 1967). In languages with the vowels [i, e, ɛ, æ], it has become customary to view both [e] and [ɛ] as [−high, −low]. The vowel [e] is generally viewed to be [+tense], while the vowel [ɛ] is considered [−tense]. In some cases, this may in fact be internally motivated by the phonological properties of a language. If, for instance, /i, e, u, o/ are pronounced [ɪ, ɛ, ʊ, ɔ] in closed syllables in a language, a rule such as the following can be written (where $ represents a syllable boundary):

$$[+\text{syll}] \rightarrow [-\text{tense}] \; / \; \_\_ \; [-\text{syll}] \; \$$$

Just as [+tense] /i/ becomes [−tense] [ɪ] in closed syllables, so does [+tense] /e/ become [−tense] [ɛ]. Thus, the proportion *i:ɪ = e:ɛ* appears to be justified.

If on the other hand, a language were to have a four-way phonemic contrast between /i/, /e/, /ɛ/, and /æ/ in CV (that is, open) syllables, it would appear necessary to recognize four contrasting vowel heights. Recognizing this possibility, Wang (1968:701) suggests replacing Chomsky and Halle's features High and Low with the new features High and Mid, which define *four* vowel heights in the following way:

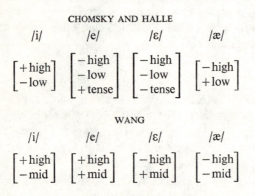

But if one has to redefine the features in such a way (and there is even a slight hint [Wang, 1968:700n] that a third feature may occasionally be needed to distinguish a fifth vowel height), one might raise the question again: why binary features? Why not simply view the four vowels *i–e–ɛ–æ* as what Trubetzkoy called a gradual opposition?

Jakobson, Fant and Halle state (1952:3): "Any minimal distinction carried by the message confronts the listener with a two-choice situation." That is, the speaker has to decide between two opposites, presence of a feature in the speech signal versus its absence. Thus, the binary principle is a way of conceptualizing the task of the listener, who must decide what he hears.[22] Fant (1967:361) states that it is possible to view Swedish vowels as having four distinct values of the same feature (height), although he argues for a binary approach "in order to allow a consistent use of the binary principle within the whole system." Thus it seems to be an important argument that since many features (for example, Nasal, Voice) are binary, it is advantageous to view all features as such (though Fant labels this approach "a matter of coding convenience only"). Viewed slightly differently, it is easier to compare and evaluate like features than unlike ones. Thus, Halle (1964: 396) counts the number of distinctive features necessary to define natural classes. In Chapter 4 we shall see the importance of feature counting in the so-called "simplicity metric." It should be clear that we can count much more easily if everything is stated in the same terms (but see Contreras, 1969).

2.5.4 Conclusion

Needless to say, there is much that remains to be resolved in distinctive feature theory. Recent attacks on distinctive features have been made by Foley (1970) and Vennemann (1972a), who argue for gradual phonological features representing the relative strength of various consonants and vowels (for example, [p] is "stronger" than [t], which is "stronger" than [k], etc.). On another front, Ladefoged (1971) has proposed that the feature Voice, often cited as one of the clearest binary features, be replaced with a continuum characterizing the degree of Glottal Stricture. He proposes a scale based on the states of the glottis, ranging from voiceless to glottal stop, including the intermediate states breathy voice, murmur, lax voice, voice, tense voice, creaky voice, creak. Finally, Halle (1972:180ff) has proposed replacing the feature Voice with the two features Stiff Vocal Cords and Slack Vocal Cords (see **6.2.2.5**). Unfortunately the implications of nonbinary features have not been revealed as yet, since few if any complex phonological descriptions have attempted to apply, for example, Ladefoged's (1971) multivalued features in phonological rules.

In the remaining chapters of this book, phonological processes will be presented wherever possible with notational abbreviations, for example, *C* instead of [−syll], *V* instead of [+syll, −cons], *N* instead of [−syll, +nas]. Where necessary, however, reference will be made to features, for example, Voice, Grave, Palatal, Nasal. It will be generally assumed that the inventory

---

[22] Recall that the binary features which were first developed were defined primarily in their acoustic aspects, with their articulatory definitions only secondary in importance.

of phonological features is identical to the inventory of phonetic features, and that languages implement these universal phonetic features in various linguistic ways. In other words, phonetic features can be "phonologized" by individual languages. Of course, it may be that a phonetic feature is used phonologically by one language but not by another. In stating phonological rules, features will be chosen which seem to best explain the motivation of the processes in question.

3

PHONOLOGICAL ANALYSIS

3.0 Different Views of the Phoneme

In Chapter 1 the difference between phonetics and phonology was discussed. It was shown that in some cases phonological representations are not identical to phonetic transcriptions. In addition, the notion of distinctiveness was discussed in Chapters 1 and 2. It was claimed, for instance, that two languages can have exactly the same inventory of phonetic sounds (or phones), but significantly different phonological systems. That is, the same sounds can be organized in different ways. Just how much emphasis is to be given to these "different ways" is a matter of much debate, as we shall see.

In this chapter we shall examine the nature of phonological analysis. Since phonologists disagree in their basic assumptions about the nature of phonology, we shall see that the specific analysis of the phonetic data of a language greatly depends on the phonological *theory* underlying the analyst's work, a fact which must be constantly kept in mind. All phonologists agree that it is necessary to recognize both phonetic units (phones) and phonological units (phonemes). But there are many differences beyond this basic agreement. In **1.3** the *phoneme* was defined as a minimal unit of sound capable of distinguishing words of different meanings. Both /p/ and /b/ are phonemes in

English, because they are capable of making a meaning difference, as in the words *pin* and *bin* or *cap* and *cab*. The exact interpretation of the fact that the word *pin* means something different from the word *bin* depends crucially on one's conception of what a phoneme is.

In the following sections we shall present three views of the phoneme. In **3.1** we shall see that some linguists (particularly in America in the 1940s and 1950s) attempted to assign sounds to phonemes on the basis of their distributional properties. In **3.2** we shall see that other linguists (particularly those of the Prague School in Europe in the 1930s) assigned sounds to phonemes on the basis of their functioning within a system of oppositions. Finally, in **3.3** it will be seen that a third group of linguists view the phoneme as a psychological sound unit. Each of these approaches has provided insights into the nature of phonology, and the discussion will, hopefully, provide a historical perspective.

3.1 The Phoneme as a Phonetic Reality

The first view asserts that the phoneme represents a physical phonetic reality. That is, sounds which belong to the same phoneme share important phonetic properties. Thus Daniel Jones (1931:74) defines the phoneme as "a family of sounds in a given language, consisting of an important sound of the language together with other related sounds, which take its place in particular sound-sequences." Similarly, Gleason (1955:261) defines the phoneme as "a class of sounds which: (1) are phonetically similar and (2) show certain characteristic patterns of distribution in the language or dialect under consideration." Under this view the phoneme is seen as a convenient label for a number of phonetic units. Thus /p/ may stand for [p], [pʰ], [p:], [p'], etc.

3.1.1 Minimal Pairs

The major task, then, for a phonologist holding this view of the phoneme is to determine which sounds belong in the same class. In order to do this, it is necessary to examine the *distribution* of the sounds in question. If two sounds which are phonetically similar occur in the same phonetic environment, and if the substitution of one sound for the other results in a difference in meaning, then these sounds are assigned to *different* phonemes. Thus, to continue the same example, if [pʰ] is substituted for the [b] in *bin*, a different word results (namely *pin*). On the other hand, if [pʰ] is substituted for the [p] in *spin* (see Chapter 1), we do not obtain a different word but rather just a slightly distorted mispronunciation, which is likely to be interpreted as [spɪn] in any case. We conclude that [pʰ] and [b] belong to different phonemes, while [pʰ] and [p] belong to the same phoneme.

It can easily be demonstrated that two sounds belong to different phonemes if we find two words which differ only in that one word has one of these two sounds in a given position (for example, at the beginning of the word), while the other word has the other sound in the same position. Two such words, which differ only by one sound, are said to constitute a *minimal pair*. Thus *pin* and *bin* are a minimal pair, since they differ only in their initial consonant, just as *cap* and *cab* are a minimal pair, since they differ only in their final consonant. On the other hand, *pin* and *bit* do not constitute a minimal pair, since they differ in both their initial *and* final consonants. Finally, *pin* and *nip* are not a minimal pair, since, although they involve the same three sounds, there are actually *two* differences between these two words: initially, *pin* has [pʰ] while *nip* has [n], and finally, *pin* has [n] while *nip* has [pʰ] (pronounced alternatively as an unreleased [p]).

We thus conclude that whenever we can establish a minimal pair, the two different sounds are phonetic manifestations of two different phonemes. The above examples involving *pin*, *bin*, and *spin* are consistent with our earlier definition of the phoneme as a *minimal unit of sound capable of making a meaning difference*. The sounds [pʰ] and [p] do not make a meaning difference in English, and so we assign them to the same phoneme, let us say /p/. This phonological unit, on the other hand, contrasts with the [b] in *bin*, and this latter sound must therefore be assigned to a different phoneme, namely /b/. The following minimal pairs illustrate the pervasiveness of the opposition between /p/ and /b/ in English:

INITIAL	MEDIAL	FINAL
pin	rapid	rip
bin	rabid	rib

It should be noted, relevant to the discussion in Chapter 2, that establishing such minimal pairs reveals what the distinctive features of the language are. Thus, we can see from the above examples that voicing is distinctive in English. Such minimal pairs as *tin : din* and *c[k]ot : got* reveal the distinctiveness of voicing in other consonantal oppositions.

3.1.2 Complementary Distribution

The existence of minimal pairs facilitates the work of the linguist seeking to establish phonemic contrasts in this way. As Hockett (1955:212) puts it: "minimal pairs are the analyst's delight, and he seeks them whenever there is any hope of finding them." This implies that it is not always possible to find minimal pairs, and this may be due to a variety of factors. It may simply be an accident that a language does not have in its vocabulary a minimal pair which distinguishes two sounds which theoretically could in fact be found in exactly the same position. In such cases it is necessary to rely on "near-minimal pairs." The German words *Goethe* [gø:tə] and *Götter* [gœtər] 'gods' are a near-minimal pair for the vowel phonemes /ø:/ and /œ/. They differ not only in their first vowel, but also by the presence vs. absence of a final /r/ phoneme. However, one can assume that the final /r/ of *Götter* is not likely to have an influence on the first vowel—and can therefore be disregarded in assigning [ø:] and [œ] to different phonemes.[1]

There is, however, sometimes a structural reason why two sounds cannot occur in the same environment. We have already seen, in Chapter 1, that the sounds [pʰ] and [p] are generally not found in the same environment. Since this is the case, it will be impossible in English to find a minimal pair in which one word differs from the other only in that it has [pʰ] instead of [p]. When two sounds are found in different environments, this is termed *complementary distribution*; the two sounds are found in mutually exclusive environments.

These environments may be stated in terms of syllable, morpheme, or word structure or in terms of adjacent segments. An example involving both comes from standard Spanish dialects. Although the words *saber* 'to know,' *nada* 'nothing,' and *lago* 'lake' are written with *b, d, g*, they are pronounced respectively [saβer], [naða], and [layo], that is, with the voiced nonstrident fricatives [β], [ð], and [ɣ]. On the other hand, these letters are pronounced [b], [d], and [g] in the words *banca* 'bench,' *demora* 'delay', and *gana* 'desire.' If one were to look closely at the facts of Spanish, one would discover that the sounds [β, ð, ɣ] are in complementary distribution with the sounds [b, d, g]. While the details are somewhat more complicated (see Harris, 1969:38–40), in these examples voiced stops appear at the beginning of a word, while voiced fricatives appear between vowels. That it is the intervocalic environment that is conditioning the voiced fricatives is seen from the following examples:

la banca	[la βaŋka]	'the bench'
la demora	[la ðemora]	'the delay'
la gana	[la ɣana]	'the desire'

When one adds the feminine definite article *la*, the voiced stops are then in intervocalic position (that is, between vowels), and must therefore "spirantize" to become [β, ð, ɣ]. Since these voiced fricatives (or spirants) are in complementary distribution with the voiced stops, we have only one series of phonemic consonants and not two. In a phonemic analysis based on the

---

[1] While the vowel of *rib* is actually longer than that of *rip* (see **5.2.5**), thereby disqualifying [rɪ:b] and [rɪp] as a true minimal pair, it is often necessary to factor out such low-level phonetic detail in phonemic analysis.

distribution of sounds, [b] and [β] would be said to be *allophones* of the
same phoneme /b/, just as [d] and [ð] are allophones of /d/, and [g] and
[ɣ] allophones of /g/. An allophone is, then, a phonetic realization of a
phoneme in a particular environment. The voiced fricative [β] is the allophone
of the phoneme /b/ found between vowels, just as the voiced stop [b] is the
allophone of /b/ found at the beginning of a word.

   In more recent approaches to phonology, such statements of allophonic
distributions have been superseded by the explicit formulation of phonological
rules. Thus, a rule such as the following,

$$\begin{bmatrix} b \\ d \\ g \end{bmatrix} \rightarrow \begin{bmatrix} \beta \\ \eth \\ \gamma \end{bmatrix} / V - V$$

would be postulated for Spanish, by which underlying (or phonemic)
/b, d, g/ are converted to [β, ð, ɣ] between vowels. In terms of distinctive
features, this rule would be formulated as follows:

$$\begin{bmatrix} +\,voice \\ -\,nasal \end{bmatrix} \rightarrow [+cont] / [+syll] - [+syll]$$

An oral voiced consonant becomes continuous (that is, a fricative) between
vowels (see **4.3.1.2** for the abbreviatory conventions used in this rule).

   Another case of complementary distribution comes from Standard German.
Note the distribution of the fricatives [ç] and [x] in the following German
words (see **1.4**):

siech	[ziːç]	'sickly'	*Buch*	[buːx]	'book'
mich	[mɪç]	'me'	*hoch*	[hoːx]	'high'
Pech	[pɛç]	'pitch'	*noch*	[nɔx]	'still'
			Bach	[bax]	'brook'

The velar fricative [x] appears after the back (and rounded) vowels [uː, oː, ɔ],
as well as after the central (unrounded) vowel [a]. The palatal fricative [ç]
is found after front (palatal) vowels, including front rounded vowels, for
example, *Bücher* [büːçər] 'books.' Since the central vowel [a] is specified
[+back] in distinctive feature theory (see **2.3.3.2**), this complementary distribution is based on the distinction between preceding front and back
vowels. Notice that it also extends to the diphthongs written *ai/ei, eu/äu*,
and *au—reich* [raɪç] 'rich,' *räuchern* [rɔɪçərn] 'to smoke (meat),' *Rauch* [raux]
'smoke.' Since plural formation in German often involves the fronting (or
umlauting) of a vowel, there will be numerous nouns with [x] in the singular
(after a back vowel) and [ç] in the plural (after a front vowel). In addition to
the alternation between [x] and [ç] seen in *Buch* and *Bücher* above, other
examples are *Dach* [dax] 'roof,' pl. *Dächer* [dɛçər], and *Loch* [lɔx] 'hole,'

pl. *Löcher* [lœçər]. The palatal fricative [ç] is therefore an allophone of the phoneme /x/ after front vowels, as stated in the following rule:

$$x \rightarrow ç \ / \ [-back] \ \underline{\quad}$$
$$V$$

Since only [ç] can occur after a consonant, for example, *Storch* [stɔrç] 'stork,' or at the beginning of a word, for example, *Chemie* [çemi:] 'chemistry,' the exact distribution of [x] and [ç] is somewhat more complicated than the above rule would indicate.

3.1.3 Phonetic Similarity

While complementary distribution is generally a clue to the phonological analysis of a language, there are cases where one might wish to maintain phonemes in complementary distribution. That is, it may be necessary to view some sounds in complementary distribution as belonging to separate phonemes. One well-known case concerns the distribution of [h] and [ŋ] in English. As seen in such words as *head*, *heart*, *enhance*, and *perhaps*, [h] occurs only at the *beginning of a syllable* (*enhance* and *perhaps* are syllabified as *en-hance* and *per-haps*). On the other hand, as seen in such words as *sing* [sɪŋ], *singer* [sɪŋ-ər], and *finger* [fɪŋ-gər], [ŋ] always occurs at the *end of a syllable*. Just as there are no English syllables ending in [h], there are no English syllables beginning with [ŋ]. It would thus appear that [h] and [ŋ] are in complementary distribution and should therefore, as suggested in **3.1.2**, be assigned as allophones of the same phoneme.

While we shall ultimately argue that [ŋ] should be recognized as the phonetic reflex of a phonemic /ng/ sequence (see **3.3.1**), let us ignore this analysis for the time being. A solution which would assign [h] and [ŋ] to the same phoneme would appear unsatisfactory to most phonemicists, since the two sounds appear to have very little in common. While [pʰ] and [p] are both voiceless labial stops in English, just as [b] and [β] are both voiced labial obstruents in Spanish, [h] and [ŋ] have little more in common than that they are both consonants. [h] is voiceless, while [ŋ] is voiced; [h] is a fricative, while [ŋ] is a (nasal) stop; [h] is oral, while [ŋ] is nasal; [h] is glottal, while [ŋ] is velar, etc. In order to rule out a solution which would assign these two sounds to the same phoneme, one must appeal to the notion of *phonetic similarity*. As Hockett (1942:103) puts it, "if *a* and *b* are members of one phoneme, they share one or more features."

The whole question of phonetic similarity is a complex one. In particular, it is not quite clear whether this criterion for assigning sounds to the same phoneme means that these sounds must share a phonetic property not shared by other sounds or simply that they must share a phonetic property. A good example comes from Gwari (Hyman, 1972a:190). The phoneme /l/ is realized as a voiced palatal stop /ɟ/ before /i/, /e/, and /y/. Thus, /li/ 'to eat' is pronounced /ɟí/ and written orthographically as *gyi*. On the other hand, the phoneme /g/ is realized as [j] before /i/ and /e/. It seems clear that the palatal stop (which is a realization of the phoneme /l/) is more phonetically similar to [g] (as the main allophone of /g/) than is [j], and yet it is [j] and not [ɟ] which belongs to the /g/ phoneme. Thus, while allophones share constant phonetic properties, there is no way of assigning sounds to phonemes on this basis alone. Since we shall argue for the psychological reality of phonemes in **3.3**, we can restate this problem in the following terms: while allophones of the same phoneme share phonetic properties, it is not possible to determine which sounds speakers of a language will judge as most similar by means of examining the phonetic data alone. Instead, it is necessary to evaluate the phonetic data on the basis of the entire phonological system, as will be seen in **3.2**.

3.1.4 Free Variation

Thus far we have discussed cases where two phones are assigned to one phoneme. In all of these cases the two allophones have been seen to be conditioned by context. For this reason they are sometimes referred to as *contextual variants* or *combinatory variants* (Trubetzkoy, 1939:49). However, it is possible that two phones may appear in the same context without causing a change in meaning. In this case they are usually analyzed as *free variants* or optional variants (Trubetzkoy, 1939:46). In English, final voiceless stops occur both aspirated and unaspirated, for example, [mæpʰ] or [mæpº] 'map,' [mætʰ] or [mætº] 'mat.' In these words two phones are found in the same context, and no meaning difference results. We therefore cannot assign [pʰ] and [pº] or [tʰ] and [tº] to different phonemes. These differences would appear to have no effect on the establishing of phonemic contrasts, and the same speaker may sometimes use one phonetic realization of a phoneme and sometimes the other.

Recently this notion of free variation has come under attack by sociolinguists (for example, Labov, 1971:432–437). Labov points out that free variants often have sociological significance, and that these variants should be accounted for quantitatively. That is, rules should be provided which account for the relative frequency of "free variants." The same speaker may use one variant in one sociological situation, while he may use the other in another situation. A number of examples have been pointed out in the literature. For example, it is well known that some French speakers use an alveolar trill [r] when they are home in a small town or village, but a uvular fricative [ʁ] when they visit Paris. This particular example illustrates that some variants are due to sound changes which have not been uniformly diffused throughout a community. One group, which enjoys greater prestige throughout the community, may acquire one variant, while another group of lesser status may acquire another variant. When a speaker of the second group comes in contact with speakers of the first group, the result is "dialect mixture." In some cases, however, the two forms coexist in the same dialect as the result of continued contact.

It is sometimes necessary to speak of free variation among phonemes. Thus, the difference between /i/ and /ɛ/ normally makes a meaning difference, for example, *beat* and *bet*. However, the word *economics* can be pronounced with either initial /i/ or /ɛ/, without a consequent meaning change. Similarly, although /u/ and /ʊ/ contrast in words such as *kook* and *cook*, the words *roof* and *root* can be pronounced with either of these vowels. It is therefore possible not only to have noncontrasting allophones in the same context but also to have noncontrasting phonemes in the same context in isolated words.

3.1.5 Discovery Procedures

A number of American linguists of the 1940s and 1950s, who held the view that the phoneme should be defined as a class of sounds, attempted to provide a methodology or set of discovery procedures for establishing phonemes. Harris (1951) devotes several chapters to the way phonemic analysis should be done, but avoids a general theoretical statement as to what the concept of the phoneme represents (for example, is it psychologically real in the sense of **3.3**). Pike (1947a:63) succinctly defines the phoneme as follows: "a *phoneme* [his emphasis] is one of the significant units of sound arrived at for a particular language by the analytical procedures developed from the basic premises previously presented." Similarly, Hockett (1942:100) defines the phoneme as "a class of phones determined by six criteria." These criteria, which are treated in **3.4**, include similarity, nonintersection (that is, no phonemic overlapping), contrastive and complementary distribution, completeness, pattern congruity, and economy. In the writings of such linguists, as argued by Chomsky (1957, 1964), emphasis is placed on the way a language should be analyzed, rather than on the way a language *is*. While most theorists have been concerned with whether the phoneme represents a phonetic reality, a phonological reality, or a psychological reality (as discussed in this chapter), it is possible to avoid the question of what the phoneme is and ask only whether a given sound belongs to one or another phoneme. Consistent with this approach is Twaddell's argument (1935) that the phoneme should be regarded as a convenient fictitious unit whose reality is yet to be proven. Chao (1934:38) on the other hand, states: "given the sounds of a language, there are usually more than one possible way of reducing them to a system of phonemes, and . . . these different systems or solutions are not simply correct or incorrect, but may be regarded only as being good or bad for various purposes." One such purpose, for instance, is clearly stated by Jones (1931:78): "The main object of grouping the sounds of a language together into phonemes is to establish a simple and adequate way of writing the language." In stating the goal of phonemic analysis as such, Jones has reduced the discussion of what a phoneme is or represents to the question of how one can best write a language phonemically. As we shall see in **3.2** and **3.3**, other linguists have asked more of their phonemes.

3.2 The Phoneme as a Phonological Reality

The definition of the phoneme in purely phonological terms is characteristic of the Prague School. Trubetzkoy (1939:36) defines the phoneme as "the sum of the phonologically relevant properties of a sound." For him, phonemes are defined in terms of *oppositions* in a phonological system. The important notion in Prague School phonology is "function": "The phoneme can be defined satisfactorily neither on the basis of its psychological nature [see **3.3**] nor on the basis of its relation to the phonetic variants, but purely and solely on the basis of its function in the system of language" (Trubetzkoy, 1939:41). Thus, a phoneme is a minimal unit that can *function* to distinguish meanings. It is not a sound or even a group of sounds, but rather an *abstraction*, a theoretical construct on the phonological level. It is defined in terms of its contrasts within a system. For example, we saw in Chapter 1 that the /b/ phoneme in English is very different from the /b/ phoneme in Berber, since in the latter case there is no /p/ to contrast with. Approaching the phoneme as a class of sounds, one would miss the fact that although [b] is assigned to /b/ in both languages, there is a basic difference between this phoneme in English and in Berber.

3.2.1 Phonemic Overlapping

In several of the examples discussed, two phones were assigned to the same phoneme, for example, [x] and [ç] in German. One issue which reveals a fundamental difference between defining the phoneme as a class of sounds and defining it by its function within a phonological system of oppositions is the question of whether one phone can be assigned sometimes to one phoneme and at other times to another phoneme. Such a possibility, termed *phonemic overlapping*, is raised by Bloch (1941) and is discussed by a number of European phonologists (for example, Martinet, 1947; Fischer-Jørgensen, 1956:591). An example discussed by Jakobson, Fant and Halle (1952:5) concerns Danish /t/ and /d/. In syllable-initial position these phonemes are pronounced, respectively, [t] and [d], for example, [tag] 'roof' and [dag] 'day.' In syllable-final position, however, /t/ is pronounced [d] and /d/ is pronounced [ð], as seen in the following words:

/hat/ → [had] 'hat'
/had/ → [hað] 'hate'

We must recognize for Danish a rule which "weakens" consonants in syllable-final position. The result is that the [d] of 'day' must be assigned to the phoneme /d/, but the [d] of 'hat' must be assigned to the phoneme /t/. Thus, one phone is assigned to one of two phonemes, depending on the context.

Such examples of overlapping pose a problem for adherents of the phonetic similarity criterion in phonemic analysis. What it means is that it is not possible to predict what phoneme a given phone will be assigned to on the basis of its phonetic character alone, since we have seen [d] to be assigned once to /t/ and once to /d/. The idea that phones and phonemes could be identified on a one-to-one basis, that is, that a given sound will always belong to a given phoneme and a given phoneme will always be associated with a given sound, is termed *biuniqueness* by Chomsky: "the biuniqueness condition . . . asserts that each sequence of phones is represented by a unique sequence of phonemes, and that each sequence of phonemes represents a unique sequence of phones" (1964:94). If one were to adhere to phonetic similarity as an overriding principle in assigning phones to phonemes, one would be forced to say that syllable-final [d] is a realization of the phoneme /d/, and that syllable-final [ð] is the realization of a third phoneme /ð/, which is found only in this position.

Just as Chomsky showed that it is necessary in phonological analysis to allow for phonemic overlapping of the kind just illustrated (and therefore argued against the biuniqueness condition), most European phonologists noted the consistency of overlapping with their view of the phonemes in a system of oppositions. Thus, Jakobson, Fant and Halle (1952:5) state: "Two patterns are identical if their relational structure can be put into a one-to-one correspondence, so that to each term of the one there corresponds a term of the other." In other words, [t] is to [d] in syllable-initial position as [d] is to [ð] in syllable-final position. In the terms of Martinet (1960:60), physical identity does not necessarily imply linguistic identity.

Examples of phonemic overlapping are not particularly difficult to find. One, from Danish again, is discussed by Martinet (1947:43). As seen in the following diagram,

before /n/   *before /r/*

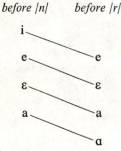

there are four contrastive vowel heights in Danish. The four front unrounded vowels are normally realized (indicated in the diagram as before /n/) as [i, e, ε, a]. However, before /r/ a rule of vowel lowering applies, yielding the phonetic series [e, ε, a, ɑ]. While this process has modified the phonetic characteristics of each vowel phoneme, it can easily be seen that the relation between the four vowels has remained constant. Thus, the vowel [e] of [er] sequences is assigned to the /i/ phoneme, even though the vowel [e] of [en] sequences is assigned to the /e/ phoneme. Danish is analyzed in this way because the phoneme /i/ is defined not in *phonetic* terms but rather in terms of its *function* within the total vowel system. In particular, rather than defining /i/ as consisting of a particular class of sounds, we define /i/ as the highest front vowel in Danish. Similarly, we define /e/ as the second-highest front vowel. Thus, when we have to assign the [e] of [er] sequences to a vowel phoneme, we choose /i/, since [e] here represents the highest front vowel before /r/. As in the case of Danish /t/ and /d/, we can apply Jakobson, Fant and Halle's notion of relational structure: [i] is to [e] before /n/ as [e] is to [ε] before /r/.

3.2.2 Neutralization

Bloch (1941:66–67) makes the distinction between *partial overlapping* and *complete overlapping*: "The intersection or overlapping of phonemes will be called partial if a given sound x occurring under one set of phonetic conditions is assigned to phoneme A, while the same x under a different set of conditions is assigned to phoneme B; it will be called complete if successive occurrences of x under the same conditions are assigned sometimes to A, sometimes to B." The two examples discussed in the preceding section both represent cases of partial overlapping.

A case of complete overlapping pointed out by Bloch involves English /t/ and /d/. Intervocalically, /t/ and /d/ are both pronounced as an alveolar tap [ɾ]. Thus, for many speakers of American English, the words *betting* and *bedding* are pronounced identically, that is, as [bɛɾɪŋ]. One might, however, attempt to assign different phonemic representations to the two words on the basis of the fact that *betting* contains the word *bet* and *bedding* contains the word *bed*. Assuming that the velar nasal should be phonemicized as /ng/ (see **3.3.1**), the two phonemic representations would then be /bɛtɪng/ and /bɛdɪng/. In this case, however, it would be necessary to state that both /t/ and /d/ have the allophone [ɾ] in the *same* environment, namely in intervocalic position. What this means in terms of Prague School phonology (see **2.2.3**) is that an opposition has been *neutralized* in this position.

While /t/ and /d/ contrast initially, as in the words *tin* and *din*, and while they contrast finally, as in the word *bet* and *bed*, they do not contrast intervocalically (with the additional restriction that the preceding vowel is stressed).

In **2.2.3**, such an opposition was termed *neutralizable*. On the other hand, the contrast between /p/ and /b/ is, at least with respect to initial, medial, and final position, a *constant* opposition (see, however, footnote 3, Chapter 2). Trubetzkoy (1939:78) differentiates *positions of neutralization*, where the neutralization takes place, and *positions of relevance*, where the opposition is realized phonetically. Thus, in the above example, the intervocalic position is the position of neutralization, while the initial and final positions are the positions of relevance.

Notice that if phonemic forms such as /bɛtɪŋ/ are to be permitted for English, then the phonological analysis will be possible only if the phonologist goes beyond the phonetic data. In particular, it must be known whether there is a word *bet* that exists independently, and whether this word exists as a morpheme in a word such as *betting*. This consideration clearly goes beyond the distributional analysis inherent in discovering complementary distribution. In this case we not only need to know whether two forms are the same (one phoneme) or different (two phonemes), but also we must establish exactly which morpheme (for example, *bet* or *bed*)) is present. In otherwords, we must introduce *grammatical* information into the phonological analysis. In terms of the positions outlined in **3.3.2**, this amounts to "mixing levels."[2]

To combat the problem of neutralization, Prague School phonologists introduced the *archiphoneme*. Consider a language such as Feʔfeʔ–Bamileke, which has the following sequences:

	ku	či	ču
ke	ko	če	čo
	ka	ča	

Since both [k] and [č] are found before /e/, /a/, /o/, and /u/, we conclude that they belong to separate phonemes, that is, /k/ and /č/. However, there is a problem concerning the vowel /i/, since only [č] is found before it. There are sequences of [či] in this language, but *[ki] is not found. If we were to analyze [či] as /či/ phonemically, Praguians would point out that this /č/ is not the same as the /č/ found in other positions. The phoneme /č/ is defined in part by the fact that it stands in opposition to /k/. Before /i/, however, this part of the definition is destroyed, since the difference between [k] and [č] cannot be used here to make a meaning difference.

Instead of calling [č] before /i/ another instance of /č/, a separate phonological unit is set up which is neither /č/ nor /k/, but which consists of all of the phonological properties *shared* by /č/ and /k/. This unit, termed an archiphoneme, is by convention written as a capital letter, here /K/. /K/ stands for a voiceless noncontinuant, which would be specified in terms of

---

[2] In a phonemic analysis emphasizing the distributional properties of sounds, it would probably be necessary to recognize a third phoneme /ɾ/, because of its unique distribution (it occurs only intervocalically and after certain sonorant consonants, e.g., *party* [pɑɾɾi]).

distinctive features as [+high] (that is, either palatal or velar), but which would not be specified with respect to backness. In other words, its specifications would be as seen below, with [0 back] indicating that this feature is irrelevant (left blank), since it is neutralized:

$$
/K/ \quad : \quad \begin{bmatrix} +\text{cons} \\ -\text{syll} \\ -\text{son} \\ +\text{high} \\ 0\ \text{back} \\ -\text{ant} \\ -\text{cor} \\ -\text{voice} \\ -\text{cont} \\ -\text{nas} \\ 0\ \text{strid} \\ 0\ \text{del rel} \end{bmatrix}
$$

In addition to [0 back], the features Strident and Delayed Release are not specified, since the archiphoneme does not specify whether the noncontinuant is a stop or an affricate.

Since [č] before /i/ represents the neutralization of the opposition between /k/ and /č/, it would be incorrect in this framework to phonemicize [či] as /či/. Trubetzkoy (1939:78) draws support for this approach from linguistic performance: "In neutralizable distinctive oppositions perception fluctuates: in positions of relevance both opposition members are clearly distinguished; in positions of neutralization, on the other hand, it is often not possible to indicate which of the two had just been produced or perceived." Phonemes which participate in neutralizations are thus felt by speakers to be closely related. We might presume, as a result, that speakers of the above language will regard /č/ and /k/ as more closely related than they will /č/ and /t/.

An example of neutralization often cited in the literature was discussed in **2.2.3.** In Standard German, voiced obstruents are devoiced syllable-finally. While the phonemes /t/ and /d/ contrast initially (for example, *Tier* [ti:r] 'animal' vs. *dir* [di:r] 'to you') and intervocalically (for example, *leiten* [laɪtən] ' to lead' and *leiden* [laɪdən] 'to suffer'), there is no possible contrast syllable-finally. Thus, the words *Rat* 'advice' and *Rad* 'wheel,' which are written differently, are both pronounced [ra:t]. Notice, however, that in the plurals, where a suffix is added (which causes a vowel change as well), the contrast been /t/ and /d/ resurfaces: *Räte* [rɛ:tə] 'advices' and *Räder* [rɛ:dər] 'wheels.' The question is how the final [t] of *Rat* and *Rad* should be analyzed.

Phonologists maintaining a definition of the phoneme as a class of phonetically similar sounds often disallowed complete overlapping (neutralization) and were therefore forced to analyze both 'advice' and 'wheel' as

/raːt/. Prague School phonologists, who saw the phoneme as a unit in a system of oppositions, could not analyze the final stop of these words as /t/, since, unlike its counterpart in initial and intervocalic position, it cannot stand opposed to /d/. Therefore, an archiphoneme would be set up. As stated by Trubetzkoy, "In German the bilateral opposition d–t is neutralized in final position. The opposition member which occurs in the position of neutralization from a phonological point of view is neither a voiced stop nor a voiceless stop but the 'non-nasal dental occlusive in general'." Thus the underlying representation of both 'advice' and 'wheel' is /raːT/, where /T/ is specified [0 voice], representing an archiphoneme sharing all of the properties common to /t/ and /d/. The words *Rat* and *Rad* thus end in a dental stop which is *redundantly* voiceless.

3.3 The Phoneme as a Psychological Reality

The original mentalist position, as espoused by Badouin de Courtenay, defined the phoneme as "a mental reality, as the intention of the speaker or the impression of the hearer, or both" (Twaddell, 1935:56). Since each time a speaker pronounces the sound [p] it is acoustically never quite the same as the last [p], the speaker must have internalized an image or idealized picture of the sound, a target which he tries to approximate. Badouin de Courtenay spoke of the phoneme as "a sound imagined or intended, opposed to the emitted sound as a 'psychophonetic' phenomenon to the 'physiophonetic' fact" (Jakobson and Halle, 1956:11). Thus, according to the argument, in Nupe (where /si/ is realized as [ši]), when a speaker pronounces [ši] 'to buy,' his real intention or abstract image is /si/. Similarly, when a speaker of American English says [aɪ mɪšə] 'I miss you,' his real intention is [aɪ mɪs yu], and so forth.

This view of the phoneme as a psychological unit was subject to attack by phonologists holding the views of the phoneme discussed in **3.1** and **3.2**. The following statement of Twaddell (1935:57) is perhaps representative of American reaction against mentalistic definitions of the phoneme: "Such a definition is invalid because (1) we have no right to guess about the linguistic workings of an inaccessible 'mind,' and (2) we can secure no advantage from such guesses. The linguistic processes of the 'mind' as such are quite simply unobservable; and introspection is notoriously a fire in a wooden stove."

Representative of the Praguian reaction to Courtenay, Trubetzkoy (1939:38) states: "Reference to psychology must be avoided in defining the phoneme, since the latter is a linguistic and not a psychological concept."

To Trubetzkoy, the phoneme is a characteristic of the linguistic system, and not of the minds of speakers:

> The fact that the concept "phoneme" is here [in Courtenay's writings] linked with such vague and nondescript notions as "psyche," "linguistic consciousness," or "sensory perception" cannot be of help in clarifying the phoneme concept. If this definition were to be accepted, one would never know in an actual case what to consider a phoneme. For it is impossible to penetrate the "psyche of all members of a speech community" (especially where extinct languages are involved). (1939:39)

Although perhaps most phonologists reacted to the strong psychological wording of Courtenay's pioneering work, this does not mean that they completely refrained from discussion of psychological (for example, perceptual) aspects of the phoneme. Virtually all theorists agree that the phonemic system of a language exerts a behavioral effect on its speakers. Few phonologists fail to make some remark about the role of the phonemic system in the perception of foreign sounds. In the words of Trubetzkoy,

> The phonological system of a language is like a sieve through which everything that is said passes. . . . Each person acquires the system of his mother tongue. But when he hears another language spoken he intuitively uses the familiar "phonological sieve" of his mother tongue to analyze what has been said. However, since this sieve is not suited for the foreign language, numerous mistakes and misinterpretations are the result. The sounds of the foreign language receive an incorrect phonological interpretation since they are strained through the "phonological sieve" of one's own mother tongue. (1939:51–52)

Even Harris (1954:36), who devoted so much attention to distributional analysis, wrote: "Clearly, certain behaviors of the speakers indicate perception along the lines of the distributional structure, for example, the fact that while people imitate nonlinguistic or foreign-language sounds, they *repeat* [his emphasis] utterances of their own language." While the antimentalist phonologists of the 1930–1950 era were quick to reject all psychological terminology, they did not refrain from pointing out that their nonpsychological phonemic systems have psychological validity for speakers.

The classic article on the psychological reality of phonemes is Sapir's (1933) article bearing exactly this title. In this article Sapir reports the following anecdote:

> When working on the Southern Paiute language of southwestern Utah and northwestern Arizona I spent a little time trying to teach my native interpreter . . . how to write his language phonetically. . . . I selected *pa:βah*. . . . I instructed Tony to divide the word into its syllables and to discover by careful hearing what sounds entered into the composition of each of the syllables. . . . To my astonishment Tony then syllabified *pa:*, pause, *pah*. I say "astonishment" because I at once recognized the paradox that Tony was not "hearing" in terms of the

actual sounds (the voiced bilabial β was objectively very different from the initial stop) but in terms of an etymological reconstruction: *pa:* 'water' plus postposition *–*pah* 'at.' The slight pause which intervened after the stem was enough to divert Tony from the phonetically proper form of the postposition to a theoretically real but actually nonexistent form. (pp. 23–24)

What this means is that Tony had knowledge of the underlying /p/ in the postposition 'at,' which by rule becomes the voice spirant [β] intervocalically. In other words, the /p/ in the phonemic representation is psychologically real.

3.3.1 Levels of Adequacy

Examples such as the above reveal that phonology goes well beyond the systematizing of phones into phonemes. There has been much recent discussion of the goals of phonology. Chomsky (1964:62ff), for example, distinguishes phonological analyses which are *observationally adequate* from those which are *descriptively adequate*. A phonological analysis is observationally adequate if it accurately transcribes the data and nothing more. It is descriptively adequate if, in addition to transcribing the data, it accounts for the knowledge (which Chomsky refers to as *linguistic competence*) of the native speaker. Let us say, for instance, that one description of English phonology states that there is a word *play* [ple] and a word *clay* [kle], but no word **tlay* (presumably to be pronounced [tle]). Such a description reaches the level of observational adequacy, since it correctly states that certain forms are observed while other forms are not.

This description cannot be said to reach the level of descriptive adequacy, however, unless it accounts for the fact that *tlay* not only is not observed but could not be a possible word in the language. The native speaker intuitively knows that it is not possible to have a [tl] cluster at the beginning of a word in English. Thus, a related fact is that English has the words *pluck* [plək] and *cluck* [klək], but no word **tluck* [tlək]. A descriptively adequate phonological description of English must include numerous constraints on consonant sequences (see **1.4.1**). Much more will be said about such constraints. For the moment it is important only to note that native speakers have knowledge of these constraints. Greenberg and Jenkins (1964) have experimentally demonstrated the native speaker's ability to judge non-existent forms for their well-formedness, both in terms of sequences which do or do not "sound English" and in terms of the distance of such forms from good English-sounding words.

An example of a phonological analysis reaching the level of descriptive adequacy concerns the velar nasal consonant [ŋ] in English. Many phonologists have observed that the velar nasal, which is written *ng* as in *sing* [sɪŋ], does not occur word-initially in English, although [m] and [n] do. A phonological analysis of English could merely state this constraint, but there is good reason to believe that such an analysis remains too superficial. In particular, once this constraint is stated, one might further ask *why* there is such a constraint to begin with. We might hypothesize that the sound is too difficult to pronounce in this position, but then there are many languages which do in fact allow [ŋ] word-initially, as the spelling of the Vietnamese name *Nguyen* suggests. Thus, while [ŋ] is difficult for an English speaker to pronounce at the beginning of a word, its absence in this position in English cannot be explained in universal terms.

Rather, the reason we do not find word-initial [ŋ] is that it derives historically from an earlier *[ŋg]. Thus, the reason we find words such as *meat* [mit] and *neat* [nit], but not *ngeat* [ŋit], is a *historical* one. The velar nasal derives historically from [ŋg] at a stage where there was not only no word *ngeat* [ŋgit] but also no word *mbeat* [mbit] or *ndeat* [ndit]. That is, a word could not begin with a nasal consonant followed by a voiced stop. What is interesting is that although the [g] of *[ŋg] has dropped, [ŋ] continues to function *as if* there were a [g] after it.

In fact, Sapir (1925:19) proposed that the sound [ŋ] be analyzed phonologically in English as /ŋg/:

> In spite of what phoneticians tell us about this sound (*b:m* as *d:n* as *g:ŋ*), no naïve English-speaking person can be made to feel in his bones that it belongs to a single series with *m* and *n*. Psychologically it cannot be grouped with them because, unlike them, it is not a freely movable consonant (there are no words beginning with *ŋ*). It still *feels* like *ŋg*, however little it sounds like it. The relation *ant : and = sink : sing* is psychologically as well as historically correct.

Chomsky and Halle (1968:85n) propose that [ŋ] should be described phonologically as /ng/. Two rules are necessary:

1 $n \rightarrow \eta \,/\, \_ \{k, g\}$
2 $g \rightarrow \emptyset \,/\, \eta \_ \#$

Rule 1 assimilates /n/ to [ŋ] before a velar consonant, for example, /sɪnk/ becomes [sɪŋk]; Rule 2 deletes [g] after [ŋ] and before a word boundary (see **3.3.2** and **6.1.2.2** for discussion of boundaries). Thus, the full derivation of *sing* is as follows:

/sɪng/ → sɪŋg → [sɪŋ]   (by rules 1 and 2)

Given this /ng/ analysis, a general sequential constraint can be formulated: in English, no words begin with *mb*, *nd*, or *ng*, that is, no word begins with a nasal consonant followed by another consonant. It is this constraint on the *phonological* level which explains the failure of [ŋ] to occur at the beginning of English words.

The /ng/ solution reaches the level of descriptive adequacy because it provides a principled reason for the exclusion of word-initial [ŋ]. In addition,

Fromkin (1971:34–35) presents evidence from speech errors for this analysis. She reports that someone, instead of saying *Chuck Young* (the Chancellor of UCLA), said *chunk yug*. Phonetically, this represents a change from the intended [čək yəŋ] to the speech error [čəŋk yəg]. If it is assumed that [ŋ] is phonologically /ng/, then this error (as well as others) can be explained by saying that the nasal consonant was transferred to the first word, thereby leaving a [g] sound stranded in the second word. The possibility of using data from speech errors to help choose among competing analyses seems very promising.

3.3.2 Grammatical Prerequisites to Phonology

One of the basic disagreements in the history of phonology has to do with what is referred to as "mixing levels." According to some phonologists, a phonological analysis would have to be justified on the basis of the phonetic variants alone. In particular, information from a grammatical level (that is, morphology, syntax) could not be used to justify an analysis. Hockett (1942:20–21) sums up this position: "There must be no circularity; phonological analysis is assumed for grammatical analysis, and so must not assume any part of the latter. The line of demarcation between the two must be sharp." This position was sometimes maintained by phonologists focusing on discovery procedures (see **3.1.5**). Procedures were developed by which sounds could be assigned to phonological units (phonemes), which in turn could, by other procedures, be assigned to grammatical units (morphemes, words).

We have already mentioned Chomsky's criticism (1957:50–53) of discovery procedures. However, all one needs to disprove the claim that phonological analysis can be done without recourse to grammatical information is to find a language where the phonology cannot be described without reference to the grammar, where "grammar" is used as a cover term for both morphology (word structure) and syntax (sentence structure).

Such examples are not hard to find. Specifically, many phonological descriptions require information such as (1) morphological boundaries and (2) class categories, such as nouns and verbs. A good example of the latter occurs in English. It is generally assumed that part of a complete phonology of English will deal with stress phenomena. However, the placement of stress in a word is partly dependent on whether that word is a noun or verb, as seen in the following examples:

NOUN	VERB
pérvert	pervért
súbject	subjéct
cónduct	condúct

While there are exceptions (for example, *to rámble, a lamént, a babóon*), some of which can be explained in terms of syllable structure and vowel tenseness (see Chomsky and Halle, 1968), the above noun and verb forms suggest a generalization: stress falls on the first syllable in nouns, but on the second syllable in verbs. Thus, for a particular set of noun–verb pairs, stress can only be accounted for with reference to grammatical information.

Another example is found in Nupe (Hyman, 1970a). In Nupe, the phoneme /s/ is pronounced [š] before /i/; for example, /sī/ 'to buy' is pronounced [šī], but /sá/ 'to cut' is pronounced [sá]. Thus, it would appear that the difference between [s] and [š] is completely redundant, since we can predict which one is found on the basis of the following vowel. Phonemic /s/ is palatalized to [š] before the front vowel /i/ (as well as before /e/ and /ɛ/). There is, however, one exception. There is a process of reduplication in Nupe which creates nouns from verbs, for example, [šī] 'to buy' becomes [šīšī] 'buying.' The vowel in the reduplicated prefix is frequently [i] (but see Hyman, 1970a:67–69 for a fuller statement; also **3.3.5**). The exception to the palatalization of /s/ to [š] before /i/ arises when a verb such as /sá/ 'to cut' is reduplicated as [sīsá] and not *[šīsá]. If we were to base ourselves entirely on the phonetics, we would be forced to say that the difference between [s] and [š] is a distinctive one, since the utterance [šī sá] (from /sī/ + /èsá/ 'to buy a chair') is also found. Thus, [sīsá] and [šī sá] would constitute a minimal pair. Such a minimal pair, which is possible only when one of the forms is a noun derived through reduplication, should not be allowed to destroy the complementary distribution of [s] and [š] in the language, which is otherwise completely general. With a minimum of grammatical information, we can still predict when we will find [s] and when we will find [š]. Nupe speakers palatalize /s/ to [š] before /i/, *except* in such cases of reduplication (see Wilbur, 1973, for theoretical discussion).

In addition to grammatical categories such as noun and verb, it is frequently necessary to refer to grammatical boundaries in phonological analyses. The boundaries which are used in phonology (see **6.1.2.2**) include the full-word boundary ($\#\#$), the internal word or stem boundary ($\#$), and the general morpheme boundary ($+$). An example of the relevance of such boundaries comes from Feʔfeʔ–Bamileke. Consider the following data:

(a) pǒ   'hand'   mbǒ   'hands'
     pē: 'accept'   mbē: 'and accept'
     púa   'two'   ntām púa   'two hearts'
     pì: 'profit'   tūm pì: 'send the profit'

(b) vāp   'whip'   vābī   'whip him/her'
     ŋgǎp   'hen'   ŋgābà   'my hen'
     pū: 'children' pē: pū: 'accept the children'

In several of these examples there is an alternation between [p] and [b].

Let us assign [p] and [b] as allophones of the phoneme /p/ (see Hyman 1972b, Chapter 3, for discussion of this solution). In (a), /p/ is realized as [b] only in the first two examples in the right-hand column, as the result of a rule which voices /p/ after [m]:

$$p \rightarrow b \ / \ m \ \underline{\hspace{1em}}$$

However, in the third and fourth examples in the right-hand column, voicing does not take place. The above rule is in effect *blocked* by the full-word boundary in the phrases 'two hearts' and 'send the profit.' Since there is only an internal word boundary in 'hand' and 'and accept,' that is,

/m#pǒ/	'hands'	/ntām##púa/	'two hearts'
/m#pē:/	'and accept'	/tūm##pì:/	'send the profit'

the rule is not prevented from applying.

Similarly, the first two examples in the right-hand column of (b) show /p/ becoming [b] intervocalically, as in the following rule:

$$p \rightarrow b \ / \ V \ \underline{\hspace{1em}} \ V$$

Since there is a full word boundary in /pē:##pū:/ 'accept the children,' no voicing takes place. On the other hand, the internal word boundary of /vāp#í/ 'whip him/her' and /ŋgāp#à/ 'my hen' does not block the above rule. Thus the distribution of [p] and [b] in Feʔfeʔ–Bamileke can only be accounted for if it is possible to refer to word boundaries. Otherwise we would be forced to conclude that the difference between [mp] and [mb] is a distinctive one, necessitating the positing of two phonemes /p/ and /b/.

Although grammatical boundaries play a role in phonology, some linguists attempted to introduce "phonological" junctures in order to avoid mixing levels. The junctures are responsible for phonetic differences in such phrases as *why try* [wa:ɪ tʰraɪ] and *white rye* [waɪt raɪ]. Thus, Z. Harris points out (1951:88): "Many of the junctures set up ... without reference to morphologic boundaries turn out nevertheless to come precisely at morphologic boundaries." While many of the phonologists eschewing the use of grammatical information did not follow their own advice in practice, not all of the linguists of the descriptivist era of the 1940s and 1950s in the United States were even theoretically in agreement, as is evident from the following statement made by Pike (1947b:158): "If language actually works as a unit, with grammatical configurations affecting phonetic configurations, why should we not describe the language and analyze it in that way? If forced to do so, why pretend we are avoiding it?" The consequences, however, show that one cannot proceed by operational steps from the physical sounds to the phonemes and from the phonemes to the morphemes, etc. Since no alternative hypotheses or criteria were advanced, this particular theory breaks down.

3.3.3 Morphophonemics

It is thus possible that the phonetic reflexes or realizations of phonemes not only reveal phonetically determined oppositions but also are determined by grammatical facts. We have discussed two possible solutions to the German case of final devoicing (**3.2.2**). The first solution, that characteristic of American phonemics, is to identify the phonetic shape of the segment found in the position of neutralization with the phonological representation. Thus, *Rat* and *Rad* will both be represented as /ra:t/. The second solution, that characteristic of the Prague School, is to posit an archiphoneme in the position of neutralization. Thus, German *Rat* and *Rad* are both represented as /ra:T/. Both of these solutions fail to give an explicit account of the fact that one instance of [ra:t] (let us say [ra:t]$_1$) alternates with a plural form with [t], that is, [rɛ:tə] 'advices,' while the other instance of [ra:t] (let us say [ra:t]$_2$) alternates with a plural form with [d], that is, [rɛ:dər] 'wheels.' The fact that there are basically two kinds of final *t*s in German is overlooked.

Clearly, there is a certain relationship between [t] and [d] in German. Since this relationship is missed by phonemic analysis, a separate, more abstract level is recognized, called the *morphophonemic* level, whose basic unit is the *morphophoneme*. The basic motivating principle is that it should be possible to give one representation to each morpheme (minimal meaningful unit of grammar) and derive all of the allomorphs from this one "base form" (barring, of course, the possibility that two allomorphs may not be phonologically related to one another, for example, *go* and *went*). The morpheme 'wheel' has two alternate phonemic forms or *allomorphs* in German: it has the allomorph /ra:t/ when the final consonant is followed by pause, but the allomorph /rɛ:d/ when the final consonant is followed by a vowel. This is no accident. The same could be said about the noun *Bund* [bʊnt] 'union' and its plural form *Bunde* [bʊndə]. This morpheme has the allomorph /bʊnt/ when the alveolar consonant is before pause, but the allomorph /bʊnd/ when there is a following vowel.

The base forms of these morphemes are {raT} and {bunT}, respectively. These capital letters are employed to represent morphophonemes and should not be confused with the archiphonemes discussed in **3.2.2**. Here {T} is the morphophoneme which is sometimes represented by the phoneme /t/ and sometimes by the phoneme /d/. As Z. Harris states: "Each morphophonemic symbol thus represents a class of phonemes and is defined by a list of member phonemes each of which occurs in a particular environment" (1951:225). The example he discusses concerns the alternation between /f/ and /v/ in

English, as exemplified in the forms *knife/knives*, *wife/wives*, *leaf/leaves*, *thief/thieves*, etc. For such allomorphs Harris proposes the morphophoneme {F}, for example, {naɪF} 'knife,' which is sometimes realized as the allomorph /naɪf/ (in the singular) and sometimes as the allomorph /naɪv/ (in the plural). Notice that while a word such as *thief* will have the base form {θiF} (since its plural *thieves* is formed with /v/), a word such as *chief* will have the base form {čif} (identical with its phonemic representation /čif/), since its plural is *chiefs* and not **chieves*.

3.3.4 Systematic Phonemics

This notion of one base form per morpheme is carried over into the models of generative phonology presented as early as Halle (1959) and still characterizing most of the work being done in this theory.[3]

The view is expressed in generative phonology that native speakers of a language *tacitly* know (that is, the knowledge is not necessarily conscious) that certain forms are related and that this relatedness must be captured somehow in the grammar. These phonologists propose that highly abstract systematic phonemic representations (equivalent in many respects to morphophonemic representations) be postulated, from which rules derive the various surface realizations. By postulating one underlying form at the systematic phonemic level, from which surface alternants are derived, the tacit knowledge speakers have of general or systematic relationships (termed *linguistically significant generalizations*) in the phonological structure is accounted for. Chomsky and Halle (1968) point out that, as a result of the Great English Vowel Shift, there are vowel alternations such as those seen in the following words (we shall limit this discussion to front vowels only):

[iy]	:	ser*e*ne	[ɛ]	:	ser*e*nity
		obsc*e*ne			obsc*e*nity
[ey]	:	prof*a*ne	[æ]	:	prof*a*nity
		in*a*ne			in*a*nity
[ay]	:	div*i*ne	[ɪ]	:	div*i*nity
		subl*i*me			subl*i*mity

On the basis of these alternations (and various other arguments), Chomsky and Halle propose the following abstract systematic phonemic representations of these morphemes:

/serēn/   /profǣn/   /divīn/
/obsēn/   /inǣn/   /sublīm/

---

[3] For a thorough statement of the "standard model" of generative phonology, i.e., of systematic phonemics, see Chomsky and Halle (1968); for a more simplified and concise introduction, see Schane (1973a).

That is, tense vowels (indicated by $\overline{V}$) are set up. Notice how closely these underlying forms resemble English orthography. This comes as no surprise, since these abstract forms coincide with historical reconstructions, which are preserved in the orthography.

Three rules are required to produce the correct phonetic forms. First, there is a vowel laxing rule, which for our purposes applies before the *–ity* suffix.[4] Thus, /serēn/ becomes *seren* before the *–ity* suffix. Second, there is a vowel shift rule which changes /ī/ to $\bar{æ}$, /ē/ to $\bar{\imath}$, and /$\bar{æ}$/ to $\bar{e}$. Finally, there is a diphthongization rule by which $\bar{æ}$ becomes [æy], $\bar{\imath}$ becomes [iy], and $\bar{e}$ becomes [ey]. The derivations for [sɔriyn] and [sɔrɛnıti] are given below:

/serēn/	/serēn + iti/	
	seren + iti	Laxing before *–ity*
serīn		Vowel shift
seriyn		Diphthongization

In Chomsky and Halle's framework, lax *i* and *e* are to be identified with phonetic [ı] and [ɛ], respectively. The schwa found in the words *serene* and *serenity* is due to a rule that reduces unstressed vowels to schwa.

The vowel shift rule is also used in conjunction with other alternations in the language. Chomsky and Halle point out (p. 234) that alternations such as *resign : resignation* and *paradigm : paradigmatic*, where the simple form has [ay] and the complex form [ıg], must be accounted for, since these forms are related. This relatedness is accounted for by providing a unique base form for each morpheme. Looking at the word *resign*, Chomsky and Halle argue for the systematic phonemic representation /rē = sign/. A number of observations are relevant here. The equal sign (=) represents a special morpheme boundary which is necessary in the following rule (p. 95):

$$s \rightarrow z / V = \_\_ V$$

The reason Chomsky and Halle wish to posit an /s/ in the underlying form is that the same morpheme, they claim, occurs in words such as *consign*, where the same = boundary is recognized. They argue that this boundary must function in the rule voicing /s/ to [z], since when there is no boundary, or when there is a full + morpheme boundary (or perhaps a word boundary #), /s/ remains [s] (for example, *reciprocate*, *re-sign* /rē#sign/ 'to sign anew').[5]

---

[4] This rule actually laxes the vowel of the third syllable from the end of the word. Thus, the vowel of the syllable directly preceding *–ity* will automatically become lax.

[5] There are, however, important exceptions. While *design* is pronounced with [z], as predicted by the above rule, *desist* is pronounced with [s] by some speakers. Since this word is represented underlyingly as /dē-sist/, it should undergo the same intervocalic voicing of /s/ as /rē-sist/, which is pronounced [rizıst]; cf. *consist*, which is pronounced with [s], since /s/ is not in intervocalic position.

Addressing ourselves now to the problem of the /g/ in *resignation* and its absence in *resign*, Chomsky and Halle propose a *g*–deletion rule, the effect of which is to tense the preceding vowel. (They discuss certain possibilities, in particular an intermediate [ɣ] which tenses the preceding vowel and later drops.) Let us state the *g*–deletion as follows: /g/ falls when it occurs before a syllable–final /n/.[6] Thus, since the word–final /n/ of *resign* is also syllable–final, the /g/ falls. However, since *resignation* is syllabified as *re–sig–na–tion*, the /g/ remains. The derivation for [riyzayn] is as follows:

/rē=sign/	Underlying (systematic phonemic) form
rē=zign	Voicing of /s/
rē=zīn	Drop of /g/ with concomitant tensing
rī=zǣn	Vowel shift
[riyzæyn]	Diphthongization

(The resulting diphthong [æy] is slightly modified to [ay] (= [aɪ]) by another rule.)

3.3.5 Phonological Abstractness

It should be clear from the previous section that considerable "abstractness" is achieved by Chomsky and Halle and others in setting up underlying forms. The resulting systematic phonemic representations are considerably more distant from the surface phonetics than any other school of phonology ever would have tolerated.

Systematic phonemics, however, goes beyond proposing an abstract morphophonemic level, since, in developing this theory of phonology, Halle (1959) proclaimed the nonexistence of both the traditional phoneme and the phonemic level. That is, between the systematic phonemic level (resembling the old morphophonemic level) and the (systematic) phonetic level there would now be no linguistically significant level corresponding to the old phonemic level.

Chomsky (1964) and Postal (1968) devote much time to supporting this view. While phonology has experienced since *The Sound Pattern of English* a shift back in the direction of a less abstract phonological level (see Kiparsky, 1968a; Schane, 1971; Stampe, 1972a), it would be worthwhile to briefly examine the kind of argument given against what has come to be known as the "autonomous" or "taxonomic" phoneme (autonomous because some phonemicists refused to admit grammatical information into their phonological analysis, and taxonomic because sounds were merely classified, ignoring important phonological generalizations expressible by rule).

[6] Chomsky and Halle do not speak of syllables, but rather propose that /g/ falls before an /n/ which is followed by either a full or internal word boundary (i.e., ## or #).

Perhaps the best-known argument against a level intermediate between the systematic phonetic and systematic phonemic is presented by Halle (1959: 22–23) and reproduced in Chomsky (1964:100–101). The claim is made that recognizing a phonemic level will, in the words of Chomsky (1964:100), "destroy . . . the generality of rules, when the sound system has an assymetry." The example comes from Russian, which has the following phonological rule:

$$[-\text{son}] \rightarrow [+\text{voice}] / \underline{\quad} \begin{bmatrix} -\text{son} \\ +\text{voice} \end{bmatrix}$$
C

An obstruent becomes voiced before a voiced obstruent. Thus, a sequence of /t/ followed by /b/ will be pronounced [db], but a sequence of /t/ followed by /l/ will be pronounced [tl], since [l] is a sonorant. The problem Halle points out is that while there is a phonemic contrast between /t/ and /d/ in Russian, there is no contrast between the phoneme /č/ (which exists in Russian) and the phoneme /ǰ/ (which does not exist). And despite the fact that there is no voice contrast in the palatals, the same facts are observed with respect to the voicing rule. That is, a sequence of /č/ followed by /b/ will be pronounced [ǰb] (and, of course, /č/ followed by /l/ will remain [čl]). Since a strict phonemic analysis adhering to phonetic similarity (biuniqueness) would be forced to analyze [db] as /db/ (although the [d] represents a neutralization of /t/ and /d/ in Prague School terminology), the following rule is a *morpho-phonemic* rule:

$$\{t\} \rightarrow /d/ \qquad / \underline{\quad} \begin{bmatrix} -\text{son} \\ +\text{voice} \end{bmatrix}$$

That is, it changes a morphophoneme into a phoneme. The following rule, however, is a *phonemic* rule, since it merely states the allophonic distribution of the phoneme /č/:

$$/č/ \rightarrow [ǰ] \qquad / \underline{\quad} \begin{bmatrix} -\text{son} \\ +\text{voice} \end{bmatrix}$$

Thus, although these two rules are clearly instances of the same rule (as formalized in features above), they must be stated at different places in the grammar. Assuming both a morphophonemic and a phonemic level, the first rule converts a morphophonemic representation to a phonemic one and the second converts a phonemic representation to a phonetic one. In order to avoid this duplication (or lack of generality), it is necessary to reject the level of autonomous phonemics and recognize only a systematic phonemic level and a systematic phonetic level.

It would be unwise to suggest that all of Chomsky's (1964) criticisms apply to all schools of phonemics. The above argument is of course limited, since many phonemicists allowed neutralization of just the type found in Russian.

Thus it would appear that it is not so much a question of establishing a difference between a systematic phonemic level and a phonemic level, the first of which is valid and the second invalid, but rather a question of properly defining what the characteristics of the one valid *phonological* level are.

While it is clear that the phonological level can differ considerably from the phonetic representation, generative phonologists themselves are now debating the question of just how "abstract" phonology is. Probably most generative phonologists would agree that the words 'advice' and 'wheel' in German, both pronounced [ra:t], should be represented phonologically as /ra:t/ and /ra:d/, respectively (see Vennemann, 1968a). But representing [riyzayn] as /rē = sign/ is quite another story, for here we have to (1) represent the high front diphthongized vowel [iy] as abstract /ē/, (2) accept a special morphological boundary (=), and (3) represent [ay] as /ig/, that is, a radically different vowel with a consonant which is not realized phonetically (in this allomorph, at least).

There seem to be no constraints on the degree of abstractness allowable in generative phonology. For example, Lightner (1971) considers the possibility of taking the underlying forms of English back to a Proto-Germanic stage (before the application of Grimm's Law). He points out that there are alternations such as the following between [f] and [p], [ð] and [t], and [h] and [k]:

*f*oot	:	*p*edestrian
*f*ather	:	*p*aternal
*f*ull	:	*p*lenary
mo*th*er	:	ma*t*ernal
fa*th*er	:	pa*t*ernal
bro*th*er	:	fra*t*ernal
*h*eart	:	*c*ardiac
*h*orn	:	uni*c*orn
*h*ound	:	*c*anine

Perhaps the root of 'foot' should be recognized as the Latin-looking /ped-/? While almost no one would accept Lightner's proposal, his question is right to the point: "Where does one stop? And why?"

One way of trying to limit the powers of generative phonology is by looking at the nature of the rules that would be required. It is hard to imagine an environment for changing underlying /ped/ to [fʊt] other than by an arbitrary diacritic, for example, [+ X]. The rule could then be written as follows:

$$p \rightarrow f / [+X]$$

But since there is no phonological or morphological correlate to this diacritic, this kind of rule would be equivalent to simply listing two forms in the lexicon, /fʊt/ and /pədɛstriən/.

Kiparsky (1968a) presented the first principled attempt to limit the powers of generative phonology. He distinguished between *contextual* and *absolute* neutralization. Contextual neutralization is the kind of situation we have seen in English (intervocalic /t/ and /d/ are neutralized), Feʔfeʔ (/k/ and /č/ are neutralized before /i/), and German (/t/ and /d/, among others, are neutralized syllable–finally). Typically, when there is a rule of the form,

A → B / __ C   (that is, AC → BC)

and there are already [BC] sequences coming from another source, we say that /A/ and /B/ are neutralized before /C/. Absolute neutralization, on the other hand, occurs when there is a rule of the form

A → B

and there are other instances of [B] coming from another source. The main difference between the two types of neutralization, then, is that in absolute neutralization the rule that accounts for the neutralization takes place without any context. That is, all instances of underlying /A/ merge with underlying /B/.

A concise example of absolute neutralization, which Kiparsky cites, comes from Sanskrit, which has the following CV sequences:

či   ku
ča   ka

Since there are no instances of *ki or *ču, /k/ and /č/ are in near complementary distribution—they contrast only before /a/. However, it would be possible to represent sequences of phonetic [ča] as underlying (systematic phonemic) /ke/, since there is no short [e] in Sanskrit, with the following derivations:

/ki/ → [či]
/ke/ → če → [ča]

The /k/ of /ke/ could be said to palatalize just like the /k/ of /ki/, yielding intermediate če. At this point a rule of the form

e → a

would convert all instances of /e/ to [a], causing absolute neutralization with /a/.

Kiparsky argues that rules of this form, which create context-free neutralizations, should be disallowed, and he presents arguments from historical linguistics to support his position. Notice, first, however, that it is not the *form* of this rule of absolute neutralization that makes it so objectionable. This rule can in fact be rewritten with a context, as follows:

e → a / č __

In a sense this restatement is a trick, since it just so happens that all instances of underlying /e/ will occur after [č] at this stage in the derivation; /e/ is posited only after /k/ (which will in turn palatalize to [č]). The real objection seems to be simply calling something what it is not. That is, the argument should be stated as one against "imaginary" segments (Crothers, 1971).

One such imaginary segment is the /œ/ which Chomsky and Halle (1968) posit as the phonological representation of the English diphthong [ɔɪ]. While a rule of the form

œ → ɔɪ

does not involve neutralization (since there is no other source of [ɔɪ]), the postulated /œ/ of *boy* /bœ/ is at least as "abstract" as the underlying /e/ considered for Sanskrit.

This reinterpretation of the problem is visible in the Yawelmani case raised in the argument against Kiparsky by Kisseberth (1969). In Yawelmani, the following surface phonetic vowels are found:

i   u
  a ɔ   e: a: ɔ:

Kisseberth argues that all instances of [e:] should be represented phonologically as /i:/, and some instances of [ɔ:] should be represented as /u:/, others as /ɔ:/. This would produce the more symmetric inventory of both long and short /i, a, u, ɔ/. His arguments are as follows.

First, there is a class of verbs of the underlying structure /CCV(C)/ which Kuroda (1967) terms "echo verbs." A phonological rule inserts a vowel between the first two consonants in the following way:

a CCe:(C) → CiCe:(C)
b CCa:(C) → CaCa:(C)
c CCɔ:(C) → CuCɔ:(C)
d CCɔ:(C) → CɔCɔ:(C)

Notice that cases **b** and **d** involve complete copying of the stem vowel, though the copied vowel is always short. Having noticed this, if we were to analyze verbs of class **a** as underlying /CCi:(C)/, then this /i:/ would also be copied as [i]. Similarly, if those verbs of the form [CuCɔ:(C)] were recognized as underlying /CCu:(C)/, then the copying rule would be completely general:

$$\emptyset \to \begin{matrix} V_i \\ [-\text{long}] \end{matrix} \quad / \# \, C \_\_ \, C \, V_i, \quad \text{where } V_i = V_i$$

A short version of the underlying vowel (V_i) of echo verbs is copied by this rule.

Another argument Kisseberth (1969) gives for his /i:/ and /u:/ solution comes from vowel harmony. While the aorist (past indefinite) suffix is represented phonologically as /hin/, it is converted to [hun] after some instances of phonetic [ɔ:]:

čuyɔ:hun   'urinated'
hɔyɔ:hin   'named'

As seen from the copied vowel [u] in 'urinated,' this verb is represented phonologically as /čyu:/. First the vowel /u:/ is copied to yield intermediate čuyu:, and then the long vowel /u:/ is lowered to [ɔ:]. This solution ties in neatly with the vowel harmony occurring in the aorist suffix. It is just those verbs with underlying /u:/ which harmonize /hin/ to [hun]. That this is correct is seen from the fact that short /u/, but not short /ɔ/, also harmonizes /hin/ to [hun]:

hudhun   'recognized'
gɔphin   'took care of an infant'

Thus, /hin/ becomes [hun] after the stem vowels /u:/ and /u/.

This solution requires a rule of the following form:

$$\textbf{a} \quad \begin{bmatrix} i: \\ u: \end{bmatrix} \rightarrow \begin{bmatrix} e: \\ ɔ: \end{bmatrix}$$

Notice that only part **b** of this rule involves absolute neutralization, since /u:/ and /ɔ:/ merge as [ɔ:] in all environments, while no merger occurs when /i:/ is converted to [e:]. Although only the latter part of the rule involves absolute neutralization, both involve setting up "imaginary" forms, that is, phonological forms which do not exist on the surface and which are converted to phonetic forms in a context-free fashion. The derivations for 'urinated' and 'named' are therefore as follows:

/čyu: + hin/   /hyɔ: + hin/
čuyu:hin   hɔyɔ:hin   (by vowel copying)
čuyu:hun   (by vowel harmony)
[čuyɔ:hun]   [hɔyɔ:hin]   (by vowel lowering)

So-called "imaginary" phonological representations characterize, at least to some extent, probably all schools of phonology. Consider, for example, the following phonetic vowel system of Nupe:

i   u   ĩ   ũ
e   o   ɔ̃
  a

Although Nupe has five phonetic oral vowels, it has only three phonetic nasalized vowels (Smith, 1967; Hyman, 1970b). The question, however, is how the vowel [ɔ̃] should be interpreted. Since there is an oral vowel /a/, pattern considerations suggest representing this vowel as /ã/, the decision reached by Smith (1967). Since /ĩ/ and /ũ/ tend to be pronounced [ĩ] and [ũ], a low-level phonetic rule is postulated which changes all nasalized vowels to [−tense]. In a sense this amounts to recognizing an imaginary segment. While in this case the distance between the phonological and phonetic representations may seem negligible, no satisfactory way of measuring such "distances" has been proposed.

In the absence of theoretical constraints on abstractness, such as the one proposed by Kiparsky, a number of competing analyses will be possible of the data of many languages, for example, a very abstract analysis, a not-too-abstract analysis, a very nonabstract analysis. Since generative theory attempts to provide the one descriptively adequate grammar of a language, which is said to have psychological reality, proposals which limit the number of possible analyses for any given data represent claims about the nature of sound systems, which can in part be experimentally tested (see M. Ohala, 1974).

Since Kiparsky's unpublished paper, a number of papers, in addition to Kisseberth (1969), have defended certain "abstract" analyses. A final example of a possible abstract solution, again from Nupe, is presented in Hyman (1970a), where it is suggested that [Cʷa] and [Cʸa] should be represented, phonologically, as /Cɔ/ and /Cɛ/, respectively. Since consonants are normally labialized before /u/ and /o/, and since they are normally palatalized before /i/ and /e/, we can simply extend the labialization and palatalization processes to include /ɔ/ and /ɛ/, as seen in the following rules:

$$C \rightarrow C^w / \_ \begin{Bmatrix} u \\ o \\ ɔ \end{Bmatrix} \qquad \text{(LR)}$$

$$C \rightarrow C^y / \_ \begin{Bmatrix} i \\ e \\ ɛ \end{Bmatrix} \qquad \text{(PR)}$$

After /Cɔ/ and /Cɛ/ have undergone the labialization rule (LR) and the palatalization rule (PR), respectively, the following absolute neutralization (AN) rule applies:

$$\begin{Bmatrix} ɔ \\ ɛ \end{Bmatrix} \rightarrow a$$

Since /ɔ/ and /ɛ/ neutralize in a context-free fashion with /a/, this is a case of absolute neutralization, as defined by Kiparsky (1968). We can, however, provide a context for this rule, as follows:

$$\begin{bmatrix} ɔ \\ ɛ \end{bmatrix} \rightarrow a / \begin{bmatrix} C^w \\ C^y \end{bmatrix} \_$$

The rule now states that /ɔ/ becomes [a] after [Cʷ] and /ɛ/ becomes [a] after [Cʸ]. This rule not only directly incorporates the motivation for the rule (that is, the fact that the labiality and palatality of /ɔ/ and /ɛ/ have been transferred to the consonant), but also captures the fact that each instance of [a] can be easily identified as deriving from /ɔ/, /ɛ/, or /a/ on the basis of the preceding consonant, as seen in the following derivations:

/tɔ́/ → tʷɔ́ → [tʷá] 'to trim'
/tɛ́/ → tʸɛ́ → [tʸá] 'to be mild'
/tá/   → [tá] 'to tell'

Two kinds of evidence for this /ɔ/ and /ɛ/ solution were proposed. First, it was claimed that reduplication provides evidence for the underlying vowel /ɔ/. As seen in the following examples,

tí	'to screech'	→ tītí	'screeching'
tē	'to break'	→ tītē	'breaking'
tá	'to tell'	→ tītá	'telling'
tú	'to ride'	→ tūtú	'riding'
tò	'to loosen'	→ tūtò	'loosening'

the reduplicated vowel is [i] if the stem vowel is [−round], that is, /i/, /e/, or /a/; or [u] if the stem vowel is [+round], that is, /u/ or /o/. Notice, however, the following forms:

tʷá 'to trim' → tūtʷá 'trimming'
tʸá 'to be mild' → tītʸá 'being mild'

The expected form for 'trimming,' if /tʷ/ is taken to be an underlying consonant, is *tʷītʷá. If, on the other hand, we recognize the underlying form /tɔ́/, this /ɔ/ naturally falls into the same class with /u/ and /o/, and the automatically chosen reduplicated vowel is [u].

The second argument is based on the findings of Hyman (1970b) concerning the nature of foreign sound assimilations in borrowing. It was argued in Hyman (1970a) that since Yoruba [Cɔ] and [Cɛ] come into Nupe as [Cʷa] and [Cʸa], the rule of absolute neutralization must be considered productive. Some relevant examples are:

Yor.	[kɛ̀kɛ̆]	> Nupe	[kʸàkʸá]	'bicycle'
Yor.	[ɛ̀gbɛ̀]	> Nupe	[ɛ̀gbʸà]	(a Yoruba town)
Yor.	[tɔ̄rɛ̄]	> Nupe	[tʷārʸā]	'to give a gift'
Yor.	[kɔ́bɔ̂]	> Nupe	[kʷábʷà]	'penny'

According to this argument, the rule of absolute neutralization is responsible for these borrowings, and for the fact that Nupes, when they speak Yoruba, frequently replace Yoruba [Cɔ] and [Cɛ] with Nupe [Cʷa] and [Cʸa]. For justification of this kind of argumentation see Hyman (1970b) (and also Ohso, 1971, and Lovins, 1973, for more recent work on this subject).

The question of how Nupe should be analyzed has been raised a number of times since the original abstract solution was proposed (see, for instance, Harms, 1973, and, for a reply, Hyman, 1973d; also Crothers, 1971; Vennemann, 1973; Krohn, 1974). Just how abstract phonology is remains a question that has yet to be answered in a manner satisfactory to all.

3.4 General Considerations in Setting Up Underlying Forms

In preceding sections we saw basically three approaches to phonological analysis, which can be summarized here by means of the following example from English. As seen in the following forms,

im–possible
in–determinate
iŋ–congruous

the prefix meaning 'not' is pronounced [ɪm] before labials, [ɪn] before alveolars, and (at least optionally) [ɪŋ] before velars. The question is, how should these forms be represented phonologically? In a strict phonemic approach one might argue that the phonetic and phonological representations are identical, that is, that these prefixes should be analyzed as the allomorphs /ɪm/, /ɪn/, and /ɪŋ/, respectively. Such phonologists would point out that since the words *ram* [ræm], *ran* [ræn], and *rang* [ræŋ] show a three-way nasal contrast, the phonemes /m/, /n/, and /ŋ/ are required in English. It should be recalled that in this first view the phoneme was defined as a class of sounds having phonetic similarity (see **3.1**). Thus, by the principle of "biuniqueness" (see **3.2.1**), the sounds [m], [n], and [ŋ] are assigned to the phonemes /m/, /n/, and /ŋ/ of the negative prefix, just as they are in the case of *ram, ran,* and *rang*.

A second solution invokes the notion of neutralization from Prague School phonology. Since nasals do not contrast before such consonants, this morpheme can be represented as /ɪN–/, that is, with an archiphoneme nasal which is specified as [+cons, +nasal], but which is left unspecified for place of articulation. This solution then captures an important fact missed by the strictly phonemic solution, since it recognizes /m/ and /n/ only where these two phonemes contrast, and recognizes /N/ where there is no contrast.

A weakness of both these solutions, however, is the fact that when this prefix is followed by a vowel, its realization is [n]. If one were to start with underlying /m/, /n/, and /ŋ/, then there would be no way to capture the fact that the basic or unassimilated form of this prefix is [ɪn], as in the word *inability*. The same problem is inherent in the archiphoneme approach. On the other hand, if one were to start with the representation /ɪn/, a rule of homorganic nasal assimilation, written as follows,

$$n \rightarrow [\alpha \text{ place}] / \_\_ \begin{bmatrix} \alpha \text{ place} \\ C \end{bmatrix}$$

would state that /n/ assimilates to the place of articulation of the following consonant. Thus, underlying /ɪn/ is realized as [ɪm] before labial consonants (*im-possible*) and as [ɪŋ] before velar consonants (*in-congruous*). Before alveolar consonants and before vowels (*in-determinate* and *in-ability*), it is realized as [ɪn].

Setting up one basic underlying form from which predictable allomorphs or alternations can be derived runs into some difficulty, however, since, as pointed out above, there seems to be no constraint as to how "abstract" the base form can be. For example, while there is a productive rule of homorganic nasal assimilation of the type seen above, we are faced with the problem of what to do with words such as *illegal* and *irregular*, where the assimilation of the /n/ of this same negative morpheme is complete. That is, /n/ assimilates to [l] before [l] and [r] before [r], and presumably the resulting [ll] and [rr] sequences are later simplified to [l] and [r], respectively. Are the underlying representations *in-legal* and *in-regular* too distant from the phonetic representations? While phonologists disagree about the permitted degree of abstractness, all those working in the framework of generative phonology accept the notion of a base "underlying form" from which allomorphs are derived by phonological rules. With this in mind, we can now ask, what are the general considerations in determining underlying forms?

3.4.1 Predictability

Given a phonological alternation, such as the alternation between [t] and [d] in the German words *Rad* [raːt] 'wheel' and *Räder* [rɛːdər] 'wheels,' how does one decide which of the two phonetic realizations is closest to the underlying representation? Or, in other words, how does one determine the "basic allophone"? While there is no foolproof rule or "discovery procedure," there are some general criteria which are sometimes cited by phonologists. The first criterion is *predictability*. Often there is little cause for hesitation, since the various alternations can be phonologically predicted (that is, by rule) only if one starts with one of the allophones—but could not be predicted if one started with the other. The German case of final devoicing is an example. If the word 'wheel' is represented with a /d/ underlyingly, that is, /raːd/, then a rule of final devoicing would change /d/ to [t] in [raːt], but not in the plural form [rɛːdər]. The rule that converts /b, d, g, v, z/ to [p, t, k, f, s] can be written as follows:

$$[-\text{son}] \rightarrow [-\text{voice}] / \_\_ \$$$

Voiced obstruents are devoiced in syllable-final position. If, on the other hand, 'wheel' were to be represented with underlying /t/, that is, /raːt/, then a rule would be required which would convert /p, t, k, f, s/ to [b, d, g, v, z] in some environment, so that /raːt/ + /ˮər/ (where ˮ represents the um-lauting process that fronts [aː] to [ɛː]) is realized as [rɛːdər] and not as *[rɛːtər]. However, notice that the plural of Rat [raːt] 'advice' is *Räte* [rɛːtə]. Since both 'wheel' and 'advice' would presumably be recognized as /raːt/ in this analysis, there would be no way of predicting which cases of final /t/ become [d] and which remain [t]. Since we can predict the alter-nations in one direction only, we assume that 'wheel' should be represented phonologically as /raːd/ and that there is a rule of final devoicing.

Of course, it would be possible to maintain both 'wheel' and 'advice' as /raːt/ if we used some arbitrary diacritic mark, say [+D], to identify those morphemes whose final /t/ becomes [d] by rule. By using such diacritics, the claim is made that this is not a purely phonological alternation, but rather a partly morphological one, since morphemes must be identified. Phonologists have generally argued that diacritics, while necessary to capture irregularities in languages, represent complexities and should be used only when strictly phonological solutions (that is, ones using distinctive features only) cannot be motivated. Since the German rule can be written in strictly phonological terms, the use of diacritics is ruled out.

A second example of the predictability criterion comes from Maori (Hale, 1971, as reported in Kiparsky, 1971). In Maori there is an alternation between certain consonants and Ø (that is, zero), as seen in the following examples:

VERB	PASSIVE	GERUND	GLOSS
hopu	hopukia	hopukaŋa	'to catch'
aru	arumia	arumaŋa	'to follow'
tohu	tohuŋia	tohuŋaŋa	'to point out'
maatu	maaturia	maaturaŋa	'to know'

As seen in the leftmost column, the active form of these verbs ends in a vowel, in this case [u]. In the passive and gerund forms, however, different consonants appear on the surface, in this case [k, m, ŋ, r]. There are two possible solutions. First, one might set up underlying forms which end in consonants. In this case we would recognize the underlying forms /hopuk/, /arum/, /tohuŋ/, and /maatur/, and a rule which deletes word-final consonants:

$$C \rightarrow \emptyset \:/ \:\_\_ \#\#$$

The second solution recognizes the underlying forms /hopu/, /aru/, /tohu/, and /maatu/, and a rule of consonant insertion. However, in this case there is a problem in predicting the exact identity of the consonant which will appear. There is no reason in this solution why /hopu/ should take a [k] but /aru/ should take an [m]. In other words, we are again forced into marking such forms with diacritics, for example, [+K], [+M], etc. Since Ø can be predicted from underlying final /k, m, ŋ, r/, but since [k, m, ŋ, r] cannot be phonologically predicted from Ø, the first solution is preferred. Notice also that there are some cases of verb forms ending in [u] which do not take *any* consonant, for example, [patu] 'to strike,' passive [patua], gerund [patuŋa]. (The expected passive [patuia] and gerund [patuaŋa] are simplified by rule.) This verb will therefore be represented as /patu/. (For more discussion of this Maori data, see **5.2.8.**)

3.4.2 Economy

In phonemic analysis, a solution is judged to be more economical than another if it recognizes fewer phonemes. While this notion has not been explicitly incorporated into generative phonology, it is sometimes invoked in terms of overall "simplicity" (see **4.1**) by generative phonologists. One example is English *ng*. A solution recognizing a word such as *sing* as /sɪŋ/ is forced to admit an additional phoneme. A solution representing this word as /sɪng/, since it avoids a phoneme /ŋ/, is more economical. However, economy in the number of phonemes or underlying segments frequently entails a greater complexity in the phonological rules. As seen in **3.3.1**, if we recognize /sɪng/ we need to apply a rule of homorganic nasal assimilation (which we already know characterizes English—compare /ɪn–/), which yields the intermediate form [sɪng]. At this point we need to introduce a rule *not* previously needed, namely, one which deletes the [g] of *sing*, thereby giving the phonetic form [sɪŋ]. Notice that neither solution can be argued for by the criterion of predictability. If we recognize an underlying /ŋ/, then a [g] will have to be inserted into the word *longer* [lɔŋgər] (compare *long* [lɔŋ]), but not in the word *singer* [sɪŋər]. If we recognize only /ng/, then the /g/ will have to be deleted in *singer*, but not in *longer*. Thus, both solutions require nonphonological information, namely boundary information. As proposed by Chomsky and Halle (1968:85n), the underlying forms of *longer* and *singer* are recognized with different internal grammatical boundaries, /sɪng#ər/ and /lɔng+ər/. Post-nasal /g/ is deleted before a word boundary (#), as in *sing* and *singer*, but not when there is only a morpheme boundary (+), as in *longer*, or no boundary, as in *finger* [fɪŋgər] (see **6.1.2.2.**).

3.4.3 Pattern Congruity

This criterion was cited by certain American phonemicists (for example, Swadesh, 1934:36), who saw the phoneme as a (psychological) point in a *pattern* (compare Sapir, 1925). In this view, a solution can be argued for on the basis that it conforms to the overall pattern of the phonological system. The /ng/ solution is a good example. If a separate phoneme /ŋ/ were recognized, we would have to ask why it, unlike /m/ and /n/, cannot appear at the beginning of a word. If, on the other hand, /ng/ is posited, the failure of [ŋ] to appear at the beginning of words in English can be explained by reference to a more general overall pattern; namely, just as /mb/ and /nd/ sequences do not occur initially, neither does /ng/ (whose phonetic reflex is sometimes [ŋ]).

The use of pattern congruity as a criterion has led many phonologists to seek segments to fill "holes" in the pattern. For example, the following consonants represent the phonetic consonant system in Feʔfeʔ–Bamileke (ignoring aspirated consonants):

p	t	č	k	ʔ
b	d	ǰ	g	
f	s	š		h
v	z	ž	ɣ	
m	n	ɲ	ŋ	
	l			
w		y		

The columns represent places of articulation, the rows manners of articulation (respectively, voiceless stops, voiced stops, voiceless fricatives, voiced fricatives, nasal consonants, liquids, and glides). A number of holes in the pattern are observed in the above chart. In addition, a number of consonants stand by themselves (for example, [l]). Thus, typically, the consonants which are isolated are frequently moved into positions which are vacant in the more general pattern. For example, Feʔfeʔ has no voiceless velar fricative [x]. It does, however, have a glottal fricative [h], which we can conveniently move into the velar slot to complete the series. Other rearrangements can be effected to yield the following phonetic chart:

p	t	č	k
b	d	ǰ	g
f	s	š	h
v	z	ž	ɣ
m	n	ɲ	ŋ
w	l	y	ʔ

Other movements are the following: since the glides [w] and [y] are made at a different point of articulation from [l], the two series are collapsed; since there is no back glide, the glottal stop has been moved into that position. Notice that the bottom row contains segments which Chomsky and Halle (1968) regard as [+son], though the case for treating a glottal stop as a sonorant is weak. While the consonant system has been made to look symmetric, this has been at the expense of calling some phonetic segments something they are not—for example, [ʔ] is not a sonorant, [h] is not velar. While by Sapir, who viewed phonemic structure as points in a pattern, such arrays of sounds as seen above were accorded theoretical status, to other phonologists such patterns merely summarize the phonetic segments of a language. Thus, as reported in Hyman (1972b), the underlying (systematic) phonemes of Feʔfeʔ are as follows:

	t	č	k	ʔ
b	d	ǰ	g	
f	s		h	
v	z			
m	n		ŋ	
(w)				

(The /w/ is of questionable status.) Thus, phonemically, a number of holes do exist in the pattern.

This manipulation is most frequently observed, perhaps, in the way phonologists present vowel systems. In vowel systems with the three vowels /i, u, a/, the five vowels /i, e, u, o, a/, or the seven vowels /i, e, ɛ, u, o, ɔ, a/, /a/ is often represented as a low *central* vowel, thereby giving the impression of symmetry:

```
i   u      i   u      i   u
  a          e   o      e   o
             a        ɛ   ɔ
                        a
```

In vowel systems with the four vowels /i, u, o, a/, the chart is usually presented as

```
i u                       i   u
a o    rather than
                            o
                          a
```

even though /a/ is lower in vowel height than /o/ and is not necessarily a front vowel. In this case, however, the symmetric vowel chart captures the the fact that in such languages there is phonologically only a two-way vowel height contrast and a two-way front/backness contrast. But to be consistent, three-vowel systems should be written as in **a** or **b**:

```
a  i  u     b  i  u
     a            a
```

Such diagrams represent the two possibilities for the phonological patterning of /i/, /u/, /a/: in **a** /u/ and /a/ pattern together, as opposed to /i/, since they are both [+back]; in **b** /i/ and /a/ pattern together, since they are both [−round]. In the first language we should expect /u/ and /a/ to function together in phonological rules, while in the second language we should expect /i/ and /a/ to function together.

One of the most frequent references to pattern congruity in phonemic analysis concerns the question of whether something should be analyzed as one phoneme or two. For instance, in a language with an aspiration contrast, such as Thai, one might ask whether the contrast should be represented as /p/ vs. /pʰ/ or as /p/ vs. /ph/. In the case of palatalization, one might wonder whether to set up a series of palatalized consonants (for example, /pʸ/) or a two-phoneme sequence of consonant followed by /y/ (for example, /py/). Such questions can frequently not be answered by the phonetics alone, but only by referring to the overall pattern of the language—in particular, the general canonical shape of syllables. In Igbo, for instance, syllables generally consist of a single consonant followed by a single vowel (that is, CV). The major exception to this pattern is the presence of labialized velars, which could possibly be analyzed as /kw/, /gw/, and /ŋw/. However, if they were to be analyzed as /kʷ/, /gʷ/, and /ŋʷ/, that is, as single consonants with a secondary articulation, then they would not violate the syllable structure of the language. If, on the other hand, we were to accept the two-phoneme analysis, then the system would be broken, and we would have no explanation of why /w/ only occurs after /k/, /g/, and /ŋ/. In the one-phoneme solution we simply say that the language has labialized velars, and, since labialized velars are much more frequent and expected in languages than labialized labials or labialized dentals, no further statement is required.

Another consideration in deciding whether to derive a given phone or phones from one or two phonemes is whether the individual components are found in isolation in the language. For instance, we could not analyze aspirated stops as /ph/, /th/, and /kh/ in a language where /h/ does not appear alone. Similarly, the phonological representations /py/ and /pw/ would be avoided in languages that do not exhibit /y/ and /w/ functioning as independent consonants. This consideration is an extension of what is known in European phonology as the *commutation test* (Fischer-Jørgensen, 1956; Martinet, 1960:73). From a minimal pair such as *lamp* and *ramp* in English we conclude that there is a distinctive contrast between the two phonemes /l/ and /r/. Now, from a minimal pair such as *ramp* and *cramp*, we conclude that there is a distinctive contrast between Ø and /k/, and that *cramp* must therefore be analyzed as having an initial consonant cluster, rather than a single initial consonant. Finally, the minimal pair *ramp* and *amp* shows that *ramp* must be analyzed as having four phonological units, since /r/ contrasts with Ø (compare *camp* and *amp*). Martinet (1960:74) applies this test to the English *ch* sound. The question is whether this should be analyzed as /č/ or /tš/, that is, as one phoneme or two. He points out that English has not only the word *chip* [tšɪp], but also the word *ship* [šɪp]. From this opposition of č:š (where č = tš phonetically), we conclude that the [t] of [tšɪp] contrasts with Ø. From the opposition between *chip* and *tip* [tɪp], we conclude that the [š] of [tšɪp] contrasts with Ø. Therefore, *chip* should be analyzed by this criterion as /tšɪp/. On the other hand, since Spanish has this alveo-palatal affricate (for example, *mucho* 'very') but does not have the corresponding fricative [š], *mucho* must be analyzed as /mučo/.

While the commutation test yields these results, Martinet rightly rejects the two phoneme /tš/ for English. He again appeals to the notion of pattern congruity. He points out that this [tš] sound must be analyzed exactly as the corresponding voiced *j* [dž] in English. Now, while there is a word *gyp* [džɪp] and a word *dip* [dɪp], there is no word *[žɪp] in the language. In other words, [ž] must always be preceded by [d] when it occurs at the beginning of a word. Since this is the case, [dž] must be analyzed as one phonological unit, that is, as /ǰ/. And since Martinet wants to analyze the *ch* sound in like fashion, he argues that the first argument from commutation should be given up in favor of the pattern, and so we recognize underlying /č/. (For more on the question of one vs. two phonemes, see **4.4.1**.)

This, of course, points out the arbitrariness of this criterion, since it is possible that each of two conflicting analyses breaks the pattern in a different way. One wonders, for example, why /ǰ/ should not be reanalyzed as /dž/, on analogy with /tš/, and not vice-versa. Notice, finally, that patterns change through time. The Grebo language (Innes, 1966) generally exhibits a CVCV pattern, but it has begun to syncopate vowels in fast speech (for example, /fodo/ 'emptiness' becomes [flo] in rapid speech), such that there are now syllables of the form CLV. With time we can expect the CLV forms to take precedence over and eventually drive out the CVCV forms. In fact, there are some forms, mostly borrowed, which only exist in their CLV form, for example, [fli] 'flea.' Thus, whenever an argument is made for conforming to a pattern, for example, CVCV, we have to be sure that the language is not on the way to establishing another pattern. It may be that the old pattern is no longer the criterion for congruity.

3.4.4 Plausibility

A fourth criterion that is often invoked is *plausibility*. Given two possible solutions, is there one which in some sense is more plausible (or "natural"—see Chapter 5)? Consider, for example, a language which has the following phonetic sequences (Nupe comes close, although it also has [ša]):

ši	su
še	so
sa	

The alveopalatal fricative [š] is found before [i] and [e] and the alveolar fricative [s] before [u], [o], and [a]. Thus, we have a classic case of complementary distribution. There are two possible solutions. First, we can recognize underlying /si, se, su, so, sa/ and posit a rule such as

$$s \rightarrow \check{s} \ / \ \underline{\quad} \begin{Bmatrix} i \\ e \end{Bmatrix}$$

which converts /si/ and /se/ to [ši] and [še], respectively. Or we can recognize underlying /ši, še, šu, šo, ša/ and posit a rule such as

$$\check{s} \rightarrow s \ / \ \underline{\quad} \begin{Bmatrix} u \\ o \\ a \end{Bmatrix}$$

which converts /šu/, /šo/, and /ša/ to [su], [so], and [sa], respectively. The first solution is plausible, while the second solution is implausible. Recognizing only /s/ is plausible, because the rule which derives [š] before /i/ and /e/ is a natural assimilation rule. That is, when /si/ becomes [ši], the alveolar /s/ assimilates to the frontness (or palatality) of /i/. Similarly, when /se/ becomes [še] the same assimilatory process is observed. On the other hand, if we start with underlying /š/, the rule which is required to derive [s] before /u/, /o/, and /a/ is not a natural assimilation rule. While the process of a palatal consonant becoming nonpalatal before a nonpalatal vowel would appear to be assimilatory in nature, the question is why /š/ should become more fronted (that is, to [s]) rather than backed (to, say, [x]) before the back vowels in question. Thus, this rule seems to be unmotivated from a phonetic point of view.

Rule plausibility usually refers to *phonetic naturalness*. Certain phonological rules are found to occur frequently in languages, and the reason for this frequency is the fact that segments tend to assimilate to neighboring segments, and they do so in fairly predictable ways (see Schachter, 1969; Schane, 1972). The notion which is usually brought forth to explain these phenomena is *ease of articulation*. It is claimed to be easier to pronounce [ši] than [si], since in the first case both segments agree in palatality.

What this means is that plausible phonological rules are usually unidirectional. Thus, one can use this criterion in phonological analysis and try to establish an inventory of underlying segments from which the surface segments can be derived by plausible rules. This criterion, like the other criteria, is subject to other considerations. In particular, some languages do have implausible or "crazy" rules (Bach and Harms, 1972). As discussed in **5.2.3**, the most phonetically natural rule is not necessarily the most simple rule. However, as a general principle, plausibility or rule naturalness is an important criterion in conducting phonological analyses.

PHONOLOGICAL SIMPLICITY

4.1 Simplicity, Economy, and Generality

In **3.4.2**, the notion of economy was said to be one of the criteria often used as a guide in phonemic analysis. A solution with fewer phonemes is judged more economical than a solution recognizing more phonemes. Similarly, we might say that a solution using fewer rules is more economical than a solution requiring more rules, and so on. Economy, then, is a quantitative measure by which a given solution can be evaluated as requiring fewer or more mechanisms (phonemes, rules, conventions, etc.) than another solution. This notion is characteristic of phonemic approaches to phonology, and, as we shall see, has its application in the history of generative phonology as well.

While one might be tempted to view a solution recognizing fewer phonemes as "simpler" than a solution recognizing more phonemes, there is another view which equates simplicity with generality. In terms of the phonemic inventory, the following argument might be made:

S₁			S₂		
i	ü	u	i	ü	u
e		o	e	ø	o
ɛ		ɔ	ɛ	œ	ɔ
	a			a	

The vowel system of S_1 is more economical, because it involves fewer vowel phonemes. The vowel system of S_2, on the other hand, is more general, because it makes greater or more general use of the distinctive features of vowels. Looked at a little differently, S_1 will require a phonological constraint to the effect that the only front rounded vowel is /ü/; S_2 will contain no such constraint, since the front rounded series /ü, ø, œ/ is exactly parallel to the front unrounded series /i, e, ε/ and the back rounded series /u, o, ɔ/. Numerous examples of this sort can be found. For example, compare the consonant systems of the following two hypothetical solutions of the same language:

S_3			S_4		
p	t	k	p	t	k
b	d	g	b	d	g
m	n		m	n	ŋ

In terms of the number of consonant phonemes, S_3 is more economical than S_4, since it lacks an /ŋ/ phoneme. However, in terms of generality, S_4 is simpler than S_3, since it makes greater use of the place of articulation features. When applied to phonemic inventories, generality can usually be equated with the notion of pattern congruity discussed in Chapter 3.

Since the more economical phonological systems, that is, those lacking phonemes, often require phonological constraints, they are *uneconomical* in this particular sense. S_1 requires a constraint which forbids the feature combination [−high, −back, +round, V] (that is, /ø/ and /œ/), and S_3 requires a constraint forbidding the feature combination [+nasal, +back, C] (that is, /ŋ/). Since S_2 and S_4 do not require any such constraints, they are in this sense more economical.

4.1.1 Lexical Simplicity vs. Rule Simplicity

This contrast points out a crucial problem in the assessment of phonological economy/simplicity: an economy in one part of the phonology may create a complexity in another part of the phonology. This means that in order to arrive at some judgment as to the simplicity of an analysis, it is necessary to take into consideration the *whole* analysis, and not just the inventory of phonemic segments, for instance.

Nowhere is this fact more blatantly clear than in the relationship between simplicity in the lexicon (or phonological level, since lexical items are entered in their phonological form) and simplicity in the phonological rules, which convert the lexical (that is, phonological) representations into phonetic ones. Let us, for example, return to the /ng/ solution, which was argued for (see **3.3.1**) in preference to an /ŋ/ phoneme in English. First, it is clear that positing

/ng/ in words such as *sing* [sɪŋ] and *long* [lɔŋ] permits a great economy, since we do not need an /ŋ/ phoneme, and since we can now equate /ng/ with /mb/ and /nd/ and achieve greater generality there. But two complications arise as a result. First, a hole in the pattern is created, as in S₃ above, since a phonological constraint will be necessary to rule out the possibility of combining the consonant features [+nasal] and [+back] in English. And second, although they turn out to be well-motivated, rules will be required to convert underlying /ng/ to [ŋ] in the appropriate environments.

4.1.2 The Simplicity Metric

While notions of economy and simplicity have always been implicit in linguistic analysis, the concept of simplicity has gained theoretical significance within the framework of generative grammar (in this case, generative phonology). In Chapter 3, reference was made to the levels of adequacy explicitly differentiated by Chomsky and other generative grammarians. *Observational adequacy* is said to be achieved by a grammar "if it correctly describes the data on which it is based and nothing more— if, in other words, it gives a compact one–one organization of this data" (Chomsky and Halle, 1965:458). If, on the other hand, the grammar achieves the higher goal of capturing the "tacit knowledge" of native speakers, it is said to reach the level of *descriptive adequacy*. In other words, such a grammar is said to be *psychologically real*. In phonology, as in other areas of linguistics, our goal is to write grammars which are psychologically real. In order to do so, our theory of phonology must be developed in such a way that when alternative solutions to a problem are proposed, it leads us to choose the one solution which captures the native competence of speakers. In other words, an *evaluation procedure* is necessary to judge the relative merits of alternative proposals in analyzing a given language.

In the early period of generative theory, an approach similar to Occam's Razor was outlined. Thus Chomsky (1962:223) wrote: "we must apparently do what any scientist does when faced with the task of constructing a theory to account for a particular subject-matter—namely try various ways and choose the simplest that can be found." However, in order to do this, it is necessary to have a good idea of what simplicity is, or of what makes one solution simpler than another. As we have already seen, simplicity in one part of the phonology may lead to complexity in another part. Thus the notion of simplicity must be refined and formalized if it is to be of any use in phonological analysis.

Simplicity is a technical term defined by the theory, and not a loosely conceptualized intuitive notion. Originally Chomsky (1955) stated that "simplicity correlates with 'maximal degree of generalization'." Linguistic theory therefore provides a *simplicity metric* which will automatically assign simplicity coefficients to alternate solutions so that the correct solution is chosen. In this way the theory reaches the level of *explanatory adequacy*, that is, it motivates the choice of the best grammar from all the descriptively adequate grammars. In later writings this simplicity metric becomes the second part of a "two-pronged attack":

> Suppose that we are concerned to develop a linguistic theory that meets the level of explanatory adequacy. It seems that a two-pronged attack on this problem offers some hope of success. In the first place, we attempt to enrich the structure of linguistic theory so as to restrict the class of grammars compatible with the data given—in other words, we attempt to make the strongest legitimate universal claim about the structure of language. Second, we attempt to construct an evaluation procedure for selecting one among the various grammars permitted by the proposed linguistic theory and compatible with the given data. (Chomsky and Halle, 1965:106–107)

In singling out simplicity as an evaluation procedure, the claim is made that phonologies which are maximally simple (as defined by the theory) are preferred by speakers, or are perhaps more easily learned by children. For as Chomsky (1960) makes clear, linguistic theory is designed "to exhibit the built-in data organizing capacities of the child which lead him to develop the specific linguistic competence characterized in a fully explicit grammar." Thus, every claim about the nature of simplicity is necessarily a claim about the nature of one's innate language faculty.

The ability of children to construct a grammar of their language upon exposure to it has been schematized by Chomsky as follows:

Corpus → | LAD | → Grammar

On the basis of a corpus of raw data and guided by the innate constraints on language (as represented by the LAD, that is, language acquisition device), the child constructs a grammar. Since we do not at present have great insight into how children discover this grammar, the possibility of developing a "discovery procedure" was deemed too ambitious a project by Chomsky. Instead as seen in the following schema,

$$G_1 \quad \rightarrow$$
$$G_2 \quad \rightarrow \quad | \ EM \ | \quad \rightarrow G_1 \text{ or}$$
$$\text{Corpus} \rightarrow \qquad\qquad \rightarrow G_2$$

an evaluation metric (EM) is proposed which, on receiving input from two grammars (two solutions) and the corpus upon which the grammars are based, will tell us which of the two is preferred. This, then, is termed an "evaluation procedure," and the proposed criterion is simplicity. It is hypothesized that the child, upon exposure to a given language, will construct the *simplest* grammar of that language compatible with the data. It is for this reason that so much attention has been paid to simplicity and the simplicity metric.

Of course, if linguistic theory becomes sufficiently developed so that the constraints placed on it are strong enough to pick out the right grammar for any language, such an evaluation procedure may not be necessary. While there is much disagreement today among linguists over the merits or usefulness of a simplicity metric (especially as developed so far—see below), most linguists seem to work under the assumption that such a metric is a necessary part of the metatheory.

4.2 Feature Counting

In phonology, simplicity has been equated with the number of features required to capture a phonological generalization. The fewer features required, the simpler (or more highly valued) the phonology. The concept of such an evaluation metric is possible only if we assume that phonological descriptions should be made in terms of (distinctive) features and not in terms of indivisible segments (for example, phonemes). The first statements concerning the simplicity metric dwell on this point. Thus, Halle (1962:381–382) mentions two rules similar to R_1 and R_2 given below:

$$R_1: \qquad\qquad R_2:$$

$$k \to \check{c} \, / \, \underline{\quad} \left\{ \begin{matrix} i \\ e \\ æ \end{matrix} \right\} \qquad k \to \check{c} \, / \, \underline{\quad} \left\{ \begin{matrix} p \\ r \\ a \end{matrix} \right\}$$

In terms of segments, each rule is stated with five symbols. But, as Halle points out, a rule such as R_1 is considerably more highly valued in a phonology than a rule such as R_2. Using indivisible units such as /k/, /i/, /p/, /r/ does not reveal the fact that a phonological process can be conditioned by the front vowels /i, e, æ/, but not by the voiceless stop /p/, the liquid /r/, and the low back vowel /a/ functioning as a single class.

Halle notes that if these rules are translated into distinctive features, then the simplicity of R_1 is revealed, as compared to the complexity of R_2:

$$R_1: \qquad k \to \check{c} \, / \, \underline{\quad} \begin{bmatrix} +\,\text{syll} \\ -\,\text{back} \end{bmatrix}$$

$$R_2: \quad k \to \check{c} \; / \; \underline{\quad} \left\{ \begin{array}{l} \begin{bmatrix} +\text{cons} \\ +\text{ant} \\ -\text{cor} \\ -\text{voice} \\ -\text{cont} \end{bmatrix} \\ \begin{bmatrix} +\text{cons} \\ +\text{son} \\ +\text{ant} \\ +\text{cor} \\ +\text{trill} \end{bmatrix} \\ \begin{bmatrix} +\text{syll} \\ +\text{back} \\ +\text{low} \\ -\text{round} \end{bmatrix} \end{array} \right\}$$

In R_1, the environment /i, e, æ/ is expressible in terms of the feature specifications [+syllabic] and [−back], that is, two features. In R_2, however, when one attempts to express the environment /p, r, a/ in terms of features, the result is a disjunction involving *fourteen* feature specifications. A simple formulation is achieved in the first case, but an astounding complexity is found in the second case. This is what is desired. Thus, simplicity can be quantified by counting features, and only a theory which requires that segments are composites of features will differentiate between real and spurious generalizations.

What this procedure reveals is that certain segments constitute *natural classes*, whereas others do not. Thus, /i/, /e/, and /æ/ constitute a natural class expressible as [+syll, −back]. Halle states that *two (or more) segments constitute a natural class when they can be specified by fewer features than any one member of the class*. Thus, /i/ is specified as [+syll, +high, −back] (three features), /e/ is specified as [+syll, −high, −low, −back] (four features), and /æ/ is specified as [+syll, +low, −back] (three features). In each case, at least one more feature is required to specify any one member of the class than the class as a whole.

4.2.1 Feature Counting in the Lexicon

There are two places where features have been counted to assess the simplicity of a phonological system: the lexicon (lexical or phonological representation, that is, underlying forms) and the phonological rules. As we saw in Chapter 1, there are numerous phonological constraints characterizing any language. Thus, there are often redundancies created in the phonological representations by constraints on sequences of phonemes. Examples of such *sequential constraints* in English are: (1) if a word-initial segment is an affricate, that is, either /č/ or /ĵ/, then the following segment must be a vowel; (2) if the second of two word-initial consonants is a stop (oral or nasal), then the first consonant is /s/. Both of these sequential constraints are language-specific, since there are languages which violate them. Thus, the word /dᶻrá/ 'to sell' in Ewe breaks the first sequential constraint since the affricate /dᶻ/ is followed by something other than a vowel. Similarly, Gwari breaks the second sequential constraint by allowing a variety of /CNV/ sequences, for example, /bmà/ 'to break,' /dná/ 'to be in.' There are, however, *universal* sequential constraints which characterize all languages. One possible universal constraint is suggested by Gwari. While Gwari has an implosive /ɓ/ phoneme, for example, /ɓà/ 'to beg,' there are no instances of /ɓmV/ in the language (see Hyman, 1972a:187). This is presumably because of the phonetic complexity which would be involved in pronouncing an egressive nasal consonant after an ingressive implosive (at least in the same syllable).[1] While some linguists have spoken of "nasally released implosives" (for example, Williamson, 1973:117), reported phonetic transcriptions such as [ɓma] probably represent something other than implosion.

4.2.1.1 Morpheme Structure Rules (MSRs) Because of sequential constraints, certain features of one segment can be predicted on the basis of certain features of another segment. That is, certain feature specifications are rendered redundant by sequential constraints. According to the theory of *morpheme structure rules* proposed by Halle (1959:30ff), redundant feature specifications are to be left blank in the underlying representations of morphemes. Consider the word *chat* [čæt], which has the following phonetic feature specifications:

[č]	[æ]	[t]
+cons	−cons	+cons
−syll	+syll	−syll
−son	+son	−son
+high	−high	−high
−back	−back	−back
−low	+low	−low
−ant	−ant	+ant
+cor	−cor	+cor
−voice	+voice	−voice
−cont	+cont	−cont
−nasal	−nasal	−nasal
+strid	−strid	−strid
+del rel	+del rel	−del rel
−round	−round	−round

[1] Sequences of C + N in Gwari can be referred to as single nasally released consonants, i.e., C^N. As argued in Hyman (1972a), a nasally released implosive may be phonetically impossible, since what is involved in the production of an implosive is the rarefaction or lowering of the air pressure inside the mouth by a downward movement of the whole glottis. If the air pressure is lower within the mouth, it should not be possible for air to be released through the nose.

On the basis of the first sequential constraint given above, it can be predicted that any segment following a [−cont, +del rel] segment (that is, an affricate) will be a vowel. Thus, the major category features for vowels, that is, [−cons, +syll, +son], are predictable and are therefore left blank in the underlying form of *chat*. Formally, the unspecified features are entered with zeros, that is, [0 cons, 0 syll, 0 son], which are filled in with pluses and minuses by a morpheme structure rule such as the following:

$$
\begin{bmatrix} 0 \text{ cons} \\ 0 \text{ syll} \\ 0 \text{ son} \end{bmatrix} \rightarrow \begin{bmatrix} -\text{cons} \\ +\text{syll} \\ +\text{son} \end{bmatrix} / + \begin{bmatrix} -\text{cont} \\ +\text{del rel} \end{bmatrix} \underline{\quad}
$$

However, the distinctive feature matrix obtained after specifying the redundant vowel features as [0 cons, 0 syll, 0 son] is still full of redundancies. In addition to sequential constraints of the type just discussed, languages are characterized by extensive *segmental constraints*. It has been seen that the feature specifications [−cons, +syll, +son] of /æ/ are redundant as a result of the [−cont, +del rel] specifications of /č/. In addition, the specifications [−cont, +del rel] allow us to predict all of the remaining features of /č/ except [−voice]. Since there are only two affricates in English, namely /č/ and /ǰ/, we know a lot about a segment once we know that it is an affricate. (Needless to say, the same does not apply to a language having other affricates in addition to /č/ and /ǰ/, for example, /pf/, /ts/, /kx/.) We can predict that it is [+cons, −syll, −son] (that is, an obstruent); that it is [+high, −back, −low, −ant, +cor, −round] (that is, an unrounded alveopalatal); that it is [−nasal] (that is, oral); and that it is [+strident] (as opposed to the [−strident] affricate [tᶜ]). Thus, in phonological representations, such features are left unspecified (via zeros) and are filled in by segmental morpheme structure rules such as the following:

$$
\begin{bmatrix} 0 \text{ cons} \\ 0 \text{ syll} \\ 0 \text{ son} \\ 0 \text{ high} \\ 0 \text{ back} \\ 0 \text{ low} \\ 0 \text{ ant} \\ 0 \text{ cor} \\ -\text{cont} \\ 0 \text{ nasal} \\ 0 \text{ strid} \\ +\text{del rel} \\ 0 \text{ round} \end{bmatrix} \rightarrow \begin{bmatrix} +\text{cons} \\ -\text{syll} \\ -\text{son} \\ +\text{high} \\ -\text{back} \\ -\text{low} \\ -\text{ant} \\ +\text{cor} \\ -\text{cont} \\ -\text{nasal} \\ +\text{strid} \\ +\text{del rel} \\ -\text{round} \end{bmatrix}
$$

Only the [−voice] of /č/ is not predictable, since the phoneme /ǰ/ also satisfies the segmental constraints of English.

While this segmental morpheme structure rule is designed to capture a redundancy in the segmental inventory of English phonemes, at least two *universal* redundancies have been confused with the language-specific redundancies. First, affricates are automatically [−nasal], since it is phonetically impossible to have a nasal affricate.[2] Thus, this part of the redundancy found in English is not a property of English, but rather a property of universal phonetics, and should be stated as such. The following segmental constraint on feature combinations is therefore universal:

$$\begin{bmatrix} -\text{cont} \\ +\text{del rel} \\ 0\ \text{nasal} \end{bmatrix} \rightarrow [-\text{nasal}]$$

A second universal segmental constraint concerns the features High and Low. According to these features a segment cannot be [+high, +low], since it is impossible for the tongue to be both raised and lowered simultaneously from the neutral position.[3] Thus, two universal segmental morpheme structure rules are required:

$$\begin{bmatrix} +\text{high} \\ 0\ \text{low} \end{bmatrix} \rightarrow [-\text{low}]$$

$$\begin{bmatrix} 0\ \text{high} \\ +\text{low} \end{bmatrix} \rightarrow [-\text{high}]$$

Since /č/ is [+high], it is automatically [−low].

We can continue to remove the redundant feature specifications from the underlying representation of *chat*. Concerning the vowel /æ/, we can predict [−high] from the [+low] specification, as just seen, as well as the feature specifications [−ant, −cor, +voice, +cont, −nasal, −strid, +del rel]. All vowels are universally [−ant, +cont, −strid, +del rel]. In addition, all underlying vowels in English are [−cor] (since there are no underlying [+cor] retroflex vowels), [+voice] (since there are no underlying voiceless vowels), and [−nasal] (since there are no underlying nasalized vowels). Finally, /æ/ is redundantly [−round], since all [−back] vowels in English are unrounded, that is, there is no /œ/.

Turning to the /t/ of *chat*, a number of features are redundant here too. The feature specifications [+ant, +cor] tell us that we have an alveolar consonant. The feature specification [−voice] is necessary to distinguish /t/ from /d/, and the feature specification [−cont] is necessary to distinguish it from /θ/ or /s/. All of the remaining features can be predicted from the

---

[2] A nasal affricate (i.e., nasal stop followed by a fricative release) is impossible because of the difficulty of building up oral pressure if the nasal passage allows a steady release of air.
[3] In some recent work, however, Krohn (1972a,b) has suggested that such contradictory feature specifications as [+low, +high] be "sequenced" within a segment, as in the diphthong /aⁱ/, pronounced [aɪ].

redundancies of English. The feature specifications [+cons] and [−del rel] are predictable from the [+ant] specification, since only obstruents and liquids can be [+ant] in English, and since the only affricates ([+del rel]) in English are alveopalatals ([−ant]). The features [−syll, −son, −nasal] are predictable from the [−voice] specification, while the features [−high, −back, −low] are all predictable from the [+ant, +cor] specifications. Finally, the [−strid] is redundant, since the segment is neither [+cont] (for example, like /s/) nor [+del rel] (for example, like /č/). Thus, the complete redundancy-free underlying phonological matrix for the word *chat* is as given below:

/č/	/æ/	/t/
0 cons	0 cons	0 cons
0 syll	0 syll	0 syll
0 son	0 son	0 son
0 high	0 high	0 high
0 back	− back	0 back
0 low	+ low	0 low
0 ant	0 ant	+ ant
0 cor	0 cor	+ cor
− voice	0 voice	− voice
− cont	0 cont	− cont
0 nasal	0 nasal	0 nasal
0 strid	0 strid	0 strid
+ del rel	0 del rel	0 del rel
0 round	0 round	0 round

4.2.1.2 Morpheme Structure Conditions (MSCs) As pointed out by Stanley (1967) and others, there are a number of problems inherent in this approach to phonological redundancy. This is particularly evident in the above analysis of the redundant feature specifications in the /t/ of /čæt/. It turns out that some feature specifications predict more redundancies than others. For example, knowing that a segment is [−voice] automatically tells us that it is a voiceless obstruent in English, since there are no voiceless liquids, glides, nasals, or vowels in the language. (We are considering /h/ to be a fricative). Since this is the case, the [−voice] specification automatically predicts [−syll, −son, −nas], that is, three features. However, the opposite specification, that is, [+voice], does not tell us anything about the redundancies in the segment, since the segment can be either [−syll] or [+syll], [−son] or [+son], and [−nas] or [+nas]. Thus, one value of a given feature often carries more information than the opposite value (see **5.1.1**).

In addition, the specification of one feature within a segment frequently carries more information than the specification of another feature. For example, the feature specification [+low] automatically narrows us down to the phonemes /æ/, /a/, and /h/ in English. On the other hand, the feature specification [+cont] includes voiced and voiceless fricatives, liquids, glides, and vowels. The feature specification [−syll] is even more inclusive.

Thus, in assessing the redundancies and presenting them in the framework of morpheme structure rules, it is often necessary to look for those feature specifications from which the greatest number of other specifications can be predicted. In assessing the simplicity in the underlying forms, *only pluses and minuses are counted*; zeros do not count. Thus, according to the evaluation metric, the more zeros in the phonological representations, the more highly valued the solution. In English, the word *chat* has a complexity of 9. In a language where a corresponding word *chlat* were possible, the word *chat* would have a much greater complexity, since so many of the feature specifications of /æ/ are predicted on the basis of the fact that only a vowel can follow word-initial /č/ and /ǰ/ in English. Similarly, in a language permitting other affricates (for example, /pᶠ/, /tˢ/), /čæt/ would be more complex ("cost more"), because so many of the feature savings in the above analysis depend on the absence of a full series of affricate consonants in English. Thus, by factoring out all of the redundancies from lexical entries, only the idiosyncratic (or unpredictable) features will have to be specified—and counted by the evaluation metric. In this way linguistically significant generalizations are captured by formulating morpheme structure rules which fill in blank (or zero) feature specifications.

A problem sometimes arising within this framework occurs when a feature specification [+F] can be predicted on the basis of a feature specification [+G], and vice-versa. Should [+F] be entered phonologically as [0 F], and be predicted on the basis of [+G], or should [+G] be entered phonologically as [0 G] and be predicted on the basis of [+F]? An example of this arises whenever a language has the typical five-vowel system:

$$
\begin{array}{ccc}
i & & u \\
e & & o \\
& a &
\end{array}
$$

There is a redundancy with respect to the features Back and Round. Both features are predictable in the /a/ case:

$$
\begin{bmatrix} 0\ \text{back} \\ +\text{low} \\ 0\ \text{round} \\ V \end{bmatrix} \rightarrow \begin{bmatrix} +\text{back} \\ -\text{round} \end{bmatrix}
$$

That is, since /a/ is the only [+low] vowel in the language, it is possible to predict both the [+back] and the [−round] specifications that make up this vowel. In the [−low] vowels, it is not as straightforward. In the case of nonlow vowels, we have only two possibilities: front unrounded (that is, [−back, −round]) and back rounded (that is, [+back, +round]). There are no front rounded vowels (for example, /ü/) and no back unrounded vowels (for example, /ɯ/) among the nonlow vowels. The question is, should we predict the frontness/backness on the basis of the roundedness/unroundedness, or should we predict the roundedness/unroundedness on the basis of the frontness/backness? We clearly cannot start with [0 back, −low, 0 round], that is, with both features unspecified, since we would have no way of distinguishing [−back, −round] from [+back, +round] in underlying forms.

While phonologists have sometimes asserted that it is possible to determine which feature is dominant or more basic, it is sometimes impossible to provide evidence for choosing one feature over the other. In fact, it is entirely possible that neither feature determines the other, but rather that the two features determine each other. That is, the true generalization may be that the two features *agree* with one another, and not that one feature is distinctive and the other redundant. Such a notion of agreement of features is difficult to express within the framework of blank-filling morpheme structure rules.

For this and other reasons (mostly formal difficulties associated with MSRs), Stanley (1967) proposed that MSRs be replaced with *morpheme structure conditions* (MSCs). Stanley pointed out that the blank-filling morpheme structure rules are different from phonological rules in that only the latter are capable of changing features, deleting and adding segments, etc., while the former only express redundancies on the phonological level. In other words, MSRs are basically static in that they do not convert one level of representation into another, but rather simply enumerate the details of the phonological representation. Quite to the contrary, phonological rules convert phonological representations into phonetic ones.

Thus, a crucial distinction was drawn between a *constraint* on a given level of representation (for example, phonological or phonetic) and a *rule* converting one level of representation into another level. Morpheme structure conditions were designed to capture the redundancies of the underlying phonological level, but without the notion of blank-filling. Instead, blanks in the underlying matrices were prohibited, thereby making it impossible to have "archiphonemes," that is, incompletely specified segments (see **3.2.2**). While many phonologists still argue for archiphonemes (especially grammatical morphemes such as the incompletely specified /N/ aspect marker in Akan [Schachter and Fromkin, 1968] or the "floating" high tone /′/ associative marker in Igbo [Voorhoeve, Meeussen and de Blois, 1969; Welmers, 1970; Hyman, 1974]), virtually all generative phonologists have given up MSRs for MSCs.

Stanley (1967:426–428) enumerates three kinds of morpheme structure

conditions: *if–then conditions, positive conditions,* and *negative conditions.*
An example of an if–then condition can be found in the above language with
the vowel system /i, e, u, o, a/, and is stated as follows:

$$
\text{If} \quad : \quad [-\text{low}]
$$
$$
\text{V}
$$
$$
\Downarrow
$$
$$
\text{Then} \quad : \quad \begin{bmatrix} \alpha \text{ back} \\ \alpha \text{ round} \end{bmatrix}
$$

This example of a segmental MSC says that if a vowel is $[-\text{low}]$ (in this case,
anything but /a/), then the features Back and Round agree. This agreement
is captured by means of the alpha variable notation. If $\alpha = +$, then we obtain
$[+\text{back}, +\text{round}]$; if $\alpha = -$, then we obtain $[-\text{back}, -\text{round}]$. Nothing
is said about whether one feature is predictable on the basis of the other.
Instead, only the *agreement* (and not the exact content for any given morpheme) is revealed. This generalization, then, is said to capture a regularity
in the underlying forms of this language.

Examples of sequential if–then MSCs were given in Chapter 1. Consider
now the example from English stop + /l/ combinations. English allows
initial /pl/, /bl/, /kl/, and /gl/, but does not allow */tl/ and */dl/ (for example,
play and *clay*, but not **tlay*). A sequential if–then MSC can be written as
follows:

$$
\text{If} \quad : \quad \#\# \quad \begin{bmatrix} -\text{cont} \\ \text{C} \end{bmatrix} \quad \text{l}
$$
$$
\Downarrow
$$
$$
\text{Then} \quad : \quad [-\text{cor}]
$$

If a word-initial noncontinuant is followed by /l/, then it must be either
labial or velar—and not alveolar.

Positive MSCs are used to capture the canonical shapes of underlying
forms. As is explicit in the term "morpheme structure condition," this means
the canonical shapes of morphemes. However, since *grammatical morphemes*
(for example, noun prefixes, tense/aspect markers, inflectional markers),
which are frequently affixes, often do not show the same phonological shape
as *lexical morphemes* (for example, nouns, verbs, adjectives), it is clear that
these regularities refer to so-called "content," as opposed to "function,"
words. The basic assumption in generative phonology has been that the
lexicon consists of morphemes which by rules are combined into words.
Positive MSCs have been used to capture the phonological shape of morphemes, rather than the derived shape of words. In a model of generative
phonology recognizing the *word* as the structural unit of the lexicon, it
would be quite consistent to distinguish between phonological and phonetic

word structure conditions, as opposed to morpheme structure conditions (see **6.1.2.1**). An example of a positive MSC is the following from Igbo:

+ C (y) V +

Each (lexical) morpheme in Igbo consists of an initial consonant, an optional /y/, and a vowel, for example, /bà/ 'enter,' /byá/ 'come.' With few exceptions, morphemes are monosyllabic in Igbo, and the above formula captures the basic underlying generalization characterizing the language. The above positive condition is definitely a morpheme structure condition (that is, a condition on *morphemes*), since words can be longer than one syllable (and almost always are). Thus, since nouns are typically VCV, we therefore need a word structure condition on nouns of the following kind:

$$\#\# \text{ V C (y) V} \#\#]_{\text{noun}}$$

As stated above, many grammatical morphemes do not conform to the positive MSC given above. Thus, the infinitive prefix consists of the single vowel /Í/, realized as [í] or [ị], depending on vowel harmony.

An example of a negative condition is the following (where $\sim$ = "not"):

$$\sim \begin{bmatrix} +\text{cons} \\ -\text{syll} \\ +\text{back} \\ +\text{nasal} \end{bmatrix}$$

This MSC states that there is no phoneme /ŋ/ in this language. Schachter and Fromkin (1968) have suggested that negative conditions are not needed, since they can always be replaced by an if–then condition. This segmental condition can be restated as follows:

$$\text{If} \quad : \quad \begin{bmatrix} +\text{cons} \\ -\text{syll} \\ +\text{nasal} \end{bmatrix}$$
$$\Downarrow$$
$$\text{Then} \quad : \quad [-\text{back}]$$

Thus, it may be that only positive and if–then conditions are required by the theory of morpheme structure conditions.

The abandonment of MSRs in favor of MSCs has had a serious effect on the evaluation of complexity in the lexicon. It is no longer possible to add up zeros and see what kind of a savings is attained by filling in feature values by rule. However, as Stanley (1967:434) himself points out, the savings that were possible in the MSR approach are still recoverable in the MSC approach. He suggests as an evaluation procedure that the "weight" or generality of a morpheme structure condition be judged by the maximum number of feature specifications that could theoretically be removed from an underlying matrix and predicted by an MSC. Thus, while the shift from MSRs to MSCs has actually been accompanied by a shift away from adding up points in underlying representations, the same procedure is still theoretically possible.

4.2.2 Feature Counting in Phonological Rules

Relatively little attention has in practice been paid to lexical feature counting as opposed to rule feature counting (see, however, the discussion of Harms, 1966, in **4.4.1**). As will be discussed in **4.3**, feature counting has had a profound effect on the whole conception of rules in phonology. The basic assumption is that a rule with fewer features specified is a simpler rule than a rule with more features specified. This assumption has led some phonologists to propose serious departures from the standard model of phonology. Thus, Contreras (1969:1) states: "Adherence to the binary principle in phonology conflicts with the simplicity criterion proposed by Halle, in the sense that rules which are intuitively more general are not consistently simpler than less general rules," that is, in terms of feature counting. This assumption has, on the other hand, been challenged by other phonologists. For example, Zimmer (1970:97–98) states: "The fairly widespread assumption that feature counting will automatically lead us to choose the preferable description from two or more competing ones, as long as they use the same features and the same conventions for writing rules, has never, to my knowledge, really been supported by detailed and convincing arguments. . . ." Nevertheless, the idea of a simplicity metric based on feature counting, with the goal of distinguishing linguistically significant generalizations from spurious ones, is one of the trademarks of generative phonology.

It has already been demonstrated that a rule converting /k/ to [č] before /i, e, æ/ is simpler in the number of features required to specify it than a rule converting /k/ to [č] before /p/, /r/, and /a/. In this particular case, feature counting is capable of discriminating between possible and impossible phonological rules—or, in weaker terms, between "natural," and "unnatural" or "crazy" rules. On the other hand, feature counting has been used to distinguish between phonological rules which are both possible and natural. The question here is which rule is simpler (more highly valued)?

Consider the following two rules of palatalization:

a $k \rightarrow č / \_\_ i$

b $k \rightarrow č / \_\_ \begin{Bmatrix} i \\ e \\ æ \end{Bmatrix}$

In terms of phonemes, rule **a** is much simpler than rule **b**, since fewer symbols are required (namely, three symbols, as opposed to five). However, when the two rules are translated into distinctive features,

$$\textbf{a}' \quad k \rightarrow \check{c} \, / \, \underline{\quad} \begin{bmatrix} +\text{high} \\ -\text{back} \end{bmatrix}$$
$$\textbf{V}$$

$$\textbf{b}' \quad k \rightarrow \check{c} / \, \underline{\quad} \, [-\text{back}]$$
$$\textbf{V}$$

rule **a**′ now requires *two* features to specify the environment of the rule, while rule **b**′ requires only *one*. Thus, the simplicity metric says that rule **b** is simpler than rule **a**. In the sense of simplicity = generality, this is certainly the case, since the environment has been generalized in **b** to include all front vowels. However, as we shall see in Chapter 5, rule **a** is a much more frequent and "natural" rule than rule **b**. If simplicity were the criterion used by children in acquisition, then we would expect rule **b** to be more common. On the other hand, it is conceivable that the simplicity metric is not correct, because it should tell us that **a** is simpler than **b**. Other such examples of where the simplicity metric goes astray will be dealt with in Chapter 5.

Another problem inherent in the simplicity metric, as discussed so far, is that only distinctive features are counted. Special diacritic features such as [+ablaut] and [+noun], which are sometimes needed in phonology, as well as grammatical boundaries, must also be evaluated somehow. While certain proposals have been made much remains to be worked out in this area.

4.3 Consequences of Feature Counting

The decision to base one's judgment of simplicity on feature counting has to a great extent determined the history of generative phonology, since the aim is to make explicit what is a real generalization. In particular, the very design of phonological rules has been determined so as to *minimize* the number of features which will be required to specify them.

4.3.1 Rule Formalisms

A number of formalisms have been introduced into the literature. These formalisms constitute tentative hypotheses concerning the nature of simplicity, which in turn provide an evaluation procedure by which a child, on being exposed to raw data, constructs a phonology of his language.

4.3.1.1 Feature-Saving Formalisms   Phonological rules are written in such a way that unnecessary repetition of feature values is avoided. For example, a rule such as

1   A → B / __ C

which says that /A/ becomes [B] before /C/, is a simpler way of writing

1′   A C → B C

That is, the formalism, which places the environment to the right of the /, is designed so that the environment need not be repeated. Thus, in assessing the simplicity of a rule in terms of the number of features required, one need not count the environment twice.

It is claimed that a rule by which AC is converted to BC is more general than a rule of the form:

2   A C → B D

Since two segments, A and C, are changed, this rule is equivalent to the simultaneous application of *two* rules:

2′   A → B / __ C

    C → D / A __

Since *two* separate conditions must be met in order for AC to become BD, rule **2** represents a complexity over rule **1**. However, in the formalization of the first rule as **1′** this difference in complexity is not revealed. On the other hand, by stating the environment once, as in **1**, the simplicity metric assigns the right relative values to these rules.

A number of conventions are built into the rule formalism in just this way. Consider, for example, the following rule:

3   [+F] → [+G] / [+H] __

A segment which is [+F] acquires the feature specification [+G] when it is found after a segment specified [+H]. This formalism is quite different from one which is stated in terms of segments (for example, A → B / C __). In the latter example, A *becomes* B, that is, it is no longer A; in the above rule written in features, the segment marked [+F] does in fact acquire the feature specification [+G], but it remains [+F]. That is, one of the feature-saving formalisms is that features whose values do not change are not repeated on the right of the arrow. Stated somewhat differently, *only those features whose specifications change are included on the right of the arrow*. Thus, the above rule is an abbreviation for the following:

3′ $[+F] \rightarrow \begin{bmatrix} +F \\ +G \end{bmatrix} / [+H]$ __

Rule 3 implies that the [+G] segments are still [+F]. It also implies that there were at least some instances of [+F, −G] segments prior to the operation of the rule. Thus, another feature-saving formalism is that *when a feature change is stated on the right of the arrow, its opposite (input) value is not stated on the left of the arrow.* Rather, it is implicitly there. Thus the original rule is actually an abbreviation for the following:

$$\textbf{3}'' \qquad \begin{bmatrix} +F \\ -G \end{bmatrix} \rightarrow \begin{bmatrix} +F \\ +G \end{bmatrix} / \ [+H] \_\_$$

Finally, note that this rule implies that there were at least some instances of [−H] segments followed by [+F, −G] segments, in which case the input to the rule was not met. If one now states the most expanded redundant formalization of this rule, as follows,

$$\textbf{3}''' \qquad [+H] \begin{bmatrix} +F \\ -G \end{bmatrix} \rightarrow [+H] \begin{bmatrix} +F \\ +G \end{bmatrix}$$

it is observed that instead of a rule consisting of *three* features (as obtained following the conventions just discussed), a rule consisting of *six* features must be written (if these conventions are not followed). The claim is that rule **3**, which expands as in **3**''', is more general than rule **4**,

$$\textbf{4} \qquad [+H] \begin{bmatrix} +F \\ +G \end{bmatrix} \rightarrow [+I] \begin{bmatrix} +J \\ +K \end{bmatrix}$$

where six different features are involved. Unless the discussed feature-saving conventions are incorporated into the theory, rules **3**''' and **4** will be judged of equal complexity by the simplicity metric, and a generalization will have been missed.

4.3.1.2 Abbreviatory Conventions While the above formalism is designed to capture the generality of a rule by minimizing the number of features which need to be expressed, additional conventions have been adopted whose effect is to *collapse* structurally similar rules into one rule. In a sense the distinctive feature system already accomplishes this. For example, the rule palatalizing /k/ to [č] before /i, e, æ/ was claimed to be a single rule written as follows:

$$\textbf{5a} \qquad k \rightarrow č / \_\_ \ [-\text{back}] \\ \phantom{\textbf{5a} \qquad k \rightarrow č / \_\_ \ [} V$$

Logically, however, three subrules can be distinguished:

$$\textbf{5b} \qquad k \rightarrow č / \_\_ \begin{bmatrix} +\text{high} \\ -\text{back} \end{bmatrix} \quad (\text{that is, /i/}) \\ \phantom{\textbf{5b} \qquad k \rightarrow č / \_\_ } V$$

5c $k \rightarrow \check{c} / \underset{V}{\_\_ \begin{bmatrix} -high \\ -back \\ -low \end{bmatrix}}$ (that is, /e/)

5d $k \rightarrow \check{c} / \underset{V}{\_\_ \begin{bmatrix} -back \\ +low \end{bmatrix}}$ (that is, /æ/)

Thus, the distinctive features serve the purpose of collapsing three subrules into one rule. This is possible only when there is some structural similarity between the subrules, here meaning that the three segments in the environment of the rule constitute a "natural class." We have already seen that it is only with great difficulty that three equivalent rules can be collapsed when the environment consists of /p/, /r/, and /a/.

The question arises whether two processes are subparts of the same rule or are two separate rules. While it is obvious that the above processes should be analyzed as subparts of one rule, it is equally obvious that the following two processes should be analyzed as separate rules:

6 $k \rightarrow \check{c} / \_\_ i$

7 $V \rightarrow \tilde{V} / \_\_ N$

The palatalization of /k/ to [č] before /i/ has nothing structurally in common with the nasalization of vowels before nasal consonants. Hence the two rules are not collapsible. Thus, formalisms are sought which permit the collapsing of rules to achieve a real generalization, but which prevent the collapsing of rules when a spurious generalization would result.

4.3.1.2.1 Brace Notation   While the palatalization and nasalization rules just given are structurally unrelated, the following two rules of Korean share obvious formal properties with one another:

8a $r \rightarrow n / \#\# \_\_$

8b $r \rightarrow n / C \_\_$

In **8a**, /r/ becomes [n] at the beginning of a word (that is, directly following the full word boundary ##); in **8b**, /r/ becomes [n] after a consonant. These rules put into effect the phonetic sequential constraint in Korean which disallows [r] except when preceded by a vowel (Hyman and Kim, in prep.).[4] Thus, we observe in the following forms that the morpheme /rak/ 'pleasure'

---

[4] This constraint actually applies only to single /r/. Geminate [ll] occurs corresponding to nongeminate [r].

is pronounced [rak] after a vowel, but [nak] at the beginning of a word or after a consonant:

UNDERLYING   PHONETIC

/kʰwɛ#rak/	[kʰwɛrak]	'pleasure-pleasure'
/rak#wən/	[nagwən]	'pleasure-garden'
/kɯk#rak/	[kɯŋnak]	'extreme-pleasure'[5]

In order to capture the relatedness of rules **8a** and **8b**, the two rules are conflated into one by means of brace notation, as seen in **8c**:

8c $r \rightarrow n / \begin{Bmatrix} \#\# \\ C \end{Bmatrix} -$

The fact that **8a** and **8b** can be abbreviated as in **8c** reveals that a solution which includes rules **8a** and **8b** is more "costly" than a solution with the one rule **8c**. In terms of feature counting, the notation in **8c** permits a great savings, since it is no longer necessary to state /r/ on the left of the arrow and [n] on the right of the arrow twice. That is, while seven symbols are required to state **8a** and **8b**, only five symbols are required in the single conflated rule in **8c**. The theory therefore *requires* that **8c** occur in the phonology of Korean, and not **8a** and **8b**. This requirement "forces" the preferred solution, since a phonological analysis with **8a** and **8b** would miss a generalization.

One of the requirements which must be met in order to conflate two phonological rules is that the rules be *structurally related*, as seen in the Korean example. A second requirement is that no third phonological rule be ordered *between* the two rules. That is, if it can be demonstrated that there is a third rule, say **8d**, which must be ordered after **8a** but before **8b**, then this would constitute an argument *against* collapsing the two rules. We would in this case be dealing with *two* rules rather than one, although **8a** and **8b** would still exhibit striking structural similarities (namely, the fact that both convert /r/ to [n]). As will be seen in **4.3.2**, most work in generative phonology is based on the position that phonological rules must be linearly ordered.

   4.3.1.2.2 Bracket Notation   Braces have been seen to involve a disjunction—thus, in the rule

9 $A \rightarrow B / - \begin{Bmatrix} C \\ D \end{Bmatrix}$

A becomes B before either C or D. That is, AC becomes BC and AD becomes BD. In a slightly more complicated example,

10a $\begin{Bmatrix} A \\ E \end{Bmatrix} \rightarrow B / - \begin{Bmatrix} C \\ D \end{Bmatrix}$

[5] In the derivation of [kɯŋnak], /kɯk#rak/ first becomes intermediate *kuknak* by the rule changing /r/ to [n] after a consonant; then a second rule nasalizes /k/ to [ŋ] before a nasal consonant, yielding [kɯŋnak].

AC becomes BC, AD becomes BD, EC becomes BC, and ED becomes BD. In the following rule, however,

11a $\begin{bmatrix} A \\ E \end{bmatrix} \to B \, / \, — \begin{bmatrix} C \\ D \end{bmatrix}$

the *bracket notation*, which is used by some generative phonologists, requires that the segments be matched along the same horizontal row. Thus, this rule states that AC becomes BC and ED becomes BC. In other words, the brace notation in 10a abbreviates the following four rules:

10b   A → B / — C

10c   A → B / — D

10d   E → B / — C

10e   E → B / — D

while the bracket notation in 11a abbreviates only the following two rules:

11b   A → B / — C

11c   E → B / — D

Thus, the bracket notation incorporates the notion of "respectively" and is therefore more restricted.

      4.3.1.2.3 Parenthesis Notation   A third notational device used to conflate rules is the *parenthesis notation*. In this case, the optional presence of a segment can be expressed. Thus, the rule

12a   A → B / — (C) D

collapses the two following rules:

12b   A → B / — C D

12c   A → B / — D

Again, a tremendous savings is obtained, since it takes *seven* segments to specify the two rules, but only *four* to specify the one collapsed rule.

    To observe the use of parentheses, consider the following data from Ewe reduplication (see Ansre, 1963):

VERB		REDUPLICATED NOUN	
φo	'to beat'	φoφo	'beating'
k͡plɔ	'to lead'	k͡pɔk͡plɔ	'leading'
syá	'to dry'	sásyá	'drying'
dᶻrá	'to sell'	dᶻádᶻrá	'selling'

The forms φɔ, ƙplɔ, syá, and dᶻrá reveal that verb roots can have any one of three phonological shapes: CV, CLV, or CGV. In the nouns derived by reduplication of the corresponding verb root, the (prefixed) reduplicated syllable is always CV.[6] Following the formalism developed for Akan by Schachter and Fromkin (1968), the Ewe reduplication rule can be written as follows:

13a $RED \rightarrow C_i V_i / \underline{\quad} C_i \left(\left\{ \begin{matrix} L \\ G \end{matrix} \right\} \right) V_i$

where $C_i = C_i$ and $V_i = V_i$

This rule copies a consonant (C_i) and vowel (V_i) identical to those found in the verb root. The parenthesis notation in the environment of this rule indicates the possibility of this rule applying to verb roots of the form $C_i L V_i$ and $C_i G V_i$. Notice also the brace notation indicating that the segment found between C_i and V_i in verb roots can be either a liquid or a glide.[7] With these notations it is thus possible to state Ewe reduplication as one rule with the following three subparts:

13b $RED \rightarrow C_i V_i / \underline{\quad} C_i L V_i$

13c $RED \rightarrow C_i V_i / \underline{\quad} C_i G V_i$

13d $RED \rightarrow C_i V_i / \underline{\quad} C_i V_i$

where $C_i = C_i$ and $V_i = V_i$

4.3.1.2.4 Angled Bracket Notation

Angled bracket notation is used to show an interdependency between two optional feature specifications. As an example, consider the following two rules from Nupe (Hyman, 1970b):

14 $\left\{ \begin{matrix} \varepsilon \\ \mathrm{ɔ} \end{matrix} \right\} \rightarrow [a]$

15 $\left\{ \begin{matrix} \tilde{\varepsilon} \\ \tilde{\mathrm{ɔ}} \\ \tilde{\mathrm{a}} \end{matrix} \right\} \rightarrow [\tilde{\mathrm{ɔ}}]$

As originally argued in Hyman (1970a), the two abstract underlying segments /ɛ/ and /ɔ/ are realized phonetically as [a], though they respectively palatalize

---

[6] The vowel of the reduplicated syllable is always [−nasal], even if the underlying vowel of the verb is [+nasal], e.g., /sɛ̃/ 'to be hard' reduplicates as [sɛ̃sɛ̃] (see Stahlke, 1971; Hyman, 1972a).

[7] Notice, of course, that the disjunction {L, G} can be replaced by the distinctive feature specifications [−syll, +son, −nas].

and labialize the preceding consonant (see **3.3.5**). In addition, underlying /ɛ̃/, /ɔ̃/, and /ã/ are all realized as a nasalized schwa, that is, [ə̃]. The rule changing both oral and nasalized low vowels to [a] or [ã] is written as follows:

16 $\begin{bmatrix} +\text{low} \\ V \end{bmatrix} \rightarrow \begin{bmatrix} +\text{back} \\ +\text{round} \end{bmatrix}$

A second rule now converts both /ã/ and the cases of [ã] deriving from /ɛ̃/ and /ɔ̃/ to [ə̃], as follows:

17 $\begin{bmatrix} +\text{nasal} \\ V \end{bmatrix} \rightarrow [-\text{low}]$

All nasalized vowels in Nupe are phonetically [−low]. We can now collapse **16** and **17** by means of angled bracket notation:

18a $\begin{bmatrix} +\text{low} \\ \langle +\text{nasal} \rangle \\ V \end{bmatrix} \rightarrow \begin{bmatrix} +\text{back} \\ -\text{round} \\ \langle -\text{low} \rangle \end{bmatrix}$

This rule states that while all [+low] vowels become [+back, −round], if the low vowel is also [+nasal] it must also become [−low]. That is, this rule schema collapses two rules. First, when the features within angled brackets are evaluated, the following rule converts low nasalized vowels to [ə̃]:

18b $\begin{bmatrix} +\text{low} \\ +\text{nasal} \\ V \end{bmatrix} \rightarrow \begin{bmatrix} +\text{back} \\ -\text{round} \\ -\text{low} \end{bmatrix}$

Second, when the angled brackets are not evaluated (since the interdependent features within them are optional), the following rule converts /ɛ/ and /ɔ/ to [a]:

18c $\begin{bmatrix} +\text{low} \\ V \end{bmatrix} \rightarrow \begin{bmatrix} +\text{back} \\ -\text{round} \end{bmatrix}$

The ordering of **18b** before **18c** is dictated by the notation, which says first read the rule with the bracketed features and then read it without them.

It should be clear that angled bracket notation also leads to an economy of features. Thus, the collapsed Nupe rule is stated with *six* features, while the two rules taken separately require *seven* features.

4.3.1.2.5 *Alpha Notation*   Among the other feature-saving devices are *alpha notation* conventions. Suppose a language has the phonemic vowel inventory /i, e, u, o, a/. A common redundancy is that nonlow vowels agree in backness and roundness. The vowels /i/ and /e/ are [−back, −round], while the vowels /u/ and /o/ are [+back, +round]. In the absence of an appropriate convention, two segmental constraints would have to be stated:

19a If   : $\begin{bmatrix} -\text{low} \\ -\text{back} \end{bmatrix}$
                      V
                      ⇓
         Then : [−round]

19b If   : $\begin{bmatrix} -\text{low} \\ +\text{back} \end{bmatrix}$
                      V
                      ⇓
         Then : [+round]

Eight features are required to state the two constraints. However, these two constraints are clearly related and should be stated as a single constraint. The use of phonological variables permits the collapsing of these two constraints as follows:

20 If   : $\begin{bmatrix} -\text{low} \\ \alpha\ \text{back} \end{bmatrix}$
                     V
                     ⇓
        Then : [α round]

Now only *four* features are needed (though we avoid the problem of counting pluses and minuses as opposed to alphas). The alpha in this constraint means that either both are + or both are −, that is, all occurrences of alpha carry the same value. Some of the formal uses of variables are summarized below, alongside the feature values they abbreviate:

[αF, αG]   : [+F, +G] or [−F, −G]

[αF, −αG] : [+F, −G] or [−F, +G]

[αF, βG]   : [+F, +G], [−F, −G], [+F, −G], [−F, +G]

The notation [αF, −αG] indicates that the two features must have *opposite* values, while [αF, βG] simply states that there is no required relationship between the specifications of the two features.

4.3.1.3 The Problem of Notational Equivalence Even with the well-defined formalisms so far developed by the theory, it sometimes is the case that a given phonological process can be formalized in more than one way. As an example, consider the following two structurally related processes:

21a u → o / __ C $

21b o → ɔ / __ C $

In Feʔfeʔ–Bamileke, for instance, /u/ is realized as [o] in "closed" syllables (that is, in syllables ending in a consonant) in many dialects, while /o/ is realized as [ɔ] in closed syllables in all dialects. These two processes can be abbreviated either with angled bracket notation or alpha notation:

22a $\begin{bmatrix} -\text{low} \\ \langle -\text{high} \rangle \\ V \end{bmatrix} \rightarrow \begin{bmatrix} -\text{high} \\ \langle +\text{low} \rangle \end{bmatrix} / \underline{\quad} C\,\$$

23a $\begin{bmatrix} -\text{low} \\ \alpha\text{high} \\ V \end{bmatrix} \rightarrow \begin{bmatrix} -\text{high} \\ -\alpha\text{low} \end{bmatrix} / \underline{\quad} C\,\$$

Rule **22a** has the following two expansions:

22b $\begin{bmatrix} -\text{low} \\ -\text{high} \\ V \end{bmatrix} \rightarrow \begin{bmatrix} -\text{high} \\ +\text{low} \end{bmatrix} / \underline{\quad} C\,\$$

22c $\begin{bmatrix} -\text{low} \\ V \end{bmatrix} \rightarrow [-\text{high}] / \underline{\quad} C\,\$$

The first expansion converts /o/ to [ɔ], and the second expansion converts /u/ to [o]. **23a** has the following two expansions:

23b $\begin{bmatrix} -\text{low} \\ +\text{high} \\ V \end{bmatrix} \rightarrow \begin{bmatrix} -\text{high} \\ -\text{low} \end{bmatrix} / \underline{\quad} C\,\$$

23c $\begin{bmatrix} -\text{low} \\ -\text{high} \\ V \end{bmatrix} \rightarrow \begin{bmatrix} -\text{high} \\ +\text{low} \end{bmatrix} / \underline{\quad} C\,\$$

The first expansion converts /u/ to [o] and the second expansion converts /o/ to [ɔ].[8]

In terms of redundancy, both rule formalisms are overspecified. In both **22b** and **23c** [−high] appears on both the left and right of the arrow, although generally only feature *changes* are expressed in phonological rules (see **4.3.1.1**). This is unavoidable, if the lowering of /u/ and /o/ are to be captured in one rule with the features High and Low. In any case, where there are alternative ways of writing a rule, evidence must be sought to determine which formalization is correct.

It might be argued, on the other hand, that two formalisms, for example, angled bracket and alpha variable notation, are equivalent, that is, they make the same claims about phonological structure, and it will therefore be impossible to argue for one over the other. In attempting to choose one

---

[8] In expanding alpha notation, it is conventional to take the + value of alpha as the first expansion and the − value as the second.

formalism over the other for the vowel-lowering example, one quickly becomes embroiled in a number of theoretical issues. In **22a**, /o/ is first lowered to [ɔ] and then /u/ is lowered to [o]. The second expansion applies "vacuously" to the [ɔ], which is derived from the first expansion, since [ɔ] is already [−high]. In **23a** /u/ is first lowered to [o] and then /o/ is lowered to [ɔ]. However, the [o] which results from the first expansion must not undergo the second expansion or else underlying /u/ will also be realized as [ɔ].[9] It is therefore necessary to introduce a principle which has wide acceptance in phonological theory, namely that the two subparts of **23a** are *disjunctively ordered* with respect to each other. If one expansion applies, the other expansion cannot apply to the same form (input). The opposite of disjunctive ordering, *conjunctive ordering*, is found when two expansions of a rule (or two rules which are conjunctively ordered with respect to each other) apply to the same form. From **22a** one might conclude that **22b** and **22c** are either disjunctively or conjunctively ordered, since the same output is obtained in either case. Rules **22a** and **23a** are in this sense somewhat different. While the formalism in **23a** imposes disjunctive ordering, that in **22a** does not. Should it ever be demonstrated that phonological rules are not disjunctively ordered, then the formalism in **22a** would necessarily be chosen over that in **23a**. On the other hand, it should be noted that rules collapsed by angled brackets have also been claimed to be disjunctively ordered, a position which in the light of evidence can always be reversed.

4.3.1.4 Summary In this section we have seen how various abbreviatory conventions lead to an economy in the number of features required to describe phonological processes. Among the formalisms discussed were brace notation, bracket notation, parenthesis notation, angled bracket notation, and alpha notation. A final formalism, which does not in itself reveal greater simplicity in terms of feature counting, allows us to rewrite rule **24a** as **24b**:

24a $\begin{bmatrix} +F \\ +G \end{bmatrix} \rightarrow [+H]$

24b $[+F] \rightarrow [+H] / \overline{[+G]}$

Rule **24a** says that a segment which is [+F, +G] changes an understood [−H] specification to [+H]. **24b** says that a [+F] segment also becomes [+H] if it is [+G]. That is, placing an environment bar *over* a feature value indicates that this feature value is part of the specification of the input

---

[9] It turns out that some dialects of Feʔfeʔ allow historical /tūm/ to become [tɔ̄m] (and even [tōm]). While it has been argued (Hyman, 1972b) that historically *tūm became [tōm] and then optionally lowered again to [tɔ̄m], the difficulty in discussing this reapplication of the lowering rule in a synchronic framework arises from the problem of maintaining /tūm/ as the underlying form in all dialects. Since there is no alternation, once *tūm is pronounced [tɔ̄m] it can just as well be recognized as underlying /tōm/.

segment. While these rules are exactly equivalent and involve three features each, this convention is particularly revealing in collapsing rules such as **24b** with other rules. Let us say, for instance, that the same language in question has a rule of the following form:

25 $[+F] \rightarrow [+H] / \_\_ X$

Rule **25** applies not only to a segment which is $[+F, +G]$ but also to one which is $[+F, -G]$. While it is not readily collapsible with **24a**, it can easily be collapsed by means of brace notation with the equivalent rule **24b**:

26 $[+F] \rightarrow [+H] / \left\{ \begin{matrix} [+G] \\ \_\_ \ X \end{matrix} \right\}$

That is, $[+F]$ becomes $[+H]$ if it is either $[+G]$ or followed by X.

As written, rule **26** requires *four* features, while **24b** and **25** require *six* features in total. While there has been a saving of two features, the convention which allows **24a** to be rewritten as **24b** is not in itself a feature-saving notation.[10]

4.3.2 Rule Ordering

Consider the following hypothetical rules taken from Schane (1969):

27 $/ti/ + /a/ \rightarrow [tya]$
       $/te/ + /a/ \rightarrow [ta]$
       $/tu/ + /a/ \rightarrow [twa]$
       $/to/ + /a/ \rightarrow [ta]$
       $/ta/ + /a/ \rightarrow [ta]$

In this hypothetical language, when the high vowels /i/ and /u/ are followed by a vowel (in this case /a/), they are converted into the respective glides [y] and [w]. Whenever a nonhigh vowel is followed by a vowel, it is deleted. These two processes can be formalized as follows:

28a $[+\text{high}] \rightarrow [-\text{syll}] / \_\_ V$
         V

28b $[-\text{high}] \rightarrow \quad \emptyset \quad / \_\_ V$
         V

As written above, the two rules require *eight* features (if we count V and $\emptyset$ as one feature each). These rules can also be applied in either order, since their environments are mutually exclusive. Thus, if **28a** is applied first, then /tia/ and /tua/ become [tya] and [twa], and then **28b** applies, converting /tea/, /toa/, and /taa/ to [ta]. If **28b** is applied first, then the same results are obtained, but in reverse order.

[10] It should be noted, however, that McCawley (1971) has argued against the use of braces in phonology, especially in such cases as **26**.

Such a solution, therefore, does not require any constraint on rule ordering. The rules are written out in such a form that they can be applied in *random sequential ordering*; that is, whenever the appropriate input is met, they apply.

On the other hand, imposing a definite (or *extrinsic*) ordering on rules allows us to simplify their structural description, sometimes dramatically. Thus, imagine that rule **28a** were to apply before rule **28b**. This would mean that all [+high] vowels followed by a vowel would be converted into glides *before* the operation of **28b**, which deletes nonhigh vowels before vowels. Since this is the case, the feature specification [−high] is redundant in **28b**. Instead, **28b** should be written as follows:

28b′   V → Ø / __ V

Since the only VV sequences which could possibly serve as input to this rule have the first vowel [−high] (because of the prior operation of **28a**), the correct output is obtained. And in the process one feature specification, namely [−high], is economized.

An appropriate example of this relationship between rule ordering and simplicity comes from Shona (Tom Hinnebusch and Theo Vennemann, personal communication). In this Southern Bantu language there are alternations between [p] and [h], [t] and [h], and [k] and [h], as informally represented by the following subrules:

29   p → h / m __
         t → h / n __
         k → h / ŋ __

That is, voiceless stops become [h] after homorganic nasals. Since these nasal consonants derive from an underlying /n/ prefix, two rules are required: homorganic nasal assimilation and conversion of voiceless stops to [h]. If the rules are ordered, they can be specified as follows:

30a   [+nasal] → [α place] / __ [α place]
          C   C

30b $\begin{bmatrix} -\text{voice} \\ -\text{cont} \\ \text{C} \end{bmatrix}$ →   h   / [+nasal] __
                                                          C

Rule **30a** converts /n/ to [m] before labials and [ŋ] before velars. The notation [α place] is an abbreviation for the place of articulation features, for example, [α ant, α cor], and should therefore be counted as several features rather than as one. Rule **30b** says that a voiceless stop becomes [h] after a nasal consonant. Since **30a** has already made all preconsonantal nasals homorganic, it is not necessary to specify the nasal consonant as to place of articulation. Thus the following derivations are obtained:[11]

31   /np/ → mp → mh
　　　/nt/ → nt → nh
　　　/nk/ → ŋk → ŋh

Rules **30a** and **30b** follow all the feature-saving conventions discussed in **3.1.1**. This is made possible by the imposition of rule ordering. If **30b** were to *precede* **30a**, then the following would be the result:

32   /np/ → nh →
　　　/nt/ → nh → ?
　　　/nk/ → nh →

First, /p, t, k/ would be converted to [h], since they are found after a [+nasal] consonant. But then it is not clear how homorganic nasal assimilation would apply to intermediate *nh*, since the point of articulation of the following consonant is now glottal, and a "nasal glottal stop" is the only possible output of rule **30a**. Thus it is clear that if these rules are to be ordered, **30a** must precede rule **30b**.

If, on the other hand, more information is incorporated into **30b**, then rule ordering is unnecessary:

$$\textbf{30b}'\quad \begin{bmatrix} -\,\text{voice} \\ -\,\text{cont} \\ \alpha\,\text{place} \\ C \end{bmatrix} \to h\; / \begin{bmatrix} +\,\text{nasal} \\ \alpha\,\text{place} \\ C \end{bmatrix}\, -$$

Rule **30b′** says that a voiceless stop becomes [h] when it is preceded by a *homorganic* nasal consonant. Since the output of **30a** is now incorporated into the input of **30b′**, it is no longer necessary that the two rules have the ordering restriction placed on. Instead, the two rules can apply whenever their structural description is met. If **30a** applies before **30b′**, then of course the derivation is straightforward. If **30b′** applies first, then it can only apply to /nt/, since this sequence alone has a consonant following a homorganic stop (as opposed to /np/ and /nk/). But then, after **30b′** has applied, **30a** can apply and convert /np/ and /nk/ to *mp* and *ŋk*, respectively, and now **30b′** can reapply, as in the following derivations:

```
           30b′     30a       30b′
33   /np/   →              →   mp   →   mh
     /nt/   →     nh
     /nk/   →              →   ŋk   →   ŋh
```

---

[11] The rule of homorganic nasal assimilation in **30a** applies vacuously to underlying /nt/, since the underlying nasal is already homorganic with the following voiceless stop.

In the first approach, each rule is designed to apply *once* at a specific point in the derivation. In the second approach, a rule can apply any time its structural description is met, randomly until there are no longer any forms which are subject to it. This may mean that the rule will apply several times before it has run its course. Even the first approach has recognized the need for so-called "persistent" rules (see Chafe, 1968:131), which can apply at several points in a derivation. In the second approach, *all* rules operate in this manner.

The consequences are significant. First, while **30b** requires only *six* features to specify it, **30b′** requires *eight* features. Thus, if rules are to be randomly ordered, it will be necessary to complicate the rules—and, most likely, to give up the evaluation measure as so far conceived. Second, the random sequential ordering approach seriously affects the abstractness of underlying forms (see **3.3.5**). Consider, for example, the following situation, which is found in Sea and Land Dayak (Scott, 1957, 1964).

Sea Dayak has two rules: **34a**, a rule nasalizing vowels after nasal consonants; and **34b**, a rule deleting voiced stops after homorganic nasal consonants (see Kisseberth, 1973a:427–428):

34a $\quad V \to \tilde{V} / N \underline{\quad}$

34b $\quad \begin{bmatrix} b \\ d \\ g \end{bmatrix} \to \emptyset / \begin{bmatrix} m \\ n \\ \eta \end{bmatrix} \underline{\quad}$

Thus, /naŋa/ 'to straighten' is pronounced [nãŋã], while /naŋga/ 'to set up a ladder' is pronounced [nãŋa].[12] What this means is that the underlying contrast between Ø and /g/ is realized on the surface as a nasalized versus an oral vowel, a clear violation of the *linearity condition* rejected by Chomsky (1964:93).[13] This state of affairs is adequately accounted for by requiring that **34a** apply before **34b**, as in the following derivations:

		34a	**34b**	
35	/naŋa/	→ nãŋã		'to straighten'
	/naŋga/	→ nãŋga	→ nãŋa	'to set up a ladder'

If, however, **34b** were to apply before **34a**, then **34a** would incorrectly nasalize the second vowel of /naŋga/:

		34b	**34a**	
36	/naŋa/	→	→ nãŋã	'to straighten'
	/naŋga/	→ naŋa	→ *nãŋã	'to set up a ladder'

---

[12] The underlying form /naŋga/ 'to set up a ladder' is well-motivated, since the rule of consonant deletion is optional. Thus this underlying form will be realized as either [nãŋga] or [nãŋa].

[13] This condition says that a given string of underlying phonemes /ABC/ should be realized phonetically as a corresponding string [abc], rather than as [acb] or [ac], for instance.

Since phonological rules have access in this theory only to the immediately preceding stage of the derivation, there is no way to nasalize /naɲa/ without nasalizing the second vowel of the intermediate form *naɲa* derived by **34b**. Instead, **34a** must precede **34b**.

Unlike the previous case, there is no way that the rules can be rewritten with random sequential ordering and still maintain the underlying forms /naɲa/ and /naŋga/. The reason is that once /naŋga/ becomes *naɲa*, there is no way short of rule ordering (but see **4.3.3**) to keep **34a** from applying to it to yield the incorrect *[nãɲã] 'to set up a ladder.' A theory not allowing extrinsic rule-ordering can be salvaged, however, by recognizing forms such as 'to straighten' with underlying vowel nasalization, that is, /nãɲã/. In this case, **34a** is replaced with a phonological constraint stating that in underlying forms, vowels after nasal consonants are automatically [+nasal]:

37   If   : N   V
                         ⇓
        Then :   [+nasal]

This is not necessarily undesirable in itself. In fact, as noted in Chapter 3, there has been a recent shift toward less abstract phonological representations. In this case, adhering to random sequential ordering decreases the distance between the phonological and phonetic representations (see Vennemann, 1973).

There has been considerable discussion concerning the need for extrinsic rule ordering. The original conception of a sequence of ordered rules, each applying once in a derivation, has been seriously challenged (Koutsoudas, Sanders and Noll, 1974; Vennemann, 1973). A distinction has been drawn between *intrinsic* and *extrinsic* rule ordering. Intrinsic ordering is that imposed by the system of rules itself; given the *form* of two rules, they can only be applied in one way. Extrinsic ordering is imposed by the language in question; given the form of the two rules, one must consult the particular data to see if a given rule precedes or follows another rule.

In order to explicate these notions, it is necessary to draw another distinction often made in the study of rule-ordering relations. Kiparsky (1968b) draws the distinction between *feeding* and *bleeding* rule ordering (see Chafe's [1968] equivalent distinction between *additive* and *subtractive* rule ordering). A rule **a** is said to *feed* into a rule **b** when it creates new environments for **b** to apply to. Thus, if [ɲa] deriving from /ŋga/ were to become [ɲã], one could say that the rule deleting /g/ *feeds* into the rule nasalizing [a] to [ã] after nasal consonants, since it creates new environments for the latter rule's application. (Of course, we saw that this was not the case.) A rule **a** is said to *bleed* a rule **b** if it removes environments that could have undergone rule **b**. Thus, if our hypothetical language had a rule of the form

38   V → Ø / ŋ __ #

by which vowels are deleted word-finally after [ŋ], this rule would *bleed* the rule that nasalizes vowels after nasal consonants, since if this rule had not applied, the vowel in question would have undergone the nasalization rule.

Having drawn this distinction, it is now possible to distinguish *absolute feeding* and *absolute bleeding* relationships. A rule **a** is said to *absolutely feed* a rule **b** if it creates all of the inputs to rule **b**. A rule **a** is said to *absolutely bleed* a rule **b** if it removes all of the inputs to rule **b**. Absolute bleeding must of course be prohibited in phonology, since if one rule removes all of the inputs to another rule, then there is no need for the second rule. Thus, if we have two rules, and if they stand in a potential absolute bleeding relationship, they must automatically be reordered so that the more general rule applies after the less general rule. This is one type of intrinsic rule ordering.

A good example of such a possibility comes from Schane's (1968) analysis of French. Two rules are relevant:

39a $V \rightarrow \tilde{V} \, / \, \_\_ \, N \, \$$

39b $N \rightarrow \emptyset \, / \, \_\_ \, \$$

Rule **39a** says that a vowel is nasalized before a syllable-final nasal. Rule **39b** says that a syllable-final nasal is deleted. If **39a** precedes **39b**, then the following derivations are correctly predicted:

40   /bɔn/   → bɔ̃n   → bɔ̃   'good' (m.)
         /bɔnte/ → bɔ̃nte → bɔ̃te 'goodness'

If, on the other hand, **39b** were to precede **39a**, the following incorrect derivations would be obtained:

41   /bɔn/   → *bɔ
         /bɔnte/ → *bɔte

That is, the syllable-final nasal would be deleted, and the rule nasalizing vowels before syllable-final nasals would have nothing to apply to. In other words, this would be a case of absolute bleeding, and could therefore not possibly be correct. Thus, given that we know French to have the two rules **39a** and **39b**, there is only one possible ordering of these rules. In this sense, the ordering can be said to be *intrinsic*. The rules order themselves.

While this is the definition of intrinsic ordering used by Schane (1969), others have restricted this term to apply only to cases of absolute feeding. Since the above rules can possibly give the wrong output, it is necessary according to this second view to modify **39b** so as to permit random sequential ordering. This can be done by incorporating the output of **39a** into the input of **39b**:

39b′ $N \rightarrow \emptyset \, / \, \tilde{V} \, \_\_ \, \$$

Rule **39b′** now states that a syllable-final nasal drops, but only when preceded by a nasalized vowel. Since, according to Schane's analysis, there are no underlying nasalized vowels, all nasalized vowels derive from **39a**. In other words, **39a** absolutely feeds **39b**. It must apply before **39b** or else **39b** will have nothing to apply to. But in the random sequential ordering (intrinsic ordering), if **39b** is selected first, it does not apply; **39a** then applies and creates nasalized vowels; now **39b** applies, and so on. The result, again, is that the rule must be complicated to include mention of the nasalized vowel preceding the syllable-final nasal consonant.

While extrinsic rule ordering can be seen as a means of minimizing the number of features required to specify a rule, the more crucial question arises over whether there are rules that can only be accounted for by such rule ordering. One case, originally cited by Chomsky (1964:96) in his demonstration against the linearity condition, concerns the pronunciation of the English words *writer* and *rider*. Many American English speakers pronounce these words [raɪɾər] and [ra:ɪɾər], that is, with a vowel length contrast, but no consonant contrast phonetically. Two rules are required:

42a $V \rightarrow V: / \_\_ [+\text{voice}]$

42b $\begin{Bmatrix} t \\ d \end{Bmatrix} \rightarrow ɾ / V \_\_ V$

First, a vowel becomes lengthened before a voiced consonant, and second, /t/ and /d/ become [ɾ] (a voiced tap) intervocalically, when the first vowel is stressed. If the rules are ordered **42a–42b**, then the forms [raɪɾər] and [ra:ɪɾər] are obtained. If they are ordered **42b–42a**, then the forms [ra:ɪɾər] and [ra:ɪɾər] are obtained. Since both possibilities exist, depending on the dialect, it is impossible to determine the ordering intrinsically, that is, on the basis of the form of the rules alone. Rather, one must extrinsically impose the rule ordering depending on which dialect one is describing.

Perhaps one way of avoiding extrinsic ordering in the first dialect (with a vowel-length contrast) is to recognize /aɪ/ and /a:ɪ/. Such an analysis is argued by Vennemann (1972d, 1973). For an alternative approach, see Koutsoudas, Sanders and Noll (1974), who argue for simultaneous rule application, maintaining the notion that rules apply only once in a given derivation. Despite all the current research into the nature of rule ordering, the issue seems far from settled.

4.3.3 Global Rules

A number of recent studies have proposed that languages have rules which can refer back to earlier (often erased) stages of a derivation (Kisseberth, 1973a,b). In the standard approach to generative phonology, all that is necessary for the application of a phonological rule is the information put into it from the immediately preceding stage in the derivation. In this modified approach, information from the systematic phonemic level is available at all stages of the derivation. For example, while an earlier rule can delete a vowel in a certain context, a later rule may have to make reference to this vowel, even when it is no longer present at the stage where this later rule applies. This kind of rule is termed a *global rule*.

While the status of global rules is being debated in current phonological discussions, the effect of this powerful device on phonology is clear. While global rules would still permit the kind of abstract phonological representations made possible by extrinsic rule ordering, it would now be difficult to make any solid argument for such rule ordering—if this alternative is available. Returning to the Sea Dayak example, Kisseberth (1973a:428) and Dinnsen (1974:38) argue that vowel nasalization should be treated as a global rule. As stated by Kisseberth (1973a:428): "a vowel nasalizes in Sea Dayak after a nasal element provided that nasal element does not arise as a consequence of the simplification of clusters of nasal plus voiced stop." Nasalization of the second vowel of /naŋga/ 'to set up a ladder' will therefore never occur, since there is an underlying /g/ between the nasal element /ŋ/ and the potentially affected vowel /a/. Similarly, in the *writer:rider* distinction, vowel-lengthening before a voiced consonant could be blocked before a voiced consonant which was not voiced at an earlier stage (presumably in the phonological representation). Thus, it appears that global rules can replace extrinsic rule ordering. It is possible that such rules do exist, since the implication is that speakers have access to underlying forms at all stages of the derivation. If the underlying forms are indeed "psychologically real," then this seems to be a reasonable claim to make.

4.4 An Evaluation of Feature Counting

As has already been said, there is much disagreement over the validity of a simplicity metric based on feature counting. While some phonologists would advocate the rejection of this notion entirely, other phonologists would simply assert that because of serious flaws (see Chapter 5), the simplicity metric should be modified or refined.

The idea of basing one's judgment of the simplicity of a given analysis on feature counting has serious consequences, since it makes certain claims about the nature of language and human language ability. For example, consider two solutions for the same language, which recognize the following vowel systems:

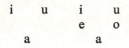

The first solution posits the three-vowel system /i, u, a/, the second the five-vowel system /i, e, u, o, a/. Now, let us say that this language has a rule palatalizing /k/ to [č] before /i/. In terms of distinctive features, the same rule would be expressed as **43a** in the three-vowel system and as **43b** in the five-vowel system:

43a $k \rightarrow č / \underline{\quad} \begin{bmatrix} -\text{back} \end{bmatrix}$
$\qquad\qquad\qquad\quad V$

43b $k \rightarrow č / \underline{\quad} \begin{bmatrix} +\text{high} \\ -\text{back} \end{bmatrix}$
$\qquad\qquad\qquad\quad V$

That is, since in the second solution there is a mid front vowel /e/, it is necessary to include two feature specifications, [+high] and [−back]. The first solution requires only one specification, namely [−back], since there is only one back vowel in the language. Thus, the same rule costs one feature more in the second solution, solely because of the inventory of segments. This is the claim that is made by feature counting. Feature counting always favors more general processes, and where a process is restricted (for example, to only *high* front vowels), a cost is assigned to it. Perhaps this claim is correct. Like other claims inherent in the simplicity metric, it is subject to empirical verification.

4.4.1 One Phoneme or Two?

Every time a decision is made on the basis of feature counting, an empirical claim is made about language—and this claim must be carefully investigated as to its implications. One appropriate example of this concerns the question of whether a given phonological entity should be analyzed as one or two underlying phonemes (see **3.4.3**). As proposed by Harms (1966) (and applied to Igbo by Carrell, 1970), such questions can be resolved by reference to the lexical complexity of the two solutions. Harms argues that in one language it may be more economical to set up /Cʰ/ vs. /C/, or /Cʷ/ vs. /C/, but in another language it may be more economical to set up /Ch/ and /Cw/, that is, sequences of two phonemes. As noted in the previous chapter, this question was of considerable importance in phonemic analysis.

Working within the framework of morpheme structure rules (see **4.2.1.1**), Harms proposes that indeterminate cases be resolved by calculating the number of features that must be specified within the lexicon in both the one-phoneme and the two-phoneme solutions. Consider, for example, the difference between a solution that recognizes an aspiration contrast between voiceless stops, that is, /Cʰ/ vs. /C/, and a solution which recognizes a sequence of /C/ + /h/ vs. /C/. This second solution, according to the commutation test discussed in Chapter 3, would have credibility only if there were an independent /h/ in the language, which could occur even if not preceded by /C/.

Now, calculating the number of feature specifications required to determine a given consonant, Harms assigns the arbitrary integer n to /C/. That is, in the matrix for any given consonant, he is assuming that it will take n features to specify it. If this is the case, then if an additional feature, say [aspirated], is introduced, it will take $n + 1$ features to specify /C/, since it will now contrast with /C^h/, which also requires $n + 1$ features. The two will differ in that /C/ is [−aspirated] while /C^h/ is [+aspirated]. Thus, each will take $n + 1$ features, or (taken together) $2n + 2$.

In the /Ch/ vs. /C/ solution, /C/ requires n features, but now /Ch/ requires n features (for the /C/), *plus* however many features are required to unambiguously specify /h/ in the lexicon. Let us say that /h/ requires *two* features (for example, [−syll, +low]). Now /Ch/ will require the n features for /C/ and *two* features for /h/, that is, $n + 2$. Since the nonaspirated /C/ also requires n features, /Ch/ + /C/ taken together require $2n + 2$ features, just as in the one-phoneme solution.

Thus, in terms of economy (judged by the number of features which must be specified in the lexicon), the result is a standoff. Harms suggests, at this point, that the relative number of forms exhibiting /C^h/ or /Ch/ vs. /C/ be incorporated into the calculation. Let us say that in our corpus we have 100 forms with /C^h/ and 200 forms with /C/. We now calculate as follows:

	/C^h/	/C/	/Ch/	/C/
	$n + 1$	$n + 1$	$n + 2$	n
100 Ch	100n + 100	200n + 200	100n + 200	200n
200 C				
Total	300n + 300		300n + 200	

As seen from the above calculation, 100 feature specifications can be economized if the opposition is analyzed as one between /Ch/ and /C/. If, on the other hand, we had the opposite proportion (namely, 200 forms with /C^h/ and 100 forms with /C/) in our corpus, the following tabulation would give the opposite results, as seen below:

	/C^h/	/C/	/Ch/	/C/
	$n + 1$	$n + 1$	$n + 2$	n
200 Ch	200n + 200	100n + 100	200n + 400	100n
100 C				
Total	300n + 300		300n + 400	

In this case we can economize 100 feature specifications in the lexicon if we analyze the opposition as one between /Cʰ/ and /C/. In fact, it will generally work out to be the case that when the consonant with secondary articulation (for example, /Cʷ/, /Cʸ/) occurs in more forms in the lexicon than the simple consonant, it will be more economical to analyze it as /Cʰ/, etc. Whenever it occurs in fewer forms than the simple consonant, it will be more economical to analyze it as /Ch/, etc. Thus this procedure suggested by Harms makes a very strong claim about the way language works—in particular the way children might go about constructing a phonology of their language. This approach claims that children will assess the numerical proportion of forms in assigning a phonological representation to the phonetic sounds they are exposed to.

The question of whether this claim is correct is, of course, difficult to answer. One can imagine various interferences or external factors that might have an effect on this analysis. For example, if /C/ occurs in more basic vocabulary and /Cʰ/ only in learned words, one might hypothesize that this could affect the analysis. Also, if the few words that have /Cʰ/ in a language are very frequent words, for example, function words like *that*, *this*, *there*, *then*, *those*, which all contain the rare English phoneme /ð/, this might also be a factor. Briefly, then, while simplicity has been put to the use of deciding between alternate solutions, in this case one vs. two phonemes, there seems to be little empirical support for either the criterion of simplicity or the more specific criterion of feature counting.

4.4.2 Derivational Constraints

However, the desire to make common or high valued phonological properties look simple formally has led to a number of other proposals. As will be seen in Chapter 5, Schachter (1969) proposes a formalism for natural rules which is designed in part to show the high value of certain kinds of assimilatory rules as opposed to others. To a great extent, the theory of *markedness* developed by Chomsky and Halle (1968), which is discussed also in Chapter 5, received its impetus from a desire to make the naturalness of segments, systems, and rules formally explicit.

A further example is provided by the work of Kisseberth (1970a) on phonological "conspiracies." Kisseberth points out that languages frequently have rules which "conspire" to turn out the same output. In Yawelmani, for instance, he describes a rule which deletes short vowels in the following environment:

$$[-\text{long}] \rightarrow \emptyset \ / \ V \ C \underline{\quad} C \ V$$
$$V$$

A vowel which is [−long] is deleted if it is both preceded and followed by a vowel separated from it by exactly *one* consonant. Thus, a word of the form

$CV_1CV_2CV_3$ will become CV_1CCV_3 if V_2 is $[-\text{long}]$. If, on the other hand, there is no preceding vowel (that is, there is a word-initial consonant, $\#C-$) or no following vowel (that is, there is a word-final consonant, $-C\#$) the deletion will not occur. Also, if the preceding or following vowel is separated by *two* consonants, deletion will not occur. These constraints are designed to guarantee that no instance of $\#CC$, $CC\#$, or CCC will result from the deletion rule. These three disallowed sequences have in common the necessity of assigning two successive consonants to the same syllable. A word-initial consonant sequence is automatically syllable-initial, just as a word-final consonant sequence is automatically syllable-final. Finally, any sequence of three consonants must be syllabified with *two* of the consonants in one syllable. It thus appears that Yawelmani has a surface phonetic constraint against two successive consonants within a syllable.

There is a second rule in Yawelmani which is also related to this constraint (Kisseberth, 1970a:296). A rule of vowel epenthesis (which inserts [i] in the regular case, [a] in the irregular case) applies in the following environment:

$$\emptyset \to V \,/\, C \_ C \begin{Bmatrix} \# \\ C \end{Bmatrix}$$

A vowel is inserted in order to break up sequences of $CC\#$ and CCC (that is, sequences of two consonants within the same syllable). Kisseberth argues that the rule deleting $[-\text{long}]$ vowels and the rule inserting vowels are *functionally* related in that their form depends crucially on the same phonetic constraint.

We have already seen that various notations have been devised to capture *structural* relatedness among rules, but there is no formalism to capture *functional* relatedness. In other words, the rule of vowel deletion (which "costs" *seven* features) could be just as related to the epenthesis rule as any other rule requiring seven features to specify it. In terms of simplicity, there should, according to Kisseberth's argument, be some feature-saving formalism for the above two rules, since it should be easier for a child to learn two functionally related rules than two unrelated rules.

To achieve this end, Kisseberth introduces the notion of *derivational constraints* into phonology. There is a derivational constraint in Yawelmani to the effect that no rule may produce a sequence of $\#CC$, CCC, or $CC\#$. With this derivational constraint in effect, the rule of vowel deletion can be rewritten as follows (Kisseberth, 1970a:304):

$$[-\text{long}] \to \emptyset \,/\, C \_ C$$
$$V$$

A short vowel is deleted between consonants—the vowels on the far sides of the consonants need not be included in the rule, since the derivational constraint will require that they be there anyway—or else the rule will not apply, since it will violate the constraint.

Thus, if the rule is rewritten in this fashion, the two features required to specify the two vowels in the environment of the rule can be economized. The rule now takes *five* features to specify it instead of *seven*. If the proposal were to stop here, the claim would be made that this rule is as related to the rule of epenthesis as is any other rule that takes five features to specify it. But, as Kisseberth hints, it may be possible to devise a formalism to take care of the epenthesis rule as well. In fact, since the epenthesis rule exists only to break up unacceptable clusters, perhaps the whole rule can be economized. Whenever a CCC or CC# is met in a derivation, a vowel is automatically inserted, having been triggered by the derivational constraint.

While derivational constraints have been proposed in a number of recent phonological studies, there is some question whether this functional related-ness between rules should be formally expressed. Heretofore the collapsing of rules implied that the two processes were *one* (inseparable) rule. In this case, the two rules are not subparts of the same rule, but are quite different rules. As suggested by Kiparsky (1972), the bond between two functionally related rules does not seem to be as tight as that between two structurally related rules (which are collapsed). For example, a rule can be ordered between two functionally related rules, and it is apparently possible for a language to lose one rule without losing a functionally related rule. This question, like so many others, has yet to be resolved in phonological theory.

5

PHONOLOGICAL NATURALNESS

5.1 Naturalness

In Chapter 4 it was seen that simplicity, as measured by feature counting, has played a large role in the development of generative phonology. Since the early years of this theory of phonology, there has been a noticeable shift away from simplicity and feature counting. Instead, phonologists have addressed themselves to the *naturalness* of phonological properties. Thus there is not only concern with what is simple (that is, general, noncomplex), but also concern for what is natural or plausible in a phonetic sense (see **3.4.4**). Certain aspects of phonology are not necessarily (or exclusively) *simple*, but are rather (or in addition) *natural*. As a result, these aspects are frequently attested in language after language. The new concern is to be sure that what is "natural" is formally revealed as "simpler" than what is "unnatural." Where a natural property of a phonological system is, by the criterion of feature counting discussed in Chapter 4, not revealed to be simple, the evaluation metric is assumed to be wrong and must be revised (see Chomsky and Halle, 1968, Ch. 9).

5.1.1 Natural Classes

In order to demonstrate the potential difference between simplicity (generality) and naturalness, let us return to the notion of natural classes, mentioned briefly in **4.3.1.2**. Two or more segments are said to constitute a *natural class* if fewer features are required to specify the class than to specify any one member of the class. Consider as an example the class of voiceless stops in English. To specify the class /p, t, k/, three features are required: [−voice, −cont, −del rel].[1] On the other hand, the following feature matrices are required in order to uniquely specify /p/, /t/, and /k/ individually:

/p/   /t/   /k/

$$
\begin{bmatrix} -\text{voice} \\ -\text{cont} \\ -\text{del rel} \\ +\text{ant} \\ -\text{cor} \end{bmatrix}
\begin{bmatrix} -\text{voice} \\ -\text{cont} \\ -\text{del rel} \\ +\text{cor} \end{bmatrix}
\begin{bmatrix} -\text{voice} \\ -\text{cont} \\ -\text{del rel} \\ -\text{ant} \end{bmatrix}
$$

/t/ and /k/ require *four* features and /p/ requires *five* features in order to distinguish each from the others and from all of the other phonemes of English.[2] As a second example, the segments /p, b, f, v, m, w/ in English are specified as [+ant, −cor], but any one of these segments will require one or more additional features to uniquely distinguish it from all the other segments.

Given this definition of a natural class, one should expect to find language-specific evidence to support the contention that two or more given segments constitute a natural class. While the sharing of a phonetic property, as ascertained in the phonetics laboratory, is in itself considerable evidence, one looks to find phonological corroboration of any phonetic relationship established by other means.

In general, we can say that two segments belong to a natural class when one or more of the following criteria are met in a number of languages:

a the two segments undergo phonological rules together;

---

[1] The feature [− del rel] is required to differentiate the stops /p, t, k/ from the affricate /č/.
[2] As mentioned in **2.5.1**, the feature [+labial] can be substituted for [+ant, −cor], in which case /p/, /t/, and /k/ have an identical complexity of 4.

b the two segments function together in the environments of phonological rules;

c one segment is converted into the other segment by a phonological rule;

d one segment is derived in the environment of the other segment (as in cases of *assimilation*).

While these criteria are not foolproof, they more often than not serve as the basis for establishing natural classes.

Consider as an example the following phonological rule:

1
$$\begin{bmatrix} k \\ g \end{bmatrix} \rightarrow \begin{bmatrix} \check{c} \\ \check{j} \end{bmatrix} / \underline{\quad} \begin{Bmatrix} i \\ e \end{Bmatrix}$$

Recalling the conventions discussed in **4.3.1.2.1** and **4.3.1.2.2**, this rule is an abbreviation for the following four subrules:

2
$$k \rightarrow \check{c} / \underline{\quad} i$$
$$k \rightarrow \check{c} / \underline{\quad} e$$
$$g \rightarrow \check{j} / \underline{\quad} i$$
$$g \rightarrow \check{j} / \underline{\quad} e$$

By criterion **a**, /k/ and /g/ constitute a natural class (the class of velar stops), since they undergo this phonological rule together. By criterion **b**, /i/ and /e/ constitute a natural class (the class of front unrounded vowels), since they function together in the environment of this rule. By criterion **c**, /k/, /g/, /č/, and /ǰ/ constitute a natural class (the class of [+high] noncontinuants), since the first two are converted into the second two by this rule. And, finally, by criterion **d**, /č/, /ǰ/, /i/, and /e/ constitute a natural class, since the first two are derived by this phonological rule in the environment of the second two. We can refer to this class as the class of palatals, although it should be noted that the Chomsky and Halle (1968) specification [+high, −back] excludes /e/ from the class.

It is important to note that these criteria are valid only if the rule in question is "natural" (see **5.2**). That is, we must make sure that the rules upon which we base our supporting evidence for natural classes are frequent and plausible, and not unnatural or "crazy" rules. (For a discussion of how unnatural rules, that is, rules which are not phonetically plausible, come into a phonology, see **5.2.6**).

Having established these criteria for natural classes, we can now examine the relationship between simplicity and naturalness. Since natural classes are formally defined by the feature-counting simplicity metric, it should generally be the case that classes which require fewer features to specify them are more natural than classes which require more features. While this sometimes turns out to be true, there are a number of cases where the simplicity metric breaks down.

Consider, for example, the following possible natural classes, arranged vertically:

CLASS A	CLASS B	CLASS C	CLASS D
b	b	b	b
d	d	d	d
g	g	g	g
	v	v	v
$\begin{bmatrix} +\text{voice} \\ -\text{cont} \\ -\text{nas} \end{bmatrix}$	z	z	z
	$\begin{bmatrix} +\text{voice} \\ -\text{son} \end{bmatrix}$	m	m
		n	n
		l	l
		r	r
		w	w
		y	y
			a
		$\begin{bmatrix} +\text{voice} \\ -\text{syll} \end{bmatrix}$	e
			i
			o
			u
			[+voice]

As one goes from left to right, the natural class gets simpler (or more general). Thus, it takes *three* features to specify class A (the class of voiced stops), but only *one* feature to specify class D (the class of all voiced segments). Classes B and C are intermediate, each requiring *two* features. As can be seen from the list of segments, class C (the class of voiced nonvowels) is more general or inclusive than class B (the class of voiced obstruents), though this is not directly revealed by the simplicity count.

If feature counting suffices in itself as a criterion for evaluating the naturalness of a class, then class D should be the most natural and class A the least natural. We should then expect class D to satisfy the four criteria stated above more readily than classes A–C. However, upon close examination, it becomes increasingly difficult to find phonological rules referring to the classes A through D as one goes from left to right. That is, it is easiest to find rules which refer to class A and class B, but it is less easy to find rules which refer to class C, and almost impossible to find rules which refer to class D. The voiced stops of class A, for instance, are required as a class in order to state the process of intervocalic spirantization found in many languages. Its general form is as follows:

$$3 \qquad \begin{bmatrix} b \\ d \\ g \end{bmatrix} \rightarrow \begin{bmatrix} \beta \\ \delta \\ \gamma \end{bmatrix} / V \_ V$$

The voiced obstruents of class B are required as a class to state the process of syllable-final devoicing in German and other languages:

$$
\mathbf{4} \qquad
\begin{bmatrix} b \\ d \\ g \\ v \\ z \end{bmatrix}
\rightarrow
\begin{bmatrix} p \\ t \\ k \\ f \\ s \end{bmatrix}
/ \underline{} \$
$$

It is difficult to find a phonological rule which has as its input the class of voiced nonvowels (class C), while no language appears to require the class of all voiced segments (class D) in phonological rules.

Feature counting thus fails to provide an adequate hierarchy of natural classes. The most simple class (that is, requiring the fewest features) is the least natural (judging from the four criteria proposed above); similarly, the least simple class is the most natural (see Chen, 1973a:226).

Another indication of the weaknesses inherent in the feature-counting approach to natural classes is found in cases where opposite feature values define classes of differing degrees of naturalness. For example, the class of [+nasal] segments in many languages includes /m/, /n/, and /ŋ/. This class is considerably more natural than the class of [−nasal] segments, which includes non–nasal stops, fricatives, affricates, glides, liquids, and vowels. While the following commonly attested rule of vowel nasalization reveals that /m, n, ŋ/ constitute a natural class,

$$
\mathbf{5} \qquad V \rightarrow \tilde{V} / \underline{} \begin{Bmatrix} m \\ n \\ \eta \end{Bmatrix} \qquad \text{or} \qquad V \rightarrow [+\text{nasal}] / \underline{} [+\text{nasal}]
$$

it is hard to imagine a phonological rule affecting all segments *except*/ m, n, ŋ/. Similarly, the feature [+glottalic] may define a class of implosives in a language (for example, /ɓ/ and /ɗ/). While these segments do constitute a natural class and are expected to function together in phonological rules, the class of [−glottalic] segments, that is, all segments *except* the implosives, is not natural. This asymmetry in the feature specifications characterizes most oppositions which were defined as *privative* by Trubetzkoy (see **2.2.2**). That is, whenever a class of segments carries a "mark" which other segments do not carry, the "marked" class is a natural one, but the "unmarked" class is not as natural (and in fact can be quite unnatural). As will be seen below, the theory of *markedness* developed by Chomsky and Halle (1968) is an attempt to remedy some of the problems created by feature asymmetries.

5.1.2 Natural Segments

Since the evaluation of natural *classes* by feature counting failed to take account of the "intrinsic content" of the various feature specifications being evaluated, phonologists turned their attention next to natural *segments*.

As pointed out in Chapter 1, certain segments are more frequently attested in languages than others. Thus, the vowels /i/ and /u/ are more frequent (and hence more "natural") than the vowels /ü/ and /ɯ/. In general, a language will not have /ü/ or /ɯ/ unless it already has /i/ and /u/. Similarly, it is hypothesized that children acquiring native Turkish (which has all four high vowels) will first learn /i/ and /u/ and only later the less natural vowels /ü/ and /ɯ/. Historically, we expect these less natural segments to merge (context-free) with more natural segments; for example, /ü/ has become /i/ in Yiddish (compare German [füsə], Yiddish [fis] 'feet').

5.1.2.1 Prague School Markedness

Since much of the discussion of naturalness in recent works centers around the notion of "markedness," it is helpful to trace the evolution of this concept. The original Prague School notion of "markedness" owes its existence to the phenomenon of neutralization discussed in **2.2.3** and **3.2.2**. It is recalled that, in Trubetzkoy's terminology, certain oppositions are constant while others are neutralizable. In addition, when two phonemes are neutralized in a given position, it is the "unmarked" member of the opposition which is found phonetically. Since German neutralizes /p, t, k, f, s/ and /b, d, g, v, z/ syllable-finally as [p, t, k, f, s], the voiceless obstruent series is said to be unmarked (in German). Since voiced and voiceless obstruents do not contrast in this position in German, Prague School phonologists would set up five *archiphonemes* (see **3.2.2**) /P, T, K, F, S/, that is, phonological units which are unspecified for voice but otherwise contain all of the feature specifications shared by voiceless and voiced obstruents. Frequently, it is the opposition member which "lacks" some phonetic property (in the sense of Trubetzkoy's *privative* oppositions—see **2.2.2**) which is found in the position of neutralization. Thus, Trubetzkoy (1939) distinguishes between an archiphoneme plus null (unmarked member of the opposition, for example, /t/ in German) and an archiphoneme plus a certain feature (marked member of the opposition, for example, /d/ in German).

In general, then, the unmarked member of an opposition is found in positions of neutralization. Translated into distinctive features, according to this view, the + value will usually be the marked value (since it indicates the presence of some phonetic property in privative oppositions), while the − value is the unmarked value (since it indicates the absence of some phonetic property in privative oppositions). However, this is not always the case. For example, some languages exhibit an opposition between oral and nasalized vowels only after oral consonants (for example, Nupe and some dialects of Chinese [Yen, 1968]). Thus, the following oppositions are found in Nupe (Hyman, 1972a:186):

[ba]	'to cut'	[da]	'to get wet'
[bã]	'to break'	[dã]	'to be in'
[mã]	'to give birth'	[ná]	'to shine'

As seen in these examples, /a/ and /ã/ contrast after the oral stops /b/ and /d/ but not after the nasal stops /m/ and /n/. Instead, only nasalized vowels are found after nasal consonants. In other words, the vowels /a/ and /ã/ are neutralized after nasal consonants as [ã].[3] Must we therefore conclude that /ã/ is unmarked and /a/ marked?

What is important is that the expected member of an opposition should be viewed as unmarked *in a specific environment*. Thus /p, t, k, f, s/ are unmarked syllable-finally but may be marked intervocalically, since many languages show a tendency to voice intervocalic consonants. The nasalization example in Nupe shows, however, that marked does not necessarily mean +, nor does unmarked mean −.

In the Prague School conception, markedness was a language-specific property. While later phonologists have emphasized the universality of markedness judgments (for example, /t/ is universally unmarked, /d/ universally marked), the evaluation of an opposition as one between marked and unmarked members depends crucially, in Prague School phonology, on the presence of neutralization. Trubetzkoy (1936:192) states this principle as follows:

> I emphasize that *unmarked* and *marked* members of an opposition exist only in the case of neutralizable oppositions. Only in such cases does the distinction between unmarked and marked members of an opposition have an objective phonological existence. Only in this case is it possible to determine the feature of a phonological opposition with complete objectivity and without the assistance of extralinguistic means of investigation. If a phonological opposition is constant, the relationship between its members may sometimes be thought of as a relationship between unmarked and marked. However, this remains only a logical or psychological fact but is not a phonological fact. [translation by L. M. H.]

In this passage, Trubetzkoy's view of the phoneme as a *phonological* (rather than *phonetic* or *psychological*) reality becomes evident (see **3.2**). In a language such as Nupe, which never neutralizes /p/ and /b/, there is no *phonological* reason to speak of /b/ as being marked. In English, on the other hand, since /p/ and /b/ are neutralized as [p] after /s/, for example, *spin*, this constitutes a phonological criterion for labelling /b/ as marked and /p/ as unmarked.

Phonetically, of course, /b/ carries voicing while /p/ lacks voicing. Also, speakers may "feel" that /b/ is marked, in that it is phonetically more complex. However, because of Trubetzkoy's position on phonological reality, the solution must be dictated by the sound system and not by universal phonetic or psychological criteria. According to him, where there is no language-specific evidence for setting up a markedness contrast, such an analysis is unwarranted. Martinet (1936:52), a disciple of Trubetzkoy, sums

---

[3] A low-level rule converts [ã] to [ɔ̃] (see **4.3.1.2.4**).

up essentially the same position: "Where the phonologist has not found any neutralization, he can of course indicate the existence of two parallel phonological series, but would be better off not to speak of markedness and archiphonemes." [translation by L. M. H.]

The assignment of markedness values is not always as straightforward as it may seem, however. Martinet (1936) argues that /t/ is marked in French and /d/ unmarked. He cites examples such as [metsɛ̃] *medecin* 'doctor,' where he claims that the [t] is lax and unvoiced. Normally, /t/ and /d/ have the following feature specifications in French:

/t/   /d/

$$\begin{bmatrix} -\text{voice} \\ +\text{tense} \end{bmatrix} \quad \begin{bmatrix} +\text{voice} \\ -\text{tense} \end{bmatrix}$$

Thus, from a logical point of view, /t/ could be unmarked (because it lacks voicing) or marked (because it is fortis, or [+tense]). Martinet argues for the second interpretation.

In addition to the above problem in analyzing markedness values, a further problem arises when there is neutralization in two different positions, and when the phonetic realizations in the two positions are not identical. Such an example is found in German. We have already seen that /s/ and /z/ neutralize in syllable-final position as [s]; /s/ and /z/ also neutralize in word-initial position in German, but this time as [z]. Just as no words end with [z] in German, no German words begin with [s]. In fact, it is only intervocalically that /s/ and /z/ contrast, for example, *reissen* [raɪsən] 'to tear' vs *reisen* [raɪzən] 'to travel.' On the basis of the final neutralization, one might suggest /s/ as the unmarked member of the opposition, but on the basis of the initial neutralization, /z/ would be the unmarked member. In brief, then, in Prague School markedness, as in other approaches, there are indeterminate cases which do not fall neatly into place.

5.1.2.2 Universal Markedness   The notion of markedness developed by the Prague School has been elaborated and applied in a number of ways. To Praguians, markedness is defined in a language-specific way. Of course, it may be possible to look for universal tendencies in the way marked and unmarked values are assigned cross-linguistically, and in fact, such a study has been begun by Greenberg (1966b). On the other hand, the exact usage of the term "marked" has not been uniform.

At least four interpretations are assigned to the term "marked." The first view of markedness is that something which is marked is characterized by the *addition* of something, for example, /kʷ/ carries lip-rounding, while /k/ does not. In distinctive features it is [+round].

A second view of markedness is *frequency*. The unmarked member of an opposition occurs more frequently than the marked member. Thus Maddieson

(1972:959) suggests that in a tone language, high tone is unmarked if it is more frequent than low tone; similarly, low tone is unmarked if it is more frequent than high tone. Proponents of this view of markedness will argue that /a/ is the unmarked vowel in a language where it has greater lexical (that is, in morphemes) and textual frequency than other vowels.

A third view of markedness is *neutrality*. In French, the epenthetic (inserted) vowel occurring nonetymologically as in *Arc de Triomphe* [arkə də triɔ̃f] is [ə]. Thus, schwa is the unmarked or zero (neutral) vowel in French, as opposed to [i] in Nupe (Hyman, 1970b) and [u] in Japanese (Lovins, 1973). As seen in the following examples (taken from Lovins, 1973:123),

ENGLISH   JAPANESE

paprika   pap*u*rika
public   pab*u*rikk*u*
pulse   par*u*s*u*

the vowel [u] is generally inserted in Japanese when English words with unacceptable consonant sequences are borrowed.[4] This also applies when the English word ends in a consonant, since Japanese permits only /n/ in final position.

A fourth view of markedness states that the unmarked member is the *productive* or *regular* one. In English, the unmarked (regular) pattern for di-syllabic nouns is to have stress on the first syllable (for example, *clímax*, *sérpent*). In this fourth view, exceptions such as *ellípse* and *cemént* are marked with respect to stress.[5]

5.1.2.3 Markedness in Generative Phonology   Starting with Chomsky and Halle (1968, Ch. 9) and Postal (1968, Ch. 8), markedness theory has come to play a central role in generative phonology (see also Cairns, 1969).

---

[4] There are two exceptions to the generality of *epenthetic* /u/ in Japanese. First, /i/ is frequently found instead of /u/ after palatal affricates, e.g., English *match* becomes Japanese [matči], and sometimes after palatal fricatives as well, e.g., English *brush* becomes Japanese [buraši] (Lovins, 1973:122). The second exception occurs after /t/ and /d/. Very frequently, since Japanese converts /tu/ and /du/ to [tˢu] and [dᶻu], the vowel /o/ is used as an epenthetic vowel after these consonants, e.g., English *stroke* becomes Japanese [sutorooku]. While the inserted vowel is sometimes [i] and sometimes [o], it is quite clear that unless the preceding consonant exerts a contrary effect, the inserted vowel will be /u/, which, it should be noted, tends to be pronounced [ɯ], i.e., [−round].

[5] Chomsky and Halle (1968:147–148) attempt to explain the irregularity of these forms by adding a final vowel. Their underlying forms are /ēlipse/ and /sēmente/, where /ē/ is a tense mid vowel which by rules of vowel shifting and diphthongization will become [iy] (see **3.3.4**). Since stress is expected to fall on the penultimate syllable (i.e., second from end), as in *climax* and *serpent*, the same rule will assign a stress to /ēlipse/ and /sēmente/. Finally, a later rule is needed to delete word-final /e/ (which by a vowel-reduction rule would be pronounced [ə] just prior to deletion).

While generative markedness theory has its roots in Prague School phonology, there is at least one crucial departure: to generative phonologists, markedness values are universal and innate. Voiceless stops, as suggested by the implicational universal of Jakobson (1941), are *universally* less marked than voiced stops, voiceless fricatives, etc. (see **5.1.2.1**). Thus, markedness is no longer treated as a property of the phonologies of individual languages, but rather as part of general phonological theory, which aims to capture the linguistically significant generalizations characterizing sound systems. It derives its support from studies of universals in language acquisition, linguistic typologies, and linguistic change. Unmarked sounds are said to be generally acquired earlier than marked sounds by children. They are also generally required in the inventory of sounds of a language before marked sounds can be added. In linguistic change, sounds are seen as changing from marked to unmarked (for example, a *context-free* change from implosive *ɗ to [l]) or from unmarked to marked (for example, the *context-sensitive* change of *V to [Ṽ] before nasal consonants).

In their epilogue, Chomsky and Halle (1968) propose that pluses and minuses be replaced by u's (for unmarked) and m's (for marked) in underlying representations. This theoretical reorientation is designed to resolve certain difficulties in the older approach. For instance, we saw in **5.1.1** that feature counting does not always lead to the establishing of clear natural classes. As a further example, compare the two natural classes given below, which are both statable using alpha notation (**4.3.1.2.5**):

$$\begin{bmatrix} \alpha\text{back} \\ \alpha\text{round} \\ -\text{low} \\ \text{V} \end{bmatrix} = \text{e.g., /i, e, u, o/}$$

$$\begin{bmatrix} \alpha\text{back} \\ \alpha\text{high} \\ -\text{low} \\ \text{V} \end{bmatrix} = \text{e.g., /e, ø, u, ɯ/}$$

The first class of vowel segments is one which frequently needs to be specified, as was seen in the discussion of morpheme structure conditions in **4.2.1.2**. The second class is highly unnatural and unexpected in languages. However, if the relative naturalness of these two classes is assessed in terms of the number of features required to specify them, we would have to conclude that the two classes are of equal naturalness. Since we know that this is not the case, the evaluation measure must be either revised or discarded.

To remedy this situation, Chomsky and Halle (1968) introduce marking conventions which are designed to evaluate the "intrinsic content" of the features. These conventions will judge [αback, αround] as more highly valued than [αback, αhigh], etc. Consider, for example, their marking conventions **X** and **XI** for vowels:

X [u back] → [+back] / [$\overline{+\text{low}}$]

XI
$$[u \text{ round}] \rightarrow \begin{cases} [\alpha\text{round}] \ / \ \begin{bmatrix} \overline{\alpha\text{back}} \\ -\text{low} \end{bmatrix} & \textbf{a} \\ [-\text{round}] \ / \ [\overline{+\text{low}}] & \textbf{b} \end{cases}$$

Convention **X** says that the unmarked (expected) value of the feature Back is [+back] if the vowel is [+low]. The reason for this is that the unmarked low vowel is /a/, which is [+back]. This vowel is more common and basic than the [−back] vowel /æ/ or the [+round] vowel /ɔ/ (which is also [+back], however).

Convention **XI** says that the unmarked value of the feature Round is (part **a**) identical with the feature specification for Back if the vowel is [−low], or (part **b**) [−round] if the vowel is [+low]. With the introduction of convention **XI**, the underlying specification for the vowel /i/ is now [−back, u round, −low], just as the vowel /u/ is now [+back, u round, −low]. In this new version of the theory, pluses and minuses cost one point each, as do *m*'s. But *u*'s are costless. Therefore, the above convention allows us to substitute a *u* for a + or − and thereby decrease the lexical complexity of items having the vowels /i, e, u, o/.

On the other hand, a vowel which is [−low] but which does not have the same feature value for Back and Round will be marked for the feature Round. We therefore have the following possibilities:[6]

/i, e/	/ü, ø/	/ɯ, ə/	/u, o/
$\begin{bmatrix} -\text{back} \\ u \text{ round} \\ -\text{low} \end{bmatrix}$	$\begin{bmatrix} -\text{back} \\ m \text{ round} \\ -\text{low} \end{bmatrix}$	$\begin{bmatrix} +\text{back} \\ m \text{ round} \\ -\text{low} \end{bmatrix}$	$\begin{bmatrix} +\text{back} \\ u \text{ round} \\ -\text{low} \end{bmatrix}$
V	V	V	V

While vowels which are [−low] but not [αback, αround] will automatically cost more than those which have the agreeing specifications for backness and roundness, there is no convention which assigns less cost to a [−low] vowel which is [αback, αhigh]. That is, there is no convention corresponding to Chomsky and Halle's convention **XIa**. Thus, this combination of alpha variables will automatically cost more than [αback, αround], and the evaluation measure is thereby retrieved. Furthermore, as Chomsky and Halle (1968:403) note, since the marking conventions are universal and not part of

---

[6] Chomsky and Halle put off any decision about whether [−back] or [+back] is less marked for nonlow vowels; see, however, Chen (1973a:232), who suggests that [u back] should be [−back] for [−cons] segments.

an individual phonology, they are not assigned any cost, just as the brace and arrow notations are free and clear.

Turning to part **b** of convention **XI**, it is observed that the unmarked value of Round is [−round] if the vowel is [+low]. This results from the fact that /a/, which is [−round], is the unmarked low vowel. The vowel /ɔ/, on the other hand, will be marked [m round], costing more than the [u round] vowel /a/.

This same approach is extended to a variety of features in 39 tentative marking conventions (Chomsky and Halle, 1968:404–407), for example, to the various places of articulation (where labial and dental articulations are less marked than velar articulations), to manners of articulation (where [u cont] is usually [−cont]),[7] and to nasality ([u nasal] → [−nasal]).

5.1.3 Natural Systems

Having provided these marking conventions by which the *u*'s and *m*'s of underlying forms are converted into pluses and minuses, Chomsky and Halle turn to the naturalness of *systems*. Their concern is to account for the naturalness of vowel system (a) and the unnaturalness of vowel system (b):

(a) i		u	(b) ü		ɯ
	e	o			ʌ
	a		œ		a

The set of marking conventions they give for vowels defines the following matrix for the various vowel sounds examined:

	a	i	u	æ	ɔ	e	o	ü	ɯ	œ	ø	ʌ
low	u	u	u	m	m	u	u	u	u	m	u	u
high	u	u	u	u	u	m	m	u	u	u	m	m
back	u	−	+	m	u	−	+	−	+	m	−	+
round	u	u	u	u	m	u	u	m	m	m	m	m

From this table it is clear that /a/ is the unmarked vowel. This is well supported from acquisition studies, where [a] is found to be the earliest acquired vowel, as reported by Jakobson (1941). Cross-linguistic typological studies of vowel systems also reveal that /a/ is apparently never lacking in any language.

The vowels /i/ and /u/ are considered to be only slightly marked, with a markedness value of 1 each, and the naturalness of these segments, as revealed by the marking conventions, accounts for the frequently attested

---

[7] The one exception mentioned by Chomsky and Halle is when a segment occurs before a "true consonant," i.e., obstruent or nasal. In this case the unmarked consonant is /s/, which is [+cont].

triangular vowel system /i, u, a/ (Jakobson, 1941), which children construct early in their development. These vowels are also quite frequent and occur in nearly all languages. A number of vowels have a complexity of 2, and the last three vowels have a complexity of 3.

Chomsky and Halle (1968:409) propose the following principle to account for natural vowel systems: "The complexity of a system is equal to the sum of the marked features of its members." Thus, returning to the two five-vowel systems, /i, e, u, o, a/ has a complexity of 6 $(1 + 2 + 1 + 2 + 0)$, while /ü, œ, ɯ, ʌ, a/ has a complexity of 10 $(2 + 3 + 2 + 3 + 0)$. The first vowel system is therefore seen to be more natural than the second.

However, there is a problem with this procedure, as Chomsky and Halle note, since the vowel system /i, ü, u, ɯ, a/ has a complexity of 6 $(1 + 2 + 1 + 2 + 0)$, yet is not as natural as the vowel system /i, e, u, o, a/, which also has a complexity of 6. A second principle is therefore required. The difference between the two systems is that the more natural system, after choosing the three least marked vowels /i, u, a/, chooses the vowels /e/ and /o/, which are marked with respect to height only. No judgment is made about whether [+back] or [−back] is less marked for nonlow vowels (see footnote 6). Thus /i/ and /e/ are entered simply as [−back] and /u/ and /o/ as [+back].[8]

The second system also chooses the three least marked vowels /i, u, a/ and then chooses the vowels /ü/ and /ɯ/, which are marked not for *height*, as in the case of /e/ and /o/, but rather for *roundness*. In other words, what makes /e/ and /o/ more marked than /i/ and /u/ is that they are [−high], rather than [+high]; what makes /ü/ and /ɯ/ more marked than /i/ and /u/ is that /ü/ is [+round] rather than [−round] and /ɯ/ is [−round] rather than [+round].

While the two systems have an equal complexity, it is clear that the system with /e/ and /o/ is more natural and expected than the system with /ü/ and /ɯ/. Since counting marked features does not reveal this difference in naturalness, another principle is necessary, which Chomsky and Halle (1968: 410) state as follows: "No vowel segment can be marked for the feature 'round' unless some vowel segment in the system is marked for the feature 'high'." This condition, as stated in absolute terms, rules out a vowel system /i, ü, u, ɯ, a/; stated less absolutely, it correctly accounts for the relative unnaturalness of this system as compared to /i, e, u, o, a/.

Chomsky and Halle suggest that other such conditions may be needed. However, since there will be a number of principles, it is likely that the product of markedness feature counting, namely, the correct specification of

---

[8] Recall that roundness is predictable from the specification of Back—i.e., [u round] is [−round] for nonlow [−back] vowels, and [+round] for nonlow [+back] vowels.

/i, u, a/ as the unmarked three-vowel system, can also be captured by a principle. One could state that before any segments with an *m* specification are chosen, the two vowels not having an *m* specification (/i/ and /u/), which are marked respectively [−back] and [+back], must be chosen. In other words, feature counting is replaceable by other notions.

Of course, one problem is that it is not always clear which of two systems (for example, vowel systems) is more natural or highly valued. For example, which of the following two vowel systems is more expected?

i	ĩ		ũ	u		i		u
	ã						e	o
	a						æ	a

The system on the left has the unmarked three-vowel system, but also the corresponding three nasalized vowels /ĩ, ũ, ã/. The system on the right has the unmarked five-vowel system, but also the vowel /æ/. In terms of markedness, the first system has a complexity of 5 (since [u nasal] is [−nasal] for all segments), while the second system has a complexity of 8. Both are six-vowel systems, and yet it is not clear how nasalized vowels should be evaluated with respect to other relatively marked vowels. According to Chomsky and Halle's conventions, /ã/ has a complexity of 1, that is, [m nasal], while /i/ also has a complexity of 1. The same procedure of feature counting would lead one to conclude that the vowels /e/ and /o/, which have a complexity of 2, are more marked (that is, less natural) than /ã/. This conclusion appears to be false, since the vowels /e/ and /o/ are more widely attested in languages than is /ã/. It is even more clear that /i/ is not equally marked with /ã/, since /i/ is one of the vowels which is found in almost all languages, while /ã/ is not found in most languages.

What this means is that [m nasal] represents more of a complexity than, say, [m high]. We are therefore faced with either assigning differential coefficients to the various features Nasal, High, etc., or seeking another condition or principle which would explain the greater complexity of certain nasalized vowels over certain oral vowels. It must be borne in mind, however, that some vowel systems may simply not be comparable, since their organizing principles are so different. Chomsky and Halle (1968) were careful to compare systems such as /i, e, u, o, a/ and /i, ü, i, ɯ, a/, where the parameters are relatively constant, that is, front/backness, height, and roundness. Introducing the parameter of nasality is not directly comparable, just as the introduction of retroflexion, pharyngealization, or tense/laxness may not be. While certain segments are less natural than others, it is not likely that this observation will lead to a foolproof formula for evaluating the naturalness of systems.

The reason for this is that the complexity of a system is *not* a function of the complexity of the segments contained in it—at least not directly. Rather, natural classes and systems are natural because of the *relationship* between the segments. Consider the following matrix of *u*'s and *m*'s, provided for consonants by Chomsky and Halle (1968:412):

	p	t	k	b	d	g	f	s	x	m	n	ŋ
ant	u	u	m	u	u	m	u	u	m	u	u	m
cor	−	+	u	−	+	u	m	u	u	m	u	u
cont	u	u	u	u	u	u	m	m	m	u	u	u
voice	u	u	u	m	m	m	u	u	u	u	u	u
nasal	u	u	u	u	u	u	u	u	u	m	m	m
Complexity	1	1	1	2	2	2	2	1	2	2	1	2

A number of observations can be made from this matrix. First, unmarked consonants are noncontinuant and unvoiced. That is, /p/ is considered to be less marked than either /b/, which is [m voice], or /f/, which is [m cont]. Second, anterior (labial and dental) consonants are less marked than non-anterior (palatal and velar) consonants. Thus, /p/ and /t/ are [u ant], while /k/ is [m ant]. Finally, no decision is made about whether the labial position is more or less marked for non–nasal stops than the dental position. Thus, as in the case of the front/backness distinction in nonlow vowels, the feature value for Coronal is entered as [−cor] for /p/ and /b/ and [+cor] for /t/ and /d/.[9]

By the conventions Chomsky and Halle propose, there are five consonants which are marked for one feature only, namely /p, t, k, s, n/, about which they remark: "It is significant that these five consonants are rarely absent in the phonological system of a language" (1968:413).

This minimal consonantal system can of course be reinforced by consonants having a complexity of 2 each, as in the following two systems:

```
a  p  t  k      b  p  t  k
   b  d  g         f  s  x
      s               m  n
      n
```

Each of these two eight-consonant systems has a complexity of 11. Each also appears to, be a natural system. While **a** has established a voice contrast, **b** has established a stop/fricative contrast as well as a nasal/oral contrast in two positions. The low figure of 11 reveals this naturalness. However,

[9] Schane (1973a:113) suggests that /t/ is the unmarked stop and that [u cor] is therefore [+cor] for consonants. Chen (1973a:230), on the other hand, suggests that labials are unmarked in syllable-initial position, while velars are unmarked in syllable-final position. Dentals are intermediate in both positions. It should be clear that the specific content of the marking conventions is constantly undergoing revision.

both **c** and **d** also add up to systems of a complexity of 11:

```
c  p t k    d  p  t  k
   b                 g
     s x        f  s
     n ŋ        m  n
```

Feature counting fails to reveal the naturalness of **a** and **b** as opposed to **c** and **d**. The latter two systems are unnatural because, unlike **a** and **b**, they are not organized according to principles of optimal contrast. The systems in **c** and **d** have arbitrarily incomplete series, for example, /s/ and /x/, but no /f/; /b/, but no /d/ or /g/. Thus, although **c** and **d** contain segments of equal naturalness to those in **a** and **b**, the resulting systems are not as natural.

Conversely, classes of segments can be equally natural even though they involve individual segments of greatly differing markedness values. The class of voiceless stops /p, t, k/ has a complexity of 3; the two classes /b, d, g/ and /f, s, x/ each have a complexity of 6, since voiced stops are marked for voice and voiceless fricatives are marked for continuance. The class of voiced fricatives /v, z, ɣ/ has a complexity of 9, since these segments are [m voice] and [m cont]. However, each of these four classes is *equally* natural. A class (or system) is not defined by the complexity of the individual segments, but rather by the relationship between them. The segments /ɓ/, /ɗ/, and /ɠ/, which are implosives, are highly marked and unnatural. Their occurrence in languages is considerably more restricted than that of any of the other classes discussed above—in fact, /ɠ/ is very rarely attested (Greenberg, 1970). However, if a language has these three implosive sounds, they constitute a class of equal naturalness to the class of voiceless stops.

5.2 Natural Rules

With the introduction of markedness theory into generative phonology, it became possible to formalize not only the naturalness of segments and systems, but also the naturalness of phonological rules, thereby distinguishing linguistically significant generalizations from spurious or nonsignificant ones. The first attempt to deal with natural rules was in the framework of *linking conventions*.

5.2.1 Linking Conventions

Chomsky and Halle (1968:401) express the view that in the following examples the **a** rule is more natural as a phonological process than the **b** rule:

6a   i → u   **7a**   t → s

6b   i → ɯ   **7b**   t → θ

However, as they point out, it is the rules in **b** which are simpler in terms of the number of distinctive features required to specify them:

6′a $\quad \left[\begin{array}{c} +\text{high} \\ V \end{array} \right] \rightarrow \left[\begin{array}{c} +\text{back} \\ +\text{round} \end{array} \right]$

6′b $\quad \left[\begin{array}{c} +\text{high} \\ V \end{array} \right] \rightarrow [+\text{back}]$

7′a $\quad \left[\begin{array}{c} +\text{ant} \\ +\text{cor} \\ C \end{array} \right] \rightarrow \left[\begin{array}{c} +\text{cont} \\ +\text{strid} \end{array} \right]$

7′b $\quad \left[\begin{array}{c} +\text{ant} \\ +\text{cor} \\ C \end{array} \right] \rightarrow [+\text{cont}]$

Rules **6′a** and **7′a** each require one more feature than rules **6′b** and **7′b**. If Chomsky and Halle's judgments concerning the relative naturalness of these rules are correct, there appears to be a discrepancy between naturalness and simplicity. The more general rules in **b**, as judged by the fewest features, are not the more expected ones.

In order to remedy this inadequacy in the theory, Chomsky and Halle propose the notion of *linking conventions*. What makes **6a** more natural than **6b** is that the unmarked value of Round for nonlow vowels is identical with the specification of Back (see **5.1.2.3**). What makes **7a** more natural than **7b** is that the unmarked value of Strident is [+strident] for nonback fricatives and affricates (see below). Chomsky and Halle propose that rules **6a** and **6b** be rewritten as follows:[10]

6″a $\quad \left[\begin{array}{c} +\text{high} \\ V \end{array} \right] \rightarrow \left[\begin{array}{c} +\text{back} \\ \text{u round} \end{array} \right]$

7″a $\quad \left[\begin{array}{c} +\text{ant} \\ +\text{cor} \\ C \end{array} \right] \rightarrow \left[\begin{array}{c} +\text{cont} \\ \text{u strid} \end{array} \right]$

In the reformulations in **6″a** and **7″a**, [+round] has been replaced by [u round] and [+strid] by [u strid]. This new formalism says that when a feature is changed (for example, [−back] to [+back] in **6″a**), all other features which are dependent upon this feature change for markedness specifications can be changed to their unmarked value without adding any cost to the rule. Since [u round] is interpreted as [+round] when a nonlow

---

[10] Chomsky and Halle actually leave [u round] unexpressed in the formalization of such a rule. When a [+high] vowel becomes [+back], the marking conventions automatically change the value of the feature Round to [−round] by means of linking. We shall incorporate [u round] into the rule formalism so as to avoid confusion with the pre–marking convention feature–saving formalisms discussed in **4.3.1.1**.

vowel is [+back], **6″a** "links up" with this marking convention and converts /i/ to [u].

Similarly, **7″a** links up with the marking convention for stridency, given below (Chomsky and Halle, 1968:407):

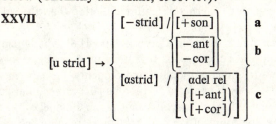

XXVII   [u strid] → $\begin{cases} [-\text{strid}] \,/\, \begin{bmatrix} +\text{son} \end{bmatrix} & \textbf{a} \\ \qquad\qquad\left\{ \begin{bmatrix} -\text{ant} \\ -\text{cor} \end{bmatrix} \right\} & \textbf{b} \\ [\alpha\text{strid}] \,\,/\, \begin{bmatrix} \alpha\text{del rel} \\ \left\{ \begin{matrix} [+\text{ant}] \\ [+\text{cor}] \end{matrix} \right\} \end{bmatrix} & \textbf{c} \end{cases}$

Part **c** of this convention states that stridency agrees with the specification for delayed release when the consonant is either [+ant] or [+cor], that is, when the primary point of articulation is prevelar (labial, dental, palatal). Affricates and fricatives are [+del rel] and so the unmarked value for Strident is [+strid] for these consonants. Since **7″a** changes /t/ to a fricative, that is, [+cont] (and redundantly [+del rel]), it automatically "feeds" into marking convention **XXVII**. Thus, in the rule converting /t/ to [s], Strident can be entered as [u strid] and therefore not be counted by the simplicity metric.

Having reformulated rules **6′a** and **7′a** as the simpler rules **6″a** and **7″a**, the question now arises: how do we formulate rules **6′b** and **7′b** in this new framework? In order to show the complexity of these rules relative to rules **6′a** and **7′a**, it is necessary to somehow *block* the application of linking. Thus, the feature values [m round] and [m strident] are incorporated into the rules, as seen in **6″b** and **7″b** below:[11]

6″b $\begin{bmatrix} +\text{high} \\ V \end{bmatrix} \rightarrow \begin{bmatrix} +\text{back} \\ \text{m round} \end{bmatrix}$

7″b $\begin{bmatrix} +\text{ant} \\ +\text{cor} \\ C \end{bmatrix} \rightarrow \begin{bmatrix} +\text{cont} \\ \text{m strid} \end{bmatrix}$

Although there is no change in the feature specification of Round in **6″b**, it is necessary to state the [m round] specification to the right of the arrow in order to correctly evaluate **6″b** as costing 4 features, as opposed to the more natural **6″a**, which costs 3 features (recall that [m F] costs one point, while

[11] Instead of [m round] and [m strid], which require an interpretation by means of the marking conventions, Chomsky and Halle use [−round] and [−strid], which will be automatically more costly than [u round] and [u strid] in rules **6″a** and **7″a**. Postal (1968: 184–185), however, discusses the use of [u F] and [m F] on the right of the arrow in phonological rules. We shall follow his proposal, since it creates less confusion with the earlier formalisms (see note 10).

[u F] is costless). Similarly, although /t/ does not undergo a change in its specification for Strident when it becomes [θ], [m strid] is included in **7″b**, so that this rule will cost 5 points, while the more natural rule **7″a** will cost only 4 points. Thus, in this new approach, the rules converting /i/ to [ɯ] and /t/ to [θ] are more complex in terms of feature counting than the rules converting /i/ to [u] and /t/ to [s].

One could, on the other hand, question Chomsky and Halle's judgments about the relative naturalness of these rules. It is difficult to evaluate these rules without some appeal to the conditioning environments. Perhaps there are some environments where /i/ is expected to become [ɯ] rather than [u] (for example, before a syllable-final velar consonant, as in Bamileke *ik > ɯk), just as there may be environments in which /t/ more readily becomes [s] than [θ] (for example, before /i/).

As an illustration, consider the case of intervocalic spirantization of [−back] voiced stops:

$$8 \qquad \begin{bmatrix} b \\ d \end{bmatrix} \rightarrow \begin{bmatrix} β \\ ð \end{bmatrix} / V \underline{\quad} V$$

This rule converts the stops /b/ and /d/ to the nonstrident fricatives [β] and [ð].[12] While Chomsky and Halle would characterize these [−strid] fricatives as more marked than the [+strid] fricatives /v/ and /z/, the following rule of intervocalic spirantization is considerably less natural than **8**:

$$9 \qquad \begin{bmatrix} b \\ d \end{bmatrix} \rightarrow \begin{bmatrix} v \\ z \end{bmatrix} / V \underline{\quad} V$$

Languages only rarely exhibit [v] and [z] as intervocalic reflexes of /b/ and /d/, and usually as the result of secondary modifications, for example, [β] becoming [v]. Thus, the more marked fricatives, that is, those which are [−strid], are more natural and expected in this particular environment.

This, then, points to a shortcoming of the markedness approach to rule naturalness as first developed, namely the fact that judgments are usually made on the basis of the complexity of the segments, and not on the basis of the process itself (see Vennemann, 1972b). Since [ɯ] is more marked than [u], a rule which yields [ɯ] in its output counts as more marked (less natural) than one which yields the more natural vowel segment [u].

5.2.2 Natural Assimilation Rules

An attempt to look directly at the process, rather than at the complexity of the output segments, is provided by Schachter (1969). Schachter points out that there are assimilatory processes which are natural and other

---

[12] The change of /d/ to [ð] is, of course, parallel to the change of /t/ to [θ] discussed in **7b** above.

assimilatory processes which are unnatural. He proposes that in the meta-theory the *n* or "natural" value of a feature will be listed for any given feature in any relevant environment. For example, the two intervocalic spirantization rules **8** and **9** would be written (ignoring linking conventions) as follows:

8′ $\begin{bmatrix} +\text{voice} \\ -\text{nasal} \\ \text{C} \end{bmatrix} \rightarrow [+\text{cont}] / V \_ V$

9′ $\begin{bmatrix} +\text{voice} \\ -\text{nasal} \end{bmatrix} \rightarrow \begin{bmatrix} +\text{cont} \\ +\text{strid} \end{bmatrix} / V \_ V$

The simplicity metric correctly reveals the first spirantization rule to be less complex than the second, since [β] and [ð] are expected intervocalically. With linking convention **XXVII** applicable, however, the rules would have to be written as follows:

8″ $\begin{bmatrix} +\text{voice} \\ -\text{nasal} \\ \text{C} \end{bmatrix} \rightarrow \begin{bmatrix} +\text{cont} \\ \text{m strid} \end{bmatrix} / V \_ V$

9″ $\begin{bmatrix} +\text{voice} \\ -\text{nasal} \\ \text{C} \end{bmatrix} \rightarrow \begin{bmatrix} +\text{cont} \\ \text{u strid} \end{bmatrix} / V \_ V$

The linking convention applies to **9″** to yield [v] and [z], while the first rule, which yields [β] and [ð], includes the specification [m strid], and therefore costs more than the second rule. In other words, the linking approach provides the wrong relative naturalness judgment in this particular case.[13]

Schachter's proposal is to replace the pluses and minuses derived by natural assimilation rules with the feature *n* (for "natural"). Thus, the two spirantization rules would be written by him as follows:[14]

8‴ $\begin{bmatrix} +\text{voice} \\ -\text{nasal} \\ \text{C} \end{bmatrix} \rightarrow \begin{bmatrix} +\text{cont} \\ \text{n strid} \end{bmatrix} / V \_ V$

9‴ $\begin{bmatrix} +\text{voice} \\ -\text{nasal} \\ \text{C} \end{bmatrix} \rightarrow \begin{bmatrix} +\text{cont} \\ +\text{strid} \end{bmatrix} / V \_ V$

[13] It is, of course, always possible that the marking convention should be revised, since Chomsky and Halle point out that their conventions are only tentative. Several of the major ones (not discussed here) have been revised by Cairns (1969), for instance.

[14] That the [−strid] specification may sometimes be needed in the resulting output of such a rule is seen from the common Bantu phenomenon by which /ǰ/ (which is [+strid]) is converted intervocalically to [y], not to the [+strid] fricative [ž]. In the few cases where the [+strid] fricative is found intervocalically, there is evidence for a secondary development by which [y] later changed to [ž].

While both rules mention the features Continuant and Strident in their outputs, the *n*, like the *u* for "unmarked," is not counted in assessing the complexity of rules. Thus, rule **8'''** costs 6 points (counting C and V as one each), while rule **9'''** costs 7 points. In order to phonetically convert [n strid] to a plus or minus, one looks at the list of *n* feature specifications and finds a statement to the effect that the natural value of Strident between vowels is [−strid].

. The real motivation for this proposal is Schachter's observation that many assimilatory processes are asymmetric in nature. One such example is palatalization. While it is a frequent phenomenon for velars to become fronted (palatalized) before front vowels, it is not a frequent phenomenon for palatals to become backed before back vowels. That is, rule **10** is natural, while rule **11** is unnatural:

10   k → č / __ {i, e, æ}

11   č → k / __ {u, o, a}

Numerous languages convert /ki/ to [či], while apparently no language converts /ču/ to [ku]. When we attempt to formalize these rules in terms of distinctive features, two equally well-motivated rules involving the same number of features result:

10'   [+back] → [−back] / __ [−back]
      C   V

11'   [−back] → [+back] / __ [+back]
      C   V

Both rules involve 5 features, and yet rule **11'** should be evaluated as infinitely more complex and unnatural than rule **10'**.

With this problem in mind, Schachter (1969) proposes the introduction of the feature specification *n* (discussed above), which is evaluated as having no cost in feature counting:

10''   [+back] → [n back] / __ [−back]
       C   V

The revised rule in **10''** now states that a back consonant takes on the natural feature value of Back, in the environment "preceding a front vowel." Included in the necessary interpretive conventions will be one stating that the *n* value of Back is [−back] before [−back] vowels. The rule as now written then carries a complexity of 4 (since *n* does not count), while the rule written as **11'** requires 5 features and is now formally more complex than the more expected rule. Notice that rule **11'** cannot be rewritten as in **11''**:

11''   [−back] → [n back] / __ [+back]
       C   V

While it is unlikely that a one-point difference can distinguish between a very natural rule **10″** and an implausible, perhaps impossible, rule **11′**, this approach yields the correct relative evaluations in the case just cited.

Further investigations of natural rules have revealed the general properties of frequently occurring phonological processes (see Schane, 1972; Chen, 1973a). The study of natural phonological processes has also been the starting point of theoretical departures from the standard model of generative phonology (Stampe, 1969, 1972a; Miller, 1972; Vennemann, 1972d, 1973).

5.2.3 The Relativity of Rule Naturalness

Studies into rule naturalness have revealed both the asymmetrical nature of assimilatory rules and the *relativity* of naturalness as a criterion for rules. The general form of an assimilation rule is seen in the following formula:

12 $X \rightarrow [\alpha F] / [\alpha F]$
$$Y$$

A segment X acquires the same feature specification as some feature F in the environment of a segment Y having that feature value. What this means is that X can become $[+F]$ in the environment of a Y which is $[+F]$, or can become $[-F]$ if Y is $[-F]$. However, many rules which are of this form are strikingly missing from phonological descriptions. One example we have already seen involves the failure of /č/ to become $[+back]$ (that is, [k]) before a $[+back]$ vowel. Another example of this type involves nasalization and denasalization.

One of the most natural rules in phonology is the nasalization of vowels before (or after) nasal consonants. As seen in **13**,

13 $V \rightarrow [+nasal] / \_\_ [+nasal]$
$$C$$

this rule is formally an assimilatory process, since a vowel acquires the feature specification $[+nasal]$ before a consonant which is $[+nasal]$. The denasalization of a consonant before an oral vowel is a less natural rule. While /an/ quite naturally is realized phonetically as [ãn], it is a rare occurrence to find /na/ pronounced [da]. As seen in rule **14**, however,

14 $C \rightarrow [-nasal] / \_\_ [-nasal]$
$$V$$

this too is of the form of an assimilatory process. However, this and other such assimilatory processes are not found, or are rarely found, in languages.

In other cases there are assimilatory rules which are each natural but differ in their *degree* of naturalness (frequency, expectancy, etc.). Chen (1973a), Stampe (1972a), and Vennemann (1972d) have pointed out that palatalization and nasalization are highly dependent on vowel height. Consider, for example, the two palatalization rules **15** and **16**:

15 $\quad$ k → č / __ i

16 $\quad$ k → č / __ $\left\{\begin{matrix} i \\ e \end{matrix}\right\}$

In **4.2.2**, it was argued that rule **16** is more simple (general) than rule **15**. Thus, when these rules are formalized using distinctive features, rule **16′** is judged to be more highly valued than rule **15′** by the evaluation metric:

15′ $\quad \begin{matrix} [+\text{back}] \\ C \end{matrix} \rightarrow [-\text{back}] / \underline{} \begin{matrix} \begin{bmatrix} +\text{high} \\ -\text{back} \end{bmatrix} \\ V \end{matrix}$

16′ $\quad \begin{matrix} [+\text{back}] \\ C \end{matrix} \rightarrow [-\text{back}] / \underline{} \begin{matrix} [-\text{back}] \\ V \end{matrix}$

Rule **15′** requires 6 features, while rule **16′** requires only 5. However, rule **15/15′** is clearly more natural than rule **16/16′**, since it is found with greater frequency in the world's languages. As in the case of natural classes, a conflict is apparent between maximally simple and maximally natural rules. The more simple rule is less natural, and the more natural rule is less simple.

The palatalization case is particularly revealing of the factors at work in determining the naturalness and simplicity of a phonological process. Palatalization is more natural when it occurs only before /i/ because the vowel /i/ is more fronted than the vowels /e/ and /æ/. Since /i/ has the highest tongue position of front vowels, the process of palatalization will always take place first before /i/. Many languages stop the palatalization process here, and this accounts for the great frequency of palatalization before /i/ only. On the other hand, some languages extend the palatalization to other front vowels, such that /k/ becomes [č] before /e/ (fairly frequently) and even conceivably before /æ/ (rare, but attested, for example, in French). The higher a front vowel, the more palatal it is, and the more likely it is to palatalize a preceding consonant. Thus, /i/ is more palatal than /e/, which is more palatal than /ɛ/, which is more palatal than /æ/. This hierarchy must be reflected in phonological theory if the correct relative naturalness values are to be assigned to the various rules of palatalization.

A similar example revolves around the nasalization of vowels, as studied by Chen (1973a). Chen points out that, of the two rules **17** and **18**,

17 $\quad \begin{matrix} \begin{bmatrix} +\text{back} \\ +\text{low} \end{bmatrix} \\ V \end{matrix} \rightarrow [+\text{nasal}] / \underline{} \begin{matrix} [+\text{nasal}] \\ C \end{matrix}$ $\quad$ (nasalization of /a/)

18 $\quad \begin{matrix} V \end{matrix} \rightarrow [+\text{nasal}] / \underline{} \begin{matrix} [+\text{nasal}] \\ C \end{matrix}$ $\quad$ (nasalization of all vowels)

rule **17** is more natural, although **18** is simpler in terms of feature counting. In his investigation of Chinese dialects, Chen reports that some dialects nasalize only /a/ in this environment and that vowel nasalization typically begins with this low back vowel. In other words, before any other vowel can become nasalized before a nasal consonant, it is necessary for /a/ to nasalize. This view has been confirmed in the experimental work of J. Ohala (1971), who reports a greater propensity to nasalize among low vowels. Vowel nasalization thus appears comparable to consonant palatalization, except that the tendency to extend the nasalization process to all vowels is much greater than the tendency to extend the palatalization process to all front vowels. Most languages appear to extend nasalization to nonlow as well as low vowels, because of timing factors involved in the lowering of the velum. While the study of rule naturalness is in its infancy, it is clear that naturalness is not a binary property. Rules are more or less natural or more or less unnatural.

5.2.4 Strengthening and Weakening

Schane (1972) mentions, in addition to natural rules of assimilation, natural rules whose function is to preserve or create preferred syllable structures. It is often observed that consonants and vowels are subject to reduction in certain positions within a syllable or word, while they are relatively stable in other positions, often becoming reinforced phonetically. In order to capture such natural processes which affect syllabic and word structure, the traditional concepts of *strengthening* and *weakening* have been recently discussed within the framework of theoretical phonology (Foley, 1970; Vennemann, 1972a; Hooper, 1973). In particular, it has been suggested that different consonant types should be assigned strength values to capture "phonological relations" between segments, particularly (though not exclusively) as they function in *syllables* (see **6.1.1.1** for discussion of the syllable).

5.2.4.1 Preferred Syllable Structure As pointed out by Jakobson (1941), the unmarked syllable type is CV, that is, an initial consonant followed by one vowel. This is the only syllable type which is found in all languages; in addition, it is the first which is learned in child language acquisition, even in languages having other syllable types. Other syllable types are more or less *marked* or unnatural. A CVC syllable is somewhat unnatural, though it is frequently attested in languages. On the other hand, a VCCC syllable is considerably less natural and is found in relatively few languages.

Evidence for the relative naturalness of one syllable structure over another is seen from the kinds of phonological processes which are introduced in order to create or avoid various syllable types. Thus, rules of insertion or deletion of segments are natural to the extent that they produce more natural syllable structures. Consider, for example, consonant-cluster simplification in Korean (Kim, 1972:162). As seen in the following examples,

19 /əps#i/ → [əp$ši] 'without'
/nəks#i/ → [nək$ši] 'the soul is'
/anč#ət⁺a/ → [an$čə$t⁺a] 'sat'[15]

Korean does not allow syllables to end with a sequence of two consonants. Thus, when a morpheme ends in two consonants and has a suffixal vowel, the second of these consonants is assigned to the following syllable, for example, [əp$ši], not *[əpš$i]. However, as seen in the following forms,

20 /əps#ta/ → [əp$ta] 'there is no'
/nəks#to/ → [nək$to] 'the soul also'
/anč#kəra/ → [an$kə$ra] 'sit!'

when underlying forms with final sequences of two consonants are followed by consonant-initial suffixes, one of the stem consonants must drop (in the above examples, the final /s/ and /č/ preceding the # boundary). These consonants are deleted by a rule of consonant-cluster simplification, since the syllable structures *[əps$ta], *[nəks$to], and *[ənč$kə$ra], which would otherwise occur, are disallowed in Korean. Since this deletion process changes CVCC and VCC syllables to CVC and VC, respectively, it is judged to be natural.

While consonant-deletion processes are widespread in languages, other languages insert segments to optimize natural syllable structures. Consider the following partial rule of epenthesis in Berber (Saib, 1973):

21 Ø → ə / __ C C V

A schwa is inserted before two consonants which are in turn followed by a vowel. Examples of the operation of this rule are seen below:

22 /gnu/ → [əgnu] 'to sew'
/rzu/ → [ərzu] 'to look for'
/fsus/ → [əfsus] 'to be light'
/frra/ → [fərra] 'to sort out'

The effect of this rule is to cause resyllabification just in case a Berber syllable would otherwise begin with two consonants; for example, *[$gnu] becomes [əg$nu]. We have already seen in the case of Yawelmani (see **4.4.2**) that there is a derivational constraint against sequences of two consonants within the same syllable. Berber disallows sequences of two consonants at the beginning

---

[15] The symbol [t⁺] represents a tense or fortis stop, sometimes said to be geminate (or double); see **5.2.4.2**.

of syllables. The resulting syllabification VC$CV is seen to be more natural than $CCV.

The unnaturalness of CC sequences within syllables should, however, be qualified, since some sequences are tolerated much more than others. Thus, some languages permit syllable-initial two-consonant sequences, but only if the second consonant is a sonorant; for example, Ewe allows CLV and CGV syllables, while Gwari allows CNV syllables. In addition, the syllable type sCV is also attested in many languages. However, here there is good evidence that a language will tend to eliminate such a structure. Spanish, for instance, has a rule of vowel insertion of the following form:

23 $\emptyset \rightarrow \varepsilon \, / \, \# \_ s\,C$

The vowel [ɛ] is inserted before word-initial sC sequences, as seen in the following examples:

24   /spaɲa/ → [ɛspaɲa]   'Spain'
      /stufa/ → [ɛstufa]   'stove'
      /skwela/ → [ɛskwela]   'school'

Thus, instead of the unacceptable syllabification *[spaɲa], we now have the acceptable syllabiffcation [ɛspaɲa] (see Hooper, 1973:166–168). Rather than a syllable beginning with sC, we now have a syllable ending with [s], which conforms to the pre-existent syllable structure of Spanish (for example, [dos$] 'two'). Other languages which show a dislike for sCV syllables include Hausa, Hindi, and Pidgin English. While Hausa has native words such as *fuska* [fús$kà] 'face' with sC sequences separated by an intervening syllable boundary, syllable-initial sC sequences borrowed from English must be separated by an epenthetic vowel; for example, [sùkó:là] 'schoolboy' (from English *scholar*). M. Ohala (1972:41) reports that the English loanword *station* appears in Hindi dialects as [isṭešən], [səṭešən], or [ṭešən]. Finally, Pidgin English modifies Standard English *stick* as [sitik], but *strong* as [trɔŋ]. Thus, different strategies are utilized to avoid (break up) undesirable syllable structures.

While rules of insertion and deletion often serve the function of making syllable structure more natural, and are therefore said to be natural themselves, counter tendencies have been noted in the literature. The following rule of short-vowel deletion in Yawelmani was mentioned in **4.4.2**:

25   [−long] → $\emptyset$ / V C __ C V
      V

However, in converting a sequence VCVCV to VCCV, the syllable structure changes from [VCVCV] to [VC$CV]. That is, three open syllables (which, recall, are favored by languages) are changed to a closed syllable followed by an open one. The relatively unnatural syllable structure VC is obtained by this rule. In Grebo, the following alternations are found (Innes, 1966:3):

SLOW SPEECH	RAPID SPEECH	
pèdè[16]	plè	'bald patch'
bòdò	blò	'chalk'
kidè	klè	'chest'
geda	gla	'divide'
kpoda	kpla	'sew'
gbudò	gblò	'room'
fodo	flo	'emptiness'

Grebo appears to be currently undergoing a vowel-deletion (*syncope*) rule by which a vowel is deleted in the environment C __ d V in rapid speech. As a secondary adjustment, resulting intermediate forms such as *pdè* and *bdò* are modified to [plè] and [blò]. Thus, two CV syllables are now becoming one CLV syllable.

In both the Yawelmani and Grebo cases, vowel-deletion rules have led or are leading to less natural syllable structures, assuming that CV is always the "preferred" syllable. These rules are not motivated by syllable structure considerations, but rather by considerations of *word* structure. In general, consonants are deleted and vowels inserted to facilitate natural syllabification. On the other hand, an unstressed vowel in a word can become reduced or deleted by a weakening process (see **5.2.4.3**). Finally, a consonant can be inserted to separate two vowels (a *hiatus*) and thereby make two natural syllables out of a VV sequence. Thus, the following Spanish data from Hooper (1973:182)

STANDARD	DIALECTAL	
	(Astorga)	
veo	veyo	'I see'
leo	leyo	'I read'
creo	creyo	'I believe'

show the need for the following consonant insertion rule:

26 $\emptyset \rightarrow y \,/\, e \_\_ o$

The result is two natural CV syllables.

   5.2.4.2 Consonant Strengthening and Weakening   It has already been noted that a consonant is subject to strengthening and weakening processes relative to its position within syllables and words. Consider first the following changes frequently observed in intervocalic position:

27   tappu > tapu > tabu > taβu > tawu > tau > to:

---

[16] The symbols [è] and [ò] represent the so-called "muffled" vowels found in Grebo and related languages.

The processes illustrated in the above derivation are, respectively, (1) intervocalic degemination, (2) intervocalic voicing, (3) intervocalic spirantization, (4) intervocalic sonorization, and (5) intervocalic sonorant deletion. Finally, it is seen that a form such as [tau] can further develop into [to:] by vowel coalescence. The above processes are frequently referred to as *intervocalic weakening*. As the form progresses from left to right, the intervocalic consonant becomes more and more weak, until it finally drops out. Many of these types of weakening occur prevocalically in Finnish, as seen in the following forms (Skousen, 1972a:571):

STRONG FORM (NOMINATIVE)		WEAK FORM (GENITIVE)	
tapa	'custom'	tavan	/tapa+n/
pato	'dam'	padon	/pato+n/
sika	'pig'	sian	/sika+n/
piippu	'pipe'	piipun	/piippu+n/
lantti	'coin'	lantin	/lantti+n/
kirkko	'church'	kirkon	/kirkko+n/

As seen in the following informal rules,

28a $p \rightarrow v / \_\_ V C \$$

       $t \rightarrow d / \_\_ V C \$$

       $k \rightarrow \emptyset / \_\_ V C \$$

28b $pp \rightarrow p / \_\_ V C \$$

       $tt \rightarrow t / \_\_ V C \$$

       $kk \rightarrow k / \_\_ V C \$$

prevocalic weakening takes place in Finnish if the following syllable is closed by a consonant (the genitive suffix −*n* in the above examples). We observe, in **28a**, intervocalic voicing of /t/ to [d], intervocalic voicing and spirantization of /p/ to [v] (a secondary development from [β]), and intervocalic loss of /k/, through historical intermediate [g] and [ɣ] stages. In **28b**, geminates become degeminated intervocalically when the following syllable is closed by a consonant.

On the basis of examples such as those above, we can propose the following definition of *weakening*: a segment X is said to be weaker than a segment Y if Y goes through an X stage on its way to zero.[17] *Strengthening*, on the other hand, refers to the reinforcement of a segment, as when a nongeminate [p] becomes geminate or double [pp]. Skousen (1972a:569) reports the following strengthening rule (in Savo dialects of Finnish),

29    $C_i \rightarrow C_i C_i / \acute{V} \_\_ VV$

which geminates a consonant following a short stressed vowel and followed

---

[17] I owe this definition to Theo Vennemann.

by a long vowel or diphthong, for example, /tékøø/ 'he does' becomes [tékkøø].

As a second criterion for defining strong and weak segments, it is suggested that stronger segments or segment types are more resistant to weakening processes. On the basis of this observation and the definition given above, consonant types have been categorized according to strength scales based on place of articulation, manner of articulation, and states of the glottis. Foley (1970:90), for instance, provides the following matrix of strength values which are necessary "for a proper interpretation of the Germanic and Spanish consonant shifts":

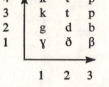

phonological strength

The horizontal strength scale arranges consonants according to their place of articulation, while the vertical strength scale arranges consonants according to manner of articulation and voicelessness/voicedness. About vertical strength 4, Foley states: "The phonological elements k^+, t^+, p^+ have diverse phonetic manifestation. They may appear as long stops kk, tt, pp (Italian, Finnish), as aspirates k^h, t^h, p^h (English), as affricates k^x, t^s, p^f (German)."

Let us first consider the contention that labials are stronger than dental/ alveolars, which are in turn stronger than velars. Foley (pp. 88–89) cites evidence from Danish and Spanish showing that /b/ is stronger than /d/ or /g/. First, from Danish, Foley states that intervocalic voiced velars and dentals become weakened, but not labials (at least not until recently): *kage* [kaɣe], English *cake*; *bide* [biðe], English *bite*; but *købe* [købe], English *cheap*. In the development of Spanish, intervocalic /g/ and /d/ have dropped, while /b/ remains (spirantized to [β]): Latin *lego* > *leo* 'I read,' *credo* > *creo* 'I believe,' but *habere* > *haber* 'to have.'

We have already seen, in our earlier discussion of intervocalic weakening, that geminates are stronger than nongeminate voiceless stops, which are stronger than voiced stops, which in turn are stronger than voiced fricatives, and which, finally, are stronger than voiced sonorants. Thus, Foley's vertical arrangement of consonant types seems motivated. Similarly, on the basis of the examples just seen from Danish and Spanish, the horizontal arrangement by place of articulation seems motivated for at least some languages. There are, however, two problems which should be singled out.

First, this hierarchy is in part language-specific. There is, in particular, good evidence that *dentals* are stronger than both labials and velars in some languages. Skousen (1972b:86), for instance, points out the following alternations between strong and weak consonants in the Adamawa dialect of Fula:

STRONG	WEAK
p	f
t	t
k	h
b	w
d	r
g	y / — [−back, V]
	w / — [+back, V]

Of the six nonimplosive stops, only /t/ does not spirantize, suggesting that it is not only by its voicelessness stronger than /d/, but also by its *dentality* stronger than /p/ and /k/. Recall from the Finnish weak consonants [v, d, Ø] that /k/ deletes entirely while /p/ voices and spirantizes. Since /t/ only undergoes one weakening process (voicing) in standard dialects, it can be argued that it is stronger here, too, that is, more resistant to loss. Interestingly, Vennemann's (1972a:6) proposed relative strength of consonants in Icelandic shows /t/ stronger than /p/ and /k/, as seen in the following scale:

1	2	3	4	5	6	7	8	strength
y	r	l	m	f	s	p	t	
v			n	b		k		
			d					
			g					

Perhaps it should not be surprising to see /p/ and /t/ play the strongest role in different languages, since it will be recalled that Chomsky and Halle (1968) did not distinguish either the labial or dental position as less marked than the other (see **5.1.3**). However, in Luganda, the following situation obtains:

STRONG	WEAK
b	β
d	l
ǰ	y
g	g

Of the four places of articulation, /g/ is the only voiced oral noncontinuant not to weaken (for example, in intervocalic position, as in [òlùgáǹdà]). Since the velar position seems so much weaker than more front articulations (for example, Chen, 1973b shows that *m and *n merge with *ŋ in final position), it is hard to predict the Luganda situation from such hierarchies. While Luganda may very well have once had a weakening of /g/ to [ɣ] and then lost it, the relative strength hierarchies fail to predict why the velar position rather than the labial or dental position should revert back to the original stop articulation.

The second problem derives from the fact that relative strength values are assigned on the basis of weakening processes of a highly specific type. In particular, not enough attention is paid to the *environment* in which the weakening takes place.[18] The following derivation represents the kind of weakening which takes place in word– or syllable-final position:

30   ab > ap > at > ak > a$^{?}$ > a

The processes illustrated are (1) final devoicing, (2) final change from labial to dental articulation, (3) final change from dental to velar articulation, (4) final change from velar to glottal stop, and (5) loss of glottal stop. Similar processes of "final consonant depletion" are discussed by Maran (1971) for Burmese, while Chen (1973b) provides the following sketch of nasal and stop developments in final position in Chinese:

The labial and dental consonants first merge as dentals, which later become velar.[19] Then final velars weaken to become a weak (almost nonexistent) nasal on the one hand or a glottal stop on the other. In the next stage, the weakened nasal and glottal stop fall, leaving respectively a nasalized vowel and a shortened vowel. In the last stage of the development, these vowels become denasalized and unshortened.

By far the most common final weakening process is devoicing. Since this process takes /b/ to [p] and *then on to zero*, /b/ must *in this environment* be interpreted as *stronger* than /p/, although in intervocalic position we have already seen it to be *weaker*. Thus, such strength scales are sensitive not only to the variations of individual languages but also to the exact environment in which the given segments occur, and strength scales such as those of Foley and Vennemann, if they are to have any use in phonology at all, must be made relative to a given *position of weakness*.

---

[18] This is not to say that there are *no* cases of context-free weakening. One good candidate may be the following set of frequently attested changes:

č > š > s > h > Ø

[19] Chen's model also allows for a merger of dentals and velars before the loss of the labials.

We have seen two positions in which weakening typically occurs: inter-vocalically and word- and syllable-finally. In a CVCVC language, these two positions have in common that the consonant appears *postvocalically*. In a language permitting consonant sequences, a consonant can become weakened postvocalically or *pre-pausally*, for example, both consonants of a VCC syllable are potentially vulnerable to weakening. On the other hand, strength-ening typically occurs *word-initially* and *postconsonantally*, that is, in positions where a consonant neither is preceded by a vowel nor occurs before a pause. A simple example from Korean will suffice.[20]

The following strengthening rule of Korean

$$31 \qquad \begin{matrix} [-\text{son}] \\ C \end{matrix} \rightarrow [+\text{tense}] \, / \begin{bmatrix} -\text{son} \\ -\text{cont} \\ C \end{bmatrix} \underline{\quad}$$

states that /p, t, k, s, č/ become tense or fortis $[p^+, t^+, k^+, s^+, č^+]$ when preceded by a noncontinuant obstruent, as in the following examples:

32   /sək#ta/   → /səkt$^+$a]   'to mix'
      /čʰɛk#putʰə/ → [čʰɛkp$^+$utʰə]   'from the book'
      /nopʰ#ke/   → [nopk$^+$e]   'highly'

This tensing of obstruents will, if anything, make $[p^+, t^+, k^+, s^+, č^+]$ less vulnerable to weakening and loss, and must therefore be seen as a strengthen-ing process.

5.2.4.3 Vowel Strengthening and Weakening

We have seen a number of cases of insertion and deletion rules whose effect is to reduce consonant sequences within syllables. Schane (1972) mentions rules whose function is to maximize the perceptual distance between segments. A well-known case is the neutralization of certain vowels in unstressed syllables in some dialects of Russian, as follows:

As seen in this somewhat simplified account, there is a five-vowel contrast /i, e, u, o, a/ in stressed syllables, but only a three-vowel contrast /i, u, a/ in unstressed syllables. /e/ becomes [i], while /o/ becomes [a], when unstressed. While the fact that /e/ moves up in vowel height and /o/ moves down may seem to be asymmetric, the result is the unmarked three-vowel system /i, u, a/. These three vowels are generally claimed to be maximally distinct from each other (Jakobson 1941; see also Liljencrants and Lindblom, 1972). Since the absence of stress on a syllable tends to obscure the identity of the vowel (see **6.2.1.2.3**), unstressed vowels may polarize around the most

[20] I owe the following rule and examples to Kong-On Kim.

perceptually distinct vowel positions, that is, high–front–unrounded, high–back–rounded, and low–central–unrounded. Thus, rules which maximize the perceptual distance between segments are natural.

More generally, vowel reductions found in unstressed syllables are seen as weakening processes. In English, unstressed vowels tend to become lax and ultimately schwa, for example, *away* [əwé], *conform* [kənfórm]. In the two pronunciations of the word *cerebral*, that is, [sérəbrəl] and [səríbrəl], notice that the unstressed vowels are pronounced with [ə]. In addition, in the history of English and French, final unstressed vowels weakened to schwa and then dropped. In French, final "*e*-muet" vowels are indicated orthographically, though usually not pronounced in the standard language; for example, *petite* [pətít] 'little (f.),' *fenêtre* [fənέ:tr] 'window.' Also, complex rules of schwa-deletion occur in the language which, for example, delete the first vowel of *petite* and *fenêtre* in the phrases *la petite* [la ptít] 'the little one (f.)' and *la fenêtre* [la fné:tr] 'the window.' Reducing a vowel to schwa is therefore one step on the way to zero and is thus a weakening process.

Just as different consonants weaken more readily than others, different vowels are more or less vulnerable to reduction and loss. It should therefore be possible to give strength values to vowels as well as to consonants. Hooper (1973:170) proposes the following strength scale for Spanish vowels:

$$\begin{array}{ccccc} e & o & i & u & a \\ 1 & 2 & 3 & 4 & 5 \end{array} \longrightarrow$$

As evidence for the relative strength of high vowels over mid vowels, Hooper cites the following weakening of high vowels in unstressed syllables:

33

LATIN		SPANISH	
díxi	>	díje	'I said.
lácus	>	lágos	'lakes'
plicáre	>	llegár	'to arrive'
lucráre	>	lográr	'to succeed'

Since /a/ has never undergone reduction or deletion, Hooper concludes that it is the strongest vowel in Spanish. /e/ is said to be the weakest vowel, since it "has been deleted in word-final position after certain single consonants, while /o/ and /a/ remain."

In general, the same remarks made about consonant strengthening and weakening apply to vowels. Thus, strength scales are both language-specific and environment-specific. There has been a considerable growth of interest in studying the processes by which segments become reinforced or reduced. Thus, the notions of *coloring* and *bleaching* developed by Miller (1972, 1973) and Stampe (1972b) are roughly comparable to the above notions of *strengthening* and *weakening*. For a critique of these notions, see J. Ohala (1974).

5.2.5 The Phonetic Basis of Natural Rules

There are probably other kinds of natural rules which do not fit neatly into one of the above categories. However, rules which linguists generally agree are natural all have in common the property of being *phonetically* motivated. While there may be cases where the phonetic explanation of a process is not known, in general the rules which are said to be natural can be attributed to either articulatory or acoustic assimilations or simplifications. Let us return to a few cases of assimilation as illustrations.

The rules in **34** and **35** are frequently cited as being natural:

34 $k \rightarrow k^y / \underline{\quad} i$

35 $V \rightarrow \tilde{V} / \underline{\quad} N$

While these processes of palatalization before /i/ and nasalization before /N/ are discussed as natural phonological processes, relatively little attention is given to the fact that **34** and **35** represent processes which are *universally* present in all languages (see, however, Stampe, 1969, 1972b). That is, a [k] will tend to be somewhat fronted before [i] and a vowel will tend to be somewhat nasalized before a nasal consonant. These universal tendencies are, as such, not part of the phonologies of individual languages, but rather belong to the realm of universal phonetics.

While the source of such assimilations is seen to be phonetic and universal, a given language may focus on one or more of these in such a way as to make them part of a language-specific phonology. Something which was automatic or "intrinsic" can thus become nonautomatic or "extrinsic" (Wang and Fillmore, 1961). In other words, something which is usually predictable from universal phonetics can become predictable only from a language-specific phonological point of view. This process of *phonologization*, whereby a phonetic process becomes phonological, can be seen from a comparison of the fronting of [k] in English and Luganda.

While the [k] of the English word *key* [ki] is somewhat fronted, it is questionable whether English has a specific phonological rule which is responsible for this. Since the fronting is slight, it seems preferable to attribute it to universal phonetic constraints on sequences of velar consonants followed by [i]. Luganda, on the other hand, pronounces [k] before [i] with a particularly noticeable palatal offglide. Thus, /èkìkópò/ 'cup' is pronounced [èk^yikópò]. Luganda has *phonologized* a phonetic variation which is usually predictable on universal grounds. While one would expect a [k] to be somewhat fronted before [i], it is up to an individual language to further modify—or exaggerate—the fronting. This is precisely what Luganda has done in this instance.

Thus, the reason natural rules are the way they are is that they are deeply grounded in the universal phonetic properties of speech. In some languages, a universal constraint on phonetic sequences, as just seen, is exaggerated—until it can no longer be predicted solely on the basis of universal phonetics but rather requires a language-specific statement (rule) in the phonology.

A particularly clear example of this involves the following rule, which frequently occurs:

36 $V \rightarrow [+long] / \underline{} [+voice]$
                        C

This phonological rule owes its existence to another phonetic universal which says that vowels are universally longer before voiced consonants than before voiceless obstruents. Numerous phonetic studies have verified this point (Chen, 1970; Lehiste, 1970; Mohr, 1971). In most languages, however, this process represents simply a low-level phonetic statement about the language—again, not a phonological rule that is language-specific, but rather a part of universal phonetics. However, some languages will phonologize this intrinsic property of vowels before voiced consonants by exaggerating the *degree* of lengthening to such a point that it can no longer be attributed to universal phonetics. English is such a language.

As shown by Chen (1970), the vowel-length difference in minimal pairs such as *bat*:*bad* exceeds the normal intrinsic variation found in other languages. The following table represents, for the languages studied by Chen, the ratio computed from the average length of a vowel before a voiceless consonant divided by the average length of a vowel before a voiced consonant (that is, V_t/V_d):

English	.61	Korean	.78
French	.87	Spanish	.86
Russian	.82	Norwegian	.82

In all six languages, it is observed that the length of a vowel found before a voiceless consonant (V_t) is less than the length of a vowel found before a voiced consonant (V_d). As computed by Chen, the closer the ratio approaches 1.0, the less the discrepancy in vowel length in the two positions. Thus, in the above figures, French shows the least difference in vowel length, while English shows the most. Furthermore, it is observed that English falls significantly below the .83 ratio obtained by averaging the remaining five languages. It thus appears that English has extended this vowel-length difference beyond the normal range predictable from the phonetics.

It is not quite clear at this time whether there is an absolute threshold or whether phonologization simply tends to enhance such a discrepancy. Notice, however, that there is an explanation for the exaggerated behavior of English vowel length. Since there is a tendency in English to devoice final voiced obstruents (such as in the word *bad*), the vowel-length discrepancy has come to assume a phonological role, and perhaps ultimately a phonemic role. As has been shown by Deneš (1955), the vowel-length difference in such pairs as *bat* :*bad* is much more important perceptually than any voicing difference which may be present in the final C. It is also relevant here to note that the initial contrast in the minimal pair *pat* :*bat* has been shown to be, perceptually, one of aspirated vs. unaspirated, rather than voiceless vs. voiced. It thus appears that English is in the process of losing its voice contrast in consonants (note the loss of the /t/–/d/ contrast in most intervocalic positions): the final voice contrast is being replaced with a length contrast and the initial contrast is being replaced with an aspiration contrast. Thus, in the terms of Jakobson (1931b), a "rephonologization" is currently taking place.

One way to show that a phonetic universal has been phonologized is to show that the language has exaggerated the *degree* of an intrinsic variation, as we have seen. Another way is to show that a further phonological process is in some way dependent upon the resulting phonetic distinction. The *bat* :*bad* example is quite appropriate. As shown by Labov, Yaeger and Steiner (1972), long vowels derived before voiced consonants (as well as long vowels derived in other contexts, for example, before /s/) have become centralized diphthongs in certain Eastern dialects. Thus, while [bæt] remains as such, [bæːd] (which tends to be pronounced [bæːt]) becomes [beᵊd]. Since the phonological process of diphthongization must refer to the vowel-length distinction, this means that the lengthening of the vowel in *bad* must be part of English phonology.

5.2.6 The Denaturalization of Natural Rules

Such examples can be extended. The basic conclusion is that universal phonetic considerations usually provide the initial motivation for phonological rules, and since this is the case, there will be many rules written in synchronic phonologies which have this aspect of phonetic plausibility. While we have witnessed considerable interest in revealing and formally accounting for the fact that some phonological rules are phonetically plausible and others are not, there has recently been a critical reaction against the use of naturalness as a phonological criterion (Bach and Harms, 1972; Skousen, 1972a). One argument which is raised in this regard is the fact that natural rules tend to lose their naturalness through time. In this section we shall discuss three mechanisms by which rules tend to become denaturalized: telescoping, morphologization, and rule inversion.

5.2.6.1 Telescoping   The phenomenon of telescoping (Wang, 1968: 708) can be defined generally as the loss of an intermediate stage in a phonological derivation. A sound change occurs which interacts with a previously existing phonological rule so as to obscure the naturalness of the latter. An example of this process can be seen in the palatalization of /k/ before [i]. While the original phonetically plausible rule is as follows,

37 $k \rightarrow k^y / \_ i$

the subsequent modification in **38** can enter into the phonology:

38 $k^y \rightarrow \check{c}$

The resulting phonological rule is the familiar one repeated in **39**:

39 $k \rightarrow \check{c} / \_ i$

We have already seen that Luganda has rule **37**, converting /èkìkópò/ 'cup' to [èk^{y}ìkópò]. The tendency of rule **38** to further convert [k^y] to [č] is seen in the dialectal pronunciation of 'cup' as [èčìkópò]. While the [i] environment has surely provided the motivation for the fronting of /k/, it has not provided the motivation for the affrication of [k^y] to [č]. Rather, two separate processes appear to be at work here. The first, as represented in **37**, is a *sequentially* motivated rule, whereby /k/ assimilates in frontness to the following vowel. The second, represented in **38**, is *segmentally* motivated, consisting of the context-free conversion of intermediate [k^y] to [č]. In the terminology of Vennemann (1972b), the first is an *I–rule*, since it *increases* the complexity of a segment, while the second is a *D–rule*, since it *decreases* the complexity of a segment. The segment [k^y] is clearly more complex than the segment [k] (though not in the context / $\_$ i). In addition, in the palatal position, affricates are more natural (or less "marked") than stops (Ladefoged, 1971:41). That it is not the vowel [i] that is directly responsible for the affrication is seen from the fact that [k^y] is just as likely to become [č] before [a] as it is to become [č] before [i]. Thus Gwari speakers, whose language historically converted [k^{y}a] to [ča], frequently repeat the Hausa word [k^{y}âw] 'beauty' as [čâw].

The resulting rule in **39** is thus the result of the telescoping of the two processes in **37** and **38**. In writing a rule such as **39**, therefore, it should be recognized that an important historical intermediate form is by-passed. While the resulting rule in **39** still maintains a general phonetic plausibility (since phonologists speak of it usually as a palatalization process with only secondary affrication), telescoping sometimes leads to rules which are not only unnatural but simply "crazy" (Bach and Harms, 1972).

One such unnatural rule in certain Bantu languages concerns consonant changes which occur before Proto-Bantu *i. We shall limit our attention to the following subpart of a rule found in certain of these languages:

40 $p \rightarrow s / \_ i$

This rule states that /p/ is realized as [s] before /i/. While certain Bantu languages show an alternation between [p] and [s] and presumably therefore a need for rule **40**, this rule is highly unnatural. While the rule of *assibilation* in **41** is attested in languages,

41   t → s / __ i

the change of a labial stop to an alveolar fricative is a relatively rare occurrence. Furthermore, if we wished to hypothesize the derivation in **42**,

42   pi → ti → si

then the change of [p] to [t] before [i] is apparently unattested in languages. Rule **40** represents a telescoping of the following sound changes:

43   pi > pʰi > pˢi > tˢi > si

The steps involved are (1) aspiration of obstruents before the high vowels /i/ and /u/, (2) affrication with an [s] release conditioned by the "grooved" vowel [i], (3) assimilation of place of articulation of the closure to the release of the affricate, and (4) deaffrication. Each of these historical changes is phonetically motivated, though the telescoped product in **40** is not natural in itself. However, since there is no reason to go through all the historical stages of **43** in a synchronic description, the form of the rule in **40** is adopted, however unnatural it may look on the surface.

5.2.6.2 Morphologization

The example just discussed shows how a phonetically plausible rule (for example, the development of a "noisy" obstruent—such as an aspirated consonant—before a high vowel) can become less plausible, and eventually implausible.[21] The resulting rule is, however, still statable as a phonological rule using only phonetic information and grammatical boundaries. A second way in which a phonetically plausible rule can become modified is for the environment to be reinterpreted as a morphological one, a process known as *morphologization* (Kiparsky, 1972; Robinson, 1972; Skousen, 1972a; Vennemann, 1972c, 1973; Hooper, 1973). The classic example is Umlaut in German, where the plural of *Gast* [gast] 'guest' is *Gäste* [gɛstə].

The derivation of the plural form [gɛstə] is seen in **44**:

44   gasti > gɛsti > gɛstə 'guests'

Historically, the plural suffix on 'guests' was, phonetically, [i]. This [i],

---

[21] Many Bantu languages obscure the original motivation for these changes by merging *i and *e as /i/. Thus, some instances of [i] will condition the consonant changes, while other instances will not.

after fronting [a] to [ɛ], was reduced to a schwa. Thus, the original rule was phonetically plausible, as in **45**:[22]

45   a → ɛ / __ C_1 i

The present-day rule must be stated in nonphonetic terms, as in **46**:

46   a → ɛ / __ morphological information such as [+pl], etc.

Since some nouns with /a/ in the singular do not take an Umlaut in the plural, as seen in **47**,

47   With Umlaut   : Gast/Gäste 'guest/guests'
          Without Umlaut   : Tag/Tage   'day/days'

it is even necessary to put a diacritic feature on *Gast* so that it will undergo the rule in **46**.[23]

Morphologization is a common phenomenon, and it is often a particular kind of telescoping. In the above example, the Umlaut rule and the schwa reduction rule have telescoped to yield the rule in **46**.

5.2.6.2 Rule Inversion   A rule which is morphologized is automatically "unnatural," since it is not phonetically motivated. In addition, a rule which changes /a/ to [ɛ] in the plural certainly cannot frequently occur in the world's languages. The third mechanism by which a natural rule can lose its phonetic plausibility is by *rule inversion* (Vennemann, 1972c). Like telescoping, an inverted rule is not necessarily unnatural, as we shall now see in a case from Feʔfeʔ-Bamileke reported by Vennemann (1972c) and discussed in detail in Hyman (1972b).

Part of a general rule of intervocalic weakening in Proto-Bamileke is given in **48**:

48   Proto-Bamileke   d → l / V __ V

Since East Bamileke dialects later introduced a rule deleting word-initial vowels, as in **49**,

49   East Bamileke   V → Ø / ## __

one of the several consonant alternations found in Feʔfeʔ involves that between [l] and [d] exemplified in **50**:

50   Feʔfeʔ   [luu] : [nduu] 'to beg' (perfective/imperfective)

---

[22] In rule **45**, C_1 signifies "at least one consonant." This formalism specifies the lower and upper limits on a sequence of identical segments, e.g., C_m^n stands for "at least *m* instances of C, but not more than *n*," such that C_0^1 means either no consonants or one consonant, etc.
[23] Alternatively, *Tag* could have a *rule exception feature* which would make it exempt from Umlaut. For the treatment of exceptions in phonology, see Chomsky and Halle (1968: 172–176), Kiparsky (1968a), Kisseberth (1970b), Schane (1973b).

This alternation can be captured by either of the following two rules:

51a d → 1 / ## __ (approx. historical rule)

51b 1 → d / n __ (inverted rule)

Rule **51a**, which takes /d/ as underlying and derives [l] word-initially, is closer to representing the original historical rule than is the inverted rule **51b**, which takes /l/ as basic and derives [d] after [n]. In this particular case it is the historical rule (slightly modified) that has become unnatural, since there is no phonetic motivation for /d/ to become [l] word-initially. On the other hand, the inverted rule is natural, since a [+cont] segment such as /l/ can assimilate to the [−cont] specification of a preceding homorganic nasal, thereby becoming [d].

Arguments for the solution in **51b** were presented by Vennemann (1972c). While the motivation for rule inversion is discussed in **5.2.8**, the following example from Schuh (1972) suffices to show that rule inversion, if a valid phenomenon, leads to rule denaturalization.

The history of Hausa and related Chadic languages has been characterized by a number of syllable-final weakenings, which Schuh (1972:390–391) summarizes as follows:

52 *P > w / __ $
     *T > r / __ $
     *K > w / __ $

Velars and labials in the reconstructed proto-language become [w] syllable-finally, while proto-alveolars become a trilled [r]. These changes, known as Klingenheben's Law, are responsible for the following alternations:

SINGULAR	PLURAL	GLOSS
juujii	jibaajee	'rubbish heap'
sawrayii	samaarii	'young man'

The etymological labial consonant /b/ or /m/ is found in the plural form, while the syllable-final reflex [w] is found in the singular form (where the [uu] of 'rubbish heap' can be analyzed as coming from intermediate [iw]). If 'rubbish heap' and 'young man' are set up with the underlying forms /jibjii/ and /samrayii/, then the singular forms can be predicted by the following rule:

53 [+labial] → w / __ $
      C

This rule is phonetically plausible, since syllable-final weakening is a widespread process in languages. On the other hand, if we were to start with the underlying forms /jiwjii/ and /sawrayii/, we would run into two problems. First, the rule required to derive the plural forms would have to be stated in such a way that /w/ sometimes would become [b], sometimes [m], that is, /jiwjii/ would have to be marked with a diacritic [+B] and /sawrayii/ with a diacritic [+M], or else the incorrect forms *jimaaje and *sabaarii might result from the rule. Second, the resulting *inverted* rule would be exceedingly difficult to state and would require considerable morphological information. In the two plural forms given, it looks as though /w/ is becoming [b] and [m] *intervocalically*. Since there is no phonetic reason for /w/ to become a stop in this position, the resulting inverted rule would therefore be unnatural. In conclusion, rule inversion can lead to either unnatural phonetically conditioned rules or morphological rules—or a combination of the two.

5.2.7 Rule Naturalness as a Phonological Criterion

To summarize thus far, it has been seen that the mechanisms of telescoping, morphologization, and rule inversion often destroy the original phonetic motivation of a phonological rule. The question might be raised at this point, why do languages permit the phonetic naturalness of processes to be destroyed? In other words, why don't they fight back?

The problem revolves around the question of whether naturalness is a valid synchronic criterion for evaluating phonological systems. Given the two hypothetical languages L_1 and L_2,

L_1		L_2	
sg.	*pl.*	*sg.*	*pl.*
ba	aβa	βa	aba
da	aða	ða	ada
ga	aɣa	ɣa	aga

no one would deny the naturalness of L_1 and the unnaturalness of L_2. The rules required are given below:

54 L_1 : $\begin{bmatrix} b \\ d \\ \dot{g} \end{bmatrix} \rightarrow \begin{bmatrix} \beta \\ \eth \\ \gamma \end{bmatrix}$ / V __ V

55 L_2 : $\begin{bmatrix} \beta \\ \eth \\ \gamma \end{bmatrix} \rightarrow \begin{bmatrix} b \\ d \\ g \end{bmatrix}$ / V __ V

It is more natural for stops to spirantize intervocalically, as in **54**, than it is for spirants to become stops intervocalically, as in **55**. The situation in L_1 is found much more frequently than the situation in L_2—which, in fact, may never be found.

The question is, is L_2 never found because of the intrinsic unlearnability of this *synchronic* (static) state or because there is no straightforward *diachronic* (historical) source for such a synchronic state? The natural system

in L_1 is obtained from a single natural sound change of intervocalic spirantization. While it is possible to imagine a chain of phonetically plausible
events which would give rise historically to L_2, as seen below,

56   sg. *aba > aβa > βa (intervocalic spirantization, loss of initial vowel)
     pl. *amba > aba   (loss of nasal mark of plurality)

it is significant that L_2 would require the convergence of several changes.
It may, then, be less frequently attested because it requires such a complex
historical source.

In order to refute this statement, it is necessary to find evidence that
naturalness does play a role in synchronic phonology. There appears to be
only counterevidence. First, we should take note of recent arguments to the
effect that speakers often do not "capture" phonological relationships in
terms of natural phonological rules. Skousen (1972a) presents cases in
Finnish where speakers appear to prefer morphologized rules to phonetically
plausible ones (see Kiparsky, 1973 for a critique of Skousen). Recall the
weakening process in Finnish, which applies when an obstruent is in intervocalic position and followed by a closed syllable:

57 $\begin{bmatrix} p \\ t \\ k \end{bmatrix} \rightarrow \begin{bmatrix} v \\ d \\ \emptyset \end{bmatrix} / V\_VC\$$

The following forms are repeated from **5.2.4.2**:

NOMINATIVE	GENITIVE	
tapa	tavan	'custom'
pato	padon	'dam'
sika	sian	'pig'

The -*n* suffix of the genitive construction closes the second syllable and
conditions the change from /p, t, k/ to [v, d, Ø].

As Skousen points out, all of the phonetic information included in **57** is
available to speakers of Finnish—and yet, he claims, speakers seem not to
have knowledge of the phonetic conditioning of the rule. Instead, they
reinterpret the rule as applying in the presence of certain grammatical
suffixes, among which are the genitive -*n* and the inessive -*ssä*, both of which
close preceding syllables. As stated by Skousen (1972a:571), speakers
"memorize that the genitive suffix *n* and the inessive suffix *ssä* take the weak
form of the stem without even perceiving that both suffixes close the syllable."

One of Skousen's arguments derives from the observation that some dialects of Finnish degeminate the -*ssä* suffix to -*sä* but still maintain the
weak consonants. The standard inessive form of /käte/ 'hand' is [kädessä],
which is syllabified as [kä\$des\$sä]. The dialectal form, where the weakened
form of /t/ is [r] instead of [d], is [käresä], syllabified as [kä\$re\$sä]. If

speakers had knowledge of the role of the closed syllable in the weakening rule, they would have changed the [r] of this form back to [t], that is, *[kätesä]. Although the second syllable is no longer closed, speakers do not show even a slight tendency to change [r] to [t]. Thus, Skousen argues that the weakening rule should be revised to include a grammatical environment:

57′ $\begin{bmatrix} p \\ t \\ k \end{bmatrix} \rightarrow \begin{bmatrix} v \\ d \\ \emptyset \end{bmatrix} / \underline{\quad} V$]genitive/inessive,etc.

It is claimed that in the standard dialect, where *-ssä* is maintained, this reanalysis has already taken place. Thus, when *-ssä* is modified dialectally to *-sä*, there is no rule change, only a phonetic change.

While Skousen's examples mostly involve morphologization as the means of capturing a phonological alternation, a more extreme case from Ngwe-Bamileke (Dunstan, 1966) suggests that speakers were not aware of an alternation at all. Ngwe, as well as other West Bamileke languages, is characterized by a rule which deletes the schwa of the class 6 *mə̀–* plural prefix when the stem begins with a labial consonant:

58 mə̀- → m̀ / __ [+labial]
        C

Thus, in the following forms from the related Mbui dialect,

59 /mə̀-búː/ → [m̀búː] 'breasts'
      /mə̀-sòŋ́/ → [mə̄sɔ̄ŋ] 'teeth'

the phonetic form of 'breasts' has lost the schwa of the /mə̀/ prefix (since the stem begins with a labial consonant), while the schwa remains in the form for 'teeth.' Ngwe dialect has modified this earlier state of affairs by replacing the *mə̀–* prefix by the more productive *bə̀-* prefix of another plural class. However, as seen in the following forms,

60 /mə̀–sòŋ́/ > [bə̄sɔ̄ŋ] 'teeth'
      /mə̀–búə/ > [m̀búə] 'breasts'

it is only *phonetic* [mə̀] which is replaced by [bə̀], and not underlying /mə̀/. Since [m̀búə] does not become *[bə̀búə], it appears that speakers failed to see the relatedness of the syllable *m̀–* prefix of 'breasts' to the *mə̀–* prefix of 'teeth.' Thus, when morphological categories such as noun classes undergo levelling, this process takes place on the basis of the phonetic shapes of the prefixes and not on the basis of the underlying morphological identity of the prefixes. Stated differently, the reality of rule **58**, which converts /mə̀/ to [m̀] before labial stems, is not revealed in language change.

The basis of Skousen's argumentation can be recapitulated as follows. It is proposed that a given language has a rule of the following form:

61   A → B / C

The conversion of A to B is conditioned by an environment C. Now, if this environment is destroyed, that is, either modified phonetically or perhaps totally lost, there are two possibilities. First, the language can continue to derive B in the new environment, say D. Or, second, the language can change B back to A, since the conditioning environment is no longer present.[24] Let us say, for example, that a language has the following rule of palatalization:

62   k → č / __ i

A form such as /paki/ will be pronounced [pači]. Now, if the language undergoes a sound change converting *i to [ə] word-finally, the language can react in one of two ways. First it can convert [pači] to [pačə], in which case palatalization appears, on the surface, to take place before [ə]. Or, second, it can change [pači] to [pakə]. In the second case, [č] has reverted back to [k], since the conditioning environment [i] is no longer present. This second alternative provides evidence for the *psychological reality* of the palatalization rule. When [i] started to change to [ə], speakers, well aware of the fact that /k/ was converted to [č] because of this [i], *undid* this rule when [i] was no longer heard phonetically. If it can be shown that speakers undo rules in just such cases, then evidence is obtained for the reality of such natural rules. It should be noted, however, that the more frequent phenomenon is for the language to leave the derived segment in the new environment, that is, [pačə].

A second type of evidence which might be sought for naturalness as a phonological criterion can be outlined as follows. Let us say that a language has the same rule of palatalization of /k/ to [č] before /i/ as in **62**, and that the same change of final [i] to schwa is about to occur. If naturalness is a valid phonological criterion, it should be possible for a sound change to be inhibited only in environments where its application would destroy the phonetic naturalness of a previously existing rule. As seen in the following hypothetical forms,

63   /papi/ → [papi] > [papə]
         /paki/ → [pači] > [pači]   (not *[pačə])

the [i] of [papi] becomes a schwa, but the [i] of [pači] does not, since the naturalness of the palatalization rule would be destroyed (that is, [č] would in the form *[pačə] be derived before the vowel [ə]). Although sound changes

---

[24] A third possibility which should be mentioned is that there will no longer be a rule at all, i.e., A and B will become contrastive or phonemic.

are sometimes blocked by considerations within a paradigm (for example, so that singular and plural forms do not merge; see Vennemann, 1968b; Kiparsky, 1972:196–206), no corresponding force has been discovered which would strive to keep rules natural. Instead, the above examples show the great tendency for rules to become unnatural (see **5.2.6**), that is, to lose their phonetic plausibility and become morphologically conditioned.

5.2.8 Rule Simplicity as a Phonological Criterion

Having questioned the validity of rule naturalness as a phonological criterion (that is, a criterion for what is more readily *learned* as a phonological rule), it is appropriate to return to the notion of phonological simplicity discussed in Chapter 4. In **5.2.6.2** and **5.2.6.3**, the phenomena of morphologization and rule inversion were introduced. The question now arises, when are rules to be represented as morphologically conditioned or as inverted rather than as phonetically conditioned?

Unfortunately, the criteria for choosing between solutions are not entirely clear, although certain clues can be isolated. For instance, consider the Turkish data discussed by Zimmer (1970:91ff):

64   /söylE + Iyor/ → [söylüyor]   'he is saying'
           not *[söyliyor]

In the underlying form, /E/ stands for the archiphoneme "unrounded non-high vowel" (that is, /e/ or /a/), while /I/ stands for the archiphoneme "high vowel" (that is, /i/, /ü/, /ɨ/ or /u/). Although the starred form *[söyliyor] is predicted from the general rules of Turkish phonology, the form [söylüyor] is found instead. To account for this fact, Zimmer considers the possibility of an additional rule of the following form:

65   i → ü / [+round] __ [+round]
                    V   V

The vowel [i] is rounded to [ü] when it appears between two rounded vowels. However, it turns out that the *Iyor* suffix is the only grammatical context which will ever satisfy rule **65**.[25] Thus it is just as easy to represent this rule as morphologically conditioned:

65′   i → ü / [+round] Iyor [__
                    V

We have seen, in the Finnish example, that speakers may attribute an alternation to grammatical rather than phonetic environments; a phonetic

---

[25] While Barbara Robson and Alan Harris have privately expressed reservations about this analysis to me, the problem of what Zimmer calls "accidental reference" to a single morpheme, which results when only one morpheme satisfies the conditions for a phonological rule, is an interesting one.

environment satisfied by only *one* suffix is even more likely to be "mis-interpreted" by speakers, as in the Turkish example. In brief, then, when given the chance to capture a phonological alternation by either a phonetically or a grammatically conditioned rule, there is a tendency toward the latter (see Hyman and Schuh, 1974:94).

In his study of rule inversion, Vennemann (1972c) states that the major factor contributing to this reanalysis is semantic. Semantically "basic" categories tend to be construed as providing the base forms for phonological representations. To reveal the problem facing generative phonology, consider the two hypothetical dialects D_1 and D_2:

	D_1		D_2	
sg.	pap	pak	pa	pa
pl.	papi	pači	papi	paki

In a standard account, we might set up the underlying forms /pap/, /pap+i/, /pak/, and /pak+i/ for both dialects. D_1 would require the phonological rule in **66**, while D_2 would require the phonological rule in **67**:

66 $k \rightarrow č$ / __ i   (palatalization)
67 $C \rightarrow Ø$ / __ ##   (final consonant deletion)

By **66**, underlying /pak+i/ becomes [pači] in D_1, and by **67**, underlying /pap/ and /pak/ both become [pa] in D_2.

Although each dialect starts with the same underlying forms and contains a phonetically-based phonological rule, the synchronic state represented in D_2 is radically more complex than that in D_1. In particular, since the under-lying final consonants can be discovered only by knowledge of the plural forms, which are morphologically and semantically more marked than the singular forms, D_2 poses a problem for the language learner which D_1 does not pose. In D_1, all the necessary information for the application of rule **66** is contained in the unmarked singular form /pak/. The plural pronunciation [pači] is therefore in a crucial way derived from the singular [pak] plus an [i] suffix. In D_2, on the other hand, the two forms [pa] are derived from underlying representations which are based on the plural forms.[26]

If simplicity is to be maintained as a synchronic criterion, and if the notion of simplicity is designed to express the intrinsic difficulty or learn-ability of a language, then the standard account of D_2 fails miserably. For

---

[26] While the [pa]–[pa] homonymity is a problem, it is important to note that we are not talking about this complexity here. Rather, the problem under consideration is the im-possibility of predicting the plural forms [papi] and [paki] from the singular form [pa]. To better understand the fact that there are two distinct problems to differentiate, consider another language where the two singular forms [pak] and [pač] are both [pači] in the plural. This language would also have the homonymity problem, but this time in the *plural* form only. It would still, however, be possible to predict the plural from the singular forms. Thus, the problem which Vennemann claims leads to rule inversion is not found in this language.

there is nothing in the analysis of D_2 that suggests that it is any more complex than D_1. In the framework of rule inversion, rule **67** would be rewritten as **67′**:

67′ $\quad \emptyset \rightarrow$ p, k, etc. / V __ V

The choice of the exact consonant would be dependent on diacritic features, such as $/pa/_p$, $/pa/_k$. Because of the intrinsic complexity of arbitrary morphological classes, this solution would reflect the less simple phonological system of D_2 as compared to D_1. While all of the discussion of Chapter 4 highlighted the attempts of linguists to reveal the *simple* and *general* properties of languages, it is important that a theory of language also reveal *complex* and *nongeneral* properties when they exist.

As a concluding example, let us return to the Maori data discussed in **3.4.1**, which are repeated below:

VERB	PASSIVE	GERUND	GLOSS
hopu	hopukia	hopukaŋa	'to catch'
aru	arumia	arumaŋa	'to follow'
tohu	tohuŋia	tohuŋaŋa	'to point out'
maatu	maaturia	maaturaŋa	'to know'

As seen in the verb stem, all of the forms end in /u/. Yet in the passive and gerund the consonants [k, m, ŋ, r] appear. In **3.4.1** it was argued that in order to predict these consonants the verbs should be represented in their underlying forms as follows: /hopuk/, /arum/, /tohuŋ/, and /maatur/. The following rule of final consonant deletion was proposed:

68 $\quad$ C $\rightarrow \emptyset$ / __ ##

This is the solution which the standard model of generative phonology would lead one to assume. However, Kiparsky (1971), basing himself on Hale (1971), presents a number of indications that speakers are not storing underlying forms with final consonants, but rather setting up distinct classes of suffixes, for example, *kia, mia*. In other words, it is argued that there is not a derivational relationship between forms such as [hopu] and [hopuk], which are found respectively word-finally and before a vowel, but rather a single form /hopu/, with the /k/ being assigned to the suffix rather than to the stem.

Following the principle of rule inversion, one could propose a rule of consonant epenthesis, whereby a consonant is inserted before certain suffixes (for example, /ia/ 'passive' and /aŋa/ 'gerund'):

69 $\quad \emptyset \rightarrow \begin{Bmatrix} k \\ m \\ \eta \\ r \end{Bmatrix}$ / $_{\substack{\text{passive} \\ \text{gerund}}}$ [__

Just as in hypothetical D_2, it would be necessary to place a diacritic on verbs stating which consonant they take. In fact, some verbs would have no diacritic, since they do not take a consonant, for example, /patu/ 'to strike, kill' has the passive form [patua], where the /i/ of the passive has dropped.

The solution representing the passive (and gerund) as a large number of suffixes (/kia/, /mia/, etc.) receives considerable support from the fact that only the /tia/ suffix (which is not illustrated above) is productive. Kiparsky (1971) gives six ways in which this productivity manifests itself:

(1) Stems which are basically nominal are often used verbally in spontaneous discourse; when they are so used, in the passive, they regularly take the ending /−tia/. (2) Derived causatives (formed with the prefix /whaka−/) take /−tia/ in the passive even if the basic verb stem takes another alternant when not in the causative. (3) There is a rule whereby certain adverbials are made to agree in voice with the verbs they modify; these adverbials take /−tia/ in the passive regardless of the shape of the passive ending which the verb itself takes. (4) Borrowings from English, including unassimilated consonant-final ones, take the ending /−tia/ in the passive. (5) Compound verbs derived by incorporating a noun from an adverbial phrase regularly form their passives in /−tia/. (6) In general, /−tia/ can be used when the conventional passive termination for a given verb is not remembered. (pp. 592–593)

Let us look, for instance, at (2). While the verb stem [mau] 'to carry' takes an [r] in the passive form [mauria], the corresponding causative form [whakamau] 'to cause to carry' takes the passive form [whakamautia], and not *[whakamauria]. If the different consonants are to be attributed to different endings on the verb stem, then there is no way to explain why hypothetical /maur/ should not be realized as *[whakamauria] in the passive causative.

It thus appears that there are different classes of suffixes with different initial consonants, and that the correct suffix is chosen with respect either to the verb stem or to a particular grammatical category (for example, causative passive). Since this solution will require diacritics on verb stems, it can be predicted that the difficulty of learning such a language will lead to eventual levelling out of the different consonant classes of suffixes. It is concluded, then, that the correct solution is a complex one, and not one which any present conception of a feature-counting simplicity metric would predict.

6

SUPRASEGMENTAL PHONOLOGY

6.0 The Study of Suprasegmentals

Much of the current research in phonology has focused on units larger than the segment. Stress, tone, and duration (vowel and consonant length) are often claimed to be properties of *suprasegmental* units such as the syllable or word, while vowel harmony and nasalization are also sometimes included under this heading (Firth, 1948; Robins, 1957b). That is, prosodic features such as those just mentioned are best seen as extending over units which can encompass more than one segment. For example, many languages require that all segments within a syllable agree in nasality. Thus, a CV sequence consisting of a voiced labial stop and a low back vowel can be realized phonetically as [ba] or [mã], but not as *[bã] or *[ma]. As seen below,

		SUPRASEGMENTAL ANALYSIS	SEGMENTAL ANALYSIS
[ba]	:	/ba/	/ba/
[mã]	:	/ba/^{N}	/bã/ or /ma/

in a suprasegmental or *prosodic* analysis a nasal *exponent* can be factored out which, by a "mapping rule" (Leben, 1973a,b), is assigned to each segment

186

within the suprasegmental unit (here, the syllable). A segmental analysis, on the other hand, would attempt to assign an underlying [+nasal] feature specification to one segment within each suprasegmental unit and then provide a rule by which neighboring segments assimilate to that feature specification. In the underlying form /bã/, nasality is assigned to underlying vowels. A rule is therefore required to nasalize oral consonants in the context of a following nasalized vowel, as seen below:

$$C \rightarrow [+nasal] / \_\_ [+nasal] \atop V$$

An equally plausible segmental analysis would recognize the underlying form /ma/, where nasality is assigned to the consonant. In this case a rule is needed to nasalize an oral vowel following a nasal consonant, as seen below:

$$V \rightarrow [+nasal] / [+nasal] \_\_ \atop C$$

While both of these rules are "natural" in the sense discussed in Chapter 5, it is also possible to analyze nasalization as a suprasegmental property, as discussed in **6.3.2**.

The issue of whether certain phonological phenomena should be analyzed segmentally or suprasegmentally (that is, prosodically, in the British terminology) has been of concern to phonologists. In addition, many of the central issues in phonological theory have been argued on the basis of suprasegmental phenomena—in particular, stress, but also tone, duration, vowel harmony, and nasalization. It is thus appropriate that the last chapter of this book address itself to questions of suprasegmentality.

6.1 Suprasegmental Units

In the preceding section it was seen that the same phonological data might be analyzed segmentally or suprasegmentally, depending on one's particular theory of phonology. We find not only this potential disagreement among phonologists, but also a second disagreement about *which* suprasegmental units are required in phonology. The term "suprasegmental" is used to refer to both phonological and grammatical units larger than the segment. In both categories there is disagreement.

6.1.1 Phonological Units

Phonological suprasegmentals are those which are defined in terms of the sound segments of which they are comprised. While the boundaries of

these units are sometimes affected by grammatical considerations, phonological units do not in themselves have a grammatical basis or function.

6.1.1.1 The Syllable   By far the most widely discussed phonological
suprasegmental is the syllable. While the study of the syllable has a long
uninterrupted history (see Allen, 1973 and Pulgram, 1970 for references),
there are typically three questions which arise in this context: (1) how does
one define the syllable? (2) how does one determine syllable boundaries?
and (3) is the syllable a necessary concept?

One can readily divide the Shona word *mùrúmé* 'man' into the three
syllables *mù, rú,* and *mé*. Since this word has a CVCVCV structure, its
division into three phonological parts creates three sequences of CV, the
optimal syllable structure. As stated by Malmberg (1963:129), "A syllable
consisting of a consonant plus a vowel represents the most primitive, and
without doubt historically the oldest, of all syllable types, the only one which
is general in all languages." Whenever languages have syllable types other
than CV, complications arise in the exact determination of syllable boundaries. For instance, should a word with the structure CVCCV be syllabified
as CV$CCV or as CVC$CV?

6.1.1.1.1 Defining the Syllable   Before anything can be determined
about syllable division, it is necessary to establish some idea of what is meant
by the syllable. In particular, is the syllable a phonological unit, a phonetic
unit, both, or neither? Most phonologists, to the extent that they have
accepted it, attempt to deal with the syllable as a phonological unit. As such,
words and larger utterances can be syllabified on the basis of the phonotactic
(or sequential) constraints of a given language, subject to certain universal
tendencies.

The syllable consists of three phonetic parts: (1) the *onset*, (2) the *peak*
or *nucleus*, and (3) the *coda*. In a syllable such as *man*, /m/ is the onset, /æ/ is
the peak, and /n/ is the coda. For phonological purposes, however, only a
single division is relevant, namely between (1) the onset and (2) the *core*,
consisting of the phonetic peak and coda combined. This analysis of the
syllable (see Pike and Pike, 1947), as represented below,

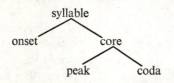

divides a CVC syllable into C-VC rather than CV-C or C-V-C. In so doing,
we are able to capture the important distinction between *open* and *closed*
syllables, as well as between *heavy* and *light* syllables (which will be discussed
in **6.2.1.2.2**). An open syllable ends in a vowel, while a closed syllable is
"checked" or "arrested" by a consonant. A CV syllable thus has a core

with a zero coda, while a CVC syllable has a core with a V peak and a C coda. The initial consonant onset is irrelevant in determining the phonological properties of a syllable.

The basic assumption in phonological approaches to the syllable is that there is an intimate relationship between word structure and syllable structure. Thus, ideally, the same sequential constraints which operate at the beginning of a word should be operative at the beginning of a syllable, even if this syllable is word-internal. Similarly, the same sequential constraints which operate at the end of a word should be operative at the end of a syllable. Attempts to provide universal principles for determining syllable structure are represented by Pulgram (1970) and Hooper (1972). Recognizing a parallel between word structure and syllable structure, Pulgram proposes (1) a principle of maximal open syllabicity, (2) a principle of minimal coda and maximal onset, and (3) a principle of the irregular coda.

By the first principle, a syllable boundary is inserted after every vowel (or diphthong) of a word.[1] Thus, words such as *rooster* and *master* are syllabified as *roo$ster* /ru$stər/ and *ma$ster* /mæ$stər/, so as to make the first syllable open. A problem arises in the form *ma$ster*, however, since the principle of maximal open syllabicity creates a sequence which violates a sequential constraint in English by which the lax vowels /ɪ, ɛ, ʊ, ɔ, æ/ are disallowed in word-final position. Since *ma$ster* contains the vowel /æ/, which does not occur word-finally, it must be resyllabified by the second principle to yield *mas$ter*. As stated by Pulgram (1970), "If a syllable cannot be kept open because its vowel does not occur in word-final position, then as many consonants as necessary—but no more—to provide the syllable with a permissible coda, thereby removing the vowel from the syllable-final position, must be detached from the onset of the next syllable and transferred to the preceding syllable" (p. 48).

A similarly motivated readjustment must occur in a second set of circumstances: " If the syllable cannot be kept open because the consonant or consonants that would form the onset of the next syllable do not occur in word-initial position, then as many consonants as necessary—but no more— to reduce the onset to a permissible word-initial shape must be detached from it and transferred to the preceding syllable as coda, thus closing the syllable" (p. 50). Thus, while *employ* would be syllabified *e$mploy* by the principle of maximal open syllabicity, this would create a syllable-initial *mpl* sequence, which cannot occur word-initially. Thus, the *m* must be sent back to the first syllable to yield *em$ploy*, where each syllable now meets the word-structure constraints of English.

Pulgram's final principle is stated as follows: "If the necessary transfer

---

[1] Pulgram actually refers to a concept of the "section," which is the domain of syllabification.

from syllable-initial to syllable-final position leads to an inadmissible syllable-final group of consonants, then the burden of irregularity must be borne by the coda rather than the following onset" (p. 51). The example which Pulgram gives is Spanish *transcribir*, which, according to the first principle, should be syllabified *tra$nscribir*. Since *nscr* (where *c* = /k/) cannot occur word-initially in Spanish, the *n* must be transferred to the first syllable to yield *tran$scribir*. However, *scr* still is not an acceptable word-initial sequence, and so the *s* must also be transferred to the first syllable, yielding *trans$cribir*. The result, however, is that the first syllable now has a final sequence (*ns*) which cannot occur word-finally in Spanish. The syllabification *trans$cribir* is preferable to *tran$scribir*, since the coda is more capable than the onset of allowing violations of word-structure constraints.

This last principle of Pulgram's correlates with the observation that many languages allow longer consonant sequences at the ends of syllables than at the beginning of syllables.[2] Thus Berber allows CC$ sequences but not $CC sequences (Jilali Saib, personal communication). However, the fact that *ns* can end a syllable but cannot end a word in Spanish illustrates the possibility that syllable-structure and word-structure constraints may occasionally differ. Vennemann (1972a:13) claims that in some dialects of German *radle* (from *radele*) '(I) go by bicycle' is syllabified *ra$dle* (pronounced [ra:dlə]), despite the fact that German does not allow word-initial *dl* sequences. Other dialects syllabify this word as *rad$le*, in which case it must be pronounced with syllable-final devoicing, that is, as [ra:tlə].

While such phonotactic approaches to the syllable define syllable breaks in terms of phonological constraints, less is said about how a word would be carefully divided into parts if spoken slowly. A word such as *bedroom* must be syllabified *bed$room*, because /ɛ/ is not a permissible word-final vowel in English. However, as pointed out by Ferguson (1962:373), many speakers of English differentiate between *bedroom* 'the room in which one sleeps' and *bedroom* 'space for a bed.' While the second is uniformly pronounced [bɛd$ruwm], with correct syllabification following Pulgram's principles, the first is often pronounced [bɛ$druwm], and even [bɛ$jruwm]. In these last two transcriptions, the syllable boundary represents the point at which a pause could conceivably be taken. What we observe is that the *d* of *bed* might be assigned to the following syllable, and that the syllable-initial *dr* sequence might even undergo affrication to [jr], exactly as observed in word-initial *dr* sequences (as in [drɛs] or [jrɛs] 'dress').

Pulgram would call *be$droom* a "nexus," while we might propose recognizing the difference between these two forms as one between different internal boundaries, that is, *bed+room* vs. *bed#room* (see **6.1.2.2**). If we attempted to define the syllable breaks according to whether or not *dr* undergoes syllable-

[2] On the other hand, certain languages, such as Ewe, have CLV (consonant–liquid–vowel) but not *CVL.

initial affrication, we would say that these two words syllabify differently. Since a word such as *excedrin* with no boundary syllabifies as [ɛk$sɛ$drɪn] or [ɛk$sɛ$jrɪn], it would appear to be the general case that VdrV syllabifies as V$drV—unless blocked by a strong boundary (#). However, the criterion of affrication is in direct conflict with phonological syllabification, according to which lax vowels such as /ɛ/ cannot end syllables.

An alternative treatment of the syllabification of VCV sequences, where the first vowel is lax, is to assign the intervocalic consonant simultaneously to both syllables. Thus, the words *bacon* and *beckon* would be syllabified as

[be$kən] and [bɛkən]. In *beckon*, the syllable boundary comes within the /k/, which is sometimes claimed to be long or geminate. In this analysis, *bed+room* would be syllabified as [bɛdrum], which is then optionally subject to affrication.

In addition to such phonological approaches to the syllable, phoneticians have attempted to provide definitions in terms of its physiological properties. While each of these has problems associated with it, the syllable has been defined acoustically in terms of sonority, articulatorily in terms of increasing and decreasing aperture, and, finally, in terms of motor theory, where each syllable is seen to correlate with a chest pulse (for discussion and references see Allen, 1973:38–45). What is clear is that while the syllable may have some physical basis, phonological syllable boundaries do not necessarily correspond to phonetic ones. Hooper (1972:539), for instance, suggests that syllabification rules apply "persistently," that is, they reapply at each stage of a derivation. It is, of course, possible to maintain a phonological syllable boundary in one place (for example, *bed+room* may syllabify as /bɛd$rum/), but a phonetic one in another place (for example, [bɛ$drum] = [bɛ$jrum]). A particularly interesting case of a discrepancy between underlying and surface syllable boundaries occurs in Maxakali (Gudschinsky, Popovich and Popovich, 1970). In this language, the following derivations are found:

/CiC/ → CiəC → CiyəC
/CoC/ → CoəC → CowəC
/CɨC/ → CɨəC → CɨɣəC
/C̃ɨC/ → C̃ɨə̃C → C̃ɨɣə̃C → C̃ɨŋə̃C

Before certain consonants (especially /t/), a rule of diphthongization converts underlying monosyllabic /CVC/ to intermediate *CVəC*. At this point a glide is inserted as follows: [y] after /i/, [w] after /o/, and [ɣ] after /a/ and /ɨ/. In the fourth line, inserted [ɣ] is converted to [ŋ] in the context of a nasalized vowel. Thus, what started out as one phonological syllable is realized phonetically as two surface syllables. In the spirit of Hooper (1972), we can propose that resyllabification must take place after glide epenthesis, for example, *CiəC* becomes [Ci$yəC].

6.1.1.1.2 The Syllable in Generative Phonology   Despite widespread use of the concept in the literature, there have been several linguists (and at least one school of linguistics) who have shown a reluctance to accept the syllable as a viable phonological unit (for example, Kohler, 1966). One argument which has been raised against phonological syllables is that, unlike segments, the location of a syllable boundary *within a morpheme* can never be phonemic. That is, two morphemes such as /a$pla/ and /ap$la/ cannot differ only in their syllable structure. Of course, we have seen in the *bedroom* example in **6.1.1.1.1** that syllable divisions can differ depending on internal morphological boundaries, but they cannot differ independently of such boundaries.[3] If morphemes could differ only in syllabic structure, then an opposition such as that between *bacon* [be$kən] and *beckon* [bɛk$ən] (or

[bɛkən]) could be reinterpreted not as a vowel contrast but as a syllable
 $
contrast, that is, /be$kən/ vs. /bek$ən/. While vowels would in this case be redundantly tense in open syllables, a problem would arise in distinguishing *bake* [bek] and *beck* [bɛk], where the only alternative to the /e/ vs. /ɛ/ opposition would be ad hoc syllable distinctions such as /be$k/ vs. /bek/. One way to prevent such misuse of syllable boundaries is to disallow their use in phonological descriptions.

Because syllable boundaries can be determined automatically from universal principles and language-specific facts about the segments contained in the syllables, generative phonologists have largely worked under the assumption that the syllable is unnecessary in phonology. Instead of writing a rule of syllable-final devoicing as follows,

$$C \rightarrow [-\text{voice}] / \_\_ \$$$

the full segmental determinants of syllable division can be incorporated into the rule. Thus, in a language where a consonant is syllable-final if it is either word-final or followed by another consonant, the devoicing rule can be written with a disjunction:

$$C \rightarrow [-\text{voice}] / \_\_ \left\{ \begin{matrix} \#\# \\ C \end{matrix} \right\}$$

While the use of $ instead of C, V, and ## sometimes simplifies phonological statements (see below), the fact that it can always be avoided is seen as evidence that it has no phonological status.

Recently, however, arguments have been presented for incorporating the syllable into generative phonology (for detailed argumentation, see Hooper, 1972, and Vennemann, 1972a). The position of these linguists is summed up

---

[3] The only reservation that need be made is that some words may function *as if* they have internal morpheme boundaries. Thus, there is a *McAuley Street* in Oakland, California, pronounced [mək$ɔli], which contrasts with *McCawley* [mə$kʰɔli], the name of a famous linguist (Francine Desmarais, personal communication).

by Vennemann (1972a), who states: "All phonological processes which can be stated in a general way with the use of syllable boundaries can also be stated without them, simply by including the environments of the syllabification rules in the formula. My contention is ... that in numerous cases such a formulation would miss the point, would obscure the motivation of the process rather than reveal it" (p. 2). (Compare the conclusion of Hoard, 1971:139–140.) A single example will suffice.

In the following Modern Icelandic data (taken from Vennemann, 1972a:3),

a *hatur*   [ha:tʰYr̥]   'hatred'
b *ofsi*   [ɔf:sɪ]   'violence'

a vowel is lengthened if followed by a CV sequence (as in **a**) but not if it is followed by a CCV sequence (as in **b**). As seen in **c**, however,

c *titra*   [tʰɪ:tʰra]   'shiver'

certain consonant sequences appear to be exceptional in that they allow the preceding vowel to be lengthened. The complete set of such sequences consists of /p, t, k, s/ in the first position and /r, j, v/ in the second. All other sequences of two consonants block vowel lengthening.

On this basis, it would be quite complex to present a rule of vowel lengthening. Vennemann's initial formulation is as follows:

$$[+\text{stress}] \rightarrow [+\text{long}] / \underline{\quad} C_1 (C_2) V$$
$$V$$

Condition: $C_2 = r, j, v$; if present,
            $C_1 = p, t, k, s$

However, the difference between *ofsi* (where vowel lengthening is blocked) and *titra* (where vowel lengthening is permitted) is one of syllabification. An underlying /VCCV/ sequence will be syllabified either VC\$CV or V\$CCV depending on the identity of the consonants involved. Thus, according to the information just given, *ofsi* will be syllabified *of\$si*, while *titra* will be syllabified as *ti\$tra*. The above rule can now be rewritten to reflect this difference in syllable structure:

$$[+\text{stress}] \rightarrow [+\text{long}] / \underline{\quad} \$$$
$$V$$

This rule is considerably simpler than the rule involving a condition on consonant sequences. Of course, in this framework, there would still have to be statements of where the syllable boundaries occur, and in a language such as Icelandic, these statements would be quite complex.

6.1.1.2 Other Phonological Suprasegmentals While the trend appears to be toward general acceptance of the syllable as a phonological unit, there has been much discussion of whether the syllable may be a unit of performance rather than a unit of competence (Fromkin, 1968). That is, un-like the phoneme, which represents an abstract distinctive unit of sound which is part of the speaker's knowledge of his language, the syllable may simply be a unit required for the production or perception of utterances. As discussed by Fromkin, it may be that phonological units larger than the syllable are also units of performance. The notion of a "breath group," for instance, seems directly tied to the speech act rather than to an underlying system of linguistic knowledge.[4] Similarly, Lehiste (1970) argues for sequences of two syllables as a phonological unit: "The disyllabic sequence, consisting of an odd– and an even–numbered syllable, appears as a basic phonological building block out of which words seem to be constructed" (p. 163). In Finnish, for instance, where stress is placed on the initial syllable of a word (and then reiterated in a weaker form on every odd-numbered syllable), Lehiste notes that "the two syllables comprising the sequences tend to have equal intensity, but each successive pair has less intensity than the preceding pair" (p. 164). She also argues that, in Estonian, statements of duration cannot be made with any insight except by reference to both the syllable and disyllabic sequences. Of course, little can be said about where these facts fit into a phonological system until general agreement is reached on what is considered to be com-petence (phonological knowledge) and what is performance (use of that knowledge).

6.1.2 Grammatical Units

It is now generally accepted that grammatical information can often exert an influence on the sound system of a language (see **3.3.2**). Although opinions vary as to what is meant by such entities as *morphemes*, *stems*, and *words*, phonologists frequently find it necessary to refer to such units in their analyses. Grammatical units have played an important role in both the statement of sequential constraints and the statement of phonological rules. For the moment we shall limit our discussion to the above three units, whose boundaries are indicated by ## (full word boundary), # (internal word or stem boundary), and + (morpheme boundary).

6.1.2.1 The Statement of (Underlying) Sequential Constraints Since the morpheme is defined as the minimal unit of meaning, most linguists assume that morphemes are listed in the lexicon. Thus every item in the lexicon has a + boundary at each end. While many linguists have accepted the notion of lexicalized words, that is, polymorphemic forms which for semantic or phonological reasons must be listed in the lexicon (for example, *sílkscreen*, as opposed to a *silk scréen*), it is clear that other words may be generated by means of productive rules of derivational morphology. In a

---

[4] The demarcation of breath groups depends, however, on syntactic phrase and clause boundaries.

recently proposed word-formation component (Halle, 1973), it is assumed that the input to these rules will be morphemes. Since speakers are claimed to have knowledge of the morphemic structure of words (for example, the word *transformational* consists of the parts *trans*+*form*+*at*+*ion*+*al*), the lexicon of a language is viewed as containing an exhaustive list of the existing morphemes. Recall from **3.3.3** and **3.3.4** that one of the aims of phonology (especially generative phonology) is to account for alternations occurring in allomorphs of the same morpheme (for example, the [aɪ] of *divine* as opposed to the [ɪ] of *divinity*).

Parallel with the question of how the lexicon is structured is the question of whether sequential constraints should be stated in terms of morphemes. Recently, Hooper (1972, 1973) and Vennemann (1972a) have argued for constraints on syllables (compare Brown, 1970). The need for syllable-structure constraints may be illustrated by Chomsky and Halle's (1968:417) examples in **a** and **b**:

a blick   **c** abnick (i.e., ab$nick)
b *bnick   **d** *agbnick (i.e., *ag$bnick, *agb$nick)

Although the nonsense form *blick* does not occur in the English lexicon (see **1.6.1**), it is well-formed with respect to the phonological properties of English. On the other hand, the nonsense form *bnick* is not well-formed, since (it is claimed) English *morphemes* do not begin with sequences such as *bn–*. In other words, *bnick* violates a *morpheme structure condition* (see **4.2.1.2**) of English.

Notice, however, that while the nonsense form in **c** is well-formed, the nonsense form in **d** is not. The reason is that the first can be syllabified as *ab$nick*, which yields two well-formed English syllables, but *agbnick* cannot be syllabified in any acceptable way (both *ag$bnick* and *agb$nick* produce unacceptable sequences within a syllable). Even if *abnick* were analyzed as /a + bnɪk/, we would not necessarily expect this to be exceptional in English. In fact, some phonologists may be tempted to analyze the word *agnostic* with a morpheme boundary (that is, *a*+*gnostic*), as in *a*+*moral*, *a*+*sexual*, etc. (compare the semantically related word *gnosis* with an initial orthographic *g*). What seems relevant, however, is not whether *bn* or *gn* begin a morpheme, but whether they begin a syllable. It may turn out that all sequential constraints should be stated in terms of syllables or words, though much work remains to be done in this area.

6.1.2.2 The Statement of Phonological Rules: Boundaries The syllable and word are found to be important in the functioning of phonological rules. In particular, many phonological rules have to be stated with grammatical *boundaries* (for example, word-final devoicing), while other phonological rules cannot assimilate one segment to another segment when certain boundaries intervene. A number of questions concern the nature of boundaries in phonology. Where do they come from? How should they be specified (for example, with features such as [+word boundary])? How many boundaries are there in phonology and what is the relationship between them? The major boundaries used by generative phonologists are ## (full word boundary), # (internal word or stem boundary), and + (morpheme boundary). In addition, a number of linguists (Harms, 1968:110ff; McCawley, 1968:52ff; Stanley, 1973:193) have proposed other grammatical boundaries, which have been represented by symbols such as @, %, &, =, *, !, and −. Some of these boundaries are language-specific and define the domain of a specific phonological process (for example, vowel harmony). Finally, Schane (1973a: 66) uses the symbol ‖ for a phrase boundary.

Different boundaries seem to have different *strengths*, according to the following scale:

$$\overset{\text{Ø} \quad + \quad \# \quad \#\#}{\underset{0 \quad 1 \quad 2 \quad 3}{\longrightarrow}}$$

Of the major boundaries, + is the weakest and ## the strongest. What this means is that ## has the greatest ability to *block* a phonological process from applying across it. One such example, from Feʔfeʔ–Bamileke, was seen in **3.3.2**. Another example occurs in Mandarin (see Cheng, 1973:82–83). In Mandarin, unaspirated noncontinuants become voiced intervocalically as in the following formalization:

$$\begin{bmatrix} -\text{son} \\ -\text{cont} \\ -\text{asp} \end{bmatrix} \rightarrow [+\text{voice}] \,/\, V \underline{\quad} V$$

As seen below in **a**, this rule applies when there is an intervening internal word boundary (#), but does not apply when there is an intervening full word boundary, as in **b**:[5]

a   /tì # tì/   → [tì di]   'younger brother'
b   /lǎu ## tì/ → [lǎu tì]   'old brother' (fig. 'buddy')

Such examples show that ## is stronger than #, since it is harder to penetrate.

That # is stronger than + is seen from the fact that the simple morpheme boundary + is *incapable* of blocking a phonological rule. Thus, Chomsky and Halle (1968:364) have proposed that any phonological rule of the form

A → B / C __ D

---

[5] While some Sinologists may be tempted to view the "neutral" tone as conditioning the intervocalic voicing, there is good evidence that the neutral tone itself owes its existence to boundary reduction (see **6.2.1.2.3**), which in turn causes the loss of stress (see Cheng, 1973).

can be expanded to include sequences of segments interspersed with +
boundaries, as seen below:

$$A \rightarrow B \ / \ C+ \ \_ \ +D$$
$$A \rightarrow B \ / \ C+ \ \_ \ D$$
$$A \rightarrow B \ / \ C \ \ \_ \ +D$$

This claim about the status of + has not been contradicted by any reported
language.

A second function of boundaries is to condition or motivate phonological
rules. That is, there are certain phonological processes which take place only
at a boundary. Some rules take place at a $\#\#$ boundary but not at a $\#$ or +
boundary, while other rules apply at both a $\#\#$ and a $\#$ boundary but not
at a + boundary. In fact, in many cases, having a + boundary is like having
no boundary at all. Recall from **3.4.2** that the rule deleting the /g/ of /ng/
sequences must be made sensitive to a boundary as seen below:

$$g \rightarrow \emptyset \ / \ \eta \ \_ \ \#$$

The following derivations are observed:

/brɪng $\#\#$ hər/ $\rightarrow$ [brɪŋər]	(full word boundary)
/sɪng $\#$ ər/ $\rightarrow$ [sɪŋər]	(internal word boundary)
/lɔng + ər/ $\rightarrow$ [lɔŋgər]	(morpheme boundary)
/fɪngər/ $\rightarrow$ [fɪŋgər]	(no boundary)

In the above forms, the /g/ of *bring her* and *singer* is deleted, since these
have, respectively, a $\#\#$ and a $\#$ boundary. In the forms for *longer* and
finger, the /g/ remains, since neither a + nor the lack of a boundary can
condition deletion of /g/. In other words, it would appear that there are two
internal word boundaries, one of which ($\#$) is like having a word boundary
and the other of which (+) is like having no boundary.

The question now is, what role does + have in phonology? Are there rules
which are conditioned by +? We see in examples such as /g/-deletion in
English that + is a weaker boundary than $\#$. This means that it is less
effective both at blocking and at conditioning phonological processes.
There are, however, certain cases where a phonological rule has been conditioned by a + boundary, for example, the formulation of "velar softening"
by Schane (1973a:95). For our purposes this rule can be formulated as
follows:

$$k \rightarrow s \ / \ \_ \ + i$$

This rule is designed to account for alternations such as the following:

electri*c* [k]	:	electri*c*ity [s]
criti*c* [k]	:	criti*c*ism [s]

If the forms on the right are analyzed with internal + boundaries (that is, *electric+ity* and *critic+ism*), then the above rule will not apply to such words as the following:

a   kill, key, kit, kite (from /kit/? See **3.3.4**)
b   spook#y, hawk#ish, pack#ing

The rule will not apply to the forms in **a** because there is no boundary preceding the high front vowel, while it will not apply to the forms in **b** because the boundary present is not the right one. However, notice that what this means is that the + boundary conditions a phonological rule which is not conditioned by the stronger # boundary. We can conclude either that this is an exception to the hierarchy presented above or that there is something wrong with this (and similar) analyses.

Since #, but not +, is capable of blocking a phonological process, it is not likely that the hierarchy is wrong. While we could simply note this English example as anomalous, there is some reason to consider rewriting the above rule to apply only to *specific* morphemes. Alternations between [k] and [s] are limited to lexicalized words (which originally were all borrowed), or to words built on analogy with these words. Thus it appears that the only productive conversion of [k] to [s] is when the word ends in *-ic*. This change takes place before a highly specific set of suffixes (for example, *-ity, -ism, -ify, -ize*). While this class of suffixes could be abbreviated by the + boundary (or by an arbitrary % boundary, if + were used for something else), it may be just as valid to write the rule as follows:

$$k \rightarrow s \: / \: \_\_\_ \: \{ity, ism, ify, ize\}$$

Or, /k/ in the suffix *ic* becomes [s] before these suffixes.[6] Although linguists like Stanley (1973) have posited numerous boundaries, it seems likely that further research will provide principled constraints on the use of boundaries in phonology.

6.1.2.3 The Transformational Cycle   A major innovation of the generative school of phonology was the introduction of the transformational cycle. Receiving its first statement in Chomsky, Halle and Lukoff (1956), it receives its fullest treatment in Chomsky and Halle (1968). Since, as we shall see, the application of the cycle depends on boundaries, and since almost all of the examples where its use has been argued involve stress, it is appropriate to consider this issue in the discussion of suprasegmentals. However, only the general motivation for recognizing the cycle in phonology will be considered here. For detailed argumentation and exemplification, the

---

[6] An alternative approach is to mark those instances of /k/ which undergo velar softening with a special diacritic, say [+VS]; or, alternatively, one could mark those instances of /i/ and /ɪ/ which *condition* velar softening with such a diacritic. In either case, the rule of velar softening would require that forms which undergo it be marked [+VS].

reader is referred to such works as Chomsky and Halle (1968), Brame (1972a, 1974), Kisseberth (1972), and, for a critique of Chomsky and Halle, Ross (1972).

The examples which will now be discussed are taken from Brame (1972a). In discussing English adjectives ending in -*atory* and -*ative*, Brame points out that there are two stress patterns, as seen below:

a	divínatory	**b**	assímilatory
	inflámmatory		congrátulatory
	oblígatory		antícipatory
	derívative		génerative
	compárative		íterative
	dispútative		ejáculative

In the words in **a**, stress is assigned to the syllable immediately preceding the -*atory* or -*ative* suffix, while in the words in **b**, stress is assigned two syllables before the adjective suffix. Since words such as *derívative* and *génerative* have identical syllable structure—but different stress patterns—one might simply conclude that stress is phonemic (that is, unpredictable) in these adjective forms.

To do this would, however, miss an important fact about stress and word structure in English. Namely, the verbs from which the adjectives in **a** and **b** are derived are consistently different, as seen below:

c	divíne	**d**	assímilate
	infláme		congrátulate
	oblíge		antícipate
	deríve		génerate
	compáre		íterate
	dispúte		ejáculate

The verbs in **d** end in -*ate*, while those in **c** are bisyllabic and do not involve the -*ate* suffix. What this means is that if we were to try to locate an internal word boundary in adjectives such as *derívative* and *génerative*, we would place them differently, that is, *deriv#ative* and *génerat#ive*. (These words may involve + boundaries, that is, *deriv#at+ive* and *géner+at#ive*, though we have already observed the minor role this boundary plays in phonology.) Similarly, two words such as *divinatory* and *sálivatory* would have an internal word boundary at different places, that is, *divín#atory* and *sálivat#ory*. Given the knowledge that adjectives ending in -*atory* and -*ative* are derived from verbs, one can predict the stress of the adjective on the basis of the verb which is contained in it.

There are two good indications that this is in fact what speakers do, that is, they predict the adjective stress on the basis of the verb stress. First, as pointed out by Brame (1972a:68), the word *obligatory* has two possible stress patterns, either *oblígatory* or *óbligatory*. In the first case, the adjective is derived from the verb *oblíge*; in the second case, it is derived from the verb *óbligate*. The word *sálivatory* cannot be pronounced **salívatory*, since there is no verb *to salíve*. Since it receives its stress on the basis of the verb *sálivate*, its stress must be *sálivatory*. A second indication that this is the correct way to view English stress is the fact that English speakers are not always sure of the stress placement in such adjectives when they cannot readily locate a verb inside them. A good example is the word *pejorative*, which has two pronunciations: *pejórative* or *péjorative*. The first stress pattern is built on the basis of a hypothetical verb *to pejóre*, while the second is built on the basis of a hypothetical verb *to péjorate*. Since *pejóre* does not exist, and since *péjorate* is not likely to be known, when English speakers see the word *pejorative* written, they are not sure which way to pronounce it. This analysis seems therefore to have support.

The basic principle of the transformational cycle is that a phonological rule (usually stress placement) operates on a "word within a word" before applying in a second cycle to the complex word as a whole. Rather than representing the internal structure of words by means of the boundaries # and +, we indicate it by means of labelled bracketing, as follows:

$$[\ [\text{deriv}]_V \ \text{at} + \text{ive} \ ]_A \qquad [\ [\text{gener} + \text{at}]_V \ \text{ive}]_A$$

In the above bracketing, V stands for verb and A for adjective. The principle of the transformational cycle is stated as follows:

> Regarding a surface structure as a labeled bracketing [which is generated by the syntactic part of the grammar] . . . , we assume as a general principle that the phonological rules first apply to the maximal strings that contain no brackets, and that after all relevant rules have applied, the innermost brackets are erased; the rules then reapply to maximal strings containing no brackets, and again innermost brackets are erased after this application; and so on, until the maximal domain of phonological processes is reached. (Chomsky and Halle, 1968:15)

In the above examples, we begin by assigning stress to the innermost brackets, that is, $[\text{deriv}]_V$ and $[\text{gener} + \text{at}]_V$. The stress rules proposed by Chomsky and Halle correctly assign the stress as indicated. The brackets are then erased, and we obtain $[\text{derívative}]_A$ and $[\text{génerative}]_A$, with no further modifications needed.

In order to show how a stress assignment rule may apply in a cyclical fashion, let us turn to a different kind of stress phenomenon. Chomsky and Halle (1968:20–22) point out that the same morphemes, *black*, *board*, and *eraser*, combine to yield three different stress patterns:

black board-eraser (board eraser which is black)
  2   1   3

blackboard-eraser (eraser for a blackboard)
  1   3   2

black board eraser (eraser of a board which is black)
  3   1   2

In these examples 1 represents primary stress, 2 secondary stress, and 3 tertiary stress (see **6.2.1.4**). In order to correctly predict these stress patterns, three mechanisms are proposed:

(1) rules for stress assignment to lexical (monomorphemic) items
(2) a compound stress rule
(3) a nuclear stress rule

We shall not discuss the details of (1) here. For our purposes a monosyllabic lexical item receives stress on its syllabic nucleus (that is, a vowel), while bi- and polysyllabic items receive stress according to other rules. The compound stress rule assigns stress as follows (1968: 18):

$$[1 \text{ stress}] \rightarrow \overset{1}{[1 \text{ stress}]} / \underline{\quad} \dots V \dots]_N$$
$$V$$

If within a noun two vowels have [1 stress] (because the noun is morphologically complex, that is, a compound), the first of these receives an additional [1 stress] specification, while the second by convention is reduced by one stress level, that is, to [2 stress]. The stress of the compound *blackboard* is thus derived as follows:

```
[ [black]_A [board]_N ]_N

[  black    board   ]_N    (by lexical stress rule)
   1        1

   black    board          (by compound stress rule)
   1        2
```

The noun *blackboard* consists of an adjective *black* and a noun *board*, as indicated by the bracketing in the first line. In the second line, [1 stress] is assigned to the vowel of each of these monosyllabic lexical items (which in this case are words). At the same time, the innermost brackets are erased. In the third line, the compound stress rule has assigned [1 stress] to *black*, while the [1 stress] of *board* is automatically reduced to [2 stress], yielding the correct stress pattern.

The nuclear stress rule applies in just those cases where two lexical items (words) come together in a phrase but are not compounded. It can be formalized for our purposes as follows:

$$[1 \text{ stress}] \rightarrow \overset{1}{[1 \text{ stress}]} / V \dots \underline{\quad} \dots]_{NP}$$
$$V$$

If within a noun phrase two vowels have [1 stress], the second of these receives an additional [1 stress] specification. Again, by convention, the

[1 stress] in first position is reduced by one stress level. The noun phrase *black board* is thus derived as follows:

[[black]$_A$ [board]$_N$]$_{NP}$

[black   board   ]$_{NP}$ (by lexical stress rule)
  1   1

     black   board   (by nuclear stress rule)
       2   1

As in the previous derivation, we begin with the words [black]$_A$ and [board]$_N$. However, this time they are joined together not as a compound noun but as a noun phrase, that is, an adjective modifying a noun. By the lexical stress rule, [1 stress] is assigned to the vowel of each of these words. The innermost brackets are then erased. At this point the compound stress rule cannot apply, since *black* and *board* are joined not as a noun but as a noun phrase. The nuclear stress rule then applies, assigning [1 stress] to *board* and reducing the [1 stress] of *black* to a [2 stress] specification.

With these rules we are able to account for the stress differences between *blackboard* (1 2) and *black board* (2 1). At this point we are ready to move on to the three stress possibilities which are observed when *black*, *board*, and *eraser* are combined. The derivations are given below (Chomsky and Halle, 1968:21):

a 'board eraser which is black'

[[black]$_A$ [[board]$_N$ [eraser]$_N$]$_N$]$_{NP}$

[black   [board   eraser   ]$_N$]$_{NP}$ (by lexical stress rule)
  1   1   1

[black   board   eraser   ]$_{NP}$ (by compound stress rule)
  1   1   2

     black   board   eraser   (by nuclear stress rule)
       2   1   3

b 'eraser for a blackboard'

[[[black]$_A$ [board]$_N$]$_N$ [eraser]$_N$]$_N$

[[black   board   ]$_N$ eraser   ]$_N$ (by lexical stress rule)
    1   1   1

[black   board   eraser   ]$_N$ (by compound stress rule)
    1   2   1

     black   board   eraser   (by compound stress rule)
      1   3   2

c 'eraser of a board which is black'

[[[black]$_A$ [board]$_N$]$_{NP}$ [eraser]$_N$]$_N$

[[black   board   ]$_{NP}$ eraser   ]$_N$ (by lexical stress rule)
    1   1   1

[black   board   eraser   ]$_N$ (by nuclear stress rule)
    2   1   1

     black   board   eraser   (by compound stress rule)
      3   1   2

In each of these derivations, stress is first assigned within the innermost brackets (that is, to units which do not have internal brackets); these brackets are then erased and stress is assigned within the remaining innermost brackets, and so on. Derivation **b** best illustrates the principle of the transformational cycle. In the first cycle, [1 stress] is assigned by the lexical stress rule to [bláck]$_A$, [boárd]$_N$, and [eráser]$_N$, as indicated. After lexical stress has been assigned, we are left with the bracketing [[bláck boárd]$_N$ eráser]$_N$. Thus, looking at the innermost bracketing, we see that the compound stress rule will apply to [black board]$_N$, changing its 1–1 stress pattern to 1–2. After the brackets around [black board]$_N$ are erased, we are left with [black board eraser]$_N$. At this point a *second* application (or cycle) of the compound stress rule applies, converting the input 1–2–1 stress to 1–3–2. That is, [1 stress] is assigned to the leftmost member of the noun compound, *black*, thereby requiring that all other stresses be reduced by one. By use of the transformational cycle, therefore, the complex stress patterns of English can be adequately accounted for.[7]

6.2 Suprasegmentals of Prominence

The word *prominence* is used as a cover term to include stress, tone, and duration (see Voorhoeve, 1973:1n). While to some linguists only these features are true suprasegmentals, other linguists have analyzed vowel harmony and nasalization suprasegmentally as well (see **6.3**). The features of stress (intensity), tone (pitch), and duration (length) are always present in all utterances (Martinet, 1960:75). Thus, any utterance in any language is characterized by differing degrees of loudness, melody, and rhythm. In addition, it is noted that these three aspects of the speech signal, corresponding respectively to stress, tone, and duration, can, unlike segmental features, be isolated and extracted as a pattern on an utterance. As such, each of these can be easily demonstrated in a medium other than speech. On a guitar, for instance, differing degrees of loudness depend in large part on the force with which a string is plucked, different melodies are obtained by plucking different notes, and different rhythms are obtained by varying the duration of each pluck. Unlike voicing, nasalization, affrication, etc., stress, tone, and duration are "overlaid functions" on segments (Lehiste, 1970:2) which can be produced independently of these segments both by the human voice (for example, humming) and by other modes of production.

---

[7] Notice, however, that the stress patterns can be modified by means of contrastive or emphatic stress. Thus, if one contrasts a *bláckboard eraser* with a *bláckboard stand*, *eraser* may receive contrastive stress (e.g., "I said *blackboard eráser*, not *blackboard stánd*).

6.2.1 Stress

Of the three suprasegmentals of prominence, stress receives by far the most developed treatment in the literature. While this can be largely attributed to the fact that most European languages are stress languages, recent intensive work on tone languages (see **6.2.2**) provides a perspective in placing stress within the wider context of prominence.

6.2.1.1 What Is a Stress Language? Stress has been defined in basically two ways: first, in terms of its *phonetic* properties; second, in terms of its *linguistic function*. We shall first emphasize the function of (word) stress and then turn to its phonetic realization (compare the approach of Garde, 1968).

In looking at various languages of the world which are said to be characterized by stress, it is quickly observed that stress has a *culminative* function. The purpose of assigning stress, as in the first syllable of *dáta* and the second syllable of *detér*, is to mark *one syllable per word* as carrying prominence. That is, there is a culmination of prominence on one syllable, and only one syllable per word (or stress unit) can receive this prominence. While in all stress languages prominence is culminative, it is at this point that stress languages begin to differ.

The major distinction that must be drawn is between *free* vs. *fixed* stress. In a language with free stress, prominence can occur on different syllables (for example, first, last), depending on the word. Thus, in Russian the two words *múka* 'torture' and *muká* 'flour' are distinguished by the fact that in *múka* stress is on the first syllable while in *muká* it is on the second (Trubetzkoy, 1939:188). That we are dealing with a stress language is seen by the fact that there are no Russian words pronounced *múká* or *mŭkă*. Since stress is culminative, there can be no word where all syllables are marked by prominence, nor can there be a word where no syllable is marked for prominence.[8] Since stress can occur on the first syllable in one word but on the second in another, stress is said to be *phonemic* in these languages.

Languages which restrict the placement of stress to one particular syllable within each word are said to have *fixed* or *nonphonemic* stress. Thus, stress is assigned to the first syllable in Hungarian, to the last syllable in Turkish, and to the penultimate (second from end) syllable in Polish. In these languages stress is completely predictable. In a language such as Russian, stress will often have to be marked on lexical items; stress therefore acquires a *lexical* function. In a language such as Hungarian, where the first syllable of every word is stressed, lexical items need not be marked for prominence. Instead, a rule of stress assignment figures among the phonological rules of the language:

$$\$ \rightarrow [+\text{stress}] \, / \, \#\# \, \underline{\quad}$$

---

[8] There are apparently languages which have words lacking stress, for example, Seneca (Wallace Chafe, personal communication), Hungarian (Robert Hetzron, personal communication), and others.

A syllable is stressed in word-initial position.[9] In Hungarian and other languages with fixed stress, stress may have a *demarcative* function (see Martinet, 1960:87). That is, stress signals a word boundary. In this respect it can be compared to languages such as German and Arabic where a glottal stop is inserted stem-initially before a vowel (that is, before the # boundary). Given a stress in Hungarian, we know that we are at the beginning of a word. Thus, it would appear that stress is an aid in processing utterances. In a language with demarcative stress, each stress tells us where we are in the word. In a language with lexical stress, we can merely correlate stress with a different word, though we do not know exactly where in the word we are.

6.2.1.2 Factors Determining Stress Placement   In languages with lexical stress, the placement of the stress within a word is part of the underlying phonological form. Therefore, no rules of stress assignment are needed. In languages with predictable stress, prominence is assigned according to grammatical and sometimes also phonological factors.

6.2.1.2.1 Grammatical Factors   The most obvious grammatical factor in determining stress placement is the word boundary (##). As noted, some languages assign stress to the first syllable, others to the penultimate syllable of each word, etc. The grammatical boundary which is relevant for stress placement may vary somewhat from language to language. Thus, in French, stress is placed on the last syllable of each *sense group*, for example, *de la mairíe* 'from the town-hall,' *la Tour Eifful* 'the Eiffel tower.' If each word were to receive stress on its last syllable we would have the incorrect **lá Toúr Eifful*. In French, then, the word is not a relevant category for stress placement. In other languages, stress is automatically placed on the *stem* of each word. In this case the relevant boundary is #, instead of the full word boundary ##.

In addition to boundary information, stress rules must sometimes make reference to grammatical categories. In **3.3.2** it was observed that in some bisyllabic noun-verb pairs in English, stress is assigned to the first syllable in nouns (for example, *cónvert*), but to the second syllable in verbs (for example, *convért*).[10] In Spanish, stress is assigned to the last syllable of infinitives (for example, *decír* 'to say', not **décir*). Since stress is expected on the penultimate syllable (subject to syllable weight; see **6.2.1.2.2**), infinitives constitute an exception to the general rule. One possibility is to have a *morphologized* stress assignment rule which would make explicit reference to the category "infinitive," much as the English rule must refer to the categories

---

[9] In generative studies such rules are usually written as

V → [+stress]

since stress is seen to be a property of syllabic segments.

[10] There are, however, important exceptions to both of these patterns, some systematic, some idiosyncratic, e.g., *to rével* vs. *to rebél*.

"noun" and "verb." On the other hand, J. Harris (1969:177ff) proposes that infinitives have an abstract final /e/, that is, *decíre* 'to say.' In this case we can first have penultimate stress assignment (*decíre*) and then final /e/ deletion (*decír*). The form *decír* would in this case be only a special exception to the general pattern of stress assignment in Spanish. Since historically there was such a vowel on infinitives, we at least gain some insight into how a morphologized rule (that is, final stress assignment in infinitives) can come into being (see **5.2.6.2**).

6.2.1.2.2 Phonological Factors While languages with fixed stress single out a particular syllable of a word for stress, that syllable may be more or less "stressable" depending on its phonological structure. Recall from **6.1.1.1.1** that the syllable was divided into an *onset* and a *core*. In a CVC syllable, C is the onset and VC the core. In many languages, a syllable whose core consists solely of a short vowel (V) cannot be stressed and stress must pass to a neighboring syllable. Such a syllable is said to be *light*. A syllable whose core consists of a long vowel (V:), a VV or VC sequence, or combinations of these, can be stressed and is said to be *heavy*. This distinction in *syllable weight* is therefore an important phonological variable in the statement of stress placement (Newman, 1972; Allen, 1973).

The best known example of syllable weight comes from Latin. As seen in the following examples (Allen, 1973:51),

a refé:cit
b reféctus
c réficit

stress is assigned to the penultimate syllable in **a** and **b**, but to the antepenultimate syllable in **c**. This difference is, of course, conditioned by syllable weight. Stress is normally assigned to the penultimate syllable in Latin, except when that syllable is light. In this case, the stress is assigned to the antepenultimate position, as in *réficit*, where the penultimate syllable *fi* is light.

In many languages stress can be assigned only to a heavy syllable. Thus, Jakobson (1931a:117) reports that Classical Arabic assigns stress to the *first* heavy syllable of a word. One important observation is that all languages with a heavy vs. light syllable dichotomy have a vowel-length contrast, that is, CV contrasts with CV:, which patterns with CVC. If this were not the case, we would simply have a contrast between open (CV) and closed (CVC) syllables. Apparently no language requires that stress be assigned only to closed syllables. Thus, in the absence of CV:, a CV syllable will always be able to accept stress. Since the same CV functions as a light syllable in languages with a vowel-length contrast and as a syllable equal in weight to CVC in languages without a vowel-length contrast, the explanation for syllable weight as a factor in stress placement cannot be purely phonetic. In **6.2.1.3**, it will be shown that stress has a tendency to lengthen vowels. Thus, if Latin *réficit* were to receive stress on its penultimate syllable, the vowel /i/ of this syllable would tend to lengthen, and /fi/ would threaten to merge with /fi:/. In order to avoid this merger, stress is shifted, hopefully to find a heavy stressable syllable. In some languages (for example, Eastern Chemeris [Itkonen, as reported in Kiparsky, 1972:190]) stress is retracted back further and further until it finds a compatible syllable. In the event that there is no preceding heavy syllable, stress is expected on the first syllable (for example, Latin *réficit*, where *re* is a light syllable).

   6.2.1.2.3 Factors Determined by Stress Placement   In the foregoing discussion we have emphasized the linguistic function of stress. Although stress is seen to be a grammatical feature (which can become part of a lexical entry), somehow speakers have to provide phonetic cues so that the stress can be identified by listeners. Since stress is culminative, it can be assumed that the intention of the speaker is to give prominence or saliency to the stressed syllable. While it was long believed that the primary phonetic cue of stress was *intensity* (that is, the energy expended in producing it), phonetic investigations have revealed that intensity is not a reliable correlate of stress (Mol and Uhlenbeck, 1956; Fry, 1955, 1958). Instead, *pitch* and *duration* (in that order) are much more effective cues of stress than intensity. This has led some scholars (for example, Bolinger, 1958:111) to conclude that "pitch is our main cue to stress."

Part of the reason that stress was viewed in terms of intensity was the feeling that it would have to be radically different from tone (see **6.2.2**). However, since pitch is seen to be the most important phonetic signal of stress, and since pitch is clearly the most important cue of tone, the difference between stress and tone is a *linguistic* one and not a phonetic one. This explains why placing a stress on a given syllable can cause modifications of the segments over which it has domain. Correlating with stress is a changing pitch (usually rising from an unstressed to a stressed syllable and falling from a stressed to an unstressed syllable), greater duration (for example, vowel lengthening in a stressed open syllable), and greater force of articulation (for example, the tendency for consonants to become aspirated or geminated). While the pitch characteristics of a word such as *data*, with stress on the first syllable, are not perceptibly different from a sequence of high followed by low tone in an African tone language, linguistic tone has not been shown to have any of the above effects. Since both stress and high tone correlate with prominent pitch, it must be concluded that the segmental effects of stress are due entirely to its *culminative* function. Both vowel lengthening and consonant fortition signal the prominence of a syllable which has culminative stress.

Since stress has these *intrinsic* properties associated with it, it is not surprising to find languages *phonologizing* (see **5.2.5**) these properties into rules of the language. Numerous cases of *strengthening* in stressed syllables and *weakening* in unstressed syllables are attested, some of which, for example, consonant fortition in Finnish, were discussed in **5.2.4.2.** In Italian, tense stressed mid-vowels undergo lengthening and then diphthongization as follows:

péde → pé:de → píede 'foot'
bóno → bó:no → búono 'good'

Stress causes vowel lengthening and long vowels tend to diphthongize or raise or both (see Labov, Yaeger and Steiner, 1972). An interesting case of weakening in unstressed syllables is reported for Mandarin Chinese (Cheng, 1973) In the following derivation,

/lí pā/ → [lí bə] 'fence'

the second syllable is unstressed. Three things happen as a result: (1) the low back vowel /ɑ/ is reduced to schwa, (2) the voiceless stop /p/ is weakened to [b], and (3) the high tone of /pā/ is reduced to "neutral" tone, which in the above example has *low* pitch. Since these three adjustments are all associated with lack of stress, Cheng (1973:83) concludes: "All the segments in a neutral-tone syllable become lax."

6.2.1.3 Natural Stress Rules Given that the function of stress is to highlight a particular syllable of a word, any rule which contributes to the identification of that syllable's prominence will be considered *natural*; by the same token, any rule which detracts from the prominence of that syllable will be considered *less* natural (or, conceivably, *unnatural*). Rules of stress placement can be evaluated for both their *conceptual* and their *phonetic* naturalness.

6.2.1.3.1 Conceptual Naturalness Conceptually, since stress ideally demarcates word boundaries, the more regular the stress assignment, the more successful it is in fulfilling its linguistic function. A stress rule which requires morphological information (that is, class categories) or which refers to syllable weight is less natural, conceptually, than a rule which operates across the board. In addition, a rule which places stress closer to a word boundary is more natural than a rule which places stress further from a word boundary, at least from a conceptual point of view. In other words, stress tends to stay close to the beginning or end of a word. We therefore do not expect to find many languages which stress the third syllable of a word, since this would require much more calculation on the part of the speaker and the hearer than would languages which place stress on the first syllable. That syllable weight adds to the conceptual complexity of a stress rule is seen from the fact that the Latin phrase *bónacalígula* allows two possible segmentations (Martinet, 1960:87):

a bóna calígula
b bónaca lígula

In **a**, *bóna* receives stress on its penultimate syllable, while *calígula* receives stress on its antepenultimate syllable (its penultimate syllable *gu* is light and therefore cannot accept stress). In **b**, both *bónaca* and *lígula* receive stress on their antepenultimate syllables, since their respective penultimate syllables *na* and *gu* are light and cannot take stress. As pointed out by Martinet, there is no way to predict that *bónacalígula* should be divided up into words as in **a** rather than as in **b**. If stress were completely regular, however, **a** would be pronounced *bóna caligúla* and **b** *bonáca ligúla*.

      6.2.1.3.2 Phonetic Naturalness While conceptual considerations would tend to have stress realized either word-initially or word-finally, penultimate position is favored over final position by languages. There appears to be an asymmetry, since the two most highly favored positions for stress are the first syllable of a word and the second syllable from the end of a word. The attraction of stress from final to penultimate position can be explained by recourse to *phonetic* naturalness. As pointed out in **6.2.1.2.3**, Bolinger (1958) and others have established that (changing) pitch is the primary acoustic cue of stress. Consider the approximate pitch values in the following English words:

perféct (verb)   [__ ⟍]

pérfect (adj.)   [⁻ __]

perféction   [__ ⁻ __]

These words exhibit stress in initial, final, and medial position, respectively. While the stressed syllable in *perféction* rises in pitch from the preceding unstressed syllable and falls in pitch to the following unstressed syllable, it appears that the fall is perceptually more salient than the rise. First, notice that since *pérfect* goes from a high pitch to a low pitch, there is no rise involved at all. Second, if the rise from an unstressed to a stressed syllable were primary, there would be no totally satisfactory way to explain the fall which is observed in *perféct*. Since a low–high sequence in a tone language does not involve such a final fall, this fall cannot be attributed entirely to the fact that this stress is in utterance-final position. In fact, if the final stress in *perféct* did not fall, that is, if the pitch pattern were [__ ⁻], linguists would probably be inclined to call English a pitch-accent or tone-placement language (see **6.2.3.1**). Since a monosyllable such as *bóy* or *gírl* is realized as [⟍] rather than as *[⟋] in stress languages, we can associate a falling pitch contour with underlying stress.

Accepting this position, we can now say that penultimate position is favored over final position, because a falling contour realized over two syllables requires less articulatory effort (note the tendency to level out contour tones in tone languages—see **6.2.2.3.1.2**) and involves greater perceptual prominence—that is, the high pitch of *pérfect* is more salient than the falling pitch of *perféct* (note the tendency of falling tones to become mid or low in tone languages). Since language is characterized by *downglide* in utterance-final position (see footnote 16), a high pitch on the penultimate syllable followed by a low pitch on the final syllable *maximizes* the fall and is thus favored over realizing the falling contour on the one final syllable. Thus, a rule which assigns penultimate stress is more natural from a phonetic point of view than a rule which assigns final stress.

That initial and penultimate positions are the most natural for stress placement is dramatically confirmed in Auca. · In this language, words consist of two parts, the stem and the suffix complex, both of which can be polysyllabic. As reported by Pike (1964:186–187), there are two primary stress rules or "wave trains." First, counting from the *end* of the word, suffixal syllables receive "alternating" stress on every *even*-numbered syllable. Thus, the penultimate syllable will be stressed, as well as the ante–ante-penultimate syllable, etc. A second rule of alternating stress assigns stress to every *odd*-numbered syllable counting from the *beginning* of the word. Thus, the first, third, etc. syllables of a stem will be stressed. A word with four stem syllables and four suffixal syllables will therefore be stressed CV́CVCV́CV#CV́CVCV́CV. In this case a perfect stressed-unstressed pattern is obtained, though Pike points out that interesting complications arise when two stresses "bump" at the stem boundary.

The Auca example reveals that stress rules can apply *iteratively* on every other syllable, starting from the syllable receiving primary stress. Similarly, Lehiste (1970:163–164) points out that Finnish receives initial stress and then weaker alternating stresses on each odd-numbered syllable, that is, CV́CVCV́CV... It appears that alternating stress facilitates the processing of stress. This is particularly clear in a language which has penultimate stress, where alternating stresses establish a rhythm which crescendoes in·penultimate position.

6.2.1.4 Degrees of Stress   In discussing the culminative nature of stress, it was stated that there can be only one (primary) stress per word. As seen in the discussion of the transformational cycle (**6.1.2.3**), however, we spoke of three levels or degrees of stress, which were indicated by the integers 1, 2, and 3 (that is, primary, secondary, and tertiary stress). It is sometimes claimed that English recognizes four levels of stress (Trager and Smith, 1951; Chomsky and Halle, 1968). It is difficult to support this claim, since stress is presumed to be a grammatical (mental) feature, and not directly a phonetic one. In other words, when one stress is judged to be more prominent than another, this decision may be made on the basis of the *grammatical* nature of an utterance rather than its *phonetic* nature. In the English utterances *fíreman* [faɪrmən] and *fíre màn* [faɪr mæn], the first (lexicalized) form is judged to have 1–0 stress while the second has 1–2 stress. We know that the second syllable of *fireman* receives less prominence phonologically than the second syllable of *fíre màn*, since its vowel is reduced to schwa. While this reduced vowel can be expected to be shorter in duration than the nonreduced vowel [æ], the two words appear to have the same pitch characteristics. As pointed out by Lehiste (1970:150), it may simply be that a syllable receiving nonprimary stress may be *heard* as stressed because at some underlying level a major stress is assigned to this syllable (see Chomsky and Halle, 1968:26n). In Lehiste's words, "we 'hear' the underlying phonological form." The words *fire* and *mán* receive [1 stress] by the lexical stress rule referred to in **6.1.2.3**. In *fíre màn* the [1 stress] of *man* is reduced to [2 stress] by the compound stress rule. In *fíreman*, an additional application of the compound stress rule may apply, since this form is lexicalized (that is, it is learned as a single form rather than created by a productive rule). The vowel therefore reduces to schwa, since the *man* syllable is felt to be less and less related to the individual word *mán*, which receives [1 stress]. Thus, speakers may feel that a syllable has greater or lesser stress according to their ability to relate this syllable to another occurrence where it has [1 stress]. In English, the less able speakers are to see such a relationship, the more likely the vowel of such a syllable will be reduced to schwa.

What this means is that speakers may rate syllables on the basis of their *potential* ability to be stressed. This may mean the possibility that a morpheme may be unstressed in one word but the same morpheme may be stressed in another word; or it may reflect that syllable's potential for receiving *emphatic* or *contrastive* stress. Thus, the only way to emphasize *fíreman* (for example, '*I said* fíreman, *not* yeóman') is by placing greater stress on *fíre*. On the other hand, stress can be shifted to the syllable *màn* of *fíre màn*, as in the sentence '*I said fire* mán, *not fire* wóman' (compare *ápple pìe* vs. *àpple píe*). Thus, the *màn* of *fíre màn* may be viewed to be more stressed than the *man* of *fíreman* because it can receive contrastive stress. Of course, it can receive contrastive stress because it retains its literal meaning 'man' as opposed to the meaning 'person' in *fíreman*.

Such demonstrations have caused scholars such as Lehiste (1970:150) to conclude (compare Weinreich, 1954 for Yiddish): "It appears probable that word-level stress is in a very real sense an abstract quality: a potential for being stressed. Word-level stress is the capacity of a syllable within a word to receive sentence stress when the word is realized as part of the sentence." For this reason, secondary stresses often have only "remnants" of primary stress characteristics. While they normally lack the pitch correlates of primary stress, they may have other segmental correlates (for example, failure of a vowel to reduce to schwa in English). A particularly clear example of this is presented from Spanish by Brame (1974). Brame points out that in Spanish, under certain conditions, when the theme vowel /e/ of the third conjugation of verbs is stressed, it becomes [i]. Thus, /débes/ 'you owe' is pronounced [déβes], while /debédo/ 'owed' (past participle) is pronounced [deβíðo]. We do not obtain *[díβes], because the first /e/ is not the theme vowel, and we do not obtain *[déβis], because the theme vowel is not stressed. The stressed vowel, of course, receives [1 stress].

An interesting problem arises in the derivation of adverbs in Spanish. The relevant adverbs are formed by suffixing *mente* to the past participle of a verb, for example, *resignáda* 'resigned,' *resignádaménte* 'resignedly.' As just indicated, the past participle would by itself receive [1 stress] on its penultimate syllable. In the adverb, however, primary stress is assigned to the *mente* suffix, and the underlying primary stress of the past participle is reduced to [2 stress]. Since the correct form involving a verb of the third conjugation is *debidamente* 'justly,' that is, with raising of stressed /e/ to [i], the following derivation is proposed:

[[debeda] mente]

[[debeda] mente]   by penultimate stress rule
      1

[debida   mente]   by vowel raising rule
      1

  debida   mente   by penultimate stress rule
    2   1

In the first cycle, stress is assigned penultimately to /debeda/ and then the stressed /e/ is raised to [i].[11] In the second cycle, penultimate stress is assigned to /mente/ and the primary stress on /debéda/ is reduced to [2 stress]. Although this [2 stress] does not necessarily carry with it the pitch characteristics of a primary stress, speakers will recognize that the syllable *bi* receives [1 stress] in the word *debída* 'owed,' and that in order for the underlying /e/ to become [i] there must be some stress associated with it. Thus, mentally *bi*² receives more prominence than either the preceding *de* or the following *da* syllable (see Hooper, 1973 for a noncyclic approach to Spanish phonology).

6.2.2 Tone

While stress was said to be of a culminative nature, having a demarcative function in many languages, tone more directly resembles segmental phenomena. Although most of the discussion of this section will focus around African tone languages, tone is found in most parts of the world (for example, Southeast Asia, Australia, Mexico).

---

[11] Brame puts the vowel-raising rule after the last cycle, although the correct output is obtained either way. By placing it within the first cycle, however, the hypothesis can be advanced that only *primary* stress has the typical segmental effects of lengthening, raising, diphthongization, etc.

6.2.2.1 What Is a Tone Language?   Pike (1948:3) defines as tonal any language "having significant, contrastive, but relative pitch on each syllable." As seen in the following examples (George, 1970:102),

high : [bá] 'to be sour'
mid   : [bā] 'to cut'
low   : [bà] 'to count'

Nupe has a phonemic contrast between high tone, mid tone, and low tone on any given syllable. The tone marks used in this section are as follows:

For African languages:

high	:	/á/ = H	rising	:	/ǎ/ = R	
mid	:	/ā/ = M	falling	:	/â/ = F	
low	:	/à/ = L	downstep	:	/'á/ = 'H	
					/'ā/ = 'M	

For Chinese (Mandarin)

tone 1 : /ā/ = [⎤] (high)
tone 2 : /á/ = [͝] (high-rising)
tone 3 : /ǎ/ = [͜] (dipping/falling-rising)
tone 4 : /à/ = [͵] (high-falling)

Unlike stress, different tones can lexically contrast in a given phonological environment. In a stress language it suffices to state where in the word (that is, on which syllable) primary stress is placed. Thus in a bisyllabic word there are two possible patterns: stressed-unstressed or unstressed-stressed. In a tone language such as Igbo (see Welmers, 1970), as seen below,

high-high : [ákwá] 'crying'
high-low   : [ákwà] 'cloth'
low-high   : [àkwá] 'egg'
low-low   : [àkwà] 'bed'

four possible tone patterns are found, since H or L can occur on either syllable. In tone languages, there *are* sometimes restrictions on the occurrence of tones, which can be either phonological (for example, the last tone of an utterance must be L) or grammatical (for example, the noun-class prefixes of Bantu have L tone).

Since these restrictions can sometimes be quite pervasive, this means that there will be a lot of redundancy in the distribution of, say, H and L tone. For this reason, Welmers (1959:2) suggests that Pike's definition of one tone per syllable is too strong. Instead, he proposes that "a tone language is a language in which both pitch phonemes and segmental phonemes enter into the composition of at least some morphemes." Thus Nupe /bá/ 'to be sour' consists of the segmental phonemes /b/ and /a/ and the pitch phoneme /'/. As we shall see, some morphemes (for example, grammatical affixes, pronouns) may lack a pitch phoneme (tone), while other such morphemes may consist solely of a tone (with no segmentals).

Pike (1948:5) draws a distinction between *register* tone languages and *contour* tone languages. In a pure register tone language, tonal contrasts consist of different levels of steady pitch heights, that is, perceptually, such tones neither rise nor fall in their production. The Nupe and Igbo examples given above are of this type. A pure *contour* tone language consists of some tones which are not level in their production but rather rise, fall, or rise and fall in pitch. In general, African tone languages are of the first type while Oriental languages are of the second. Thus, the following minimal pairs reveal that in Peking Mandarin, three of the four tones are contours:

/mā/	'mother'	[⎺]
/má/	'hemp'	[˘]
/mǎ/	'horse'	[˘]
/mà/	'scold'	[ˋ]

Since the tone on 'mother' is a level H tone, Peking Mandarin is not a pure or consistent contour tone language.

While in all of the above examples tone has been seen to exhibit a *lexical* function, in many if not most tone languages tone also has a *grammatical* function. Thus, in Shona, tone is used to distinguish between a main and a relative clause:

mwàná ákàwúyá 'the child came'
mwàná àkáwùyà 'the child who came'

In other languages, tone serves to mark different verb tenses, possession and even negation.

6.2.2.2 The Lexical Representation of Tone   Current interest in tone research can be divided into two general categories: (1) the lexical representation of tone and (2) the nature of tone rules. A number of debates have centered around the first of these.

6.2.2.2.1 Segmental vs. Suprasegmental Representation of Tone Perhaps the most lively debate in generative studies of tone centers around the issue of whether tone is a segmental or a suprasegmental phenomenon. Given the tonal contrasts of /bá/, /bā/, and /bà/ in Nupe, the question is whether H, M, and L should be features assigned segmentally to the vowel /a/ or whether tone should be assigned to units larger than syllabic segments (vowels, syllabic nasals and liquids, etc.). Although this controversy is usually stated as a debate between suprasegmentalists and segmentalists, there are at least two separate questions to be answered. The first is whether the syllable is a viable unit for tonal representation and the statement of tone rules. Although tone is sometimes maintained to be a feature on syllables (Wang, 1967:95), generative phonologists have, for reasons which we have seen, tried to avoid syllables and speak instead of syllabic segments as carrying tone. Thus, instead of saying that H tone is assigned to the entire syllable /bá/ 'to be sour' in Nupe, the underlying H tone is assigned to the [+syllabic] segment /á/. It appears that the syllable approach and the segment approach are readily translatable into each other. That is, whether we say that the H tone of [bá] is assigned to the syllable /ba/ or simply to the vowel /a/, the same insights into the tonal structure of Nupe are obtained. We can assume that this is due to the fact that syllables are defined in terms of segments and, as a result, it is always possible to avoid talking about syllables and talk instead of the segments which define them (see **6.1.1.1.2**). Thus, tone is frequently assumed to be a segmental property (Schachter and Fromkin, 1968; Woo, 1969; Maddieson, 1971).

A totally different debate centers around the question of whether tone can ever be assigned to underlying grammatical units, for example, morphemes or words. In both the segment and the syllable approach, tone is assigned to an underlying *phonological* unit, while in this case the possibility of assigning tone to a *grammatical* unit is considered. In the Igbo examples given earlier, a phonological approach would assign H or L to each syllable or syllabic unit, while a grammatical approach would assign H, L, F, or R to each word (or, conceivably, to each morpheme). In the case of F and R, a falling tone would be realized over two syllables as a H followed by a L, while a rising tone would be realized as a L followed by a H.

Depending on whether underlying tone is assigned to a phonological unit (either the syllable or syllabic unit) or a grammatical unit (morphemes, words, or perhaps tone phrases), considerably different tone systems result. Let us say, for instance, that it has been established that a certain language distinguishes H and L tone on monosyllabic words. When we look at words which are longer than one syllable, we expect one of two situations. First, if tone is assigned to a phonological unit, we expect *four* tone patterns on bisyllabic words (H-H, H-L, L-H, L-L), as seen above for Igbo. If, on the other hand, tone is assigned to words, only *two* tone patterns are expected on bisyllabic words (H-H and L-L). That is, a whole word would take either one tone (H) or the other (L), and this tone would be realized throughout the word, no matter how many syllables that word is composed of. As argued by Leben (1971b; 1973a,b), a language having only two tonal possibilities independent of the number of syllables in a word would remain unaccounted for if tone were not assigned to underlying grammatical units. Leben thus states (1971b):

> One fact about Mende [compare Dwyer, 1971] which points to the appropriateness of suprasegmental representation is that a constraint must be stated to rule out the sequence HLH on all morphemes. The following sequences, for example, are impermissible: *ĆV̌; *CV́CV̌; *CV́CV̀CV́. If the sequence of tones is represented as a feature on the morpheme [or word], a single statement of the constraint will cover all morphemes regardless of the number of their syllables; such a general statement might not be formulable if we took tone as a segmental feature. (p. 197)

Leben also shows that certain tone rules cannot be properly understood in the segmental framework, since whole (bisyllabic) morphemes are raised or lowered in pitch as a unit.

If Leben is correct in representing underlying tone suprasegmentally in some languages (for example, Mende, Maninka, Hausa), then Pike's definition of a tone language as having contrastive pitch on each syllable (see **6.2.2.1**) must be modified or abandoned (compare Welmers' definition). In a recent study of Tamang phonology, Mazaudon (1973:85–92) presents a number of arguments for recognizing word-tone in this and presumably other languages of Nepal. Tamang is characterized by four lexical tones, which are referred to as 1, 2, 3, and 4. Whether a word in Tamang consists of one, two, or three syllables, it is assigned only one of four contrastive tones. However, as seen from the following comparison of these tones on mono- and bisyllabic words,

	MONOSYLLABIC	BISYLLABIC
tone 1	[˥˨]	[＼]
tone 2	[—]	[⌄]
tone 3	[⌄]	[◞—]
tone 4	[◝]	[◡◝]

there is not always a perfect one-to-one correspondence in pitch between a given tone on a monosyllabic vs. a bisyllabic word. Thus, although tone 4 is realized on a monosyllable as a L tone (which falls in utterance final position), on two syllables it is realized as a L followed by a falling tone from H to M, that is, L-$\widehat{\text{HM}}$.[12] In addition, Mazaudon (66, 82–84) points out that associated with these different word-tones are different states of the glottis (glottalization, breathiness, etc.), as well as different degrees of duration. She considers—and convincingly argues against—various alternatives to recognizing the word as the unit of tonal representation. Thus, it is not possible to assign an individual tone to each syllable, to recognize a two-way tonal contrast with a movable accent, or to assign tone only to the first syllable of each word (with a phonological rule or rules spreading each tone over a word). Each of these alternative approaches would fail in one way or another to account for the tonal properties of Tamang.

    6.2.2.2.2 Contour Tones vs. Sequences of Level Tones In drawing the difference between the two types of tone languages, Pike (1948) states:

> Contour systems differ from register systems in a number of points: (1) The basic tonemic unit is gliding instead of level. (2) The unitary contour glides cannot be interrupted by morpheme boundaries as can the nonphonemic com-

---

[12] In this section T–T (where T = tone) stands for two tones on two separate syllables, while $\widehat{T_1T_2}$ stands for two tones on the same syllable.

pounded types of a register system. (3) The beginning and ending points of the glides [contours] of a contour system cannot be equated with level tonemes in the system, whereas all glides of a register system are to be interpreted phonemically in terms of their end points. (4) In the printed material examined contour systems had only one toneme per syllable, whereas some of the register tone languages, like the Mazateco, may have two or more tonemes per syllable. (p. 8)

We have already mentioned point 1. Thus Mandarin Chinese is considered to be a contour tone language, while Nupe and Igbo are register tone languages. However, it is not the case that register tone languages lack contour tones. In fact, such languages frequently have rules of tonal assimilation (termed "spreading") by which rising and falling tones are derived (see **6.2.3.1**). Other register languages have contour tones which are the result of two morphemes coming together. In Hausa, for instance, we find a falling tone in one of the two future tenses:

nâ: zó:	'I will come'	mwâ: zo:	'we will come'
kâ:	'you (m.)'		
kyâ:	'you (f.)'	kwâ:	'you (pl.)'
yâ:	'he'		
tâ:	'she'	swâ:	'they'

If we compare the form of these subject pronouns in the past tense,

ná: zó:	'I came'	mún zó:	'we came'
ká:	'you (m.)'		
kín	'you (f.)'	kún	'you (pl.)'
yá:	'he'		
tá:	'she'	sún	'they'

we see that it is possible to recognize a future marker /à/ with L tone, which combines with the underlying form of the subject pronouns, for example, /kí + à/ 'you (f.) will,' /mú + à/ 'we will.' Thus, these falling tones are better analyzed as a H followed by a L which come together across a morpheme boundary.

While most African tone languages with contour tones show evidence that a R should be analyzed as a $\widehat{LH}$ sequence on one syllable, and that a F should be analyzed as a $\widehat{HL}$ sequence, there are a few exceptions. Thus, in the dialect of Kru reported on by Elimelech (1973), there is a H, a L, and a F which can be analyzed as $\widehat{HL}$. However, in addition, there is a rising tone which begins at the level of a H and rises to a "super-high" level, and there is a falling tone which begins at this "super-high" level and falls to L. While these two tones could conceivably be analyzed as $\widehat{HS}$ and $\widehat{SL}$ (where S = super-high tone), this S does not exist as an independent tone. As seen in Pike's third point, this provides some evidence that we are dealing with a true contour tone rather than with a "compound" tone consisting of two level tones on one syllable.

Arguments to the effect that all phonetic contour tones should be analyzed as underlying sequences of level tones have recently been presented in the literature (Woo, 1969). Leben (1973a:123–125) presents evidence which suggests not only that Thai has segmental tone, but also that its contour tones must be analyzed as sequences of level tones, that is, L͡H and H͡L rather than R and F. Since it is languages such as Chinese which Pike refers to as contour tone languages, let us take a closer look at the contours which are found in Chinese dialects. The four tones of Mandarin are specified phonetically as follows (Chao, 1965:33):

tone 1 : [⌐] 55
tone 2 : [ꞈ] 35
tone 3 : [˅] 214
tone 4 : [꞉] 51

That is, tone 1 is realized on a high level pitch (5), tone 2 rises from a M level (3) to H (5), tone 3 falls slightly (from a 2 level to a 1 level) and then rises almost to a H (4 level), and tone 4 falls from H (5) to L (1). While Pike and most other tonologists have the intuition that the tones of Chinese are best seen as single contour units rather than sequences of levels, Chao's notation offers an important insight into the workings of tonal assimilations in Chinese.

In Mandarin there is a tonal assimilation which takes place as follows (Cheng, 1973:44): "In fast conversational speech, a second tone becomes first when preceded by first or second tone and followed by any tone other than the neutral tone." In terms of Chao's notation, this rule can be formalized as follows:

$$35 \rightarrow 55 \ / \ \begin{Bmatrix} 55 \\ 35 \end{Bmatrix} \text{—— T} \quad \text{(where T = any tone except neutral)}$$

That is, a 35 tone goes up to 55 (level H tone) when preceded by a tone which *ends* in H (5) tone. A second rule of assimilation is now presented, from Cantonese, which can be formalized as follows:[13]

$$53 \rightarrow 55 \ / \text{——} \begin{Bmatrix} 55 \\ 53 \end{Bmatrix}$$

In Cantonese a HM (53) falling tone becomes a H (55) tone when followed by a tone which *begins* with a H (5) tone. If we were to state these two rules by

---

[13] Both of these rules are discussed by Mohr (1973).

means of indivisible contours, the following two rules would result for Mandarin and Cantonese, respectively:

$$R \rightarrow H / \begin{Bmatrix} H \\ R \end{Bmatrix} - T$$

$$F \rightarrow H / - \begin{Bmatrix} H \\ F \end{Bmatrix}$$

As written, these rules suffer from several shortcomings. First, while a R becoming a H after a H may be viewed as assimilatory, no explanation is given as to why R becomes H *after* H rather than before H. Similarly, no explanation is given as to why F becomes H *before* H rather than after H. Second, no explanation is given of why R should become H after R, or why F should become H before F. Finally, using units such as R and F fails to reveal that exactly the *same* assimilatory process is responsible for both rules. That is, if we were to write these rules using Chao's number notations, in both Mandarin and Cantonese we would find that a 3 level rises to a 5 level whenever it is wedged between two 5 levels, that is,

$$535 \rightarrow 555$$

In this formulation all of the above shortcomings are avoided.[14] Of course, while this line of argument supports the division of contour tones into sequences of phonetic pitch levels, it still may be the case (subject to verification) that contour tones could represent an indivisible unit on a more abstract level.

> *6.2.2.2.3 Distinctive Features of Tone*   The first attempt in the literature to provide distinctive features of tone is Wang (1967). Closely tied to the question of the kind of features necessary to capture tonal contrasts in languages are those seen in **6.2.2.2.1** and **6.2.2.2.2**, that is, should such features be on segments or on suprasegments and should there be contour tones. In addition, before providing features of any kind, one must establish the realm of possibilities for tonal contrasts. Thus, a limit must be established on the number of possible contrasting tone levels in any given language; similarly, limits must be placed on the number of contrasting contour tones (for example, how many rising tones can a language have?) as well as the number of ups and downs possible on any given tone unit (whether the segment or the syllable).

In general, the features proposed to capture contrasts between different levels of tone mirror those that have been used to capture different vowel heights. Thus, a contrast between H and L in a two-tone language is captured

---

[14] The one remark that must be made is that in Cantonese, while $53 \# 5$ becomes 555, $5 \# 35$ does not become $*5 \# 55$. Thus the exact position of the internal boundary is important in stating the assimilation.

by calling the first [+High] and the second [−High].[15] Given a language with a three-way tonal contrast between H, M, and L, it is possible to use the features High and Low (mirroring the features High and Low used for vowel height; see **2.4.4.2.1**), or the features High and Mid. The latter features are proposed by Wang (1967:97), the former by Sampson (1969:62–63):

	WANG					SAMPSON		
	H	M	L			H	M	L
High	+	−	−		High	+	−	−
Mid	−	+	−		Low	−	−	+

In Sampson's feature notations, M is designated as sharing one property with both H and L, since both H and M are [−Low] and both M and L are [−High]. In Wang's system, M is classed with L, since M and L share a [−High] specification, while H and M share no feature in common. Should a three-tone language reveal a functional similarity between H and M, rather than between M and L, it would of course be theoretically possible to specify M as [+High, +Mid], since it would still be distinct from H.

Languages have been reported with four underlying level tones, as well as five in the questionable case of Trique (Longacre, 1952). For a language with the four tones H, M, 'M, L (where 'M indicates a lowered-mid tone), Wang's features High and Mid can be redistributed as follows:

	H	M	'M	L
High	+	+	−	−
Mid	−	+	+	−

Alternatively, another feature, which Wang calls Central, can be introduced, which could also be used in the event that a clear case is made for *five* underlying tone levels in any language. In any event, other features such as High$_1$, High$_2$, Extreme, Raised, Lowered have been proposed, as well as features intended to capture the relationship between tones and certain consonant types (see **6.2.2.5**). Note, finally, that Maddieson (1972:960) argues from numerous African languages that different tone features should be used depending on the phonological nature of otherwise identical phonetic contrasts. Thus, extending the notion of markedness discussed in **5.1.2ff** to tone, he argues that the same contrast between H and L may be analyzed as [+Raised] vs. [−Raised] in one language, but as [−Lowered] vs. [+Lowered] in another, depending on whether H or L is the marked tone in the language.

Finally, Wang (1967) also gives the contour features Rising, Falling, and Convex. A rising tone will of course be [+Rising], while a falling tone will

---

[15] In the literature tone features are sometimes written in capitals (e.g. [+HIGH]) to distinguish them from vowel height features such as [+high]. In this chapter they are written with an initial capital.

be [+Falling]. A tone which, like Mandarin tone 3, first falls and then rises is specified [+Rising, +Falling], while a tone which first rises and then falls is specified [+Convex]. Superimposed on these contour features are the features, High, Central, and Mid. Thus, [+High, +Rising] designates a high rising tone (for example, the 35 second tone in Mandarin), while [+High, +Falling) designates a high falling tone (for example, the 53 tone of Cantonese). The following formalization of the two tone rules discussed from Mandarin and Cantonese in the last section, taken from Mohr (1973), illustrates the use of these features:

$$\begin{bmatrix} +\text{High} \\ +\text{Rising} \end{bmatrix} \rightarrow [-\text{Rising}] \Big/ \begin{bmatrix} +\text{High} \\ -\text{Falling} \end{bmatrix} - [-\text{Neutral}]$$

$$\begin{bmatrix} +\text{High} \\ +\text{Falling} \end{bmatrix} \rightarrow [-\text{Falling}] \Big/ - \begin{bmatrix} +\text{High} \\ -\text{Rising} \end{bmatrix}$$

While these rules work, they are as unrevealing as the rules written with H, R, and F in the previous section. Thus it should be clear that if tone features are to reveal generalizations not captured by listing tones as units, much work will have to be done in this area. In particular, it will have to be shown that contour features are absolutely necessary and that level tone contrasts should be captured by *binary* features. At present, the evidence for both is inconclusive.

6.2.2.3 Natural Tone Rules   Two recent studies (Hyman, 1973b; Hyman and Schuh, 1974) have provided typologies of natural tone rules and have proposed various universals concerning the nature of these tonal processes. A distinction is drawn between natural tone rules which have a phonetic motivation and natural tone rules which have a grammatical basis. These will be referred to, respectively, as *phonetic* and *morphophonemic* tone rules.

6.2.2.3.1 Phonetic Tone Rules   The two kinds of phonetic tone rules which will be considered here are *assimilation* and *simplification*.

6.2.2.3.1.1 ASSIMILATION   Like rules involving segments, a tonal assimilation can be either *anticipatory* or *perseverative*. In addition, tonal assimilations group themselves according to whether the assimilation is *vertical* or *horizontal*. In a vertical assimilation, tones are raised or lowered in the environment of a higher or lower tone. In an anticipatory vertical assimilation, a tone is typically raised before a higher tone. Thus, Mbui has a rule by which L is raised to M before H:

L → M / __ H

As a result, underlying /nìbúː/ 'breast' is realized as [nībúː]. In a perseverative vertical assimilation, a tone is typically lowered after a lower tone. Thus, by the following rule,

H → M / L __

a H can be lowered to a M after a L. While this lowering process may sometimes involve a horizontal assimilation termed *spreading* (see below), the following Gwari examples show that after L, H becomes M and M becomes 'M:

/gyìwyé dā/ → [gyìwyē dā] 'possessor of money'
/jàakī dā/ → [jàaˈkī dā] 'possessor of donkey'

However, although the Mbui and Gwari examples show vertical raising and lowering, as in a L-H sequence, vertical assimilations generally do not occur when a preceding tone is higher than a following tone, as in a H-L sequence. This fact is represented in the following table:

Vertical Assimilation

NATURAL	UNNATURAL
L-H → M-H	H-L → H-M
L-H → L-M	H-L → M-L

Finally, a third possibility for vertical assimilation in a L-H sequence is that the L may rise as high as the H is lowered. In this case we obtain a M-M sequence (Meeussen, 1970).

Horizontal assimilations result from a nonsynchrony between the tones and the segments (syllables) over which they have domain. In a *partial* horizontal assimilation, a contour tone, either rising or falling, results, as seen in the following typical rules:

L H → L L͡H
H L → H H͡L

A L-H sequence may become a L-L͡H and a H-L sequence may become a H-H͡L, where L͡H represents a rising tone from L to H, and H͡L a falling tone from H to L. Examples from Gwari illustrating these two assimilations are seen below:

/òkpá/ → [òkpǎ] 'length'
/súkNù/ → [súkû] 'bone'

In these examples, the tone of the first syllable *spreads* into the second syllable, creating a contour tone. This spreading process is not complete, since a trace of the second H-tone syllable remains in the LH rise, and a trace of the second L-tone syllable remains in the HL fall.

Complete horizontal assimilation occurs when there is no remaining phonetic trace of the underlying tone of the syllable onto which spreading has occurred. Complete L– and H–spreading are seen in the following rules:

a L H H → L L H
b H L L → H H L

In **a** it is seen that a L can spread over an entire subsequent H-tone syllable only when this syllable is in turn followed by another H, as seen in the following Kikuyu derivation (Pratt, 1972:335):

/gòr/ + /írɛ́/ → [gòrìrɛ́] 'bought' (immed. past)

Similarly, in **b**, a H can spread over an entire subsequent L-tone syllable only when this syllable is in turn followed by another L. As shown by Hyman (1973b:157–159) and Hyman and Schuh (1974:98), complete horizontal assimilation normally involves a telescoping (see **5.2.6.1**) of two separate processes, *spreading* (as seen in the partial horizontal assimilations above) and *absorption*, as seen in the following rules:

L͡H H → L H
H͡L L → H L

Absorption takes place when a contour tone is followed by a tone which is identical to the end point of the contour. Thus, a L͡H rise becomes L before a H tone, and a H͡L fall becomes H before a L tone. The two steps involved in complete horizontal assimilation are therefore represented as follows:

L H H → L L͡H H → L L H
H L L → H H͡L L → H H L

First a contour is created by spreading, and then this contour is simplified by absorption.

While we have seen that vertical assimilations can be either anticipatory or perseverative, horizontal assimilations are nearly always perseverative. This fact is represented in the following table:

Horizontal Assimilation

NATURAL	UNNATURAL
L-H → L-L͡H	L-H → L͡H-H
H-L → H-H͡L	H-L → H͡L-L

Thus, we do not expect a L-H sequence to become a L͡H rise followed by a H, nor do we expect a H-L sequence to become a H͡L fall followed by a L. Spreading normally takes place in a perseverative fashion.

   6.2.2.3.1.2 SIMPLIFICATION   Simplification is the term used to refer to rules by which contour tones are simplified to level tones. The Mandarin rule by which the 35 rising tone becomes a H, and the Cantonese rule by which the 53 falling tone becomes a H are examples of simplification. The process of absorption cited in the preceding section also can be viewed as simplification. In general, tone languages tend to level out contours, though we have seen counteracting assimilations by which new contours are introduced. In the following derivation it is seen that horizontal assimilation can also apply to contours:

$$\widehat{\text{LH}}\ \text{L} \rightarrow \text{L}\ \widehat{\text{HL}} \rightarrow \text{L H}$$

A $\widehat{\text{LH}}$ rise followed by a L becomes, by spreading, a L followed by a $\widehat{\text{HL}}$ fall. By a second horizontal movement, the L of the final $\widehat{\text{HL}}$ fall is dropped at the end of the word. While languages have simplification processes operating on both rising and falling tones, rising tones seem to be less tolerated. Thus, a context-free conversion of all $\widehat{\text{LH}}$ rising tones to H is attested in certain tone languages, for example, Hausa (Leben, 1971a:203).

6.2.2.3.2 Morphophonemic Tone Rules In addition to phonetic rules of tonal assimilation and simplification, tone languages are characterized by numerous grammaticalized rules. These all have in common that they refer to specific morphemes or constructions.

6.2.2.3.2.1 DISSIMILATION Just as dissimilation most frequently is bound to certain morphemes or constructions (see Johnson, 1973), the same is true of tonal dissimilations. The only completely general tonal dissimilation which comes to mind is reported by Leben (1971a:202). As seen in Leben's formalization, in Hausa

$$\underset{[+\text{long}]}{\text{L}\quad \text{L}} \quad \#\# \quad \rightarrow \quad \text{L}\quad \underset{[+\text{long}]}{\text{H}} \quad \#\#$$

a L-L sequence dissimilates to become L-H when the vowel of the second L–tone syllable is long, and when this syllable is in word-final position. Thus, underlying /káràntà:/ 'to read' is pronounced [káràntá:]. With this rule of L-tone dissimilation, Leben is able to explain a number of apparent anomalies in the tonal structure of Hausa (see **6.2.2.3.2.3**).

6.2.2.3.2.2 COPYING Copying refers to the process by which a syllable (most frequently a grammatical morpheme such as a pronoun) is considered to have no underlying tone of its own, but rather receives its tone from a neighboring syllable. In Kru, the relative clause marker /a/ takes H tone after a H-tone verb, and L tone after a L-tone verb. Since its tone is always identical to that of the verb stem which immediately precedes it, this morpheme is represented with no underlying tone. A rule of tone copying will assign it the correct phonetic tone.

6.2.2.3.2.3 POLARIZATION As in the case of copying, rules of tone polarization assume a morpheme with no underlying tone. In this case, however, the morpheme is assigned a tone which is *opposite* to that of the neighboring syllable from which it gets its tone. In Hausa, direct-object pronouns are polarized with respect to the tone of the preceding verb, for example, [mún ká:mà ší:] 'we seized it' vs. [mún sàyé: šì:] 'we bought it.'

In the first phrase /ši:/ takes H tone, since the verb 'to seize' ends in L tone; in the second phrase, /ši:/ takes L tone, since the verb 'to buy' ends in H tone. The rule of dissimilation mentioned in **6.2.2.3.2.1** *follows* this rule of polarization, as seen below:

/mún káràntà: ši/ → mún káràntà: ší: → [mún káràntà: ší:] 'we read it'

The L-tone dissimilation raises the last syllable of /káràntà:/ to H only after the pronoun /ši:/ is polarized to this L, becoming a H tone. If the two rules were to work in the opposite order, the wrong result would be obtained:

/mún káràntà: ši:/ → mún káràntá: ši: → *[mún káràntá: šì:]

Thus the only exception to the polarization of direct-object pronouns is explained by Leben's rule of L-tone dissimilation.

　　6.2.2.3.2.4 REPLACEMENT   By replacement is meant the process by which the inherent tone of a morpheme is replaced by a grammatical tone. Thus, in Igbo, the imperative is usually constructed by replacing the first syllable with L tone and adding a suffix:

/rí/ 'eat' → [rì-é] 'eat!'

Tone replacement frequently takes place in the verb paradigm and in noun-noun compounding. For example, in Mandarin, all four tones are replaced by the so-called "neutral" tone in noun compounding (Cheng, 1973:54ff).

　　6.2.2.3.2.5 FLOATING TONES   In many cases where one might be tempted to write a morphologized rule of tone alternation, an underlying tone can be posited which has no underlying segments. Compare, for example, the following realizations of the phrase 'jaw of monkey' in two Igbo dialects:

Central Igbo : [àgbà] + [èŋwè] → [àgbá èŋwè]
Aboh Igbo   : [ègbà] + [èŋwè] → [ègbà éŋwè]

In both cases there appears to be a H-tone influence between the two nouns. Instead of writing a rule by which L becomes H in possessive constructions, an underlying H tone marker 'of' is recognized, as in the following underlying forms (see Voorhoeve, Meeussen and de Blois, 1969; Welmers, 1970):

Central Igbo : /àgbà ´ èŋwè/
Aboh Igbo   : /ègbà ´ èŋwè/

In Central Igbo this "floating" H tone is assigned to the left, while in Aboh Igbo it is assigned to the right. Such floating tones often explain otherwise baffling tonal modifications which occur when words and morphemes are strung together.

　　6.2.2.4 Terraced-Level Languages   A number of African languages exhibit tonal properties which prompted Welmers (1959:3) to distinguish between *discrete-level* and *terraced-level* tone systems. In the former, each "toneme" is restricted to a relatively narrow pitch range and there is usually no "phonemic overlapping" (see **3.2.1**). That is, given a three-tone language with H, M, and L, H will be higher than M and M higher than L anywhere in the sentence. To illustrate this, Welmers presents the following Jukun sentence meaning 'who brought these yams?'':

/áni zè súrà à syī ní bi/ → [⎺ — _ _ ⎺ _ _ — ⎺ —]

In numbers we could represent this as 3–2–1–3–1–1–2–3–2.

    6.2.2.4.1 Downdrift   In many African languages, on the other hand, a sequence H-L-H is not realized as [⎺ _ ⎺], but rather as [⎺ _ —]. That is, the two H tones are not pronounced on the same pitch level (though they are *phonologically* identical), but rather the second H is lower in pitch than the first. Stated differently, the interval from H to L is greater than from L to H. This phenomenon, known as *downdrift*, applies progressively to each H preceded by a L, as seen in the following Igbo sentence:

    ọ̀ nà áŋwà ịnyà ígwè   ' he is trying to ride a bicycle'
    H L H L H L H L

[⎺ _ ⎺ _ ⎺ _ ⎺ _]

In the above example, the downdrifting effect extends over several H-L-H sequences. As shown in phonetic brackets, the L tones which intervene between the H tones are also subject to downdrift, though the degree of lowering varies from language to language. In Hausa, for instance, a H late in a sentence can downdrift to a pitch level which is phonetically *lower* than a L which appears early in the sentence, as seen below:

    Bà lá: dà Shé: hù zá: sù zó: 'Bala and Shehu will come'
    L H L H L H L H

[_ ⎺ _ ⎺ _ _ _]

If we were to assign pitch integers to the different tones, we would have a sequence 4–6–3–5–2–4–1–3. Thus, the 4 of the initial L is higher than the 3 of the final H. Numerous formalizations of downdrift have been devised to assign such integers (Schachter and Fromkin, 1968:108; Voorhoeve, Meeussen and de Blois, 1969:82; Carrell, 1970:98; Williamson, 1970; Fromkin, 1972:56–57; Schadeberg, 1972; Peters, 1973; for theoretical discussion, see Stewart, 1971). What is consistent in the above integers is that L is always two steps below the last H. Also, H_2 in a H_1–L–H_2 sequence will be realized one step below H_1, and L_2 in a L_1–H–L_2 sequence will be realized one step below L_1. The assigning of an underlying tone will therefore not be done on the basis of absolute pitch; rather, it will be done on the basis of the relationship of a given phonetic pitch to surrounding pitches.

6.2.2.4.2 Downstep While downdrift represents an automatic lowering process (see, however, **6.2.2.4.3**), a lowered H receives phonemic status when a L which "conditions" downdrift is lost (either through deletion or through assimilation). The standard example comes from Twi (Fromkin, 1972:57):

	/mí ɔ̀bú/	'my stone'
pitch-assignment:	3 1 3	
downdrift:	2	
vowel deletion:	Ø	
	[mí Ꞌbú]	
	3 2	

First the integers 3 and 1 are assigned to H and L, respectively, in such phrases (see Fromkin, 1972; Peters, 1973 for more detailed discussion). By downdrift, the 3 of the second H is lowered to 2. At this point a rule of vowel deletion deletes /ɔ̀/, and the result is a 3–2 sequence, that is, a H tone followed by a *downstepped* ꞋH. Since on the surface we now have a phonetic contrast between H-H, H-L, and H-ꞋH, a new "toneme" has come into existence.

Many of these downsteps can be predicted morphophonemically, as in the above example. Others, however, cannot be, and must be treated as a third tone. As pointed out by Welmers (1959:3), it would be mistaken to call this tone a M, since this tone does not contrast with H after L (see Tadadjeu, 1974 for a counterexample from Dschang-Bamileke). More important, however, in languages with true M tones, a sequence H-M-H is realized [‾ — ‾], that is, 3–2–3, with the second H rising above the level of the preceding M. In a language such as Twi, however, a H–ꞋH–H sequence is realized as [‾ — —], that is, 3–2–2, with a following H realized on the same pitch level as the preceding ꞋH. In other words, a downstepped high tone establishes a terrace just like a regular H tone, and no tone can go higher than this ceiling. For this reason, Welmers refers to such languages as *terraced-level*.

6.2.2.4.3 Intonation and Tone The relationship between *downdrift*, representing an automatic lowering process, and *downstep*, representing a nonautomatic phonemic tone, is now generally acknowledged (see Stewart, 1967, 1971). While recent studies such as Voorhoeve (1971) and Tadadjeu (1974) have shown that downdrift is not a necessary prerequisite for downstep (compare Meeussen, 1970), most cases of the latter do in fact derive from the former.

A relationship which is not as well understood is that between intonation and tone. Schachter (1965) argues convincingly that downdrift is an intonational property, since in languages such as Hausa it can be suspended for purposes of emphasis or question. Virtually all tone languages exhibiting automatic downdrift have only two tones, H and L. Most dialects of Yoruba, Nupe, Ewe, and Jukun, all of which have H, M, and L, do not have downdrift. An explanation for this has recently been proposed by Hombert (1974). Hombert shows that if a three-tone language were to let the second H of a H-L-H sequence undergo downdrift, it would be likely to be confused with an underlying M (compare LaVelle, 1974). Hombert further shows that intonational lowering can, in other sequences, also be accounted for by reference to the tonal contrasts of a language. In most African languages, for instance, a sequence H-H-H is realized as [⎺ ⎺ ⎺] rather than as [⎺ — —]. That is, sequences of H tones are realized on the same pitch level. The reason is that in these languages H-H contrasts either with H-M or H-ʹH, and perceptual confusion would result if H-M were to undergo lowering. In languages such as Hausa and Shona, where there is no M and where tone is less important for lexical contrasts, sequences of H tones do in fact lower (see Meyers, 1974). Finally, sequences of L tones almost always descend in pitch; only Dschang–Bamileke (Tadadjeu, 1974) has a contrast between L-L and L-ʹL which could be potentially confused.[16] The conclusion is that it is to be expected that intonational lowering will occur, *except* where there is a tonal contrast which would be obscured. For further discussion, see Hombert (1974).

6.2.2.5 Consonant Types and Tone While the tone rules of the preceding sections have been presented without reference to segmental information, different consonant types frequently interact with natural tonal assimilations. In Nupe, as seen in the following forms,

/pá/	'peel'	:	[èpá]	'is peeling'
/bá/	'be sour'	:	[èbǎ]	'is sour'
/wá/	'want'	:	[èwǎ]	'is wanting'

L-spreading takes place only when the intervening consonant is *voiced*. In Ngizim, on the other hand, H-spreading takes place when the intervening consonant is voiceless (for example, /p/), a sonorant (for example, /w/) or an implosive (for example, /ɓ/). In other words, certain consonant types are more amenable to L-spreading or H-spreading operating through them. As proposed in Hyman and Schuh (1974:108), a voiced obstruent can *block* the spreading of a H tone through it, just as a voiceless obstruent can block the spreading of a L tone through it. Sonorants are neutral with respect to tone, since they allow both L and H to spread through them.

Such examples which are numerous in African tone languages (for example,

---

[16] According to recent investigations by the author and Jean-Marie Hombert, a phonetic fall is the primary perceptual cue for low tone. This fact is at least in part responsible for the phenomenon of *downglide* (Stewart, 1971:185) by which a L in utterance-final position is realized as a marked fall in many languages.

Ewe, Xhosa, Shona) point to the generalization that *consonant types affect tone but tone does not affect consonant types*. While a voiced obstruent shows an affinity for L tone, L tone does not voice consonants. This points to an important difference between stress and tone, since we saw in **6.2.1.2.3** that stress has many effects on segments. While a number of explanations have been proposed to capture the relationship between voicelessness and H tone on the one hand and voiced obstruents and L tone on the other, none of these has received universal acceptance by phoneticians. Halle and Stevens (1971) and Halle (1972:181) propose to capture this relationship by means of the features Stiff Vocal Cords vs. Slack Vocal Cords, as follows:

	VOWELS			OBSTRUENTS		SONORANTS
	$\grave{V}$	$\bar{V}$	$\acute{V}$	p	b	w
stiff	−	−	+	+	−	−
slack	+	−	−	−	+	−

H tone and voiceless obstruents share stiff vocal cords, while L tone and voiced obstruents share slack vocal cords. Both M tone and sonorants represent the neutral state of the vocal cords. Another set of distinctive features based on larynx height is proposed by Maran (1971:14), while others emphasize the rate of air flow through the glottis as the primary factor responsible for this interaction. (For a collection of papers dealing specifically with the topic of consonant types and tone, see Hyman, 1973c.)

Since voiceless and voiced obstruents have different pitch characteristics, a tonal contrast can reconstruct as an earlier voice contrast. Thus, Mandarin 35 reconstructs as an earlier H (55) tone with an initial voiced obstruent. This voiced obstruent lowers 55 to 35 and then devoices. If the first tone contrast in a language can be traced back to a voicing contrast, one speaks of *tonogenesis* (Matisoff, 1973:73).

6.2.3 Typologies of Prominence

In the preceding sections, stress and tone have been treated as two diametrically opposed types of prominence. Some of the differences between stress and tone systems have already been alluded to. These differences are summarized as follows:

1. In a stress language prominence is *culminative*; in a tone language prominence is *nonculminative*. Thus, while only one syllable per word can have primary stress, any number of syllables in a word can have H tone, subject to the sequential constraints of the language.

2. In a stress language prominence is *syntagmatic*; in a tone language prominence is *paradigmatic*. Thus, while in a stress language one syllable in a word is singled out for stress, each syllable of a tone language receives

tone, often choosing from a number of contrasting values (for example, H, M, and L[17]) or *kinds* of prominence.

3. In a stress language we find rules of stress reduction; in a tone language we find rules assimilating and dissimilating tones (see McCawley, 1964, 1970).

4. In a stress language, presence vs. absence of stress can condition segmental changes (for example, diphthongization under stress, vowel reduction under stresslessness); in a tone language, consonants typically affect tone, rather than the reverse.

There are other criteria which are also sometimes used to type different systems of prominence. Voorhoeve (1973), for instance, focuses on the difference between lexical and rule-governed prominence. In **6.2.1.1** a distinction was made between *free* and *fixed* stress. If stress is free, that is, unpredictable, falling on the first syllable in some words and on the second in others, then its exact position must be part of the lexical entry for each word. If stress always falls on the same syllable (for example, initial or penultimate), stress need not be a part of the lexical makeup of underlying forms. Stress languages can be of either type, or even intermediate, with stress being partially free, partially fixed. Tone languages, on the other hand, are normally assumed to have tone indicated as part of the lexical item. In this typology a language such as Russian, which has unpredictable stress, would be grouped with tone languages such as Thai or Yoruba, since each of these languages would require some indication of prominence in the lexicon.

The question of determining an adequate typology of prominence has received considerable attention from a number of linguists (Pike, 1948; Welmers, 1959; Martinet, 1960; McCawley, 1964, 1968, 1970; Woo, 1969; Voorhoeve, 1973). While stress and tone represent the logical dichotomy within such typologies, it is quite clear that many languages fall in one respect or another midway between stress and tone. First, it is quite clear that stress exists in at least some tone languages. We have already referred to Mandarin Chinese (see **6.2.1.2.3**), where the neutral tone results from the lack of stress. In many Bantu languages which are tonal (for example, Shona), there is in addition a superimposed penultimate stress which lengthens the vowel of this syllable. Stress and tone are therefore not mutually exclusive (see Woo, 1969; McCawley, 1970).

6.2.3.1 (Dynamic) Stress vs. Pitch-Accent (Musical Stress) One of the dichotomies drawn in Prague studies of prominence (for example, Trubetzkoy, 1939; Jakobson, 1931a) is that between *dynamic* and *musical* stress. Dynamic stress is what we referred to as stress in **6.2.1**. While force of articulation and the resulting intensity of the speech signal are not necessarily the major perceptual cues of stress, the term *dynamic* was chosen partly on the

---

[17] The existence of such word-tone languages as Tamang (see **6.2.2.2.1**) should, however, be borne in mind.

basis of this misunderstanding. The term *musical*, on the other hand, indicates that it is a *tone* which is assigned culminatively to a given syllable within a word. Languages such as Swedish and Serbo-Croatian, for instance, have contour tones assigned to words. In Serbo-Croatian there is both a rising and a falling tone, and either of these can be long or short. This means that in addition to the placement of this "musical accent," speakers must pay attention to the *direction* of the pitch change, since rising and falling tones contrast on potentially the same syllable. Prominence is still culminative, since only one such tone can be assigned per word. In more recent terminology, these languages would be called *pitch-accent*, as opposed to *stress-accent*. In a stress-accent language, a single culminative mark of prominence is possible on a given syllable of a word. The perceptual cues of this stress can be changing pitch, vowel duration, or greater intensity, all contributing to the highlighting of the stressed syllable. In a pitch-accent language, prominence is assigned to a given syllable of a word, but there can be two or more kinds of prominence (for example, a rising vs. a falling contour). Pitch-accent languages are thus tonal to the extent that the feature which is assigned is tone (and that this tone can contrast with another tone in the same position). Pitch-accent languages are like stress-accent languages, however, in that there cannot be more than one syllable per word which receives the tonal accent; that is, prominence in pitch-accent languages is culminative.

For a language to be called pitch-accent, it is, however, not necessary for there to be a tonal contrast. Thus, Voorhoeve (1973) for Safwa and Schadeberg (1973) for Kinga show that in these languages there is normally only one H tone per word. In Japanese, as treated in great detail by McCawley (1968), each word can be treated for prominence by indicating the placement of a "pitch fall." The following accentual possibilities for words with one, two, and three syllables are represented in Table 6.1 (McCawley, 1968:132).

Table 6.1 Accentual Patterns on Japanese Words of 1, 2, and 3 Syllables

Underlying Accent		Pitch	Following Pitch
/hí/	'fire'	[¯]	[_]
/hi/	'day'	[_]	[¯]
/sóra/	'sky'	[¯ _]	[_]
/kawá/	'river'	[_ ¯]	[_]
/take/	'bamboo'	[_ ¯]	[¯]
/kábuto/	'helmet'	[¯ _ _]	[_]
/kokóro/	'heart'	[_ ¯ _]	[_]
/ʔotokó/	'man'	[_ ¯ ¯]	[_]
/katati/	'form'	[_ ¯ ¯]	[¯]

In the forms in the table, it is observed that there is always one and only one pitch fall, which can be realized within the word or on the following syllable of the next word (or suffix). Since there is a rule by which a H-H pitch sequence at the beginning of a word in Tokyo Japanese is converted to L-H, we can recognize the following intermediate possibilities:

monosyllabic words:	H + (L)
	H + (H)
bisyllabic words:	H-L + (L)
	H-H + (L)
	H-H + (H)
trisyllabic words:	H-L-L + (L)
	H-H-L + (L)
	H-H-H + (L)
	H-H-H + (H)

As seen in the underlying forms of the table, the pitch contours of Japanese words can be predicted by placing an accent /'/ on the vowel which immediately precedes the pitch fall. If there is no pitch fall within a word, either the last syllable is accented, in which case the fall will be realized on the suffix syllable, or there is no accented syllable, in which case a suffix syllable will be realized without an accentual fall.

It should be quite clear that although we are talking about pitch and pitch falls, Japanese is not a tone language. In fact, it differs from stress languages only in that the accentual pattern is spread throughout the whole word, rather than being realized phonetically on one syllable. There are, it should be noted, stress languages which, like Japanese, have words without any stress (see footnote 8). While it would be distorting the nature of Japanese to speak of a H and a L on each syllable, Japanese should be compared with such word-tone languages as Tamang (Mazaudon, 1973), which was discussed in **6.2.2.2.1**.

6.2.3.2 Monotonic vs. Polytonic Accent The term *accent* has been used to refer to systems of prominence where the assigned feature is culminative (either stress or tone). A second dichotomy made by Jakobson (1931a) and Trubetzkoy (1939) is based on the number of contrasting culminative tones found in a language. Stress languages such as English, Russian, Japanese, and Finnish are *monotonic* since they assign only one kind of culminative accent. Safwa and Kinga, which assign one H tone per word, are also monotonic. On the other hand, languages such as Swedish, Serbo-Croatian, and all tone languages are *polytonic*, in that a contrast between at least two different kinds of prominence is possible in the same position in a word.

While this dichotomy seems straightforward, it sometimes runs into difficulties. In a language such as Greek, for instance, where there is a contrast between rising and falling accents only on a syllable with a long vowel or diphthong, it is possible to decompose these contours and assign stress to *morae*, as follows:

rising tone: CVV́
falling tone: CV́V

In this analysis, Ancient Greek is judged to be monotonic, and as a result can be viewed as a stress language which assigns prominence to morae. A mora can be defined basically as a light (that is, CV) syllable, or as each of the two parts of a heavy (that is, CV-C or CV-V) syllable. It is quite clear that if Ancient Greek is treated as having syllable prominence, it is then polytonic (with rising and falling tones); if it is treated as having mora prominence, it is monotonic. In the second case, the same division of syllables into morae that was seen in connection with stress placement in **6.2.1.2.2** is observed.

6.3 Other Suprasegmentals

While most studies of suprasegmental features center around the various kind of prominence systems (stress, tone, pitch accent), some linguists have attempted to view other phonological features as suprasegmental—at least in some languages. The two features which will be briefly treated in this section are vowel harmony and nasalization.

6.3.1 Vowel Harmony

By vowel harmony is meant that all vowels within a specified (suprasegmental) unit agree in some phonetic feature. The question is whether this feature should be interpreted as a property of segments or of grammatical units larger than the segment (for example, stems, words).

6.3.1.1 Types of Vowel Harmony   An attempt to provide a framework for typologizing vowel harmony systems is provided by Aoki (1968). Aoki first distinguishes between *partial* and *complete* vowel harmony. In complete vowel harmony, which can also be seen as a kind of reduplication, the vowel of a morpheme completely assimilates to another vowel. An example can be found in certain central dialects of Igbo, where a verb such as /mé/ 'make, do' takes in the past tense the consonant /r/ followed by a copy of the vowel of the verb stem, that is, *mèrè* 'made, did'; compare *màrà* 'knew' from /má/ 'know' plus /r/ plus a copy of the stem vowel /a/. A process of vowel harmony occurred historically, since dialects in the Onitsha area pronounce 'made' *mèlù*, revealing that the past tense suffix reconstructs as **lu*.

While complete vowel harmony is often referred to as vowel copying or vowel reduplication, most cases referred to as vowel harmony are of the *partial* variety. In this case a vowel assimilates in certain features to another vowel. The most common features assimilated are front-backness, tense-laxness and labiality. An example of front-backness harmony is found in Hungarian (Vago, 1973:581). The first person plural suffix 'we' is realized as *unk* after back vowels and *ünk* after front vowels, as seen in the following forms:

hoz-unk	'we bring'	ül-ünk	'we sit'
varr-unk	'we sew'	ver-ünk	'we beat'

However, as pointed out by Vago, there are certain verb stems with /i/ and /i:/ which exceptionally take back vowels in their suffixes, for example, *szid-unk* 'we curse,' not **szid-ünk*. In order to predict the back vowel found after such stems, we are faced with either recognizing these stems as exceptional (specifically by marking these forms with a *rule exception feature* [−vowel harmony] which would prevent /unk/ from becoming *ünk*), or with positing an abstract underlying high central unrounded vowel /ɨ/ in the stem *szid*. By a low-level phonetic rule all instances of /ɨ/ would be converted to [i], but only after vowel harmony had had a chance to apply. This second solution brings us into the abstractness controversy (see **3.3.5**), which is the concern of Vago's study of vowel-harmony systems.

The second feature which is frequently found to be assimilated in vowel harmony is tense-laxness. This feature has been treated as an opposition between tense and lax, covered and noncovered (Chomsky and Halle, 1968:314–315), and advanced vs. retracted tongue root (Stewart, 1967). Thus, in Central Igbo two sets of four vowels are found (see **2.4.2.3**):

ADVANCED TONGUE ROOT	RETRACTED TONGUE ROOT
i u	ị ụ
e o	a ọ

The vowels /ị/ and /ụ/ give the impression of a very tense closed [e] and [o], respectively, while /ọ/ resembles [ɔ]. What is important is that in constructing words in Igbo, all vowels found within # boundaries are chosen from one of these sets. Thus there are words such as /é'gó/ 'money' and /a'gụ/ 'leopard,' but no words such as */é'gụ́/ and */á'gó/. As a result, the verbal noun prefix is pronounced [e] before the stem vowels /i, e, u, o/ and [a] before the stem vowels /ị, a, ụ, ọ/, as seen in the following forms:

/sí/	'wash'	→	[èsí]	'washing'
/sị́/	'say'	→	[àsị́]	'saying'

The third feature found in vowel-harmony systems is roundness. In Turkish (Zimmer, 1967, 1970) high vowels agree in both backness and roundness.

Thus, the vowel in the momentary suffix /Iyor/ is pronounced [i] after front unrounded vowels, [ü] after front rounded vowels, [ɨ] after back unrounded vowels, and [u] after back rounded vowels, as seen in the following forms (Zimmer, 1970:90):

[istiyor]   'he wants'
[söylüyor]   'he is saying'
[anlıyor]   'he understands'
[kutluyor]   'he is celebrating (some occasion)'

6.3.1.2 Approaches to Vowel Harmony   From the above discussion it is seen that vowel harmony applies to all vowels within a given domain (normally between # boundaries). As with other phonological rules, vowel harmony can be blocked by a strong grammatical boundary. Thus, when the two Igbo verbs /gá/ 'go' and /fè/ 'cross' are compounded, the result is [gáfè] 'go across' and not *[gáfà] or *[géfè]. It is assumed that the underlying boundary in /gá#fè/ blocks the application of vowel harmony. As this boundary weakens to a +, vowel harmony may be able to penetrate it. Thus, some speakers pronounce /bú#tá/ 'to carry (away)' as [bútá] (breaking vowel harmony), while others pronounce it as [búté]. In the latter case, # has weakened to + (see the discussion of boundaries in **6.1.2.2**).

The question is whether vowel harmony is a suprasegmental or a segmental property. When there is vowel harmony across a boundary, there is no need to discuss the underlying representation of vowel harmony, since an affix vowel can be seen to assimilate to the vowel in a neighboring syllable. When the vowel harmony is within a morpheme it is not clear whether one should speak of one vowel assimilating to the other or of a suprasegmental assignment of the shared vowel feature. Thus, Finnish, which is characterized by front-backness vowel harmony, has the two words [pöütä] 'table' and [pouta] 'fine weather.' These words differ in that all of the vowels in 'table' are [−back], while all of the vowels in 'fine weather' are [+back]. Within the framework of generative phonology, there have been three approaches to the underlying representation of vowel harmony (see Kiparsky, 1968a; Vago, 1973). In the first, an underlying abstract feature such as [+Back] and [−Back] is assigned to each morpheme (Lightner, 1965). In this case, the two Finnish words would be represented, respectively, as /pouta/$_{[-Back]}$ and /pouta/$_{[+Back]}$. In the second approach, one vowel (for example, the first or last) is fully specified, while all other vowels in the same morpheme are represented by means of archiphonemes, that is, partially specified segments in the underlying form (see Bach, 1968; Carrell, 1970). In this case the two Finnish words would be represented as /pöUtA/ and /poUtA/, respectively. The archiphonemes /U/ and /A/, which are unspecified for backness (see **3.2.2**), are converted to [ü] and [ä] after front vowels, [u] and [a] after back vowels. In the final approach, as argued by Kiparsky

(1968a), all vowels within morphemes are fully specified (see Stanley, 1967), and the fact that all vowels agree in backness within a morpheme is captured by means of a morpheme structure condition (see **4.2.1.2**). In this last approach, the two Finnish words would be represented as /pöütä/ and /pouta/.

Of the three approaches, only the first treats vowel harmony as a suprasegmental property. In the second approach, vowel harmony is seen to be the property of, in this case, the first vowel of each morpheme, while in the third, it is seen to be a redundant property of morphemes. In all approaches, a rule of vowel harmony assimilates vowels across morphological boundaries.

6.3.2 Nasalization

The case for analyzing vowel harmony as a suprasegmental property has received less and less support; in contrast, recent arguments have been put forth (Leben, 1973a,b) suggesting that nasalization may be considered a suprasegmental feature in some languages. Both vowel harmony and nasalization were seen to be "prosodic" in the British (or Firthian) school, as evidenced, for example, by Carnochan's (1960) analysis of Igbo and Robins' (1957a) analysis of Sundanese. In addition to Sundanese, nasalization takes on a suprasegmental appearance in Terena (Bendor-Samuel, 1960), Desano (Kaye, 1971), and Guarani (Lunt, 1973), although Langendoen (1968) proposes a restatement of such phenomena without "prosodies." The three languages receive close attention from Leben (1973a,b), who presents Terena vowel nasalization as follows:

> In forming the first person singular:
> (a) Nasalize all vowels and semivowels in the word up to the first stop or fricative
> (b) Nasalize the first stop or fricative in the word as follows: *mb* replaces *p*, *nd* replaces *t*, *ŋg* replaces *k*, *nz* replaces both *s* and *h*, and *nž* replaces both *s* and *hy* (1973a: 142–143).

Thus, the following oral-nasal opposition is found in comparing the third person singular and first person singular forms:

emoʔu	'his word'	ẽmõʔũ	'my word'
ayo	'his brother'	ãỹõ	'my brother'
owoku	'his house'	õw̃õŋgu	'my house'
piho	'he went'	mbiho	'I went'
ahyaʔašo	'he desires'	ãnžaʔašo	'I desire'

It is quite clear from these forms that nasalization is the distinguishing feature between third and first person singular, and that nasalization (or orality) is realized potentially over several syllables. It is this latter feature which suggests a suprasegmental analysis of nasalization in Terena.

In determining whether nasalization should be viewed as segmental or suprasegmental for any given language, several factors must be considered.

First, can a *directionality* for nasal spreading be established? In the above examples, nasalization clearly spreads from left to right. Hence it is possible to recognize a nasal element 'first person singular' which is prefixed to nouns and verbs, let us say /N/ (for example, /Nemoʔu/ 'my word'), which causes the perseverative spreading of nasalization. A later rule deletes /N/. In such a fashion, one could avoid analyzing nasalization as an underlying suprasegmental property. The counterargument to such an analysis for Terena is that the exact phonological shape of this underlying nasal element is indeterminate, since its sole specified feature is [+nasal]. The same argument has been used against "floating tones" (see **6.2.2.3.2.5**), which are specified only for tonal features.

Since certain consonants (specifically nonlow obstruents) block the spreading of nasalization, a directionality can be established. It is this directionality which in turn provides the possibility of a segmental analysis of Terena nasalization. In a language such as Desano (Kaye, 1971), on the other hand, where nonlow obstruents also become nasalized (*b* becomes *m*, *d* becomes *n*, etc.), a segmental analysis is much more difficult to maintain. In Desano, morphemes are marked as a unit as either [+Nasal] or [−Nasal], or are unspecified for nasality. Thus, the morphemes [w̃ãĩ] 'name' and [wai] 'fish' differ in that the first is recognized as /wai/ with the feature specification [+Nasal], while the second is recognized as /wai/ with the feature specification [−Nasal]. Morphemes left unspecified for nasality are typically those which become nasalized in the context of another morpheme marked [+Nasal].

The motivation for recognizing a suprasegmental feature Nasal is seen from the forms [ɲõh̃sõ] 'kind of bird' and [yohso] 'kind of lizard.' Kaye analyzes these as /yohso/$_{[+Nasal]}$ and /yohso/$_{[-Nasal]}$, respectively. We have already said that nasalization is not blocked by nonlow obstruents. In addition, unspecified morphemes become [+Nasal] both before and after [+Nasal] morphemes, as seen in the following derivations (see Leben, 1973b:142):

/seda/$_{[+Nasal]}$ + /du/ → [sẽnãnũ]   'pineapple'
/go/$_{[-Nasal]}$ + /du/ → [goru]   'ball'[18]

/bü/ + /da/$_{[+Nasal]}$ → [mũnã]   'old men'
/bü/ + /gü/$_{[-Nasal]}$ → [bügü]   'old man'

Since an unspecified morpheme becomes nasalized on either side of a [+Nasal] morpheme, it is not possible to mark nasalization on only the first (or last) vowel of a morpheme and then copy nasalization throughout the morpheme. The only way to avoid analyzing nasalization as an underlying suprasegmental property is to follow Kiparsky's (1968a) suggestion for vowel

---

[18] Underlying /d/ is converted to phonetic [r] in this position.

harmony and fully specify [+nasal] on each nasalized segment of the so-called [+Nasal] morphemes, for example, /ɲõh̃sõ/ 'kind of bird.' While such underlying forms will exhibit considerable redundancy, these redundancies can be captured, as in the case of vowel harmony, by morpheme structure conditions.

In summary, then, the issue of whether vowel harmony and nasalization are suprasegmental in the same sense as stress and tone is as yet largely unsettled.[19]

---

[19] While duration (vowel and consonant length) is normally treated along with stress and tone as a suprasegmental (see Lehiste, 1970), this topic will not receive specific attention here, since we have already had occasion to refer to length in conjunction with other issues in phonology.

APPENDIXES

List of Symbols

C — *consonant*
C^h — aspirated
C^o — unaspirated
C^y — palatalized
C^w — labialized
C: — long or geminate
Ç — pharyngealized

N — *nasal*
Ņ — voiceless
Ṇ — syllabic

G — *glide*
G̦ — voiceless

V — *vowel*
Ṽ — nasalized
V: — long
V́ — stressed (or high tone)
V̄ — tense (or mid tone)
ʏ — pharyngealized
V̥ — voiceless

L — *liquid*
Ḷ — voiceless
Ḷ — syllabic

Ø — zero or null segment

/AB/ — phonemic slashes
[AB] — phonetic brackets

{AB} — morphophonemic braces
[+F] — distinctive feature brackets

*AB — unattested (either a historical reconstruction or a disallowed sequence)

A → B / __ C — A 'becomes' by phonological rule B before C
A → B / C __ — A 'becomes' by phonological rule B after C

Other Lists of Symbols: 1. rule formalisms, **4.3.1**
2. boundaries, **6.1.2.2**
3. tone marks, **6.2.2.1**

Notes on Phonetic Transcriptions

I. *Consonants*
1. Dentals are sometimes written [t̪, d̪, s̪, z̪, n̪] to distinguish them from alveolars.
2. Other symbols sometimes used are:

[ɟ] = [φ]   [tʲ] = [t̬ˢ] = [č]
[v] = [β] (although [v] may be sonorant, as   [d³] = [d̬ᶻ] = [ǰ]
[ʃ] = [š] opposed to [β] which is a fricative)   [k₁] = [c]
[ʒ] = [ž]   [ñ] = [ɲ]

3. In addition to the places of articulation indicated on the chart, the following are also found:
a. palatalized, e.g., [pʸ, tʸ, kʸ]
b. labialized, e.g., [pʷ, tʷ, kʷ]
c. retroflex, e.g., [ṭ, ḍ, ṣ, ẓ, ɹ]
d. velarized, e.g., [sᵚ, zᵚ]
e. pharyngealized, e.g., [ṭ, ḍ, ṣ, ẓ]
f. glottalized, e.g., [p', t', k' (=ƙ)] (ejectives), [ɓ, ɗ, ɠ] (implosives)
g. aspirated, e.g., [pʰ, tʰ, kʰ]
4. [w] is a labiovelar glide, that is, it has two constrictions; compare the West African labiovelar stops [k͡p], [g͡b], and [ŋm].

II. *Vowels*
1. Other symbols sometimes used: [ä] = [æ], [y] = [ü] (in which case [j] = [y]), [ö] = [ø], [ɔ̈] = [œ], [ɾ] = [ɪ], [ɷ] = [ʊ].
2. Nasalized vowels are written with a tilde, e.g., [ẽ], [ũ].
3. Voiceless vowels, liquids, and nasals are written as follows: [e̥], [l̥], [n̥], etc.
4. [a] sometimes stands for a low *front* vowel, e.g., French *patte* 'paw.'

Vowel Chart

	Front Unrounded	Front Rounded	Central Unrounded	Back Unrounded	Back Rounded
high	i	ü	ɨ	ɯ	ʊ ʋu
mid-high	e ɪ	ø		ɤ	o
			ə		
mid-low	ɛ	œ		ʌ	ɔ
low	æ		a	ɑ	ɒ

Consonant Chart

	Bilabial	Labiodental	Interdental	Dental/Alveolar	Alveopalatal	Palatal	Velar	Uvular	Pharyngeal	Glottal
voiceless stop	p			t		c	k	q		ʔ
voiced stop	b			d		ɟ	g	G		
voiceless affricate		pᶠ		tˢ	č (= tš)					
voiced affricate		bᵛ		dᶻ	ǰ (= dᶻ)					
voiceless fricative	φ	f	θ	s	š	ç	x	X	ḥ	h
voiced fricative	β	v	ð	z	ž	j	ɣ	R	ʕ	ɦ
nasal	m			n		ɲ	ŋ			
liquid				l r	ř			R		
glide	w ɥ					y ɥ	w			

SPE Distinctive Feature Matrix for Consonants (i)

	p	b	φ	β	m	pᶠ	bᵛ	f	v	θ	ð	t	d	tˢ	dᶻ	s	z	n
cons	+	+	+	+	+	+	+	+	+	+	+	+	+	+	+	+	+	+
syll	−	−	−	−	−	−	−	−	−	−	−	−	−	−	−	−	−	−
son	−	−	−	−	+	−	−	−	−	−	−	−	−	−	−	−	−	+
high	−	−	−	−	−	−	−	−	−	−	−	−	−	−	−	−	−	−
back	−	−	−	−	−	−	−	−	−	−	−	−	−	−	−	−	−	−
low	−	−	−	−	−	−	−	−	−	−	−	−	−	−	−	−	−	−
ant	+	+	+	+	+	+	+	+	+	+	+	+	+	+	+	+	+	+
cor	−	−	−	−	−	−	−	−	−	+	+	+	+	+	+	+	+	+
voice	−	+	−	+	+	−	+	−	+	−	+	−	+	−	+	−	+	+
cont	−	−	+	+	−	−	−	+	+	+	+	−	−	−	−	+	+	−
nasal	−	−	−	−	+	−	−	−	−	−	−	−	−	−	−	−	−	+
strid	−	−	−	−	−	+	+	+	+	−	−	−	−	+	+	+	+	−
del rel	−	−	−	−	−	+	+	−	−	−	−	−	−	+	+	−	−	−
round	−	−	−	−	−	−	−	−	−	−	−	−	−	−	−	−	−	−
grave	+	+	+	+	+	+	+	+	+	−	−	−	−	−	−	−	−	−
lab	+	+	+	+	+	+	+	+	+	−	−	−	−	−	−	−	−	−
pal	−	−	−	−	−	−	−	−	−	−	−	−	−	−	−	−	−	−

SPE Distinctive Feature Matrix for Consonants (ii)

	l	r	č	ǰ	š	ž	c	ɉ	ç	j	ɲ	y	ɥ	k	g	x	ɣ	ŋ
cons	+	+	+	+	+	+	+	+	+	+	+	−	−	+	+	+	+	+
syll	−	−	−	−	−	−	−	−	−	−	−	−	−	−	−	−	−	−
son	+	+	−	−	−	−	−	−	−	−	+	+	+	−	−	−	−	+
high	−	−	+	+	+	+	+	+	+	+	+	+	+	+	+	+	+	+
back	−	−	−	−	−	−	−	−	−	−	−	+	+	+	+	+	+	+
low	−	−	−	−	−	−	−	−	−	−	−	−	−	−	−	−	−	−
ant	+	+	−	−	−	−	−	−	−	−	−	−	−	−	−	−	−	−
cor	+	+	+	+	+	+	−	−	−	−	−	−	−	−	−	−	−	−
voice	+	+	−	+	−	+	−	+	−	+	+	+	+	−	+	−	+	+
cont	+	+	−	−	+	+	−	−	+	+	−	+	+	−	−	+	+	−
nasal	−	−	−	−	−	−	−	−	−	−	+	−	−	−	−	−	−	+
strid	−	−	+	+	+	+	−	−	−	−	−	−	−	−	−	−	−	−
del rel			+	+	−	−	−	−	−	−	−	−	−	−	−	−	−	−
round	−	−	−	−	−	−	−	−	−	−	−	−	+	−	−	−	−	−
grave	−	−	−	−	−	−	−	−	−	−	−	−	−	+	+	+	+	+
lab	−	−	−	−	−	−	−	−	−	−	−	−	+	−	−	−	−	−
pal	−	−	+	+	+	+	+	+	+	+	+	+	+	−	−	−	−	−
lateral	+	−																

SPE Distinctive Feature Matrix for Consonants (iii)

	k͡p	g͡b	ŋ͡m	w	q	G	X	ʁ	R	ħ	ʕ	ʔ	h	ɦ	tʷ	tʸ	tᵐ	t̪	t'
cons	+	+	+	−	+	+	+	+	+	+	+	+	+	+	+	+	+	+	+
syll	−	−	−	−	−	−	−	−	−	−	−	−	−	−	−	−	−	−	−
son	−	−	+	+	−	−	−	−	+	−	−	−	−	−	−	−	−	−	−
high	+	+	+	+	−	−	−	−	−	−	−	−	−	−	−	+	+	−	−
back	+	+	+	+	+	+	+	+	+	−	+	−	−	−	−	−	+	+	−
low	−	−	−	−	−	−	−	−	−	+	+	+	+	+	−	−	−	+	+
ant	+	+	+	−	−	−	−	−	−	−	−	−	−	−	+	+	+	+	+
cor	−	−	−	−	−	−	−	−	−	−	−	−	−	−	+	+	+	+	+
voice	−	+	+	+	−	+	−	+	+	−	+	−	−	+	−	−	−	−	−
cont	−	−	−	+	−	−	+	+	+	+	+	−	+	+	−	−	−	−	−
nasal	−	−	+	−	−	−	−	−	−	−	−	−	−	−	−	−	−	−	−
strid	−	−	−	−	−	−	+	+	−	−	−	−	−	−	−	−	−	−	−
del rel	−	−	−		−	−	−	−	−	−	−	−	−	−	−	−	−	−	−
round	−	−	−	+	−	−	−	−	−	−	−	−	−	−	+	−	−	−	−
grave	+	+	+	+	+	+	+	+	+	+	+	+	+	+	−	−	−	−	−
lab	+	+	+	+	−	−	−	−	−	−	−	−	−	−	+	−	−	−	−
pal	−	−	−	−	−	−	−	−	−	−	−	−	−	−	−	+	−	−	−

REFERENCES

References

Allen, W. Sidney. 1973. *Accent and Rhythm. Prosodic Features of Latin and Greek: A Study in Theory and Reconstruction.* Cambridge Studies in Linguistics 12. Cambridge University Press.

Anderson, Stephen R. 1971. "On the description of 'apicalized' consonants." *Linguistic Inquiry* 2.103–107.

Ansre, Gilbert. 1963. "Reduplication in Ewe." Journal of African Languages 2.128–132.

Aoki, Haruo. 1968. "Toward a typology of vowel harmony." *International Journal of American Linguistics* 34.142–145.

Bach, Emmon. 1968. "Two proposals concerning the simplicity metric in phonology." *Glossa* 2.128–149.

Bach, Emmon, and Robert T. Harms. 1972. "How do languages get crazy rules?" In Robert P. Stockwell and Ronald K. S. Macaulay, eds., *Linguistic Change and Generative Theory*, 1–21. Bloomington: Indiana University Press.

Bendor-Samuel, J. T. 1960. "Some problems of segmentation in the phonological analysis of Terena." *Word* 16.348–355. (Also in F. R. Palmer, ed., *Prosodic Analysis*. London: Oxford University Press, 1970, 214–221).

Bloch, Bernard. 1941/72. "Phonemic overlapping." *American Speech* 16.278–284. In Makkai, 1972, 66–70.

Bolinger, Dwight L. 1958. "A theory of pitch-accent in English." *Word* 14.109–149.

Brame, Michael K. 1972a. "The segmental cycle." In Brame, 1972b, 62–72.

Brame, Michael K., ed. 1972b. *Contributions to Generative Phonology.* Austin: University of Texas Press.

Brame, Michael K. 1974. "The cycle in phonology: Stress in Palestinian, Maltese, and Spanish." *Linguistic Inquiry* 5.39–60.

Brown, Gillian. 1970. "Syllables and redundancy rules in generative phonology." *Journal of Linguistis* 6.1–18.

Cairns, Charles E. 1969. "Markedness, neutralization, and universal redundancy rules." *Language* 45.863–885.

Campbell, Lyle. 1974. "Phonological features: Problems and proposals." *Language* 50.52–65.

Carnochan, Jack. 1960. "Vowel harmony in Igbo." *African Language Studies* 1.155–163.

Carrell, Patricia L. 1970. *A Transformational Grammar of Igbo.* West African Language Monographs 8. Cambridge University Press.

Chafe, Wallace L. 1968. "The ordering of phonological rules." *International Journal of American Linguistics* 34.115–136.

Chao, Yuen-Ren. 1934/57. "The non–uniqueness of phonemic solutions of phonetic systems." *Bulletin of the Institute of History and Philology*, Academia Sinica, Vol. IV, Part 4, 363–397. In Joos, 1957, 38–54.

Chao, Yuen-Ren. 1965. *A Grammar of Spoken Chinese.* Berkeley and Los Angeles: University of California Press.

Chen, Matthew. 1970. "Vowel length variation as a function of the voicing of the consonant environment." *Phonetica* 22.129–159.

Chen, Matthew. 1973a. "On the formal expression of natural rules in phonology." *Journal of Linguistics* 9.223–249.

Chen, Matthew. 1973b. "Cross-dialectal comparison: A case study and some theoretical considerations." *Journal of Chinese Linguistics* 1.38–63.

Cheng, Chin-Chuan. 1973. *A Synchronic Phonology of Mandarin Chinese.* Monographs on Linguistic Analysis 4. The Hague: Mouton.

Chomsky, Noam. 1955. *The Logical Structure of Linguistic Theory.* Mimeo. M.I.T. Library.

Chomsky, Noam. 1957. *Syntactic Structures.* The Hague: Mouton.

Chomsky, Noam. 1960. "Explanatory models in linguistics." In E. Nagel, Patrick Suppes, and A. Tarski, eds., *Logic, Methodology, and the Philosophy of Science.* Stanford University.

Chomsky, Noam. 1962/64. "A transformational approach to syntax." In A. A. Hill, ed., *Proceedings of the Third Texas Conference on Problems of Linguistic Analysis in English, 1958.* Austin: University of Texas Press. In Fodor and Katz, 1964, 211–245.

Chomsky, Noam. 1964. "Current issues in linguistics." In Fodor and Katz, 1964, 50–118. Published in slightly-revised form by Mouton, The Hague.

Chomsky, Noam, and Morris Halle. 1965/72. "Some controversial questions in phonological theory" *Journal of Linguistics* 1.97–138. In Makkai, 1972, 457–485.

Chomsky, Noam and Morris Halle. 1968. *The Sound Pattern of English.* New York: Harper and Row.

Chomsky, Noam, Morris Halle, and Fred Lukoff. 1956. "On accent and juncture in English." In M. Halle *et al.* eds., *For Roman Jakobson*, 65–80. The Hague: Mouton.

Contreras, Helas. 1969. "Simplicity, descriptive adequacy, and binary features." *Language* 45.1–8.

Crothers, John. 1971. "On the abstractness controversy." *Project on Linguistic Analysis*, Second Series, 12.CR1–CR29. Berkeley: Phonology Laboratory, Department of Linguistics, University of California.

Curtiss, Susan, Victoria A. Fromkin, Stephen Krashen, David Rigler, and Marilyn Rigler. 1974. "The linguistic development of Genie." *Language* 50.528–554.

Dell, François. 1973. *Les Regles et les Sons. Introduction à la Phonologie Générative.* Paris: Collection Savoir.

Denes, Peter. 1955. "The effect of duration on the perception of voicing." *Journal of the Acoustical Society of America* 27.761–764.

Dinnsen, Daniel A. 1974. "Constraints on global rules in phonology." *Language* 50.29–51.

Dunstan, Margaret E. 1966. *Tone and Concord Systems in Ngwe Nominals.* Unpublished Doctoral Dissertation, University of London.

Dwyer, David. 1971. "Mende Tone." *Studies in African Linguistics* 2.117–130.

Elimelech, Baruch. 1973. "On the reality of underlying contour tones." Paper presented at the Winter Linguistic Society of America Meeting, San Diego, California.

Fant, Gunnar. 1960. *Acoustic Theory of Speech Production.* The Hague: Mouton.

Fant, Gunnar. 1967/72. "The nature of distinctive features." In *To Honor Roman Jakobson*, 634–642. The Hague: Mouton. In Makkai, 1972, 360–365.

Ferguson, Charles A. 1962/72. Review of *The Sound Pattern of Russian*, by Morris Halle. *Language* 38.284–298. In Makkai, 1972, 369–379.

Ferguson, Charles A. 1966. "Assumptions about nasals: A sample study in phonological universals." In Joseph E. Greenberg, ed., 1966, 53–60, *Universals of Language.* Cambridge, Mass.: M.I.T. Press.

Firth, J. R. 1948/72. "Sounds and prosodies." *Transactions of the Philological*

Society, 127–152. Reprinted in J. R. Firth, 1957, *Papers in Linguistics*, 121–138. Also in Makkai, 1972, 252–263.

Fischer-Jørgensen, Eli. 1956/72. "The commutation test and its application to phonemic analysis." In M. Halle *et al.*, eds., *For Roman Jakobson*, 140–151. The Hague: Mouton. In Makkai, 1972, 582–592.

Fodor, Jerry A., and Jerrold J. Katz. 1964. *The Structure of Language. Readings in the Philosophy of Language*. Englewood Cliffs, N.J.: Prentice–Hall.

Foley, James. 1970. "Phonological distinctive features." *Folia Linguistica* 4.87–92.

Fromkin, Victoria A. 1968. "Speculations on performance models." *Journal of Linguistics* 4.47–68.

Fromkin, Victoria A. 1971. "The nonanomalous nature of anomalous utterances." *Language* 47.27–52.

Fromkin, Victoria A. 1972. "Tone features and tone rules." *Studies in African Linguistics* 3.47–76.

Fromkin, Victoria A., ed. 1973a. *Speech Errors as Linguistic Evidence*. The Hague: Mouton.

Fromkin, Victoria A. 1973b. "Slips of the tongue." *Scientific American* Vol. 229, No. 6 (Dec. 1973), 110–116.

Fry, Dennis. 1955. "Duration and intensity as physical correlates of linguistic stress." *Journal of the Acoustical Society of America* 27.765–768.

Fry, Dennis. 1958. "Experiments in the perception of stress." *Language and Speech* 1.126–152.

Garde, Paul. 1968. *L'Accent*. Paris: Presses Universitaires de France.

George, Isaac. 1970. "Nupe tonology." *Studies in African Linguistics* 1.100–122.

Gleason, H. A. 1955. *An Introduction to Descriptive Linguistics*. New York: Holt, Rinehart and Winston.

Greenberg, Joseph H. 1966a. "Synchronic and diachronic universals in phonology." *Language* 42.508–517.

Greenberg, Joseph H. 1966b. *Language Universals*. The Hague: Mouton. Also in T. Sebeok, ed., 1966, *Current Trends in Linguistics* 3.61–112. The Hague: Mouton.

Greenberg, Joseph H. 1970. "Some generalizations concerning glottalic consonants, especially implosives." *International Journal of American Linguistics* 36.123–146.

Greenberg, Joseph H., and James J. Jenkins. 1964. "Studies in the psychological correlates of the sound system of American English." *Word* 20.157–177.

Gudschinsky, Sarah C., Harold Popovich, and Frances Popovich. 1970. "Native reaction and phonetic similarity in Maxakali phonology." *Language* 46.77–88.

Hale, Kenneth. 1971. "Deep–surface canonical disparities in relation to analysis and change: An Australian example." To appear in T. Seboek, ed., *Current Trends in Linguistics* 11.

Halle, Morris. 1957. "In defense of the number two." In Ernst Pulgram, ed., *Studies Presented to Joshua Whatmough*, 65–72. The Hague: Mouton.

Halle, Morris. 1959. *The Sound Pattern of Russian*. The Hague: Mouton.

Halle, Morris. 1962/72. "Phonology in generative grammar." *Word* 18.54–72. In Fodor and Katz, 1964, 334–352. Also in Makkai, 1972, 380–392.

Halle, Morris. 1964/72. "On the bases of phonology." In Fodor and Katz, 1964, 324–333. Also in Makkai, 1972, 393–400.

Halle, Morris. 1972. "Theoretical issues in phonology in the 1970s." In André Rigault and René Charbonneau, eds., *Proceedings of the Seventh International Congress of Phonetic Sciences*, 179–205. The Hague: Mouton.

Halle, Morris. 1973. "Prologomena to a theory of word formation." *Linguistic Inquiry* 4.3–16.

Halle, Morris, and Kenneth N. Stevens. 1971. "A note on laryngeal features." *Quarterly Progress Report* No. 101. Cambridge, Mass.: Research Laboratory of Electronics, M.I.T.

Harms, Robert T. 1966. "The measurement of phonological economy." *Language* 42.602–611.

Harms, Robert T. 1968. *Introduction to Phonological Theory*. Englewood Cliffs, N.J.: Prentice–Hall.

Harms, Robert T. 1973. "How abstract is Nupe?" *Language* 49.439–446.

Harris, James W. 1969. *Spanish Phonology*. Cambridge, Mass.: M.I.T. Press.

Harris, Zellig S. 1951. *Structural Linguistics*. Chicago: University of Chicago Press.

Harris, Zellig S. 1954. "Distributional structure." *Word* 10.146–162. Also in Fodor and Katz, 1964, 33–49.

Hoard, James W. 1971. "Aspiration, tenseness, and syllabification in English." *Language* 47.133–140.

Hockett, Charles F. 1942/72. "A system of descriptive phonology." *Language* 18.3–21. In Makkai, 1972. 99–112. Also in Joos, 1957, 97–108.

Hockett, Charles F. 1955. *A Manual of Phonology*. *International Journal of American Linguistics* Vol. 21, No. 4, Part I. Baltimore: Waverly Press.

Hombert, Jean–Marie. 1974. "Universals of downdrift: Their phonetic basis and significance for a theory of tone." In W. Leben, ed., *Proceedings of the Fifth Annual Conference on African Linguistics, Studies in African Linguistics*, Supplement 5, 169–183.

Hooper, Joan B. 1972. "The syllable in phonological theory." *Language* 48.525–540.

Hooper, Joan B. 1973. *Aspects of Natural Generative Phonology*. Unpublished Doctoral Dissertation, University of California, Los Angeles.

Hyman, Larry M. 1970a. "How concrete is phonology?" *Language* 46.58–76.

Hyman, Larry M. 1970b. "The role of borrowing in the justification of phonological grammars." *Studies in African Linguistics* 1.1–48.

Hyman, Larry M. 1972a. "Nasals and nasalization in Kwa." *Studies in African Linguistics* 3.167–205.

Hyman, Larry M. 1972b. *A Phonological Study of Feʔfeʔ–Bamileke. Studies in African Linguistics*, Supplement 4.

Hyman, Larry M. 1973a. "The feature [grave] in phonological theory." *Journal of Phonetics* 1.329–337.

Hyman, Larry M. 1973b. "The role of consonant types in natural tonal assimilations." In Hyman, 1973c, 151–179.

Hyman, Larry M., ed. 1973c. *Consonant Types and Tone. Southern California Occasional Papers in Linguistics* No. 1. Los Angeles: Department of Linguistics, University of Southern Califormia.

Hyman, Larry M. 1973d. "Nupe three years later." *Language* 49.447–452.

Hyman, Larry M. 1974. "The great Igbo tone shift." In Erhard Voeltz, ed., *Proceedings of the Third Annual Conference on African Linguistics, 1972.* Bloomington: Indiana University Press.

Hyman, Larry Mₔ and Kong-on Kim. "Constraints on boundaries." (In preparation).

Hyman, Larry M., and Russell G. Schuh. 1974. "Universals of tone rules: Evidence from West Africa." *Linguistic Inquiry* 5.81–115.

Innes, Gordon. 1966. *A Grebo–English Dictionary.* West African Languages Monograph 6. Cambridge University Press.

Jakobson, Roman. 1931a/71. "Die Betonung und ihre Rolle in der Word– und Syntagmaphonologie." *Travaux du Cercle Linguistique de Prague* IV. Reprinted in *Roman Jakobson, Selected Writings* I, 117–136. The Hague: Mouton.

Jakobson, Roman. 1931b/72. "Principles of historical phonology." Originally in *Travaux du Cercle Linguistique de Prague* IV in German. In French translation in *Roman Jakobson, Selected Writings* I, 202–220. In English translation in Allan R. Keiler, ed., 1972, *A Reader in Historical and Comparative Linguistics*, 121–138. New York: Holt, Rinehart and Winston.

Jakobson, Roman. 1941/68. *Child Language, Aphasia, and Phonological Universals.* Originally published in German, Uppsala: Språkvetenskapliga Sällskapets i Uppsala Förhandligar. Also in *Roman Jakobson, Selected Writings* I, 328–401. The Hague: Mouton. In English translation, Allan R. Keiler, 1968, The Hague: Mouton.

Jakobson, Roman. 1960/71. "Why mama and papa?" In *Perspectives in Psychological Theory Dedicated to Heinz Werner.* New York. Reprinted in *Roman Jakobson, Selected Writings* I, 538–545. The Hague: Mouton.

Jakobson, Roman, Gunnar Fant, and Morris Halle. 1952. *Preliminaries to Speech Analysis.* Technical Report 13, M.I.T. Acoustics Laboratory. 5th printing, M.I.T. Press, 1963.

Jakobson, Roman, and Morris Halle. 1956. *Fundamentals of Language.* The Hague: Mouton.

Johnson, Lawrence. 1973. "Dissimilation as a natural process in phonology." *Stanford Occasional Papers in Linguistics* 3 (James Paul Gee, Carolyn Johnson, William R. Leben, eds.). 45–56.

Jones, Daniel. 1931. "On phonemes." *Travaux du Cercle Linguistique de Prague* IV, 74–79.

Joos, Martin. 1957. *Readings in Linguistics* I. Chicago: University of Chicago Press.

Kaye, Jonathan D. 1971. "Nasal harmony in Desano." *Linguistic Inquiry* 2.37–56.

Kim, Chin-Wu. 1972. "Two phonological notes: A–sharp and B–flat." In Brame, 1972b, 155–170.

Kiparsky, Paul. 1968a. "How abstract is phonology?" Unpublished.

Kiparsky, Paul. 1968b. "Linguistic universals and linguistic change." In Emmon Bach and Robert T. Harms, eds., *Universals in Linguistic Theory*, 171–202. New York: Holt, Rinehart and Winston.

Kiparsky, Paul. 1971. "Historical Linguistics." In William Orr Dingwall, ed., *A Survey of Linguistic Science*, 576–649. Linguistics Program, University of Maryland.

Kiparsky, Paul. 1972. "Explanation in phonology." In Stanley Peters, ed., *Goals of Linguistic Theory*, 189–227. Englewood Cliffs, N.J.: Prentice–Hall.

Kiparsky, Paul. 1973. "Productivity in phonology." In Michael J. Kenstowicz and Charles W. Kisseberth, eds., *Issues in Phonological Theory*, 169–176. The Hague: Mouton.

Kisseberth, Charles W. 1969. "On the abstractness of phonology: The evidence from Yawelmani." *Papers in Linguistics* 1.248–282.

Kisseberth, Charles W. 1970a. "On the functional unity of phonological rules." *Linguistic Inquiry* 1.291–306.

Kisseberth, Charles W. 1970b. "The treatment of exceptions." *Papers in Linguistics* 2.44–58.

Kisseberth, Charles W. 1972. "Cyclical rules in Klamath phonology." *Linguistic Inquiry* 3.3–33.

Kisseberth, Charles W. 1973a. "Is rule ordering necessary?" In Braj B. Kachru *et al.*, eds., *Issues in Linguistics*, Papers in Honor of Henry and Renee Kahane. Urbana: University of Illinois Press.

Kisseberth, Charles W. 1973b. "On the alternation of vowel length in Klamath: A global rule." In Michael J. Kenstowicz and Charles W. Kisseberth, eds., *Issues in Phonological Theory*, 9–26. The Hague: Mouton.

Kohler, K. J. 1966. "Is the syllable a phonological universal?" *Journal of Linguistics* 2.207–208.

Koutsoudas, Andreas, Gerald Sanders, and Craig Noll. 1974. "The application of phonological rules." *Language* 50.1–28.

Krohn, Robert. 1972a. "On the sequencing of tautosegmental features." *Papers in Linguistics* 5.114–123.

Krohn, Robert. 1972b. "Underlying vowels in Modern English." *Glossa* 6.203–224.

Krohn, Robert. 1974. "A rule of feature–sequencing in Nupe vowel phonology." Paper presented at Winter Linguistic Society of America Meeting, San Diego, California.

Kuroda, S.-Y. 1967. *Yawelmani Phonology.* Cambridge, Mass.: M.I.T. Press.

Labov, William. 1971. "Methodology." In William Orr Dingwall, ed., *A Survey of Linguistic Science*, 412–497. Linguistics Program, University of Maryland.

Labov, William, Malka Yaeger, and Richard Steiner. 1972. *A Quantitative Study of Sound Change in Progress.* Philadelphia: U.S. Regional Survey.

Ladefoged, Peter. 1971. *Preliminaries to Linguistic Phonetics.* Chicago: University of Chicago Press.

Langendoen, D. Terence. 1968. *The London School of Linguistics: A Study of the Linguistic Theories of B. Malinowski and J. R. Firth.* Cambridge, Mass.: M.I.T. Press.

LaVelle, Carl. 1974. "An experimental study of Yoruba tones." In William R. Leben, ed., *Proceedings of the Fifth Annual Conference on African Linguistics, Studies in African Linguistics*, Supplement 5, 185–194.

Leben, William R. 1971a. "The morphophonemics of tone in Hausa." In Chin–Wu Kim and Herbert Stahlke, eds., *Papers in African Linguistics*, 201–218. Edmonton, Alberta: Linguistic Research, Inc.

Leben, William R. 1971b. "Suprasegmental and segmental representation of tone." *Studies in African Linguistics*, Supplement 2, 183–200.

Leben, William R. 1973a. "The role of tone in segmental phonology." In Hyman, 1973c, 115–149.

Leben, William R. 1973b. *Suprasegmental Phonology.* Unpublished Doctoral Dissertation, M.I.T.

Lehiste, Ilse. 1970. *Suprasegmentals.* Cambridge, Mass.: M.I.T. Press.

Li, F. K. 1946. "Chipewyan." In *Linguistic Structures of Native America*, 398–423. New York: Viking Fund Publications in Anthropology 6.

Lightner, Theodore M. 1965. "On the description of vowel and consonant harmony." *Word* 19.376–387.

Lightner, Theodore M. 1971. "Generative phonology." In William Orr Dingwall, ed., *A Survey of Linguistic Science*, 498–574. Linguistics Program, University of Maryland.

Liljencrants, John, and Björn Lindblom. 1972. "Numerical simulation of vowel quality systems: The role of perceptual contrast." *Language* 48.839–862.

Longacre, Robert E. 1952. "Five phonemic pitch levels in Trique." *Acta Linguistica* 7.62–68.

Lovins, Julie B. 1973. *Loanwords and the Phonological Structure of Japanese.* Unpublished Doctoral Dissertation, University of Chicago.

Lunt, Horace G. 1973. "Remarks on nasality: The case of Guarani." In Stephen R. Anderson and Paul Kiparsky, eds., *A Festschrift for Morris Halle*, 131–139. New York: Holt, Rinehart and Winston.

Maddieson, Ian. 1971. "The inventory of features." In Ian Maddieson, ed., *Tone in Generative Phonology*, 3–18. *Research Notes* 3, parts 2 and 3, Department of Linguistics and Nigerian Languages, University of Ibadan.

Maddieson, Ian. 1972. "Tone system typology and distinctive features." In André Rigault and René Charbonneau, eds., *Proceedings of the Seventh International Congress of Phonetic Sciences*, 957–961. The Hague: Mouton.

Makkai, Valerie Becker, ed. 1972. *Phonological Theory. Evolution and Current Practice*. New York: Holt, Rinehart and Winston.

Malmberg, Bertil. 1963. *Structural Linguistics and Human Communication. An Introduction into the Mechanism of Language and the Methodology of Linguistics*. Berlin: Springer-Verlag.

Maran, La Raw. 1971. *Burmese and Jinghpo: A Study of Tonal Linguistic Processes. Occasional Papers of the Wolfenden Society on Tibeto–Burman Linguistics*, Vol. IV. F. K. Lehman, ed. Urbana: University of Illinois.

Martinet, André. 1936. "Neutralisation et archiphonème." *Travaux du Cercle Linguistique de Prague* 6.46–57.

Martinet, André. 1937. "La phonologie du mot en danois." *Bulletin de la Société de Linguistique de Paris* 38.169–266.

Martinet, André. 1947. "Où en est la phonologie?" *Lingua* 1.34–58.

Martinet, André. 1960/64. *Elements of General Linguistics*. Originally published in French. Paris: Librairie Armand Colin. Translated by Elisabeth Palmer. Chicago: University of Chicago Press.

Martinet, André. 1965. *La Linguistique Synchronique*. Paris: Presses Universitaires de France.

Matisoff, James A. 1973. "Tonogenesis in Southwest Asia." In Hyman, 1973c, 71–95.

Mazaudon, Martine. 1973. *Phonologie Tamang*. Paris: Société d'Etudes Linguistiques et Anthropologiques de France (SELAF).

McCawley, James D. 1964. "What is a tone language?" Paper presented at the Summer Linguistic Society of America Meeting.

McCawley, James D. 1967/73. "The role of a phonological feature system in a theory of language." Originally in French translation in *Langages* 8.112–123. In Makkai, 1972, 522–528.

McCawley, James D. 1968. *The Phonological Component of a Grammar of Japanese*. Monographs on Linguistic Analysis 2. The Hague: Mouton.

McCawley, James D. 1970. "Some tonal systems that come close to being pitch accent but don't quite make it." In M. Campbell *et al.*, eds., *Papers From the Sixth Regional Meeting of the Chicago Linguistic Society*, 526–532.

McCawley, James D. 1971. "On the role of notation in generative phonology." Unpublished. Circulated by Indiana University Linguistics Club.

Meeussen, A. E. 1970. "Tone typologies for West African languages." *African Language Studies* 11.266–271.

Meyers, Laura F. 1974. "Tone patterns in Hausa." Paper presented at Fifth Annual Conference on African Linguistics, Stanford University, March 29–31, 1974.

Miller, Patricia. 1972. "Some context-free processes affecting vowels." *Ohio State University Working Papers in Linguistics* 11.136–167.

Miller, Patricia. 1973. "Bleaching and coloring." In Claudia Corum *et al.*, eds., *Papers from the Ninth Regional Meeting of the Chicago Linguistic Society*, 386–397.

Mohr, B. 1971. "Intrinsic variations in the speech signal." *Phonetica* 23.69–93.

Mohr, B. 1973. "Tone rules and the phonological representation of tones." Paper presented at the Sixth International Conference on Sino–Tibetan Language and Linguistic Studies, San Diego, Oct. 19–22, 1973.

Mol, H., and E. M. Uhlenbeck. 1956. "The linguistic relevance of intensity in stress." *Lingua* 5.205–213.

Newman, Paul. 1972. "Syllable weight as a phonological variable." *Studies in African Linguistics* 3.301–323.

Ohala, John J. 1971. "Monitoring soft palate movements in speech." *Project on Linguistic Analysis*. Berkeley: Phonology Laboratory, Department of Linguistics, University of California.

Ohala, John J. 1974. "Phonetic explanation in phonology." *Proceedings of Parasession on Natural Phonology*, 251–274, Chicago Linguistic Society.

Ohala, Manjari. 1972. *Topics in Hindi–Urdu Phonology*. Unpublished Doctoral Dissertation, University of California, Los Angeles.

Ohala, Manjari. 1974. "The abstractness controversy: Experimental input from Hindi." *Language* 50.225–235.

Ohso, Mieko. 1971. "A phonological study of some English loan words in Japanese." Unpublished M.A. Thesis, Ohio State University.

Peters, Ann M. 1973. "A new formalization of downdrift." *Studies in African Linguistics* 4.139–154.

Pike, Kenneth L. 1947a. *Phonemics: A Technique for Reducing Language to Writing*. University of Michigan Publications in Linguistics 3. Ann Arbor.

Pike, Kenneth L. 1947b/72. "Grammatical prerequisites to phonemic analysis." *Word* 3.155–172.

Pike, Kenneth L. 1948. *Tone Languages: A Technique for Determining the Number and Type of Pitch Contrasts in a Language, with Studies in Tonemic Substitution and Fusion*. University of Michigan Publications in Linguistics 4. Ann Arbor.

Pike, Kenneth L. 1964/72. "Stress trains in Auca." In D. Abercrombie, ed., *In Honour of Daniel Jones*, 425–431. London: Longmans. Reprinted in

R. Brend, ed., *Kenneth L. Pike, Selected Writings*, 186–191. The Hague: Mouton.

Pike, Kenneth L., and Eunice Pike. 1947. "Immediate constituents of Mazateco syllables." *International Journal of American Linguistics* 13.78–91.

Postal, Paul M. 1968. *Aspects of Phonological Theory*. New York: Harper and Row.

Pratt, Mary. 1972. "Tone in some Kikuyu verb forms." *Studies in African Linguistics* 3.325–378.

Pulgram, Ernst. 1970. *Syllable, Word, Nexus, Cursus*. The Hague: Mouton.

Robins, R. H. 1957a. "Vowel nasality in Sundanese: A phonological and grammatical study." In *Studies in Linguistic Analysis*. Oxford: Basil Blackwell.

Robins, R. H. 1957b/72. "Aspects of prosodic analysis." *Proceedings of the University of Durham Philosophical Society* 1.1–12. In Makkai, 1972, 264–274.

Robinson, Orrin. 1972. *Synchronic Reflexes of Diachronic Phonological Rules*. Unpublished Doctoral Dissertation, Cornell University.

Ross, John Robert. 1972. "A reanalysis of English word stress (part I)." In Brame, 1972b, 229–323.

Saib, Jilali. 1973. "The treatment of geminates: Evidence from Berber." Paper read at the Winter Linguistic Society of America Meeting.

Sampson, Geoffrey. 1969. "A note on Wang's 'phonological features of tone'." *International Journal of American Linguistics* 35.62–66.

Sapir, Edward. 1925/72. "Sound patterns in language." *Language* 1.37–51. In Makkai, 1972, 13–21.

Sapir, Edward. 1933/72. "The psychological reality of phonemes." Originally published in French. "La réalité psychologique des phonèmes." *Journal de Psychologie Normale et Pathologique* 30.247–265. In Makkai, 1972, 22–31.

Schachter, Paul. 1965. "Some comments on J. M. Stewart's 'The typology of the Twi tone system.'" *Bulletin of the Institute of African Studies* 1.28–42. Legon University, Ghana.

Schachter, Paul. 1969. "Natural assimilation rules in Akan." *International Journal of American Linguistics* 35.342–355.

Schachter, Paul, and Victoria Fromkin. 1968. *A Phonology of Akan: Akuapem, Asante, and Fante. Working Papers in Phonetics* 9, University of California, Los Angeles.

Schadeberg, Thilo C. 1972. "[αFn]?" Paper presented at Colloquium on Prosodic Systems, Leiden, September 9–11, 1972.

Schadeberg, Thilo C. 1973. "Kinga: A restricted tone language." *Studies in African Linguistics* 4.23–48.

Schane, Sanford A. 1968. *French Phonology and Morphology*. Cambridge, Mass.: M.I.T. Press.

Schane, Sanford A. 1969. "Disjunctive or conjunctive (?) and intrinsic or extrinsic (?) ordered rules in phonology." *Linguistic Notes from La Jolla* 1.16–45.

Schane, Sanford A. 1971. "The phoneme revisited." *Language* 47.503–521.

Schane, Sanford A. 1972. "Natural rules in phonology." In Robert P. Stockwell and Ronald K. S. Macaulay, eds., *Linguistic Change and Generative Theory*, 199–229. Bloomington: Indiana University Press.

Schane, Sanford A. 1973a. *Generative Phonology*. Englewood Cliffs, N.J.: Prentice–Hall.

Schane, Sanford A. 1973b. "The treatment of phonological exceptions: The evidence from French." In Braj B. Kachru *et al.* eds., *Issues in Linguistics. Papers in Honor of Henry and Renee Kahane*, 822–835. Urbana: University of Illinois Press.

Schuh, Russell G. 1972. "Rule inversion in Chadic." *Studies in African Linguistics* 3.379–398.

Scott, N. C. 1957. "Notes on the pronunciation of Sea Dayak." *Bulletin of the School of Oriental and African Studies* 20.509–512.

Scott, N.C. 1964. "Nasal consonants in Land Dayak (Bukar–Sadong)." In D. Abercrombie, ed., *In Honour of Daniel Jones*, 432–436. London: Longmans.

Skousen, Royal. 1972a. "On capturing regularities." In Paul M. Peranteau *et al.*, eds., *Papers from the Eighth Regional Meeting of the Chicago Linguistic Society*, 567–577.

Skousen, Royal. 1972b. "Consonant alternation in Fula." *Studies in African Linguistics* 3.77–96.

Smith, N. V. 1967. "The phonology of Nupe." *Journal of African Languages* 6.153–169.

Stahlke, Herbert. 1971. "On the status of nasalized vowels in Kwa." In Chin-Wu Kim and Herbert Stahlke, eds., *Papers in African Linguistics*, 239–247. Edmonton, Alberta: Linguistic Research, Inc.

Stampe, David. 1969. "The acquisition of phonetic representation." In Robert I. Binnick *et al.*, eds., *Papers from the Fifth Regional Meeting of the Chicago Linguistic Society*, 443–454.

Stampe, David. 1972a. *How I Spent my Summer Vacation*. Unpublished Doctoral Dissertation, University of Chicago.

Stampe, David. 1972b. "On the natural history of diphthongs." In Paul M. Peranteau *et al.*, eds., *Papers from the Eighth Regional Meeting of the Chicago Linguistic Society*, 578–590.

Stanley, Richard. 1967. "Redundancy rules in phonology." *Language* 43.393–436.

Stanley, Richard. 1973. "Boundaries in phonology." In Stephen R. Anderson and Paul Kiparsky, eds., *A Festschrift for Morris Halle*, 185–206. New York: Holt, Rinehart and Winston.

Stewart, John M. 1965. "The typology of the Twi tone system." *Bulletin of the Institute of African Studies* 1.1–27. Legon University, Ghana.

Stewart, John M. 1967. "Tongue-root position in Akan vowel harmony." *Phonetica* 16.185–204.

Stewart, John M. 1971. "Niger–Congo, Kwa." In T. Sebeok, ed., *Current Trends in Linguistics* 7.179–212. The Hague: Mouton.

Swadesh, Morris. 1934/72. "The phonemic principle." *Language* 10.117–129. In Makkai, 1972, 32–39.

Tadadjeu, Maurice. 1974. "Floating tones, shifting rules, and downstep in Dschang–Bamileke." In William R. Leben, ed., *Proceedings of the Fifth Annual Conference on African Linguistics, Studies in African Linguistics,* Supplement 5, 283–290.

Trager, George L., and Henry Lee Smith. 1951. *An Outline of English Structure. Studies in Linguistics Occasional Paper* 3. Norman, Oklahoma: Battenburg Press.

Trubetzkoy, N. 1936/66. "Die Aufhebung der phonologischen Gegensätze." In *Travaux du Cercle Linguistique de Prague* 6.29–45. Reprinted in Josef Vachek, ed., *A Prague School Reader in Linguistics*, 187–205. Bloomington: Indiana University Press.

Trubetzkoy, N. 1939/69. *Principles of Phonology.* Originally published in German (*Grundzüge der Phonologie*) as *Travaux du Cercle Linguistique de Prague* 7. Translated by Christiane A. M. Baltaxe. Berkeley and Los Angeles: University of California Press.

Twaddell, William Freeman. 1935/57. *On Defining the Phoneme. Language Monograph* 16. Baltimore. Reprinted in Joos, 1957, 55–80.

Vago, Robert M. 1973. "Abstract vowel harmony systems in Uralic and Altaic languages." *Language* 49.579–605.

Vennemann, Theo. 1968a. *German Phonology.* Unpublished Doctoral Dissertation, University of California, Los Angeles.

Vennemann, Theo. 1968b. "On the use of paradigmatic information in a competence rule of modern German phonology." Paper read at Summer Linguistic Society of America Meeting.

Vennemann, Theo. 1972a. "On the theory of syllabic phonology." *Linguistische Berichte* 18.1–18.

Vennemann, Theo. 1972b. "Sound change and markedness theory: On the history of the German consonant system." In Robert P. Stockwell and Ronald K. S. Macaulay, eds., *Linguistic Change and Generative Theory*, 230–274. Bloomington: Indiana University Press.

Vennemann, Theo. 1972c. "Rule inversion." *Lingua* 29.209–242.

Vennemann, Theo. 1972d. "Phonological uniqueness in natural generative grammar." *Glossa* 6.105–116.

Vennemann, Theo. 1973. "Phonological concreteness in natural generative grammar." In Roger Shuy and C. J. Bailey, *Toward Tomorrow's Linguistics*. Washington, D.C.: Georgetown University Press.

Vennemann, Theo, and Peter Ladefoged. 1971. "Phonetic features and phonological features." *Working Papers in Phonetics* 21.13–24. University of California, Los Angeles.

Voorhoeve, Jan. 1971. "Tonology of the Bamileke noun." *Journal of African Languages* 10.44–53.

Voorhoeve, Jan. 1973. "Safwa as a restricted tone system." *Studies in African Linguistics* 4.1–22.

Voorhoeve, Jan, A. E. Meeussen, and Kees de Blois. 1969. "New proposals for the description of tone sequences in the Igbo completive phrase." *Journal of West African Languages* 6.79–84.

Wang, William S.-Y. 1967. "The phonological features of tone." *International Journal of American Linguistics* 33.93–105.

Wang, William S.-Y. 1968. "Vowel features, paired variables, and the English vowel shift." *Language* 44.695–708.

Wang, William S.-Y., and Charles Fillmore. 1961. "Intrinsic cues and consonant perception." *Journal of Speech and Hearing Research* 4.130–136.

Weinreich, Uriel. 1954. "Stress and word structure in Yiddish." In Uriel Weinreich, ed., *The Field of Yiddish: Studies in Yiddish Language, Folklore and Literature*, 1–27. New York: Linguistic Circle of New York.

Welmers, William E. 1959. "Tonemics, morphotonemics, and tonal morphemes." *General Linguistics* 4.1–9.

Welmers, William E. 1962. "The phonology of Kpelle." *Journal of African Languages* 1.69–93.

Welmers, William E. 1970. "Igbo tonology." *Studies in African Linguistics* 1.255–278.

Wilbur, Ronnie B. 1973. "The phonology of reduplication." Circulated by Indiana University Linguistics Club.

Williamson, Kay. 1970. "Downstep/downdrift." In Ian Maddieson, ed., *Tone in Generative Phonology*, 23–33. *Research Notes* 3, parts 2 and 3, Department of Linguistics and Nigerian Languages, University of Ibadan.

Williamson, Kay. 1973. "More on nasals and nasalization in Kwa." *Studies in African Linguistics* 4.115–138.

Wilson, Robert D. 1966/72 "A criticism of distinctive features." *Journal of Linguistics* 6.195–206. In Makkai, 1972, 351–359.

Woo, Nancy. 1969. *Prosodic Phonology*. Unpublished Doctoral Dissertation, M.I.T. Circulated by Indiana University Linguistics Club.

Yen, Sian L. 1968. "Two measures of economy in phonological descriptions." *Foundations of Language* 4.58–69.

Zimmer, Karl E. 1967. "A note on vowel harmony." *International Journal of American Linguistics* 33.166–171.

Zimmer, Karl E. 1969. "Psychological correlates of some Turkish morpheme structure conditions." *Language* 45.309–321.

Zimmer, Karl E. 1970. "On the evaluation of alternative phonological descriptions." *Journal of Linguistics* 6.89–98.

AUTHOR INDEX

SUBJECT INDEX

LANGUAGE INDEX